I0126966

Since Time Immemorial

YANNA YANNAKAKIS

Since Time Immemorial

Native Custom & Law in Colonial Mexico

DUKE UNIVERSITY PRESS   DURHAM AND LONDON   2023

© 2023 Yanna Yannakakis
This work is licensed under a Creative Commons Attribution-
NonCommercial-NoDerivatives 4.0 International License, available at
https://creativecommons.org/licenses/by-nc-nd/4.0/.

Designed by Aimee C. Harrison
Project Editor: Ihsan Taylor
Typeset in Garamond Premier Pro and SansBleu Kingdom
by Copperline Book Services

Library of Congress Cataloging-in-Publication Data
Names: Yannakakis, Yanna, [date] author.
Title: Since time immemorial : Native custom and law in colonial
Mexico / Yanna Yannakakis.
Other titles: Native custom and law in colonial Mexico.
Description: Durham : Duke University Press, 2023. | Includes
bibliographical references and index.
Identifiers: LCCN 2022041591 (print)
LCCN 2022041592 (ebook)
ISBN 9781478019626 (paperback)
ISBN 9781478016984 (hardcover)
ISBN 9781478024255 (ebook)
ISBN 9781478093572 (ebook other)
Subjects: LCSH: Customary law courts—Mexico—History. | Indians
of Mexico—Politics and government. | Indians of Mexico—Legal status,
laws, etc.—History. | Justice, Administration of—Mexico—History. |
BISAC: HISTORY / Latin America / Mexico | SOCIAL SCIENCE /
Anthropology / Cultural & Social
Classification: LCC KGF2200 .Y36 2023 (print) | LCC KGF2200 (ebook) |
DDC 347.72/0108997—dc23/eng/20221215
LC record available at https://lccn.loc.gov/2022041591
LC ebook record available at https://lccn.loc.gov/2022041592

Cover art: Detail of the Relaciones geográficas map of Teozacoalco.
Courtesy of Benson Latin American Collection, LLILAS Benson Latin
American Studies and Collections, the University of Texas at Austin.

This book is freely available in an open access edition thanks to TOME
(Toward an Open Monograph Ecosystem)—a collaboration of the
Association of American Universities, the support of Emory University
and the Andrew W. Mellon Foundation. Learn more at the TOME
website, available at: openmonographs.org.

For Maeve, Marianna, and Aiden

Πρέπει να θυμόμαστε και να ελπίζουμε. We must remember and hope.

Contents

A gallery appears after page 107.

Acknowledgments

This book has been a collective enterprise, a product of conversation, friendship, community, and long years of work. I will begin by thanking the staff of the archives and libraries that I have visited and consulted since I began collecting material on custom more than twenty years ago: Archivo Histórico Judicial de Oaxaca; Archivo Histórico Municipal de Oaxaca; Archivo General del Estado de Oaxaca; Archivo Histórico de la Arquidiócesis de Antequera Oaxaca; Archivo Histórico de Notarías del Estado de Oaxaca; Biblioteca Francisco de Burgoa; Biblioteca de Investigación Juan de Córdova; Archivo General de la Nación; Archivo General de las Indias; Library of Congress Indian Languages Collection; Special Collections of the Latin American Library at Tulane University; the John Carter Brown Library; and the Rosenbach Museum and Library. I owe special gratitude to Israel Garrido Esquivel, director of the Archivo Histórico Judicial de Oaxaca, where I have spent the bulk of my time. He has been an immensely helpful and kind interlocutor.

Linda Arnold provided digitized resources and sage advice. Selene García Jiménez lent her excellent archival skills, knowledge, and historical insights. At Emory, I have been blessed with wonderful research assistants who have helped me with transcriptions, data management, and bibliographies: Jon Coulis, Audrey Henderson, Marissa Nichols, Alexander Cors, Rachel Shapiro, María de los Angeles Picone, and Juan Viacava. Special thanks to Alexander Cors and Randy Mesa who produced the maps for the book; and

Emory's Center for Digital Studies for providing resources and support. Kelly Duquette helped with editing and formatting at a critical juncture.

Numerous fellowships and institutions made this work possible, including a National Endowment for the Humanities Summer Stipend, American Council of Learned Societies Faculty Fellowship, Emory University Research Committee Award, Mellon New Directions Fellowship, and Senior Fellowship at Emory's Fox Center for Humanistic Inquiry. I also benefited from the engagement of colleagues at the following institutions and symposia: Tepaske Seminar for Colonial Latin American History; Tepoztlán Institute; Symposium on Comparative Early Modern Legal History at the Newberry Library, "Meanings of Justice in New World Empires"; the *seminario permanente* at the Max Planck Institute for Legal History; "Reframing Nineteenth Century Latin America" at Yale University; the Omohundro Institute of Early American History and Culture colloquium and the William and Mary Legal History Seminar; the University of Wisconsin Department of Spanish and Portuguese Studies; "Renaissance Displacements" at Princeton University; "Tasks of the Translator" at Saint Louis University's Center for Intercultural Studies; "Indigenous (Latin) America" at the Center of Latin American and Caribbean Studies (CLACS) and Department of American Indian Studies at the University of Illinois at Urbana-Champaign; "Agents Médiateurs Dans L'Empire Hispanique" at the Institut D'Études Européenes et Globales; Université du Maine; the University of Chicago Latin American History Workshop; and the Early Modern World Seminar at the Institute of Historical Research, School of Advanced Study, University College of London.

In Oaxaca, many people provided support, inspiration, and ideas over the years. I am grateful for the friendship of Martina Schrader-Kniffki and Johannes Kniffki, who have connected me with friends and colleagues and taught me much about Oaxaca. My collaborative work with Martina on colonial Zapotec-language sources and theories of translation has deeply informed this book. I also thank María de los Ángeles Romero Frizzi, Daniela Traffano, Carlos Sánchez Silva, Francisco José Ruiz Cervantes, Michael Swanton, Sebastián van Doesburg, Flaviano Pérez Hernández, Genaro Hernández, Juana Vásquez, Kiado Cruz, Rayo Cruz, and Omar Aguilar Sánchez for illuminating conversations and guidance. Other scholars based in Mexico have enriched my work through their supportive and critical engagement: Luis Alberto Arrioja Díaz Viruell, Marta Martín Gabaldón, Antonio Escobar Ohmstede, Victor Gayol, Edgar Mendoza, Michel Oudijk, Ethelia Ruiz Medrano, and Margarita Menegus Bornemann. In the United States, Europe, and beyond, I have benefited from the intellectual and personal generosity of many colleagues who have pushed my thinking and answered questions big and small: Renzo Honores, Alcira Dueñas, Michelle McKinley, Camilla Townsend, Mónica Díaz, Pete Sigal, Kevin Terraciano, Matthew Restall, Stephanie Wood, Susan Kellogg, Robert Haskett, John Schwaller, Jerome Offner, Lisa Sousa, Owen Jones, Caterina Pizzigoni, Richard Conway, Karen Graubart, Jane Mangan, Frank Salomon, Caroline Cunill, Claire Gilbert, Frances Ramos, Martin Nesvig, Jorge Cañizares-Esguerra, Christoph Rosenmüller, Rachel O'Toole, Marcela Echeverri Muñoz, Mark Lentz, Nora Jaffary, Christina Bueno, Alexander Dawson, Eddie Wright-Rios, Sonya Lipsett-Rivera, Mark Overmyer-Velázquez, Alex Hidalgo, Brian Owensby, Richard Ross, Thomas Duve, Lauren Benton, António Manuel Hespanha, Wim Decock, Otto Danwerth, Margarita Zamora, Santa Arias, Alejandra Irigoin, and Santiago Muñoz Arbeláez. I owe special thanks to Gabriela Ramos, Laura Matthew, Joan Bristol, and Paja Faudree for long years of friendship and camaraderie, and who continue to help me grow as a scholar of colonial Latin America and Oaxaca.

Javier Villa-Flores, Bianca Premo, Karen Stolley, Nancy Farriss, Joanne Rappaport, Lorrin Thomas, and Miranda Johnson read and commented on part or all of the manuscript. I thank each of them for their astute critiques, generosity, and friendship. Arun Jones and Clifton Crais offered insightful feedback on an early version of chapter 4, Michelle Armstrong-Partida on an early version of chapter 1, and José Carlos de la Puente Luna, Tamar Herzog, Cynthia Radding, Justyna Olko, Adriana Chira, Maria Montalvo, Sharon Strocchia, and Pamela Scully, on an early version of chapter 5. Roberto González and Miranda Johnson provided helpful suggestions on an early version of the epilogue. Thank you especially to Bianca Premo for joyful and generative conversations that have sharpened my thinking, and most importantly, for her friendship and counsel through this process. I could not have done this without her. Nancy Farriss's influence is evident throughout the book, and her impeccable scholarship continues to inspire and motivate me. I thank her for many years of support and memorable visits and conversations in Oaxaca and Philadelphia. And of course, this book would not have been possible without the patience, guidance, and cheerleading of Gisela Fosado, senior editor at Duke University Press. Thank you also to Alejandra Mejía, assistant editor; Ihsan Taylor, project editor; Aimee Harrison for the cover design; and the two anonymous reviewers, who provided discerning and helpful commentary on the manuscript.

At Emory, I am lucky to have superb and supportive Latin Americanist colleagues: Javier Villa-Flores, Tom Rogers, Adriana Chira, Jeffrey Lesser,

Susan Socolow, Pablo Palomino, Xóchtil Marsilli-Vargas, Karen Stolley, Mónica García-Blizzard, María Carrión, Hernán Feldman, and Phil MacLeod. Adriana Chira has spent hours talking with me about custom, encouraging me to think broadly and comparatively across the Spanish Empire. Tom Rogers helped me survive the pandemic through our daily constitutionals around the Emory campus. Kristin Mann has pushed my work forward and served as a valued mentor. Astrid Eckert has supported me with letters for fellowships and more. Walter Melion and Keith Anthony, who run Emory's Fox Center, and my colleagues during my senior fellowship—Falguni Sheth, Miriam Udell, Michael Peletz, and Corinna Zeltsman—nourished the book at a critical moment. Gyan Pandey and David Nugent invited me to present at Emory's Colonial and Postcolonial Studies Seminar, and Arun Jones, at the seminar that he convened at Emory, "Can the Native Christian Speak?" Joe Crespino and Sharon Strocchia, my chair and interim chair, have encouraged and supported me in these final stages of research and writing. Department of History staff over the years—Kelly Yates, Becky Herring, Katie Wilson, and Allison Rollins—provided much logistical and moral support. I thank other colleagues in the department and across Emory University for their friendship and moral support, including Deboleena Roy, Sean Meighoo, Lauren Klein, Susan Gagliardi, Mariana Candido, Tehila Sasson, Malinda Lowery, Ellie Schainker, Dawn Peterson (currently an independent scholar), Jamie Melton, Brian Vick, Matt Payne, Tonio Andrade, Daniel LaChance, Don Tuten, Robert Goddard, and Carla Freeman. Julia Gaffield, Lia Bascomb, and other friends and colleagues of the Greater Atlanta Latin American and Caribbean Studies Initiative (GALACSI) commented on many fragments of this manuscript.

My family—Aiden, Marianna, and Maeve Downey—are the wellspring from which everything else flows. I thank them for their love and companionship, and the reminder to live in the present. My parents and sisters, George, Zoena, Grace, and Daphne Yannakakis; my parents-in-law, Mary Gold and Robert Gold (who passed away in November 2021); my brothers and sister-in-law, nieces, nephews, cousins, uncles, aunts, and friends underscore the importance of the past and where we come from while pointing to the excitement and promise of the future.

ACKNOWLEDGMENTS

A Note on Orthography

Historically, and in the present, there are multiple conventions for writing in the many Indigenous languages of Mexico. When I reproduce Indigenous-language words and passages from historical documents, I maintain the original spelling. In the case of Nahuatl place-names, I do not use accents (i.e., Tenochtitlan and Yanhuitlan). For the sake of consistency, I maintain this practice throughout the book, even for the later colonial period when orthographic conventions changed and accents were frequently used in Nahuatl place-names, as they are today. The only exception is when I discuss the case of present-day Teotitlán del Valle, in which case I follow the modern orthography. For the case of Ñudzahui (Mixtec) and Ayuuk (Mixe) place-names, I reproduce the original spellings in the documents. For the case of Tíchazàa (Zapotec), for which there are regional variants and a recent renaissance in Zapotec writing has produced new orthographies, I follow the recent conventions (i.e., San Juan Tabaá and San Juan Yaeé).

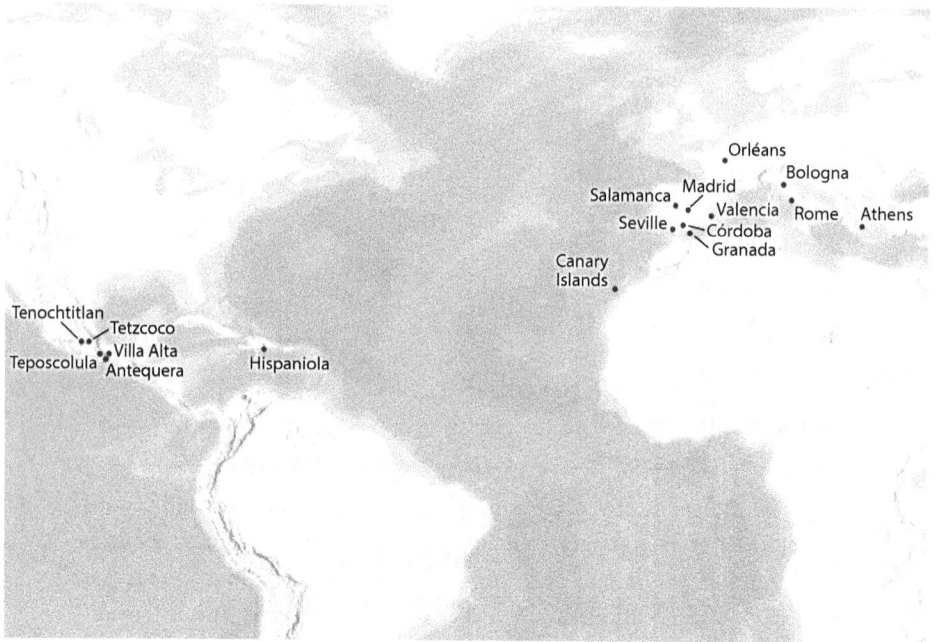

Map 1 Selected locations in the Mediterranean-Atlantic world.
Map produced by Alexander Cors and Randy Mesa.

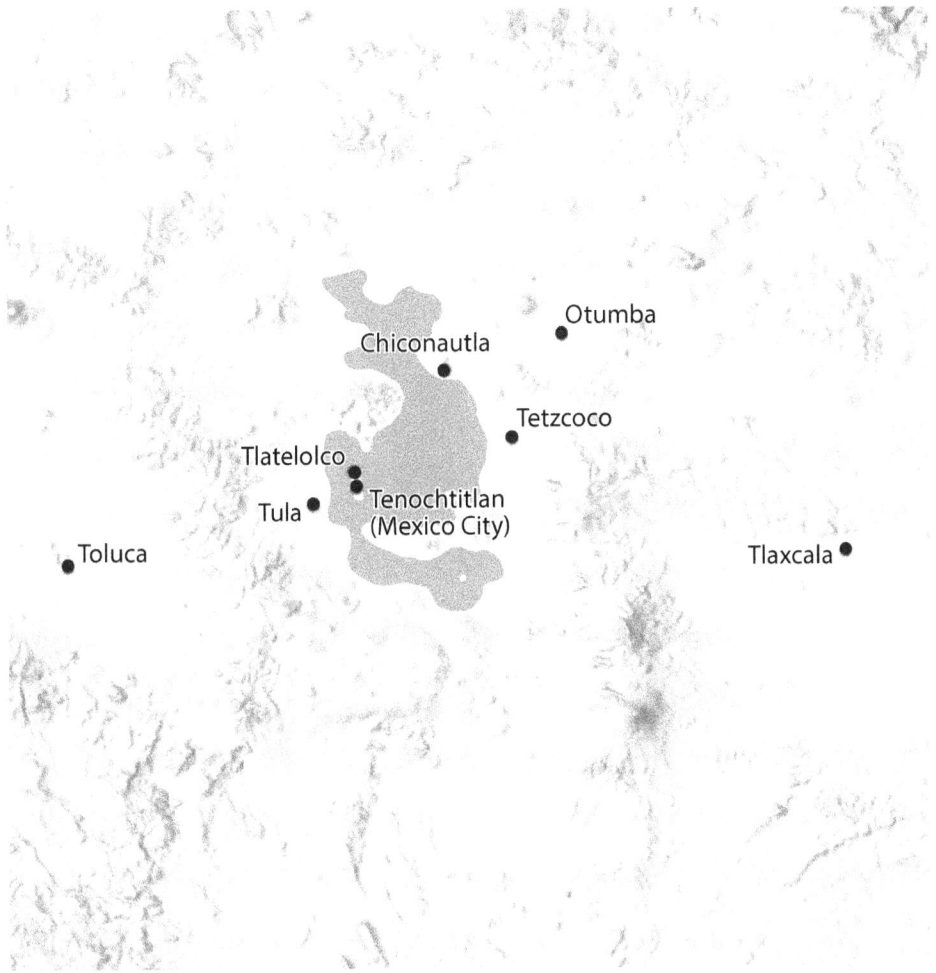

Map 2 Selected *altepeme* (Nahua ethnic states) of Central Mexico.
Map produced by Alexander Cors and Randy Mesa.

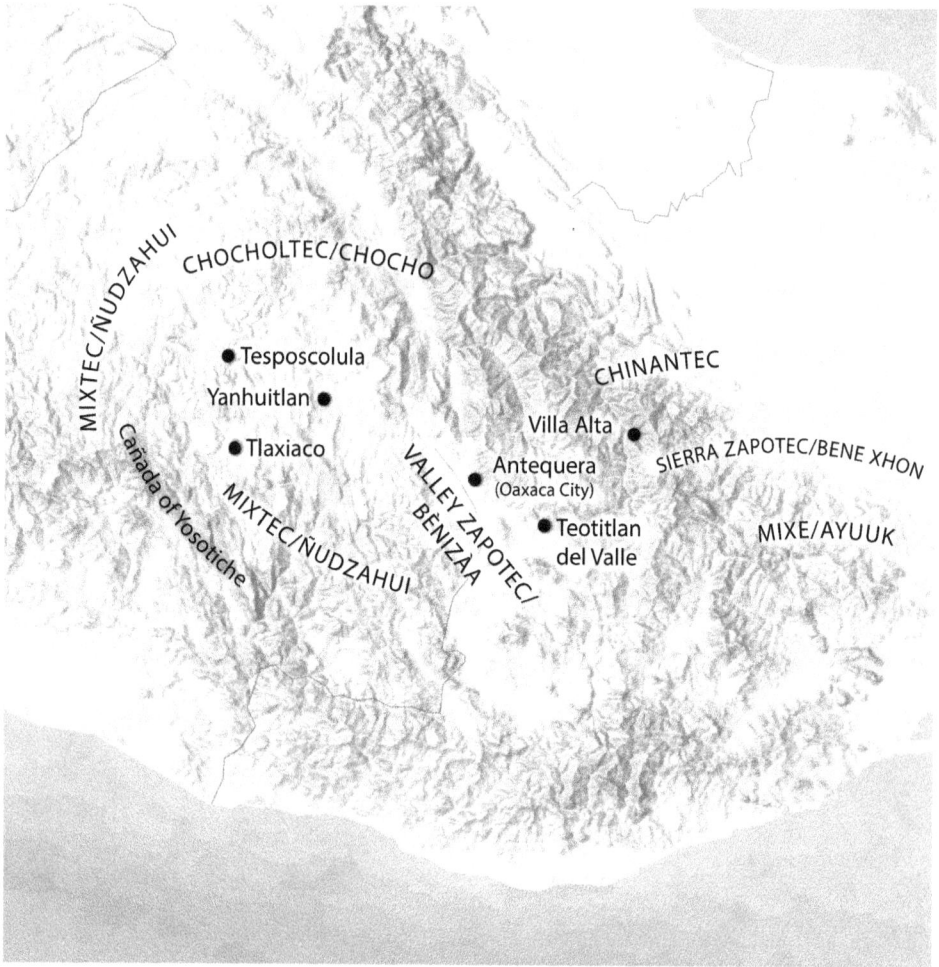

Map 3 (above) Selected urban administrative centers and ethnic groups of Oaxaca. Map produced by Alexander Cors and Randy Mesa.

Map 4 (opposite) Selected Indigenous towns of the Teposcolula district of Oaxaca. Map produced by Alexander Cors and Randy Mesa.

5

23
18

Coixtlahuaca

29

Yanhuitlan 8

Teposcolula
11 7
10
Santa María Asunción
Nochixtlan 9

19
14 16 3
20
12 2 27
17 15 13
26 6
28 4

Tlaxiaco

22

21

1

24 25

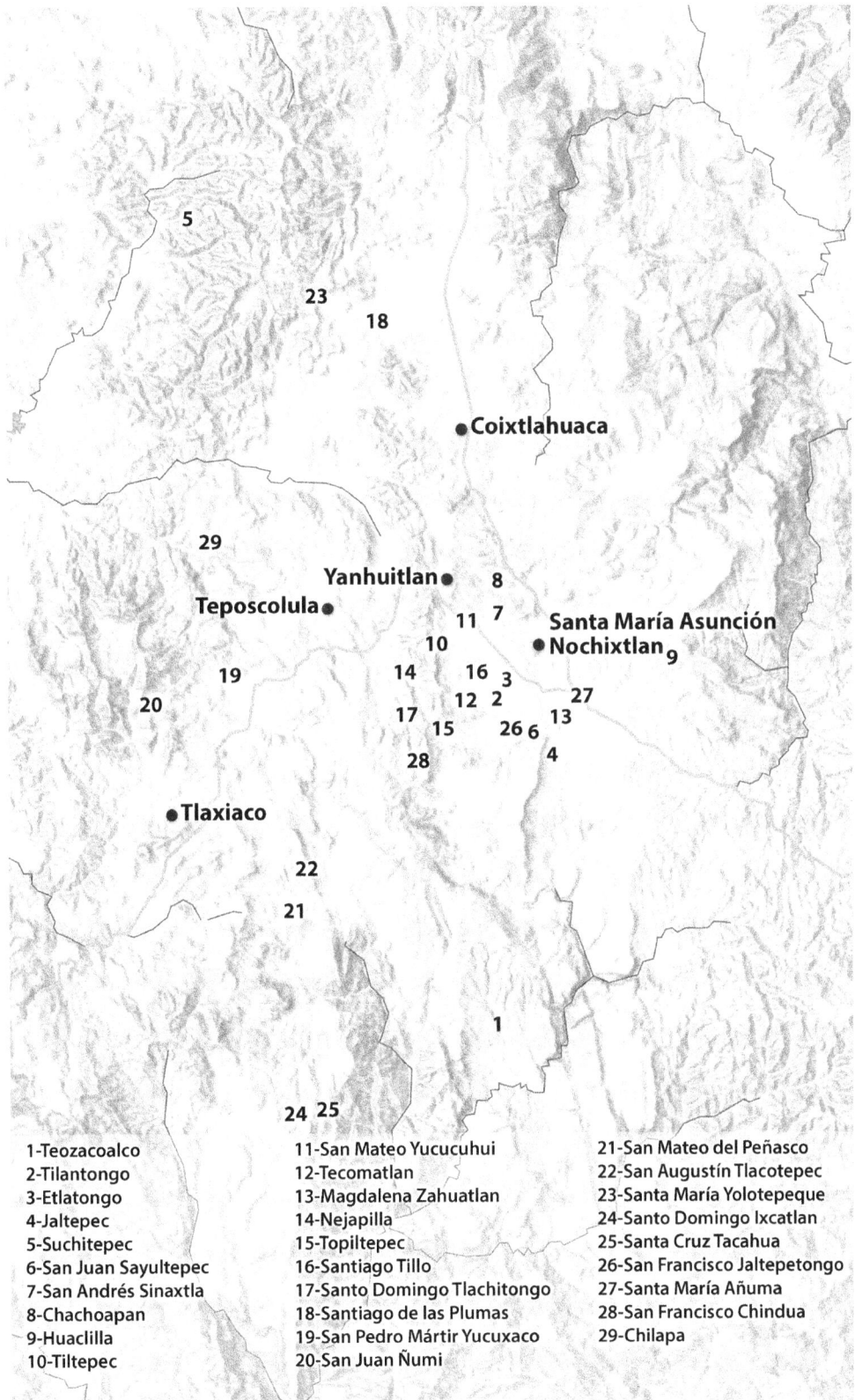

1-Teozacoalco
2-Tilantongo
3-Etlatongo
4-Jaltepec
5-Suchitepec
6-San Juan Sayultepec
7-San Andrés Sinaxtla
8-Chachoapan
9-Huaclilla
10-Tiltepec

11-San Mateo Yucucuhui
12-Tecomatlan
13-Magdalena Zahuatlan
14-Nejapilla
15-Topiltepec
16-Santiago Tillo
17-Santo Domingo Tlachitongo
18-Santiago de las Plumas
19-San Pedro Mártir Yucuxaco
20-San Juan Ñumi

21-San Mateo del Peñasco
22-San Augustín Tlacotepec
23-Santa María Yolotepeque
24-Santo Domingo Ixcatlan
25-Santa Cruz Tacahua
26-San Francisco Jaltepetongo
27-Santa María Añuma
28-San Francisco Chindua
29-Chilapa

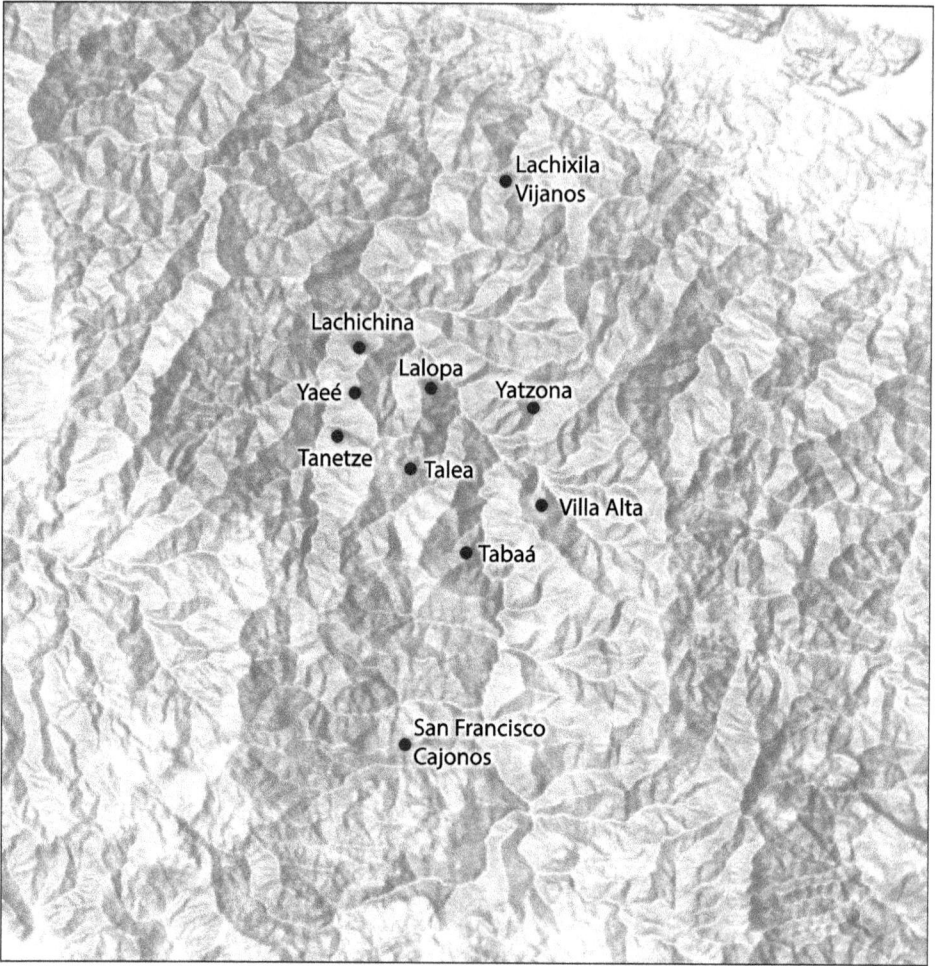

Map 5 Selected Indigenous towns of the Villa Alta district of Oaxaca.
Map produced by Alexander Cors and Randy Mesa.

Introduction

BUILDING FENCES STRONG ENOUGH to restrain cattle and oxen from trampling communal cropland is hard work. Until recently in Teotitlán del Valle, an Indigenous Zapotec town in the southern Mexican state of Oaxaca, the men of the community built and repaired the fences together as part of a customary practice of mutual aid and reciprocal labor.[1] Teotitlán del Valle sits at the gateway between one of Oaxaca's seven central valleys and the formidable Sierra Juárez to the north. Some of the town's communal lands are dispersed in the mountains above the village center. Until the 1940s when most residents were full-time farmers, it was worth the steep climb to access a small communal plot and the trouble and sweat to patch a breached fence. The labor exchange for corral construction, and for other agricultural needs like planting, weeding, and harvesting, allowed the men in the community to earn their subsistence and circumvent the exploitative practice of debt peonage.[2]

According to historical documentation, during the eighteenth century in San Juan Tabaá, a Zapotec town deep in the mountains above Teotitlán del Valle, the commoners of the town built fences around communal lands in order to keep oxen and mules of the well-to-do members of the community from trampling the crops that the commoners farmed. Although the commoners felt the custom was unjust since the livestock was not theirs, the livestock owners countered that the arrangement was reciprocal and part of the mutual bonds of obligation that held the community together. They pointed out that they allowed the town to use their draft animals to carry crops to market to earn currency to support the fiestas that punctuated the Christian ritual calendar and transport Spanish administrators when they visited the town on official business. Furthermore, they argued, the practice was just because it was ancient custom. Unable to resolve the dispute through the purview of village justice, the opposing parties brought their case to a Spanish colonial court for resolution.[3]

These examples of community norms of collective labor separated by more than two hundred years reveal distinct modes of Native custom in Mexican history: one that produced horizontal bonds of reciprocity and another that upheld social hierarchy. Broadly construed, custom refers to social practice that over time takes on the normative power of law within a territorially based community. In historical contexts across the globe, custom was at times equivalent to law; in others, a source of law; and in others, an alternative legal framework.[4] In the example from twentieth-century Teotitlán del Valle, custom regulated labor for collective benefit. Despite the onerous nature of the work, the community's peasant farmers considered the labor exchange to be worthwhile because it allowed them to expand production into marginal lands and insulate themselves from exploitation by wealthy landowners. In eighteenth-century San Juan Tabaá, the custom of building fences to protect communal lands reinforced divisions of wealth and status within the community, serving the interests of elites at the expense of commoners. When the commoners went to court to challenge the custom, they did so on moral grounds, claiming that it did not serve equity or the common good, two fundamental principles of colonial justice. The historical, social, and economic circumstances in these cases—defined by whose interests the labor exchange served—applied sharp divergences in meaning to what on the surface appears to be a similar custom across time. In both cases, however, custom's power as a communal norm and a mode of organizing labor was underwritten by the moral force of its claim to antiquity and reciprocity. The capacity of custom to produce social cohesion was in constant tension with the community's internal hierarchies and the broader economic and political systems in which the community participated. As a result, custom—in dynamic relationship with history—was subject to change and contestation.

Custom, a category of European law with origins in medieval Roman law, has not always been understood as historical, dynamic, and changing. In language evocative of timelessness and primordiality, a well-known historian of medieval Europe characterizes custom as a nexus of blood, land, and time, the coagulation of enduring communal values, and a primitive unwritten law.[5] The European idea of custom as the expression of an authentic, autochthonous popular will can be traced to the rise of nationalism in the nineteenth century and a move among elite functionaries to nationalize law according to a mythic national character. In this romantic guise, custom predates law on an evolutionary continuum in which the latter represents the apex of a process of legal modernization. Critics argue that this formulation of custom persists and reinforces a problematic association with a timeless primordiality while reproducing hierarchies between local and state-centered norms.[6] Woven into such binaries are assumptions regarding custom's irrationality versus law's basis in practical reason.[7] According to these logics, peasant communities are locked in time, fettered to tradition, and governed by norms of popular justice. As such, they are objects to be modernized and brought into line with written, codified, state-centered law.

In the context of European empire, the custom–law opposition bolstered and generated social inequalities through the production of hierarchies of difference evidenced by categories like "native." National and imperial elites have justified and consolidated violent conquest and political domination from the era of the Roman Empire to the present moment by casting the laws and norms of conquered peoples as custom, and subordinating their customs to imperial or state-centered law. The earliest generations of European and North American social scientists supported the logic of empire by characterizing the social conventions of "primitive" and "simple" societies as customs, and those of "complex," urban ones as law. Legal anthropologists have critiqued the stark opposition between law and custom by arguing that all peoples living under nation-state or imperial regimes must contend with both legal and customary norms, and that the alleged boundary between them has always been much more porous than conventional wisdom has suggested.[8] Despite this, the dichotomy between custom and law—a vestige of the romantic and primordial notion of custom—persists in the popular and scholarly imagination. Until recently, this was especially true in Latin America where anthropologists and social scientists characterized Indigenous customary law as an essential aspect of ethnic and communal identity, fundamentally opposed to state-centered positive law.[9]

Historians and anthropologists have been whittling away at these deeply ingrained assumptions for the last few decades, pointing to how peasant communities in diverse settings across time forged a dynamically plural legal culture through a synthesis of custom and law.[10] Scholars of medieval and early modern Europe, where studies of custom are densely concentrated, have revised earlier romantic formulations, demonstrating that far from being an oral tradition locked in time, custom served as a terrain for the negotiation of social norms, was often written down, and could become law or indistinguishable from it.[11] On a parallel track, scholars have disentangled the presumed linkage between custom and autochthonous Native practice in colonial and postcolonial societies. Africanist scholarship has yielded seminal work on custom as a tool of European empire, contending that rather than representing Indigenous norms based in antiquity, customary law was often an invention of Native elites, colonial authorities, and anthropologists who used it to justify indirect rule and social control.[12] For the case of Latin America, constitutional reforms across the region during the 1990s prompted a wave of research on legal pluralism that reassessed earlier positions, pointing to how law and Native custom have always influenced one other, while shaping and being shaped by the same historical processes.[13]

Taken together, recent scholarship has overturned the custom–law opposition and custom's identification with a purported peasant and Indigenous primordiality, characterizing it instead as a multifaceted legal, political, and social strategy. Depending on the historical context, it served as a tool of domination, claim regarding the allocation of privileges and obligations, and resource for local justice. It is important to note, however, that one axiom holds true across custom's many guises: historical actors across time and space have recognized that associating custom with antiquity and community lends it considerable moral force.

Indigenous Custom and Law in Pre-Hispanic Mesoamerica and Colonial Latin America

This book is about the invention, translation, and deployment of Native custom as a legal category and imperial strategy in colonial Mexico. Custom represented the primary framework through which Mexico's and more broadly Latin America's Native communities governed themselves and interfaced with authorities outside the community from the first decades following the Spanish conquest until independence from Spain. The Spanish Crown recognized the right of Native authorities to rule their communities according to their laws and customs provided that they did not contradict Christianity or Spanish law. Over three hundred years, Native communities synthesized Indigenous and Spanish norms regarding self-governance, justice, landholding, labor, sexuality, morality, and ritual life to produce the realm of colonial Indigenous custom. Through analysis of laws and legislation, missionary sources, Inquisition records, Native pictorial histories, royal surveys, and Spanish- and Native-language court and notarial records, I show how the idea of custom was given local meaning, how it became part of the fabric of Native communal life and a potent claim in Spanish courts, and how its purview changed and narrowed over time. In the hands of Native litigants, claims to custom, which on the surface aimed to conserve the past, ultimately provided a means with which to contend with rapid change in the present and the production of new rights for the future.

Spanish missionary priests and conquistadors destroyed the pre-Hispanic pictographic manuscripts that recorded the laws, legal institutions, and judicial proceedings of the Aztec city-states (*altepeme*, pl.; *altepetl*, sing.) of central Mexico during their violent campaign against Native religious authority, which as in the case of Europe was inextricably linked to political and legal authority. Ironically, the same agents of destruction who burned Native libraries, archives, and scriptoria later sought to recover Indigenous knowledge for the purposes of more effective evangelization. Friars Toribio de Benavente (Motolonía), Juan de Torquemada, Alonso de Zorita, Diego Durán, and Bernardino de Sahagún commented extensively on pre-Hispanic law and custom based on ethnographic observations and their discussions with Indigenous intellectuals.[14] So too did the descendants of Indigenous rulers, some of whom were the products of unions between Indigenous noblewomen and Spanish conquistadors, such as Fernando Alva de Ixtlilxochitl and Juan Bautista Pomar.[15] The mestizo chroniclers had their own axes to grind, including the vindication of the actions of their forebears before and after the Spanish wars of conquest. Indigenous painter-scribes (*tlacuiloque*) of the colonial period also recorded pre-Hispanic norms regarding crime and punishment in the pictorial *Mapa Quinatzin*, created in 1546.[16] Ethnohistorians have carefully cross-referenced these texts to produce histories of the laws and legal institutions of the pre-Hispanic era, most fulsomely for the cases of Tenochtitlan and Tetzcoco, the dominant altepeme of the Aztec Triple Alliance.[17]

Prior to the Spanish conquest, royally controlled legal and political bodies as well as local institutions and customs regulated matters concerning land tenure, property, inheritance, kinship relations, business, trade, contracts, slavery, crime and punishment, and local and imperial administration in Tenochtitlan and Tetzcoco. Missionary friars and mestizo chroniclers devoted special attention to the legal system of Tetzcoco, crediting the *tlatloani* (ruler, literally "speaker") Nezahualcoyotl, who governed from 1429 to 1472 with the development and expansion of the city-state's laws and court system. According to their accounts, he was responsible for a body of eighty laws divided into four parts. He designed a legal system to administer these laws that concentrated royal power while incorporating distinct social sectors through the creation of lower-level courts. Two tribunals overseen by the tla-toani sat at the apex of the system. Below these, four supreme councils, one of which was designated a Supreme Legal Council, rendered judgments that could be appealed to two higher judges who pronounced sentence with royal approval. The jurisdiction of the four councils was determined by the nature of the dispute or offense in question rather than the quality of the person being judged or the territory from which he or she hailed. In addition to these high courts, there were local-level courts overseen by the city's wards (*calpulli,* singular, *calpolleque,* plural), temples, schools for youth, and kinship groups. There were also separate legal fora for merchants, artisans, and the dependent towns subject to the authority of Tetzcoco.[18]

The jurisdictional complexity of the system, designed to control diverse ethnic groups and multiple local rulers in an era of imperial expansion, was complemented by its strong class character. Nobles and commoners had separate courts, and nobles could only be judged by other nobles. Criminal cases followed a process of official accusation, investigation of the facts of the case, sentencing, and punishment. Judgments were often rendered swiftly—cases were limited to eighty days—and punishments were harsh, especially for the crimes of theft, adultery, drunkenness, and rebellion.[19] More recent scholarship argues that missionaries and mestizo chroniclers portrayed the legal system of Tetzcoco favorably—as rational, secular, and civilized—in relation to that of Tenochtitlan, which they glossed as violent, expansionist, and religious, in order to justify the Spanish conquest of the latter. But in reality, these comparisons were overdrawn, and many of the institutions and principles of justice at work in Tetzcoco were generalizable across the Basin of Mexico.[20]

A shared feature of pre-Hispanic Nahua legal culture was the importance of local institutions, rules, and sanctions in regulating social life. In Tenochtitlan and Tetzcoco, ward officials, schoolmasters, merchant and craft guilds, and families taught and enforced proper comportment and the duties and obligations of their members.[21] As was true in Europe during the same period, custom rather than formal law provided the primary framework for dispute resolution, local justice, and social control.

Within the first years following the conquest, Spanish authorities had to confront the challenge of how to incorporate sovereign Indigenous peoples and their political and legal institutions into an imperial order. In a time of violence, dispossession, and uncertainty, Spanish officials knew one thing for sure: in order to subjugate the Indigenous population, they had to destroy Native institutions at odds with their economic and religious objectives, while maintaining those that served them. For their part, the Native ruling elite navigated between Spanish expectations and local pressures as they adapted their institutions to colonial demands. An important body of scholarship on Mesoamerica and the Andes focuses on the sixteenth-century transition from Indigenous authority, based on the customary control of Indigenous lords over land and labor to a colonial system grounded in two separate administrative and legal jurisdictions: the republic of Spaniards and the republic of Indians. The territorial jurisdictions overseen by Spanish magistrates and the jurisdiction of Indian cabildos (Spanish-style municipal councils) gave institutional expression to this hierarchical caste-based system. The dissolution of Native territory, which had provided the basis of elite Indigenous dominion, made the transition possible. The overall trajectory charted by this literature is one of destruction of the politically and socially complex autonomous Indigenous world of the sixteenth century to the making of a less stratified Native peasantry administered by their municipal councils and subordinate to Spanish colonizers in the two centuries that followed. In the process, Native custom gave way to Spanish norms of landholding, labor, and self-governance.[22]

Ethnohistorians of Mesoamerica have tempered this narrative with an emphasis on synthesis and adaptation.[23] Relying on Native-language sources produced by Indigenous authorities, scholars working in the tradition of the New Philology, an influential school of ethnohistory, have argued for greater continuity in Mesoamerican spatial-territorial organization, household composition, political authority, officeholding, kinship, religion and ritual, and gender relations.[24] Others have analyzed Indigenous-language sources to demonstrate continuities in Indigenous intellectual life, including moral philosophy and history.[25] More recently, intensive research in local archives across Mesoamerica and the Andes and imperial archives in Spain points to the production of a legal order characterized by the dynamic interplay of Indigenous and Spanish forms of justice and self-governance.[26] These studies show that rather than being divided into two republics, colonial Spanish America was a constellation of cities, towns, and diverse ethnic and racial communities that constituted their own individual republics with semiautonomous jurisdiction, governed by a wide range of imperial and local norms.[27]

Indigenous litigation in Spanish courts was a dominant feature of colonial life and a primary mode through which Native peoples sought to protect old privileges and rights or advocate for new ones. Native people appeared with frequency in front of local Spanish magistrates and in higher viceregal courts to make legal claims against Spanish colonists and other Native individuals and communities. Scholarship on Native society and colonial law contends that the law served a hegemonic function by providing a common terrain, recognized by all parties as legitimate, on which colonial authorities and Native communities struggled between and among themselves over competing interests.[28] In this context, litigation represented a form of politics at varied scales, from the local to the imperial, across the civil and ecclesiastical jurisdictions, and in fora specifically designed to facilitate Indigenous access to justice such as the General Indian Court and the Protector of Indians.[29] Law and litigation also responded to and shaped changes in colonial governance and social order, including gendered and racial hierarchies, and interethnic loyalties and allegiances.[30] In some instances, Native authorities and commoners strategically combined extralegal means, such as violence or rebellion, with legal processes to achieve diverse objectives.[31] In others, Native petitioners, claimants, and litigants—noble and commoner alike—played upon their identity as imperial subjects, sometimes in the court of the king himself or in metropolitan courts, to demand justice and protection.[32]

The Spanish Crown afforded Indigenous people special legal jurisdiction in Spanish courts dedicated to Indian litigation and in Native courts of first instance in their communities. Woodrow Borah's seminal study of the General Indian Court, which operated from 1585 to 1820, reveals how the Crown attempted to facilitate access to justice to its Native subjects by streamlining the huge volume of Native litigation, reducing its cost, and providing greater fairness in legal procedures. Borah contends that the founding of the General Indian Court marked a transition from the Crown's attempts to preserve and accommodate Native custom to a more aggressive policy of incorporating Native subjects into the imperial order through the legal category of *miserable*, which entitled them to the same protections as widows, orphans, the poor, and the wretched in Europe.[33] More recently, scholarship on local justice and the jurisdiction of Native cabildos has shown that although Spanish judges may have increasingly discounted Indigenous custom over time in disputes that reached the colony's higher courts, custom remained central to the local affairs of Indigenous communities. As evident in Native town council records, some of which were written in Indigenous languages, and legal documents from the local courts of the Spanish magistrates, Native authorities actively produced imperial legal culture by forging local ideologies of justice, participating in networks of legal knowledge, and braiding together pre-Columbian, colonial Indigenous, and European legal traditions.[34] Focus on Indian jurisdiction as constitutive of early modern legal pluralism provides an important corrective to studies that have often ignored the role of Native peoples as producers of imperial legal orders.[35]

Across the deep literature on Native people and the law in colonial Meso-america and the Andes, Native custom appears frequently as a point of reference for arguments about continuity and change during sixteenth-century transitions in colonial governance. However, it is rarely the focus of sustained in-depth analysis in legal settings and beyond, and over the *longue durée*. In studies of custom in colonial law and society in Spanish America more broadly, Indigenous custom tends to be treated tangentially.[36] On the other hand, recent groundbreaking work on colonial law and justice in Afro-descendant communities focuses on custom as a terrain for regulating and navigating the large gray zone between slavery and freedom, pushing scholars to ask new questions about how custom took on specific meanings and uses in the lives of colonial subalterns.[37]

In his seminal study of the "power of custom" in Spanish colonial law, Víctor Tau Anzoátegui demonstrates how custom became fully integrated into the thinking of elite jurists and animated the theory and practice of colonial Spanish American law. He argues against entrenched ideas that custom was subordinate or contrary to law, or outside of it, positing instead that law and custom were part of a continuum in a colonial world regulated by a plurality of norms and sources of law. This was a crucial contribution to the field of the *derecho indiano* school of historiography, in which he was a central figure. Although Indigenous custom does not feature centrally in his work, he addresses its significance to the development of Spanish colonial law. But he does so from the perspective of royal legislation, law, and the writings of jurists and legal scholars. Indigenous views of custom do not figure much in his analysis.[38]

When Native custom appears at the center of colonial historiography, it surfaces in small-scale, microhistorical, and article-length studies, most of which are concentrated in the early colonial period.[39] A pioneering work in the tradition of derecho indiano argues that Native laws and customs held the same weighty status in colonial law as did the *fueros* (laws and charters specific to localities and persons) of Castilian law. The hierarchy of legal sources for colonial judges, then, began at the top with the laws of the Indies, followed by Indigenous custom, and finally, the laws of Castile (primarily *Las Siete Partidas* and the *Recopilación de las leyes de Castilla*).[40] Subsequent studies built upon this foundational insight, arguing that due to the centrality of local custom to Iberian law and the casuistry of the judicial process that foregrounded local conditions and weighed the particularities of individual legal cases with recourse to a plethora of legal sources (including local custom), pre-Hispanic Indigenous law and custom significantly impacted colonial legislation. This vein of scholarship focuses mainly on Spanish laws, legislation, and legal treatises that equated the status of Native custom with local custom in the Iberian and Roman tradition as well as the commentaries of colonial chroniclers, jurists, and administrators who observed Native law and custom and evaluated it in relation to Spanish and Christian norms.[41] As in Tau Anzoátegui's work, Indigenous views and uses of custom remain largely invisible.

Historians have remedied this imbalance by moving from the lofty perch of legislation, law, and legal treatises to the archives of colonial courts that recorded Indigenous disputes. Important studies of sixteenth-century colonial Mexico emphasize how Native custom's validation by Spanish judges facilitated the consolidation of colonial rule through the incorporation of Native elite landholding and authority into a Spanish normative order. A preliminary work tests the argument that Native custom shaped colonial law through a sample of early sixteenth-century Indigenous disputes brought before the Real Audiencia of Mexico. The judges often found in favor of Native customary claims, which served to incorporate Native custom into colonial law and the Native elite into the colonial ruling order, while further subordinating both over time.[42] Subsequent scholarship modifies this argument through analysis of elite Native claims in Spanish courts to patrimonial lands based on custom during the 1530s, which resulted in favorable decisions for the claimants and the legitimation of Native ancestral landholding more broadly.[43] A recent study moves beyond royal legislation and the courts to explore the many meanings of Native custom produced in diverse settings in sixteenth-century central Mexico and Yucatán, including the missionary context. The authors argue that custom's conceptual and practical flexibility facilitated the legitimation of the political authority of Native elites and the consolidation of colonial rule.[44]

For the case of the sixteenth-century Andes, the scholarship suggests that colonial jurists and authorities selectively recognized elements of Native custom in keeping with their private or political interests, tipping the balance of forces more definitively toward Spanish colonists than was the case in New Spain. In northern coastal Peru, Spanish judges recognized the validity of Andean custom inconsistently, overturning it in a case regarding an ethnic lord's sexual monopoly over his wives, with the objective of removing a powerful and uncooperative Native ruler.[45] In the central Andes, when Spanish economic interests were at stake, litigation provided an impulse for Spanish jurists, officials, and *encomenderos* (recipients of royal grants of Indigenous towns) to unearth and record Inca custom, allowing for its partial recognition, distortion, and politically motivated application.[46] Beyond the purview of Spanish courts, custom served as a framework for Native self-governance and dispute resolution in the Andes, including the customary management of land, labor, and communal assets, and the changing ends to which they were directed over time.[47] Recent scholarship on the northern Andes shows that the category of custom served as a terrain for the creation of an interdependent colonial order in which Native people retained considerable power especially at the margins of empire. Indigenous and Spanish litigants invoked custom in quotidian conflicts, forging deep cross-cultural relationships and networks that transcended the purported divide between Native and Spanish worlds.[48]

Although the bulk of scholarship on custom focuses on the sixteenth century, recent studies move forward in time to the seventeenth and eighteenth centuries when Indigenous claims to custom in Native and Spanish courts centered on colonial-era as well as—or instead of—pre-Hispanic practice for their legitimacy, and written documents took precedence over claims to custom in oral testimony.[49] Multiple norms come to the fore in some of these cases, as Native authorities used Spanish and pre-Hispanic Inca law to adjudicate land disputes in the seventeenth-century central Andes, and as Native authorities navigated between local custom and law to manage communal resources and lands in eighteenth-century Oaxaca.[50] In the Northern Andean province of Quito, a series of legal cases over the same Native lands from the sixteenth through eighteenth centuries shows how the temporal referent for customary claims shifted from the pre-Hispanic period, to the conquest, to a vague invocation of time immemorial. Rather than oral testimonies recounting Indigenous knowledge of pre-Hispanic rights that was typical of sixteenth-century claims, litigants in later years presented Spanish legal instruments as proof of Native customary practice, resulting in a transformation of Native land rights and diminution of Native land tenure.[51] A comparative study of Oaxaca and the northern coast of Peru demonstrates how, during the eighteenth century, Native litigants deployed different referents for custom in disputes over local governance and elite hereditary privilege that yielded new conceptions of time, history, and merit. In the process, they produced Enlightenment discourse whose origins scholars have traditionally located in Europe.[52]

Since Time Immemorial builds upon the insights of these studies by widening the lens chronologically, spatially, and analytically to examine Native custom's entangled history as a legal category, colonial governing strategy, framework for Native self-rule, and claim for Native rights and protections in

Spanish courts. Throughout, I pay close attention to the interplay between Native custom's changing meaning as a cultural and legal category and its use by Native litigants as a strategy to claim power and resources in local courts. In this regard, my analysis tempers notions of colonial Indigenous agency that have taken hold in recent ethnohistorical scholarship. When Native litigants made claims to custom in court, they reinforced the position of the Native subject within the Spanish legal-administrative structure, a process that had consequences beyond the case at hand and that reinforced a wider system of inequality.

The narrative focuses on three crucial historical periods that move across a broad geography: transformations in medieval European and Iberian law that incorporated the Roman and Islamic legal traditions; sixteenth- and seventeenth-century cross-cultural encounters and struggles in ecclesiastical and legal settings in central Mexico and Oaxaca; and first-instance disputing in late seventeenth- and eighteenth-century Indigenous communities in Oaxaca. Juxtaposition of the Nahua altepeme of Tlatelolco, Tetzcoco, and Tenochtitlan, and of Oaxaca's ethnolinguistically diverse Native polities puts into relief the different modes in which custom developed in the century after conquest. During the early colonial period, intense cross-cultural interaction in the three Nahua city-states resulted in some of the richest documentation on pre-Hispanic Mesoamerican legal systems. These places also concentrated Indigenous, missionary, and Spanish administrative power and served as testing grounds for the creation of new colonial legal institutions based in part on Native custom. At the same time, the weight of Spanish power meant that central Mexican ethnohistorical documentation bore the heaviest imprint of Spanish colonial objectives. In Oaxaca, Spanish presence was thinner on the ground, and Indigenous ethnic states were smaller and more numerous. These factors, combined with a long-standing tradition of local autonomy, allowed multiple versions of Native custom to flourish and develop in local practice and social memory. Ethnohistorical and legal documentation about custom was therefore more diffuse, diverse, and idiosyncratic. For these reasons, the final chapters dive deeply into focused case studies from Oaxaca to analyze how Native litigants mobilized legal claims and generated rich evidence regarding custom's manifold and changing meanings and uses. By moving away from exclusive focus on central Mexico and toward Oaxaca's diversity of Indigenous places and politics, I attend to continuities in Indigenous experience across Mesoamerica's vast space while highlighting the importance of locality in the making of colonial legal institutions.

My argument aims to underscore the historical nature of Indigenous custom by grounding it in place and time. It unfolds as follows. During the sixteenth and seventeenth centuries, Indigenous authorities, missionaries, and Spanish officials translated and aligned Indigenous and Spanish norms through cross-cultural knowledge production, violence, and legal conflicts to produce new rights and protections categorized as Indian custom. The dismantling of noble polygyny was one of the most important outcomes of this process since it destroyed the means by which Native state structures and elite forms of property cohered. By the end of the sixteenth century, Native customary claims were increasingly anchored to practices and rights generated in the postconquest period and were relegated to issues that most affected the colonial economy and administration: land tenure, labor, and Native self-governance. Customary claims in these realms, however, still tended to be framed in ways that benefited the Native elite.

From the second half of the seventeenth century through the dawn of the nineteenth, Native officials and litigants reoriented the terms through which the colonial balance between exploitation and protection was legitimized, away from relations of unequal reciprocity rooted in antiquity and noble privilege and toward new forms of mutual obligation based on economic utility and defense of communal interests. A growing cadre of legally literate Native officials of commoner status challenged the old laws and customs that bolstered the position of the Native elite with new customs untethered from inherited status and tied instead to the economies and governing norms of smaller, individual pueblos. In an effort to assert their interests against those of the Native nobility, the Native officials of these reconfigured communities framed customs of communal land tenure, self-governance, and labor as contractual rather than primordial obligations to the community. The legality and instrumentality of customary arrangements came to take precedence, pointing to the ways in which Native people participated in the transformation from a justice- to law-centered Atlantic legal culture during the eighteenth century while reproducing Native difference and local particularity.

Chapter Summaries

Since Time Immemorial is organized thematically, and broadly speaking, chronologically and geographically. Part I provides a legal-intellectual history of the concept of custom that developed in the villages, towns, universities, and palaces of medieval Europe; intersected with the religious and legal pluralism of Islamic and Christian Iberia; and extended into the ethnic states and Christian missions of sixteenth- and seventeenth-century Mexico. Chapter 1 traces the elaboration of custom as a juridical category during the twelfth-century European legal revolution and Christian military expansion in Iberia. The legal, social, and political transformations of this period culminated with *Las Siete Partidas*, the Castilian legal code of Alfonso the Wise in which custom was defined as the local law of a territorially bounded community based in long-standing practice and popular will, and oriented toward the common good. The narrative then moves forward in time to analyze the use of custom as a measure of Native civility during the conquest of the Americas and the decades that followed. Although key figures in the debate over the Indies such as Francisco de Vitoria and Bartolomé de Las Casas acknowledged the civility of Native laws and customs and the sovereignty of Mexico's Indigenous lords, they did so with a strong dose of paternalism that resulted in the incorporation of Indigenous people into the empire as apprentices of Christian social and political order. These two faces of Native custom—as an extension of Spanish medieval law, and a means by which to underscore Spanish cultural superiority—were foundational to its translation in the Spanish American context.

Chapter 2 expands beyond the transatlantic networks of theologians, jurists, and administrators into the realm of Christian evangelization of the Native population in central Mexico and Oaxaca. In this crucible of the colonial encounter, Christian missionaries and Native elites generated knowledge about one another and built an ideological and practical foundation for the elaboration of intercultural ideas about justice and morality. In short, they were key players in the production of colonial legal consciousness. Translation across Spanish and Indigenous languages was central to this process since it facilitated an alignment of Spanish and Indigenous normative categories and produced a Native vocabulary tailored to the Spanish legal-administrative context characterized by the interpenetration of civil and ecclesiastical jurisdictions. While the missionaries and their elite Native interlocutors produced their bilingual dictionaries, grammars, and catechisms, they evaluated the norms and practices of the preconquest past in relation to Christianity and natural law and assigned them moral valence. The sorting of "good" and "bad" customs in these early years of the colony had long-lasting impact on how Native custom was understood and deployed in colonial courts in the following centuries.

Part II examines the production of knowledge about pre-Hispanic Native law and custom in response to debates regarding the sovereignty and civility of Native peoples and their place in the colonial order. As Native religious and sexual norms were criminalized and relegated to a "barbaric" past over the course of the sixteenth and seventeenth centuries, the ambit of legitimate colonial Native custom narrowed and was further subordinated to Spanish law and economic objectives. Chapter 3 analyzes how Indigenous and Spanish subjects framed and evaluated pre-Hispanic Native law and custom through comparison of two colonial ethnographic projects. The first is the Codex Mendoza, a Native-produced history and ethnography of the Aztec capital of Tenochtitlan, created sometime during the 1540s or early 1550s. Unlike the Florentine Codex, the monumental ethnographic work that brought together Franciscan friars led by Fray Bernardino de Sahagún and elite Nahua intellectuals, the Codex Mendoza was created by Nahua tlacuiloque (painter-scribes) of the artisan class. As such, it adopts a commoner perspective on the city's laws and customs that blends Mesoamerican sensibilities with European notions of political and social order to portray Tenochtitlan as a civilized Native republic. The Relaciones geográficas—royal geographical surveys administered in the Native provinces of New Spain and Peru from 1579 to 1585—were intended to assess the natural and human resources of Native communities so that the Crown could more efficiently exploit them. The survey also asked about pre-Hispanic customs, laws, and forms of governance. In the case of Oaxaca, the survey responses provided a more ambivalent and often negative perspective on the region's pre-Hispanic institutions, reflecting late sixteenth-century shifts in Spanish attitudes toward Native custom.

Chapter 4 traces the legal and social process of dismantling Native marital and sexual norms through analysis of Inquisition cases brought against Native lords in central Mexico and Oaxaca during the 1530s and the 1540s and criminal cases from Native tribunals in seventeenth- and early eighteenth-century Oaxaca. Elite polygyny was crucial to the production and maintenance of state-level Indigenous alliances as well as the laws of royal succession and property prior to the conquest. As such, its vigorous suppression by Christian missionaries and Spanish officials represented an attack not only on elite Native marital and sexual norms but also on the very fabric of Indigenous political order. Despite its criminalization, polygyny persisted in central Mexico in clandestine form for at least the first few decades after the conquest, and in some other regions much longer. In tandem with the missionary project of evangelization, the Inquisition applied the discourse of the "old law," used by Christian authorities in the Iberian Peninsula to characterize the customs of Jewish and Muslim converts, to the practice of Native polygyny.

Native authorities adopted the concept of the "old law" as a means of persecuting rivals who did not conform to Christian sexual morality or norms of governance. Criminal records in the Zapotec language redacted in Native courts of first instance in Villa Alta, Oaxaca, point to the ways in which the "old law" continued to be politicized until the early eighteenth century.

Part III moves forward in time to the late seventeenth and eighteenth centuries to consider how Native custom was legislated, contested, and deployed in courts of first instance in disputes over Native land, self-governance, and labor. In these final chapters, the southern Mexican region of Oaxaca takes center stage. Its large and ethnically diverse Indigenous population overseen by only a few Spanish administrators and colonists made Native custom especially important for the ongoing negotiation of colonial order. In contrast with the sixteenth century, when Native litigants made claims to custom connected to Native antiquity and noble privilege, in this later period, claims to custom were based in colonial practices and framed as contractual obligations. Crucially, over the course of the eighteenth century, communal interests were increasingly defined against those of the Native nobility. Chapter 5 shows how Native authorities deployed custom to claim or create common lands in late seventeenth- and eighteenth-century Oaxaca. From colonialism's inception, Native people appeared in front of the Spanish judges to claim and dispute land tenure based on pre-Hispanic custom. Viceroys and judges often upheld Native customary claims until the 1570s when the Crown's fiscal troubles meant that colonial demands for revenue and exploitation of Indigenous labor trumped customary claims to use rights or exemption from tribute. A second wave of customary claims to land emerged during the late seventeenth and eighteenth centuries with the Crown's land titling program that targeted Indigenous communities. In Oaxaca, where Native landholding persisted throughout the colonial period in an unparalleled fashion, Native authorities used customary claims to joint possession and usufruct as a strategy for securing the territorial integrity of their communities. They enshrined these customs in partnership agreements drawn up before Spanish judges that conferred plural ownership and shared territorial jurisdiction, thereby producing new communal property rights, often at the expense of Native caciques (hereditary lords).

Chapter 6 surveys first-instance disputes among Native communities over customs of self-governance and communal labor in late seventeenth- and eighteenth-century Oaxaca. In a sampling of eighty-three cases, I focus on the common language deployed by Native authorities and litigants to make their customary claims. Categories that were integral to the European framework of natural law came to the fore, including tyranny, servitude, force, consent, free will, and the common good. Although these concepts informed Native legal claims in earlier periods, they took on new meaning in the eighteenth century. Through their legal arguments, Native town councils, whose social makeup tilted toward commoner status as the eighteenth century wore on, sought to recalibrate the uneasy balance between the Crown's exploitation and protection of the Native population. They also sought to undermine relations of unequal reciprocity linked to the past and the prerogatives of the Native elite and replace them with new forms of mutual obligation based on economic utility and defense of communal interests through litigation. I argue that over the course of the eighteenth century, Native authorities redefined customs of self-governance and labor as contractual, a strategy that devalued inherited privilege and foregrounded a vision of communal interests anchored to a collective of commoners.

Chapter 7 trains the lens on two long-term disputes over customary labor in eighteenth-century Oaxaca, which began early in the century under the umbrella of village justice, moved to the Spanish court of first instance, and were ultimately settled in the 1760s and 1770s. In both cases, Native officials drew up a contract in their Native languages that detailed the labor expected of commoners or dependent communities and bound them to perform it by requiring them to sign. They did this because the commoners or officials of the dependent communities no longer consented to performing the labor. Aligning themselves with the interests of Native notables in one case and a powerful administrative center in another, the town officials turned to Spanish judges to uphold the contract and impose social discipline. The commoners and the officials of the subject communities continued to resist and provided legal arguments of their own against these old, customary privileges tied to the Native elite and administrative center. In one case, the town officials eventually switched sides and supported commoner claims against elite privilege. These legal battles over custom's meaning and force provide an encapsulation of the process through which unwritten norms became binding contracts, and ultimately, a provisional form of local law that served the interests of the powerful in Native communities. The existence of the Native-language contracts demonstrates that contrary to conventional wisdom, Native custom was not an exclusively oral code.

My analysis of the changing meanings and uses of Native custom answers a call to globalize legal history by focusing on the cross-cultural production of legal meaning and the engagement of Native people with a plurality of imperial institutions from the center of the viceroyalty of New Spain to its most remote corners.[53] In doing so, my narrative encompasses historical actors who have been traditionally marginalized from legal histories, including Indigenous authorities, interpreters, artisans, and peasant farmers, as well as Spanish lexicographers, missionary priests, and Inquisitors. Legal meaning issued forth from palaces, high courts, and council halls, and from the desks of jurists and theologians. But it was also forged in Native communities, parishes, missionary schools, workshops, town halls, and courts of first instance. By expanding into the social networks and spaces that coproduced colonial legal culture, I show how imperial legal orders were not just imposed from above but also built on the ground through translation and vernacularization of legal concepts and procedures, and struggle over power and resources at the local level.

Since Time Immemorial contributes to our understanding of the past while inviting the reader to consider how the legacies of imperial and colonial law continue to impact the present moment across the Americas and the so-called Global South. By historicizing the link between Indigenous identity and customary law and challenging the essentialization of Indigenous communal norms, we can move beyond the impulse to recover a romanticized Indigenous past prior to European contact. This is especially relevant for the present context of Mexico and other Latin American countries where constitutional reforms of the 1990s recognized the right of Indigenous communities to govern themselves according to local custom, much of which has been cast as ancestral and timeless. Despite the frequent association of Native custom with resistance to state-centered injustice, local governance through custom has had ambiguous effects. The Mexican state of Oaxaca provides a poignant example. By the early 2000s, 418 of Oaxaca's 570 municipalities were officially operating according to local custom, originally glossed as *usos y costumbres* and now referred to as *sistemas normativos indígenas* (Indigenous normative systems). Concretely, this meant that Oaxaca's state government recognized the right of the General Assemblies of the vast majority of its rural, Indigenous municipalities to conduct local elections, distribute communal land, organize diverse forms of mutual aid and community service, and adjudicate minor crimes and local disputes according to customary practices, as long as these did not contradict state and federal law.[54] Although it has contributed to greater autonomy and local control in some regions, in other cases it has reinforced and reproduced internal inequalities within Indigenous municipalities.[55] In light of this, we need to ask whose interests custom serves in particular historical moments, how it has endured over time, and why it is reanimated at certain moments as a legal and governing strategy. By addressing these questions for the past, I hope to illuminate their importance for the present and future.

Legal & Intellectual Foundations

Part I

TWELFTH THROUGH
SEVENTEENTH CENTURIES

Custom, Law & Empire in the Mediterranean-Atlantic World   **1**

CUSTOM WAS A CAPACIOUS IDEA that rulers, jurists, missionaries, and litigants used to make legal claims, evaluate social conventions, and legitimize local and imperial rule in the early modern world. This chapter charts the production of the concept of custom in law, theology, and political theory in the Mediterranean-Atlantic space of military conquest and intellectual exchange from the twelfth through sixteenth centuries. This early legal-intellectual history of custom is crucial to understanding its adoption and use by America's Indigenous peoples from the Spanish conquest until the present.

The idea of custom as a source of law and social convention originated in the European tradition with the ancient Greeks, but its relevance for the story I tell begins in the medieval period when Christian theologians revived Aristotle's theories of ethics and politics, realigning the concept of custom with those of reason, virtue, and natural law to create a blueprint for Christian political and social order. At the same time that the Scholastic movement infused Christianity with Greek philosophy, medieval jurists dusted off the legal code of the Roman emperor Justinian to systematize and order a European world that was rapidly urbanizing and commercializing. These twin processes, aimed at building administrative and governing institutions for Christian and secular authorities, provided a foundation for the codification of custom in Spanish law.

The broad theological and juridical trends of medieval Europe intersected with the intellectual and social history of law particular to the Iberian Peninsula, shaped substantially by the episodic warfare between Christian kingdoms and Muslim principalities, the legal codes of frontier settlements, and the policing of interfaith communities that attempted to regulate the daily interactions of Christians, Jews, and Muslims living side by side. The *Siete Partidas* (Seven-Part Code)—a product of this intersection, Castile's first legal code, and the first legal code written in a European vernacular language—articulated a definition of custom that provided for the translation and use of the concept by Mexico's Indigenous peoples in the context of Christian evangelization and legal claim making in Spanish America. But the concept of custom cut many ways and served the purposes of empire in multiple arenas. While Native litigants appealed to custom to make legal claims in the early years following the conquest, Spanish theologians and jurists used natural law to evaluate the sovereign status of Indigenous societies and produce legislation that subordinated Native people, their laws, and their customs within an imperial legal order.

Custom in Medieval Europe's Legal Revolution

The juridical concept of custom, which Mexico's Indigenous peoples incorporated into their framework of self-governance and mobilized as a legal claim during the Spanish colonial period, originated an ocean away from American shores and centuries before the conquest of Mesoamerica. For most of Europe's early medieval history, custom provided the primary means through which civil and religious authorities and common people regulated their social lives, local governance, and economic relationships. During the twelfth and thirteenth centuries, a legal and intellectual revolution swept across Italy, France, the Iberian Peninsula, and other parts of Western Europe. This process involved rethinking the relationship of custom to law and codifying its meaning by retrofitting old ideas to suit contemporary realities.[1]

The Greek and Roman traditions provided a resource to ruling elites and intellectuals in high medieval Europe who sought to develop a legal science with which to govern and regulate a changing world. The expansion of commerce had revitalized urban centers and shifted the balance of power from the countryside to cities, where universities emerged whose curricula integrated philosophy, theology, medicine, law, and rhetoric, the foundational subjects of classical humanist education.[2] For their part, theologians sought to reconcile Christian thought with ancient Greek rational philosophy, especially that of Aristotle. They founded schools that focused on the translation of ancient texts from Greek to Latin, convinced that these old writings provided a map to the attainment of truth, which in their view was the most sure-footed path to salvation. Saint Thomas Aquinas's *Summa Theologiae* (1265–74) represented the apogee of this mode of thinking, known as Scholasticism, which involved exegesis, interpretation, and debate over the foundational texts.[3] In the hands of Franciscan and Dominican theologians, Scholasticism strongly shaped legal thought in the high Middle Ages and the centuries that followed, particularly through its revival of the concept of natural law.[4]

Aristotle held that social and moral order were founded upon three principles: nature (physis), habit or custom (ethos), and reason (logos). In this formulation, custom bridged nature and reason by integrating the habitual moral behaviors of the individual and the social norms of a community, making it, in essence, the original form of law. Whereas positive law was the product of rational, stipulated norms, custom represented the unconscious practices of human communities. Custom existed, then, in dynamic tension with nature and natural law. Natural law derived its norms from a rationally ordered natural world and a purportedly universal and rational human nature. Natural law was not a legal code but a blueprint for the perfection of human society whose ultimate form was a city governed by just laws, a political theory that Aristotle elaborated in *Politics*.[5] Whereas natural law united humanity, the distinct customs of human societies produced cultural difference and hierarchies of civilization. In this view, customs made some societies more civilized than others.

In his *Summa Theologiae*, Aquinas modified Aristotle by attributing the rationality of natural law to the divine law of the Christian god, and by reducing the principles of social order to a binary: custom belonged either to nature (as unconscious habit) or to reason (as law).[6] In this reading, Christian societies represented the apex of an evolutionary civilizational process, their laws reflecting natural and divine law. In order to move toward perfecting their social order, non-Christian peoples had to be habituated to new customs through evangelization and the alignment of their laws with Christian reason.

Together with theologians' revival of ancient Greek philosophy, a new class of legal professionals known as jurists turned to Roman law as a framework for centralizing and systematizing a fragmented and decentralized legal landscape dominated by the charters and prerogatives of noble families and clergymen. Urban merchant elites and princes sent their finest legal minds to the universities of Bologna in Italy and Orleans in France. In these centers of learning, jurists from all over medieval Europe studied the *Corpus Iuris Civilis*, a compilation of Roman laws created under the direction of the Byzantine emperor Justinian (482–565 CE) as part of his effort to restore the Roman

Empire after its collapse in the West in 476 CE. By interpreting and glossing the Justinian Code, as it came to be known, the jurists produced common principles and bodies of law on the Roman foundation. The first, the *ius commune*, provided the legal and philosophical grammar of European civil law, and the second, canon law, aimed to systematize the norms and rules that governed the Church and society.[7]

As medieval jurists revived Roman law, they also revived Aristotelean political theory. The concept of custom in the Roman legal tradition—known in Latin as *ius consuetudine*—owed a heavy debt to Greek philosophy. Cicero, a philosopher, statesmen, and lawyer, and one of Republican Rome's most celebrated figures, was perhaps best known for his translations of the major works of Hellenistic philosophy into the Latin language. Through his translations, he laid the groundwork for a latent theory of the relationship between law and custom in Roman law. Drawing from Aristotle, Cicero located the foundation of all law in a rationally ordered nature. Custom (*consuetudo*) provided the intermediate step between the raw material of natural law on the one hand, and laws promulgated by rulers on the other. As a practicing lawyer, Cicero drew upon custom to justify the behavior of a client even in instances in which that behavior was contrary to a particular law. For Cicero, custom was what "age has approved by the will of all in the absence of a statute."[8] In his schema, customary norms acquired binding or disciplinary force through their practical use over time. Eventually, rulers recognized certain customs as useful and recorded them as law (*lex*).[9]

Custom's conceptual connection to a latent and time-honored collective will raised questions for medieval jurists, much as it did for their Roman predecessors. Was it a source of law, supplemental to it, or equal to it? Were there occasions in which it abrogated a legal statute? In the context of Republican Rome, although there was substantial disagreement on these questions, a consensus emerged that both custom and law were valid if they originated in the will of the people. This consensus was tested as Rome expanded into an empire starting in the first century BC. In territories that ranged from the Iberian Peninsula, to North Africa, to the southern shores of the Black Sea and to Northern Europe, Roman emperors recognized the laws of conquered populations and allowed local rulers to apply them. Since local rulers lost their legislative powers when conquered by Roman armies and could no longer promulgate their own laws, the laws that they had prior to conquest had to be classified as something else: custom (*ius consuetudinis*).[10] Despite the imbalance of power implied by imperial conquest, local custom modified Roman law in provinces across the empire. This was most evident in the practice

of testation in which conquered Roman subjects prepared their wills according to the custom of the region.[11]

Centuries of Roman legal tradition, crystallized in Emperor Justinian's
Corpus Iuris Civilis, provided the primary fodder for medieval jurists as they
reworked the relationship of law and custom in a legally pluralistic world
of feudal estates and emerging cities. The Justinian Code, written in Latin,
was composed of three parts, all of which carried the force of law: the Code,
which was a compilation of imperial legislation to date; the Digest, a collection of writings of Roman jurists; and the Institutes, which served as a
textbook for students that introduced the Code and glossed important concepts.[12] The relationship between law and custom constituted an important
thread through the *Corpus Iuris Civilis*. According to the Digest, "custom
of long standing" should be "observed as law and statute in all such matters
as are not regulated by written rules." The Digest also notes that one way in
which to determine the validity of a custom was to ask whether it had ever
been "confirmed by a judicial decision given after objections were heard." The
Digest and Institutes also allowed that law could be abrogated by custom "by
the fact of their falling out of use by common consent."[13]

The *Corpus Iuris Civilis* reproduced the pronouncements of Roman emperors on the status of custom. Emperor Alexander in the year 224 affirmed
the use of custom by the rulers of imperial provinces, stating that especially
in cities, customs should be preserved. Almost a century later, Constantine
recognized a need to assert imperial control over the recognition of local
custom as law by claiming that although custom had authority, it could not
contravene common sense, reason, or the law. Emperors Leo and Anthemius
noted that custom's validity depended on its "ancient" provenience and its
constant adherence. They added that custom should serve as perpetual law
in particular contexts, including political offices, local senates, cities, posts of
command, and guilds.[14]

It is difficult to discern the precise relationship between law (lex) and custom (consuetudo) among the many sources cited in the *Corpus Iuris*. According to some sources, it was subordinate to law, in others equal to it, and in
others, it could abrogate law. There is some consistency, however, regarding
certain attributes of custom, including the importance of its ancientness, its
association with cities and specific institutions, the significance of popular
consent in its validation, and the power of a judicial decision to give it legal force. These attributes were particularly useful to medieval jurists as they
codified and ordered civil and canon law according to the competing interests of urban elites, nobles, ecclesiasts, and feudal lords.

Legal and Religious Pluralism in Medieval Iberia

When Europe's legal revolution reached the Iberian Peninsula sometime in the twelfth century, it encountered a feudal society governed by a patchwork of local laws of varied origins, many of which were deeply influenced by Roman, Visigothic, and Islamic law. Centuries prior to the legal and cultural revival of Justinian, the Indigenous peoples of the Iberian Peninsula experienced Roman law through conquest and imperial rule and modified it through customary practice. Rome annexed Iberia into its empire in 19 BCE after almost two centuries of warfare and conquest and divided it into two provinces known as Hispania Citerior and Hispania Ulterior. In 133 CE, Rome extended its provincial law (*lex* or *formula provinciae*) to Hispania, which allowed local urban and rural residents to rule themselves according to their own laws in matters that were not covered by Roman law. Roman law enjoyed greater presence in cities, whereas in the countryside, pre-Roman customs held sway. The Visigothic invasions of the fifth century ended Roman rule and resulted in the dissolution of cities, fragmentation of commerce, and a shift of power to the countryside. The Roman society of urban citizens and slaves gave way to one of rural lords and peasants. The law of the land was the *Liber Iudiciorum*, the Visigothic legal code based on Roman law and adapted to the early medieval society that emerged after the fall of Rome. The *Liber*, alongside local custom, continued to provide the primary legal framework for the Christian kingdoms of the Iberian Peninsula until the rule of the Umayyad Caliphate, which began in 711. Despite the ascendance of Islamic law, the *Liber* served as a touchstone for local governance and judicial administration for Christian communities under Umayyad rule and during the centuries that followed.[15]

During the eighth century, the Umayyad Caliphate, based in Córdoba, consolidated its rule over just about the entire Iberian Peninsula. The Muslim-controlled territory came to be known as al-Andalus, the most ethnically diverse state in Europe. The Muslim majority was made up of a small Arab ruling elite, a much larger population of Berbers who filled out the military, and Indigenous Iberians who had converted to Islam (*muwalladūn*). Jews and Mozarabs—Christians who maintained their confessional identities while adopting many aspects of Arab culture—constituted important minorities, whose prominent social and economic roles outweighed their small numbers.[16]

Islamic law provided a means by which to manage this diverse society, especially in towns and cities. The Muslim majority of al-Andalus lived under the Malikī school of Islamic law, which in theory was inflexible, relying primarily on the central texts of Sharī'a (Islamic canon law)—the Qur'an and hadiths—while holding customary law ('urf) in low esteem.[17] Although custom may not have played as important a role as a source of law as it did in the Roman tradition, it was used by local judges (qadi) in al-Andalus and the Maghrib in the context of commercial transactions, family law and marriage, inheritance, and contracts regarding labor and land tenure.[18] In Córdoba, the seat of Umayyad rule, Islamic law proved to be much more flexible in practice than previously thought, and judges who oversaw local judicial administration interpreted the law pragmatically and resorted on occasion to custom.[19] Municipal judges relied not only on informal norms and practices as sources of law but also on a specialized body of secular customary law, known as *hisba*, used throughout the Islamic world to regulate weights and measures, artisanal production, and public hygiene and health in urban markets.[20]

Christian and Jewish communities in al-Andalus enjoyed semiautonomous status. The Qur'an constructed a hierarchical world regulated by religious difference, with Muslims, preferably Arabs, at the apex. As religious minorities, Christians and Jews were accorded status as *dhimmī* (protected people, or People of the Book), and as such had to pay a special tax (*jizya*). They were entitled to their own courts and judges who were elected by the community and to rule themselves according to their own religious laws and customs. In al-Andalus, dhimmī status took on particular dimensions: those Christians and Jews who held it were officially excluded from holding political office, though they often served in bureaucratic posts as interpreters, tax collectors, and notaries, and in some exceptional cases, they held high office. In general, though, access to political power for dhimmīs could only be secured through conversion. The Islamic government provided other enticements to convert, including exemption from the jizya and broader access to social mobility. The logic of hierarchy, tolerance, and separation produced double-edged effects. The semiautonomy of Christian and Jewish communities, defined by the right to practice their religion, observe customary norms, and be judged in their own courts, allowed a space for cultural continuity, even as their collective norms were shaped by Islamic law and custom.[21] As the historian Thomas F. Glick notes, the semiautonomous jurisdiction of dhimmī courts "was an expression of group cohesion, serving to reinforce the distinctive cultural traditions of the group."[22] In this way, the legal and religious pluralism of al-Andalus fostered cultural distinctiveness and separation while facilitating transculturation, especially in urban spaces.

Islamic law and custom left a strong imprint on the Iberian Peninsula, as evident in the civil and judicial administration of the territories ruled by

Christian forces after the fall of the Córdoba Caliphate in 1031 and the splintering of Islamic power into the *taifa* principalities. A clear example was the adoption of the hisba jurisdiction by Christian kingdoms.[23] Another example was respect for the laws and customs of religious minorities. Some Christian lords went as far as to commission translations of Muslim legal codes so that they could judge Mudejars—Islamic Iberians living under the jurisdiction of Christian lords—according to Sharī'a.[24]

Christian rulers also adapted dhimmī status for their own purposes, allowing Jews, Muslims, and non-Muslim Africans to govern their own semiautonomous communities and administer justice in their own courts. Castilian authorities referred to these communities and their institutions of self-governance as *aljamas*, borrowed from the Arabic term *al-jamāʿa*, which meant "collectivity" or "community."[25] In cities, aljamas were given spatial expression in segregated *juderías* and *morerías* (Jewish and Muslim wards). However, the guarantees of security and semiautonomy afforded to dhimmīs diminished under Christian rule. Generally speaking, although Jews and Muslims administered their own courts, Christian rulers reduced the judicial power of religious minorities over time by requiring that cases involving Christians be heard by Christian judges. And although semiautonomy and freedom of worship for religious minorities were respected in principle, the extent of such protections varied widely.[26]

The laws of Iberia's Christian kingdoms in which there was no general legal norm but rather individual pacts—known as *fueros*—negotiated between rulers and subject communities explains the inconsistent legal status of religious minorities. Fueros, which were specific to localities and akin to municipal charters, stood in contrast to the universality of Islamic law, through which dhimmī status had been normalized and made consistent across Muslim polities. Fueros spelled out the privileges and obligations of social groups in specific towns or territories in relation to the local lord and regulated aspects of commercial and social life. They served as local law and at the same time as tools of expansion, granted by Iberian kings and princes to lesser nobility who were sent to colonize territorial frontiers. Sovereigns could also issue fueros to specific corporate groups such as the Catholic Church, military, or aristocratic families, as a means of creating alliances and shoring up political support with competing powers.[27] It is important to note that fueros were distinct from customary laws because they were issued by sovereign authorities. At the same time, customs were incorporated into fueros and also existed alongside them in the countryside and in urban centers.

Royal power grew as the northern Christian kingdoms, especially Castile and León, violently challenged Muslim sovereignty to take control of cities and wide swaths of countryside. As this happened, royal authorities sought to subordinate the plethora of fueros and customs to royal law and systematize them, while urban elites petitioned their kings for confirmation of their customary privileges, leading to the redaction of municipal laws and customs. The landed aristocracy also participated in the shoring up of custom, evident in the anonymous redactions of customary laws for large territories. A crucial dynamic developed, then, in the relationship between law and custom: writing custom down became a defensive measure against the imposition of royal legislation and a means for urban and rural elites to protect their way of doing things from the king's impositions. This process led to a proliferation, diversification, and localization of written laws at the very moment when Iberian jurists brought the revival of Justinian to the peninsula, centered in the universities of Valencia and Madrid.[28]

The *Siete Partidas*: Systematizing Law, Fuero, and Custom in Castile

The cross-cultural influences of Islamic and Christian laws and customs gave Iberia's legal revolution of the twelfth and thirteenth centuries a distinct flavor. The ongoing formulation of law and custom in medieval Iberia, and the laws used by both Islamic and Christian rulers to manage ethnic and religious diversity, intersected with other processes that occurred throughout Europe. The *Siete Partidas*, a Castilian legal code completed in 1265 and compiled under the direction of Alfonso X—known as "el Sabio" (the Wise)—king of Castile from 1252 to 1284, represented a culmination of royal efforts to use the medieval revolution in legal thinking to unify a fragmentary feudal system and subordinate fueros and customs to royal law. Alfonso brought together leading jurists who worked for about a decade to produce a legal code that could apply to the entire kingdom. The Justinian Code and a newly systematized canon law provided its foundations, as did Islamic law, the *Liber*, and Castilian fueros and customs.[29] Crucially, Alfonso commissioned the work to be written in Castilian rather than Latin, making it the first European legal code ever written in the vernacular. At the time of its publication, it was also Europe's most extensive legal code.

According to historian Paola Miceli, the *Siete Partidas* provided the first systematic definition of custom as a Castilian juridical category with the objective of operationalizing it in the service of royal power.[30] The definition of "costumbre" in the *Partidas* drew upon the Justinian Code, while incorporating new aspects that reflected Alfonso X's imperative to unify and order a politically fragmented territory under his rule. The *Partidas* defined custom as an "unwritten law or privilege, which men have made use of for a long period of time, aiding themselves by means of it in matters and on occasions to which it is applicable."[31] The assertion that custom constituted "unwritten law" requires some unpacking, especially since authorities throughout medieval Iberia and Europe redacted customs in writing for a variety of purposes. As Miceli points out, "unwritten" did not necessarily equal "oral tradition." When thirteenth-century jurists invoked "ius non scriptum" (unwritten law), they were not referring to orality but rather to laws that were not present in the texts of the *Corpus Iuris*. "Unwritten law," then, encompassed customs recorded in writing and in the oral tradition of the community.[32]

The *Siete Partidas* invested custom with flexibility so that it could be applicable across diverse corporate bodies and territorially based political communities: custom could pertain to a specific thing, person, or place; to many people and places; and to distinct actions performed by many consensually.[33] Custom was also defined in relation to usage, meaning social practice and convention, time, fueros, and natural law: "usage originates from time, custom from usage, and fuero from custom," and all three were derived from natural law.[34] With regard to the latter, custom had to be reasonable, advantageous for all who were bound to observe it, and in the interest of the common good (*bien común*) and social peace in order to be recognized as valid.[35] Consistent with Roman law, custom could not be coerced; consent formed a core element of its legitimacy.

Custom's relationship to time was also quite flexible according to the *Siete Partidas*. On the one hand, the *Partidas* reproduced the importance of antiquity to custom's validity as laid out in the Justinian Code. If advantageous; born of reason, public deliberation, and consent; and practiced consistently, custom "gained force" over time.[36] On the other hand, the *Partidas* made clear that custom did not necessarily need to reach back to a distant past in order to be valid. Newer customs could be established if they were reasonable, born of the will and consent of the majority, and practiced for ten to twenty years. The establishment of custom required substantial deliberation by the community, and a public, standardized process for its founding. Popular consent had to be given freely; coercion, fear, ignorance, and error made a new custom invalid. Newer customs also had to survive a judicial test. During the ten to twenty years required for the establishment of a custom, it had to be upheld at least twice by a judge or authority without objection, and if a judge ruled against a legal challenge to it after hearing testimony from both parties, then custom could stand.[37]

By delineating how customs could be established, the *Siete Partidas* clarified some of the ambiguity of the relationship between law (lex) and custom (consuetudo) in *Corpus Iuris*. According to the *Partidas*, in the absence of a written law or statute, custom had the force of law, and when law was unclear on a particular matter, custom could interpret the law. If practiced widely, through an entire kingdom, custom could even abrogate the law of the kingdom, but if practiced in a particular place, it could only abrogate the law of that place. A custom could be abolished and replaced by a new one by the command of a lord and the consent of the people if the newer custom was more advantageous than the old, or by a written law or fuero.[38] Although a fuero consisted of usage and customs, the latter pertained to "particular matters, whether many or few countries or only certain well-known localities are concerned," whereas the former "must be absolute and relate to everything which pertains in a special way to right and justice, and therefore is more broad and general in its application than either custom or usage, for it can be stated and understood everywhere."[39] The ordering of usage, custom, and fuero in the *Partidas* facilitated the subordination of custom to fueros and, eventually, all fueros to royal law.

The *Siete Partidas* built upon the Roman concept of consuetudo, modifying it to produce "costumbre," a juridical concept in the service of ordering and systematizing a legally fragmented kingdom and bolstering royal power. Despite Alfonso X's ambition that the *Siete Partidas* would serve as a Castilian legal code, it was not much used in practice until the *Ordenamiento de Alcalá*, enacted by the courts of Alfonso XI in 1348. The *Ordenamiento de Alcalá* represented another victory for royal power and the influence of jurists and lawyers trained in medieval Roman law. It systematized and ordered the principal legislation, laws, and fueros of Castile, including the *Siete Partidas*. From that point on, the *Siete Partidas* enjoyed enormous prestige and served as one of the most important legal resources for Spanish judges and lawyers. Crucially, it enjoyed the same prestige in the Americas until the nineteenth century.[40] The key characteristics of custom in the *Partidas*—its identification with a territorial community, specific temporal parameters, and basis in popular will and consent—determined the kinds of legal claims that ordinary litigants of Iberia, and later its American empire, made across diverse courts and legal venues. Just as important, however, was the porous relationship that the *Partidas* established between custom and law. Custom—unwritten or written—provided a source of law and could also become law if recognized by a judge or a king. In this formulation, custom and law were not opposed, as is often assumed, but rather different parts of the same process of law making.

Beyond the Iberian Peninsula:
Custom, Conquest, and Indigenous Sovereignty

Custom played a central role in the military expansion of Iberia's Christian kingdoms beyond the territorial confines of the Iberian Peninsula. Just a little over half a century after the promulgation of the *Ordenamiento de Alcalá*, members of the Castilian nobility moved into the Atlantic to conquer the Canary Islands. They did this through vassalage pacts with the Castilian Crown in which the king acknowledged their right of conquest in exchange for fealty. After intermittent episodes of noble infighting, transfers of power, and rebellions by the Indigenous Guanche peoples through much of the fifteenth century, King Ferdinand of Aragón and Queen Isabella of Castile, known as the Catholic monarchs, launched their own invasion of the Canaries, and between 1478 and 1496, they conquered the well-populated islands of Gran Canaria, La Palma, and Tenerife.

The conquest of the Canaries grew directly from the warfare on the Iberian Peninsula, forming part of the same process of Castilian military, political, and economic expansion. It also allowed for further experiments with legal pluralism. As discussed earlier in this chapter, in Iberian frontier territories, confessional identities often determined what law applied, and conquerors and administrators often respected local custom. The Muslims and Jews in the peninsula to whom Christian rulers afforded dhimmī status were "people of the book" who shared common theological and legal roots with their overlords. This legal pluralism was facilitated by centuries of commercial, political, and social contact among Christians, Muslims, and Jews whose customs and laws strongly influenced one another. In the Canaries, a much greater cultural divide separated the Castilian invaders from the Indigenous Guanche people who inhabited the islands.[41] The conquerors forced the Guanche to convert to Christianity, while allowing local chieftains to govern according to custom unless a dispute involved a Spaniard, or a Native Guanche involved in a suit lived within the jurisdiction of a Spanish settlement. In such instances, a Spanish judge heard the case and generally applied Castilian law.[42] Castilian administrators also made room for local custom in economic matters. At the behest of Christian conquerors who had become sugar producers, they recognized Guanche water rights grounded in the Mālikī school of Islamic law. By incorporating customs suited to Canarian agricultural conditions and property relations, the Castilian sugar barons maximized their production for a European market.[43] Legal pluralism and economic advantage went hand in hand in this process of conquest, assimilation, and incorporation. In this regard, Spanish experience of conquest and local rule in the Canaries provided a partial model for military expansion and early colonialism in the Americas.

The invasion and conquest of the Caribbean Island of Hispaniola dovetailed with the consolidation of Castilian rule in the Canaries. In fact, Christopher Columbus's ships stopped in the Canary Islands for provisioning on their way across the Atlantic, establishing a pattern whereby the Canaries served as an important way station for Spanish galleons headed to the Caribbean and later to other ports in the Americas. The conquest of Hispaniola also followed on the heels of the Christian defeat of the Nasrid Kingdom of Granada in 1492, the last Muslim caliphate in the Iberian Peninsula.

Through territorial expansion, King Ferdinand and Queen Isabella continued to centralize the power of the monarchy and systematize the diverse sources of Castilian law, a project that culminated with the *Leyes de Toro* of 1505 following Isabella's death.[44] Violent Spanish expansion into the Americas and the incorporation of America's Indigenous peoples into the empire contributed a new dimension to the consolidation of Castilian legal order. Jurists and theologians debated over the legal status of Indigenous people and their position in a nascent Atlantic empire and widening Christian ecumene. The stakes were high. Arguments regarding Native sovereignty had direct bearing on the legitimacy of the conquest and the legality of Indigenous slavery and the *encomienda*, a system of forced labor and Christian assimilation that originated in medieval Iberia, and which Spanish conquerors and colonists imposed on the Indigenous population.[45]

The morality of the conquest was as important to the debate as its legality. If the conquest was to be determined unjust and sinful, the souls of Spanish colonists, officials, and even the Crown itself would be in peril. In 1511 Dominican friar Antonio de Montesinos excoriated his audience of Spanish colonists for their abuses of the Indigenous people on the island of Hispaniola, warning them of the dangers that their behavior posed for their salvation.

Montesinos inspired further denunciations of the mistreatment of Indigenous laborers, resulting in the Crown's promulgation in 1512 of the Laws of Burgos, which declared the Indians—the term Spaniards applied to the wide diversity of Indigenous peoples of the Americas—free people. Upon closer inspection, however, the laws only modified the earlier policy of forced labor by supporting greater regulation; in short, they upheld the encomienda while prohibiting coercion in its implementation and emphasizing the responsibilities of the Spanish encomenderos to facilitate Christian conversion. Ultimately, many encomenderos ignored both provisions.[46]

Among the thirty-five laws, almost all of which addressed the encomenderos' relationship to their Indigenous laborers, three explicitly addressed the customs of the Indigenous peoples of the Caribbean. Law 14 upheld Native custom by declaring that the Indigenous should be allowed to perform their sacred dances. Law 16, on the other hand, forbade Native polygyny, insisting that the Indigenous could not have more than one wife at a time, nor could they abandon their wives. Law 17 called for the gradual erasure of Native customs and their replacement by Christian ones by ordering that the sons of Native chiefs under the age of thirteen were to be removed from their villages under encomienda to be educated by the friars in the Christian faith and in the skills of latinized reading and writing. At age nineteen, they were to return to their villages in order to educate the others.[47]

It is notable that among Native customs identified in the Laws of Burgos, Native ritual dances were tolerated, whereas polygyny was not. Intolerance of polygyny was likely a carryover from a long struggle by medieval canonists and ecclesiasts to put an end to bigamy and concubinage in Europe. From the thirteenth century forward, canon law aggressively upheld a model of marriage that was monogamous and lifelong, undergirded by Christian sacrament, property relations, and sexual duty.[48] As will be discussed in the following chapters, Native polygyny became a matter of bitter struggle between Spanish authorities and Native peoples beginning in the sixteenth century.

As was characteristic of the Spanish Crown's policies toward the Indigenous population throughout the conquest and early colonial period, the Laws of Burgos provided for the continued exploitation of Native labor, while attempting to soften its harshest effects by insisting on the free status of the Indigenous peoples, paying lip service to curbing coercion, and emphasizing the imperial objective of Christian conversion. In practice, though, the encomenderos' abuses continued, as did denunciations by missionary friars. So too did the debate over the legal status of the Indigenous peoples of the Americas and the conquest's legitimacy. Dominican theologians and missionaries played a fundamental role in this debate. They established a legal, theological, and moral framework for defining and ordering the laws and customs of the Indigenous societies of the Americas in relation to Spanish law. And their assessments of Native customs, based in Aristotelian categories, laid the groundwork for organizing a Spanish colonial system of indirect rule that ensured the exploitation of Native labor while providing Native authorities and missionary friars with outsized influence in matters of Native governance and justice.

Francisco de Vitoria, a Dominican theologian trained in law who held a chair in theology at the University of Salamanca, was a central figure in this process. Through a revival of the teachings of Thomas Aquinas, Vitoria and his pupils turned the University of Salamanca into a center for the "Second Scholasticism" and an incubator for the most consequential theological and legal treatises of the era.[49] A key aspect of Vitoria's legal philosophy was that he did not recognize the divine right of kings, nor the pope's temporal authority. Instead, he looked to natural law as the ultimate authority governing human societies.[50]

In "De Temperantia" (1537), "De Indis" (1539), and "De iuri belli" (1539), three influential lectures, Vitoria made the most substantive theological and legal arguments of the era regarding the legitimacy of Spanish claims to dominion over the land and people of the Americas, and Indigenous peoples' legal status. Vitoria used Aristotelian philosophy, especially the framework of natural law, as a measuring stick with which to evaluate Indigenous societies and, based on that evaluation, determine whether they could be legally conquered and subjugated.[51] Crucially, in the period between the promulgation of the Laws of Burgos and the emergence of the School of Salamanca, Spanish forces had conquered much of Mesoamerica and the Inca Empire. Overawed descriptions of the Mexica capital of Tenochtitlan and the Indigenous Nahua society of the Basin of Mexico, like those found in the letters of Hernán Cortés and other observers, fundamentally changed the debate over the Indies. Spanish expansion had run up against Native societies on an entirely different scale from that of the Arawak of Hispaniola.

Vitoria never traveled to the Americas, but like other Europeans he was strongly influenced by the information that had begun to circulate throughout Europe about the Mexica and Inca Empires. Based on these accounts, he determined that Indigenous societies were characterized by what Europeans recognized as political order, including cities, civil administration, laws and a judiciary, social differentiation, rule by an elite, and a complex religion. At the same time, he acknowledged that some Native customs qualified as what Europeans considered contrary to reason, such as human sacrifice, ritual cannibalism, and sexual practices that did not align with Christian conventions. In his view, this was not evidence of the subhuman condition of Indigenous people but rather the force of custom, which compelled them to behave in ways contrary to natural law. So powerful was custom in Vitoria's eyes that it could obscure the truth that undergirded the natural order of human societies, and due to its strength, he speculated that it would take six hundred years for a custom deemed no longer binding to fall out of use.[52]

According to the Thomist vision to which Vitoria subscribed, the laws and customs of a civilized society were meant to produce a common good through the creation of virtuous citizens. By the same token, laws and customs contrary to natural law could erode the foundation of natural reason upon which all human societies rested. Aristotle's theory of habituation (*ethismos*) as laid out in his *Nicomachean Ethics* held that people were products of their social and moral environment.[53] Following Aristotle and Aquinas, Vitoria reasoned that Indigenous adherence to "unnatural customs" could be undone through Christian education. This paternalist thinking positioned Indigenous peoples as children who needed to be habituated to the good customs of a civilized polis. In Vitoria's view, the undoing of Native customs justified Christian evangelization and the cultural tutelage of Native people but could not justify Spanish conquest and dominium.[54]

Contrary to the idea that Indigenous peoples fit into Aristotle's category of natural slaves—a position taken by his fellow Dominican Juan Ginés de Sepúlveda—Vitoria argued that although the Indigenous were not as "civilized" as their Christian counterparts, they were sovereign peoples whose rulers exercised jurisdiction and possessed dominium over their lands, much as did European princes. He argued that this put the legality of Spanish conquest on shaky ground. In order to support his case, he turned to *ius gentium*, a body of customary law of ancient Roman origins that Europeans believed all people held in common, and which regulated international conduct. The doctrine of just war in the ius gentium held that war by one sovereign nation against another was permissible under very limited circumstances. The justification for the conquest given by proponents of Spanish colonialism was the purported barbarism of Indigenous peoples, evident in the tyrannical rule of Native lords who led their people to engage in human sacrifice and cannibalism. According to ius gentium, tyranny qualified as sufficient reason for just war. Vitoria countered this claim by pointing to the Indigenous peoples' reason and civility, which he argued rendered Spanish claims to dominium illegitimate. But he undercut this position with a crucial caveat. He pointed to a principle of ius gentium that guaranteed the right to travel and trade freely across sovereign territories. Not surprisingly, in many instances Indigenous authorities had prevented Spanish invaders from doing this, which Vitoria argued violated the law of nations and justified Spanish war against them.[55]

Despite the contradictions and ambivalences in his positions, Vitoria's acknowledgment of the civility and sovereignty of America's Indigenous peoples represented a radical perspective for its time and challenged the legitimacy of Spanish colonialism. His reasoning suggested that if the Native people of the Americas needed only to be educated in the matters of Christian reason in order to take their place among "civilized" nations, then once that education was complete, the Spaniards would have no justified purpose to command their labor or claim dominium over their territory. This was a scandalous proposition for Charles V, the Spanish king and Holy Roman emperor, who in 1539 prohibited further public discussion of the matter. Despite efforts at censorship, however, the School of Salamanca supported Vitoria's position, as did other theologians and missionaries.[56]

Dominican friar Bartolomé de Las Casas went even further than Vitoria did, making the strongest case among his fellow theologians and jurists for Native sovereignty based on an evaluation of their laws and customs. He arrived at this position over time, from his conversion to the Indigenist cause following Montesinos's 1511 sermon, to the authorship of his *Apologética Sumaria*, a full-throated defense of Native sovereignty that he wrote in 1555. The development of Las Casas's thinking was profoundly shaped by his four visits to the former Aztec capital of Tenochtitlan in 1535, 1536, 1539, and 1546. While in Mexico City, he participated in four meetings of New Spain's ecclesiastical leadership, which generated ideas and advocacy that shaped Spanish and papal policy toward the Indigenous.[57] At the same time, his interactions with Franciscan and Indigenous intellectuals in New Spain convinced him of the civilized status of the Nahuas whose customs and institutions he observed firsthand. Whereas he had rejected the application of Aristotelian notions of natural slavery to the status of Indigenous peoples, he came to embrace Aristotle's theory of rational political and social order as laid out in *Politics*. Using natural law and the Aristotelian ideal of the polis to evaluate Native customs and laws, he argued that the Indigenous people of New Spain should retain their legitimate and just dominium, ideas that he eventually expressed in the section on New Spain in his *Apologética Sumaria*.[58] He rejected Vitoria's advocacy of civilizational tutelage in favor of Indigenous integration into the empire through "free and voluntary consent."[59]

In his writings, Las Casas juxtaposed what he construed as evidence of Indigenous civility with observations of barbaric Spanish treatment of Native people in order to bolster his case for Indigenous sovereignty. In his *Brief Account of the Destruction of the Indies*, written in 1542 and addressed to Charles V, he lobbied for laws that would hold in check the Spanish administrators and encomenderos who abused the Indigenous people and impeded missionary efforts.[60] In response to Las Casas's exhortations and other pressures, Charles V promulgated the New Laws in December 1542, effectively cutting a middle path between the Spanish king's express commitment to protecting the Indians and ensuring their evangelization, and the profitable exploitation of their labor. The laws prohibited Indian slavery and other forms of forced labor and provided for the gradual abolition of the encomienda.[61]

The New Laws addressed the matter of the relationship between Spanish and Native law by instituting the judicial protection of Indigenous peoples and acknowledging the validity of Indigenous custom in the colonial legal system. In a Real Ordenanza (Royal Order) dated November 20, 1542, Charles V ordered Spanish judges to provide summary resolution of Indian disputes in order to avoid the expense of prolonged cases drawn out by unscrupulous lawyers. He also ordered that Spanish judges at all levels of appeal—from the high court of the Audiencias to the judges of first instance—should resolve Indian cases according to Native customs, provided that they were just.[62] In this regard, the New Laws reinforced prior policy on the matter. The Crown had issued a cédula as early as 1530 recognizing the Indians' "good" customs provided that they did not contradict Christianity.[63] Far from acknowledging legal sovereignty, this approach subordinated Native law and custom to imperial law and cast Native people as vulnerable and in need of the Crown's protection.[64]

According to Spanish colonial law, then, Native custom was designed to operate in two primary modes: as norms through which Native judges and authorities could govern their own communities and resolve disputes within their own semiautonomous and subordinate jurisdiction, and as a legal claim in Spanish courts. Native authorities, overseen by the first viceroy of New Spain, Antonio de Mendoza, were operating in the first mode by the 1530s. Mendoza was well suited to oversee this experiment in legal pluralism in the Americas. Trained in law, and having served in municipal administration in Granada, he was steeped in the Hispanic-Nasrid legal tradition of Andalusia and applied his peninsular education and experience with Islamic law and custom to colonial administration in the Basin of Mexico.[65] In order to adjudicate the competing legal claims of Native litigants, he obtained in 1537 royal authorization to name Indian judges to resolve Native disputes according to their uses and customs.[66] In 1547 he commissioned Pablo González, a Nahua *principal* (noble) from Tula, to serve as a judge to resolve a land dispute between two Native claimants in Toluca. According to the records in the case, he listened to both sides and issued a ruling based on the law imposed on the region by the Mexica *tlatoani* Moctezuma. González noted that one of the parties submitted a pre-Hispanic pictographic record in support of their claim.[67] At the end of his administration in 1550, Viceroy Mendoza recognized the rights of central Mexican Native communities to elect their own rulers—if they were well-reputed, good Christians—according to their ancient customs.[68]

Claims to custom made before Spanish judges—the second mode in which colonial law designed Native custom to operate—occurred when Native claimants faced off against a Spanish claimant or when a dispute between two or more Native claimants could not be resolved by Native judges and authorities. The Crown established the Second Audiencia of New Spain (1531–35), composed of trained jurists, as an antidote to the First Audiencia (1528–31), which was made up of conquistadors who brazenly exploited Indigenous communities. Some of the jurists of this new body, like Vasco de Quiroga, openly admired the laws and customs of central Mexico's Indigenous communities and advocated for their preservation as a means by which to create a viable social and political order in New Spain.[69] Such favorable attitudes made the Second Audiencia a sympathetic forum for Indigenous lords to lodge complaints against encomenderos regarding their customary land and labor rights.[70] The cases brought to the Real Audiencia by the hereditary nobility of Tenochtitlan, Tlatelolco, Otumba, and other central Mexican altepeme from the 1530s to 1550 laid the groundwork for the establishment of *cacicazgos*, entailed estates of Native lords that included their customary labor and tribute entitlements.[71] Another wave of Native customary claims washed over the Real Audiencia during the administration of Viceroy Luis de Velasco (1550–64). During the *juicio de residencia* (judicial investigation) conducted against Audiencia judge Lorenzo de Tejada from 1554 to 1556 for abuses committed against many central Mexican Indigenous communities, Native claimants accused Tejada of violating customary practice regarding labor, tribute, and land use. They produced painted manuscripts in a style that drew from Mesoamerican and European pictorial traditions expressly for the purpose of supporting their claims.[72]

Colonial administration of Indigenous communities via Spanish-style municipal councils (cabildos), the rearticulation of the customary prerogatives of the Native nobility via the cacicazgo, and missionary efforts at evangelization transformed the meaning and substance of Native custom during the 1550s. By this time, there was a shift in Native self-government, from the traditional rule of Native lords to that of the Native cabildo.[73] Custom became the norm through which the authority of the Indian cabildo and Indian jurisdiction were legitimized. Against this backdrop, a royal cédula dated August 6, 1555 solidified the place of Native custom in the colonial order by declaring that the Indians should observe and maintain their laws and good customs that they had in the past (meaning before the Spanish conquest), provided that they were just and preserved good government (*buen regimiento*) and Christian civility (*policía*). It also stated that the Crown recognized those customs that the Indians had created and reaffirmed more recently.[74] The legislation made it clear that Native custom had to promote Christianity and civility as measured by Spanish standards in order to be considered legitimate, while recognizing the coexistence and validity of pre-Hispanic and more recent colonial-era custom.

The 1555 cédula reflected and forecasted important changes underfoot in the relationship between Native custom and Spanish colonial law: through interaction with the colonial administration and courts, Native people were generating new customary rights whose legitimacy could not only reinforce but also compete with those of pre-Hispanic origins. As the conquest receded further into the past, pre-Hispanic practice lost its luster for Spanish judges and Native claimants. By the 1580s, Native custom was increasingly defined in terms of postconquest norms and Native claims, and by Spanish law and legal decisions.[75]

The 1555 legislation concerning the validity of Native custom was reproduced in the royal *Cedulario* that was printed and widely circulated at the end of the sixteenth century and once again in the *Recopilación de leyes de los reynos de las Indias* in 1680, ensuring its continued and broad diffusion. The 1680 version renewed the Crown's recognition of pre-Hispanic Native law and custom but added new and more precise language stating that the laws and good customs that they had observed, maintained, and made "after their conversion to Christianity" were also valid provided that they were not in conflict with Christianity or Spanish law.[76] The more specific language identified the Native Christian community as a locus for the legitimacy of colonial Indigenous custom. It also underscored a central logic of Spanish colonial rule: the Crown had extended a legal privilege to the Native population that Spanish settlers did not enjoy—the right to rule themselves according to their customs, even as those customs experienced profound transformation and depended on Spanish recognition and validation for their legitimacy.[77] This special privilege, then, came at a heavy price especially for the Native elite whose interests were most fully served by pre-Hispanic law and custom.

Conclusion

The Castilian concept of custom transplanted to the Americas drew from Europe's medieval legal revolution, which had revived and repurposed natural law and the Roman legal tradition as well as the complex dynamic of Muslim and Christian coexistence and episodic warfare particular to Iberia. As the *Siete Partidas* made clear, custom had to align with reason in order to be just, and it had to benefit the common good. Valid customs emerged from popular will and consent and could not be a product of coercion or tyranny. Written or unwritten, custom was a source of law whose validity drew from time-honored social practice, and it applied to diverse corporate groups and territorially based communities. These foundational elements of custom undergirded its meaning and use in colonial Native communities and in Native litigation in Spanish courts for centuries.

According to the proponents of the Second Scholasticism and the School of Salamanca, custom served as a tool of imperial governance and a means with which to measure societies on a civilizational scale. In keeping with Aristotle's political theory, in the eyes of imperial authorities, it was also the key to making a society more civilized; changing the social habits of a population could lead to a more rational legal and political order. At the same time, though, as collective habitus, custom was difficult to change because of its embodied nature. It is no surprise that Cicero called custom "second nature," and Saint Augustine claimed that there was no more difficult battle than against custom. These ideas informed colonial governance in the Americas and came to inform Indigenous self-government.

Spanish colonial law instantiated the subordinate status of Indigenous laws and customs within a framework designed to narrow the ambit of their legitimacy. Spanish judges recognized only the pre-Hispanic customs and new customs that aligned with Christianity and colonial law. The litmus test of Christian reason distinguished the relationship between Native custom and law in Spanish America from local custom and law in Spain. Even though the medieval Castilian society that gave rise to the *Siete Partidas* consisted of culturally and religiously diverse communities, the customs of non-Christian peoples were often compatible with Christianity or with what Christian rulers considered reason. The Jews and Muslims who lived in Castile had engaged in centuries of intimate contact with Christians, such that their customs were shaped by Christian norms. And the reverse was also true; Muslim and Jewish customs strongly influenced Castilian legal practice, and the *Siete Partidas* and later compilations of Spanish law and legislation bore the imprint of these traditions. The situation in the Americas was entirely different. How would it be possible to disentangle the "good" laws and customs of Indigenous peoples from normative orders that had no prior contact with European legal traditions and were alien to Christianity? What would remain of Native law once the non-Christian elements were culled out? Ultimately, these questions were addressed through Indigenous claims in Spanish courts during the sixteenth century and beyond as Native leaders accommodated themselves to Spanish norms of marriage, property, and inheritance. As will become clear in the next chapter, the missionary enterprise was central to this process, providing an arena in which the idea of Native custom was given meaning for the Indigenous peoples of Mexico.

Translating Custom in Castile, Central Mexico & Oaxaca **2**

COLONIAL INDIGENOUS LEGAL CONSCIOUSNESS, a process through which Native people learned to position themselves within colonial institutions and situate Native practice according to colonial norms, was produced in the crucible of the evangelical enterprise as much as it was in colonial courts.[1] Scholars have written nuanced and illuminating studies of how missionaries and their Native interlocutors fashioned a syncretic Indigenous Christianity through varied forms of translation.[2] They have paid less attention, however, to how the missionary project shaped colonial Native legal culture.[3] Native law and custom figured centrally in how the religious orders conceived of their role in the Americas. While the missionaries conceded that many aspects of Native society counted as "civilized," they were determined to make the Native people they were charged with evangelizing aware of the error of their laws and customs and convince them to abandon them in favor of Christian norms. This was not an easy proposition, and in the early decades after the conquest, the friars developed multipronged and diverse approaches to conversion that included translation between Spanish and Indigenous languages, the recording of Indigenous knowledge, Christian education, and violent destruction of the Native ritual world.

The history of Christian evangelization in Spanish America has been best documented for the case of central Mexico. In the heart of the Mexica Empire, the Franciscan order founded the Colegio de Santa Cruz Tlatelolco, a school where the children of the Nahua nobility were taught Latin, Spanish, Christian doctrine, and other European forms of knowledge.[4] Together, the Franciscan friars and young Nahua intellectuals systematized their language according to European orthography and Latin grammatical norms. They queried the older generation regarding the laws, customs, and daily habits of their people before the conquest. The twelve-volume *General History of the Things of New Spain*, also known as the Florentine Codex, coordinated and edited by Fray Bernardino de Sahagún alongside his erudite Indigenous pupils and local Indigenous leaders, represented the crowning achievement of these efforts, and stands as the most comprehensive survey of Native customs for the early colonial period.[5]

Trained in the intellectual tradition of Renaissance humanism, the missionaries valued Indigenous knowledge for its own sake, although at the same time, as missionaries, they sought to use Indigenous knowledge in the service of evangelization. They imagined that as they learned about Nahua language, history, government, ritual, medicine, education, and gender roles, among other things, they would equip themselves to transform the Indigenous population into a millennial Christian kingdom. Furthermore, they hoped that by putting Indigenous custom into conversation with Christian doctrine, their young Nahua pupils would acquire the knowledge necessary to help convert their fellow Indigenous peoples and habituate them to new customs.[6] As we know well, the moral dialogue between missionaries and Indigenous authorities, youth, and elders also implied violence.[7] The same missionaries who translated, wrote, and educated also denounced Native lords and commoners before the Inquisition, served as interpreters in Inquisition trials, and participated in the extirpation of idolatry.

The Colegio de Santa Cruz Tlatelolco was singular in its ambition and impact as a forum for the production of knowledge regarding Native custom. In the diocese of Oaxaca, distant from the colonial administrative hub of Mexico City and the centers of ecclesiastical power, the making of colonial legal consciousness occurred in a more diffuse way, in missions with fewer resources and less staffing. In the absence of a full-blown survey of Native laws and customs like the Florentine Codex, bilingual missionary literature such as dictionaries, grammars, catechisms, exempla, and confessional manuals provide the best evidence of the cross-cultural production of legal concepts. As a product of collaboration between missionary friars and elite Native interlocutors, these textual genres served as tools of conversion as well as linguistic and cultural primers for parish priests who often found themselves to be the only Spanish authorities in Native towns isolated from Spanish population centers. The missionary friars' work as translators facilitated their role as proxy imperial administrators, judges, teachers, disciplinarians, and legal advisors. Some of the more famous missionaries like Las Casas and Sahagún were formally trained in canon law at the University of Salamanca. But even those with less elite credentials were part of the "lettered city," familiar with the basic notarial genres that facilitated local administration and governance.[8] As they cajoled, advised, translated, and transcribed, they communicated not only the foundations of the Christian faith to their Native parishioners but also the core categories of Castilian law and justice, which alongside Christianity served as the primary framework of colonial rule. The expansion of Christendom into the Americas entailed the incorporation of Native peoples into an imperial administrative-legal order that governed their daily lives. It should come as no surprise, then, that Castilian legal language occupied much space in missionary dictionaries and grammars.

This chapter analyzes the translation of the Spanish concept of custom into Indigenous languages in central Mexico and Oaxaca. This process began with the standardization of the Castilian language itself and the publication of the first Spanish-language grammar and Spanish-Latin dictionary at the end of the fifteenth century. These texts provided a template for the missionary friars' translation work as well as an ancient Greek and Latin conceptual foundation for the translation of Spanish legal discourse into Indigenous languages. As the missionary friars and their Native assistants endeavored to align the Spanish ideas of law and custom—rooted in natural law and medieval practice—with Indigenous categories of knowledge, they produced new meanings unique to the colonial context. Alongside their translation work, the missionaries sought to preserve some aspects of Native moral authority while suppressing others, a process in keeping with Spanish laws that legitimized Native customs that were commensurate with Christianity as a basis for Indigenous self-governance. The sorting of "good" and "bad" customs in these early years of the colony had long-lasting impact on how Native custom was understood and deployed by Native litigants, judges, and legal agents in a wide array of colonial courts in the centuries to come.

Translating Custom into Castilian

As they translated the Castilian language into Indigenous languages, missionary friars participated in a broader intellectual project. Much as the jurists of the medieval period and the conquest era had sought to order and systematize law, in the late fifteenth and early sixteenth centuries, churchmen trained in Latin grammar standardized, ordered, and systematized European languages. In 1492—the year that Ferdinand and Isabella's forces defeated Granada, the last Muslim caliphate in the Iberian Peninsula; and the year that Columbus sailed to America—Antonio de Nebrija, bishop of Avila and a former teacher of Latin grammar and philology at the University of Salamanca, published his *Gramática de la lengua castellana*, the first Castilian grammar, and the first to be published among all of Europe's Romance languages. Nebrija followed quickly with the publication of Latin-Spanish and Spanish-Latin dictionaries: *Diccionario latino-español* in 1492 and *Vocabulario español-latino* in 1495. Nebrija's famous adage that "language has always been the perfect instrument of empire," which appears in the prologue of his *Gramática*, was put into practice by the missionary friars in the decades that followed as they fanned out across Spain's American empire to engage in the intertwined projects of accommodating Indigenous languages to latinized writing, translating the Christian doctrine, and evangelizing Indigenous peoples. Nebrija's work served as a template for their own bilingual Spanish-Indigenous grammars and dictionaries.[9]

Nebrija drew his source material from ancient Latin texts rather than medieval Latin, which he scorned as impure, and he used the same classical source material for his Spanish-Latin dictionary. Notably, all the ancient authors to whom he turned were pagan with the exceptions of Saint Augustine and John the Evangelist. His affinity for pre-Christian Latin imbued the dictionary with a strong ancient Mediterranean imprint, which missionary friars reproduced in their Native-language dictionaries. It is important to note, however, that Nebrija's Spanish-Latin dictionary was not a static record of the Castilian language, nor did the missionary friars who used it as a source mechanically reproduce it. The *Vocabulario español-latino* was reprinted thirty-four times between 1495 and 1600, each version different from the one before due to ongoing revision through which Nebrija deleted some entries and added others. The changes reflected the process of Spain's empire building and the ways in which missionary translation affected the Castilian language. For example, Nebrija incorporated the Caribbean terms for "corn" (*maiz*) and "chiles" (*axi*) into his list of Castilian entries.[10]

Nebrija's two entries for "custom"—"costumbre" and "costumbre de muger" —remained consistent across the thirty-four reprintings of the *Vocabulario español-latino*. The first entry drew primarily from the Roman legal tradition, indexing the idea of social convention becoming law through use over time, and associating custom with language and the body. His Latin equivalencies for the first entry, "costumbre," are *mos, oris,* and *consuetudo.*[11] *Consuetudo* was the Latin term used to produce the idea of customary law in the Roman tradition (ius consuetudo), and its many meanings evoke the unreflective corporeality of custom as conceived by Aristotle, including habit, practice, convention, intimacy, manner, routine, fashion, familiar acquaintance, and use. Consuetudo's meanings also included linguistic usage and chronic illness, linking its meaning more directly to language and the body.[12] The meanings of *oris,* closely associated with language, include mouth, speech, expression, face, and pronunciation. The term *mos* was tightly bound to Roman tradition, in the form of the *mos maiorum,* a set of unwritten norms that influenced the practice of law, religion, military discipline, the education of children, and public and private comportment. Domicio Ulpiano, a third-century Roman jurist, wrote that *mos* originated from the consent of the community and ancestral use and was consolidated through practice over time.[13] The meanings of *mos* also extended to linguistic usage, fashion, established practice, rule, law, and ordinance.[14]

Nebrija glossed his second entry for custom, "costumbre de muger" (woman's custom), as *menstruum* (menstruation).[15] Taken together, the first definition of custom as law, and this second one, as menstruation, reproduced Aquinas's binary principles of social order: custom as nature (unconscious habit) and custom as reason (law). In his famous *Tesoro de la lengua castellana o española* (1611), the Spanish lexicographer Sebastián de Covarrubias Orozco illuminated the complementary meanings attributed to custom by Nebrija, noting that menstruation is called custom because it is "ordinary and routine." He also noted the great challenge in changing custom, which, quoting the Greek Stoics and Cicero, is "like second nature," and quoting Saint Augustine, is the "hardest and most difficult battle." To this he added that there are good and bad customs, and that the bad ones must be "broken."[16] In both Nebrija's and Covarrubias's formulations, the bodily routine of menstruation over which the rational mind had no control was related and gave meaning to custom as political and social order—speech, law, rules, and ordinances—produced by human rationality. According to this mode of thinking, derived from Aristotelian philosophy, only through the education of reason and the application of laws could bad customs, rooted in bodily habit, be undone. This was precisely the framework with which the missionary friars approached their task of evangelizing the Native population: Christian education served as a means of breaking bad Native customs and bringing Natives into the light of reason and Christian truth.

Translating Custom into Nahuatl

The Christian missionaries who worked in colonial Mexico and other parts of the Americas used Nebrija's dictionary, which rested on an ancient Mediterranean conceptual bedrock, as a point of departure for creating their bilingual dictionaries, whose purpose was to facilitate the evangelization of the Indigenous population. They also produced bilingual grammars and catechisms, which were often redacted and published earlier than the dictionaries due to the friars' priority to convert the Indigenous. Although the missionaries' names alone appear on the bilingual literature, the texts were outcomes of decades of collaborative work between the friars and anonymous Indigenous authorities, many of whom the friars trained in Latin grammar, Spanish language, and Christian doctrine. In the case of the dictionaries, the friars determined the Spanish entries, but the complex and multiple equivalences provided in the opposite column were clearly the product of Indigenous knowledge and dialogue with the friars.[17]

Alonso de Molina's *Vocabulario en lengua castellana y mexicana*, first published in 1555 as a Spanish–Nahuatl dictionary, and in 1571 as an expanded version containing both Spanish–Nahuatl and Nahuatl–Spanish sections, was the first bilingual dictionary in the Americas based on Nebrija's model. Molina, a Franciscan friar who arrived in New Spain as a child soon after the conquest and learned Nahuatl from a young age, entered the Franciscan monastery in 1528 and taught Latin and grammar at the Colegio de Santa Cruz Tlatelolco. His dictionary served as a model for bilingual dictionaries of Indigenous languages across New Spain and continues to stand as a foundational text for the study of colonial Nahuatl by modern historians and philologists.

The work entailed in creating bilingual and Native-language texts was daunting. Molina, the friars who followed in his footsteps, and the Native intellectuals they engaged faced serious obstacles to translation, including the fact that Latin grammar did not in any way correspond to the structure of Indigenous languages. They also faced the profound problem of meaning, especially for ancient Mediterranean concepts and Christian terminology for which there were no Indigenous equivalents. To cope, they adopted a range of translation strategies, which included description, periphrasis, or circumlocution, which amounted to describing the Spanish term in the Native language in an effort to approximate meaning.[18] *Tlamelauacachiualiztli*, the Nahuatl entry for the Spanish term *justicia* (justice) in Molina's dictionary, provides an example of description. In the Nahuatl-to-Spanish section, it is glossed as "el acto de hazer alguna obra recta y justa" (the act of doing some work properly/straight and in a just manner).[19] This description was useful because it drew from metaphors resonant in Mediterranean, European, and Mesoamerican cultures. "Straight" provided the central metaphor for law and justice in the Greek and Roman ancient traditions and beyond, including the Mesopotamian and the Egyptian. In many European languages, the word for "law" is also the world for "straight," as evident in the Spanish *derecho*, the French *droit*, the Italian *diritto*, and the German *recht*. "Straight" also provided a metaphor with which missionaries translated the Christian idea of "faith and belief" in Zapotec, suggesting that it served as a bridge between European and Mesoamerican notions of truth and the sacred.[20]

When description, circumlocution, and periphrasis were insufficient, doublets—or pairs of expressions, which when combined produced a third meaning—represented another translation strategy used by the friars. Doublets may have been especially effective given their congruence with the Mesoamerican rhetorical style of parallelism.[21] Molina's entry for "law of the pueblo" in the 1555 edition, closely related to the idea of custom as local law, is defined with the doublet *altepetlalilli, altepenauatilli*.[22] In the Nahuatl-to-Castilian section of the 1571 dictionary, Molina defines *altepetlalilli* as a community that is already established and *altepenauatilli* as the ordinances or laws of the town.[23] The two terms together produced the idea of a town charter or constitution, linking the moment of founding with legal order, an idea that had currency in both Spanish and Nahua societies as evident in medieval *fueros* and Mesoamerican codices.

The varied strategies of amalgamating semi-equivalencies created an imbalance in the dictionaries between the short Spanish entries of one or more words and the elaborate Native-language entries in the right-hand column. Attempts to align meaning where full commensuration was impossible generated new meanings and word forms and allowed for the integration of Spanish into the structure of Indigenous languages.[24] Some neologisms were too clunky, though, to gain traction in the mundane arena of Native-language notarial writing.[25] Nevertheless, the friars' Spanish entries and the complex and multiple Indigenous equivalencies provide a kind of shorthand transcript for the modern scholar of the exchange of knowledge between the friars and their Indigenous interlocutors.

Spanish legal terminology often entered Nahuatl writing as loan words, especially after the mid-1540s.[26] But in some cases, there were Nahuatl equivalents derived from the Indigenous legal tradition that stuck and that appear in genres of writing beyond the dictionaries. One of the translations for "custom" listed in Molina's dictionary provides an example. Molina listed five entries for custom: "custom of the pueblo," "custom," "life habit," "woman's custom," and "to be accustomed." Custom of the pueblo, the most pertinent entry for custom as source of law, was translated as *tlamanitiliztli*, which in the Nahuatl-Castilian section of the dictionary appears as "use or custom of the pueblo, or the laws that the pueblo keeps."[27] The term *tlamanitiliztli* can be found in other literature of the era that sought to preserve the moral philosophy and rhetoric of the Nahuas. In the *Historia general de las cosas de la Nueva España*, which formed part of the Florentine Codex, Franciscan friar Bernardino Sahagún and his Nahua coauthors translated *tlamanitiliztli* as the laws and customs that the ancestors recorded in the painted books. The term appears in a Nahuatl metaphor recorded in Book 6 "Rhetoric and Moral Philosophy": "The black, the red of the ancient ones. This saying was said of the customs of the ancient ones—that which they left established, a way of life. All lived accordingly."[28] Black and red refer to the primary colors of the ink used by Nahua tlacuiloque (painter-scribes) to record their histories, genealogies, rituals, laws, and aspects of political administration in pictographic form.[29] *Tlamanitiliztli* also appears in the seventeenth-century Codex Chimalpahin: "This was the custom of our early ancestors, who were still idolaters living in darkness in those times."[30] It was used as well in a miscellaneous record regarding land in the Nahua altepetl of Cuauhtinchan in which the Nahua author wrote that certain procedures were "not in keeping with the old order."[31]

The varied uses of *tlamanitiliztli* suggest that it was a body of pre-Hispanic law recorded in pictographic text and a normative order that regulated landholding, moral comportment, and other elements of social life. The pictographic record was likely destroyed in the friars' zeal to obliterate all material objects linked with the rituals and religions of old. However, as the friars' documentation of Nahua oral tradition makes clear, knowledge of pre-Hispanic custom in the early colonial period was maintained through the rhetorical form of the *huehuetlatolli*, the "archaic word" or "words of the elders."[32] Fray Andrés de Olmos, another Franciscan friar and crucial figure in the Nahua-Christian "moral dialogue" of the mid-sixteenth century, recorded some of these orations in the last chapter of his Nahuatl grammar *Arte de la lengua mexicana*, published in 1547.[33]

Fray Andrés de Olmos's background puts the incorporation of the huehuetlatolli in his *Arte* into important context. Olmos came to New Spain in 1528 with Fray Juan de Zumárraga, who would later become bishop of New Spain and chief officer of the Mexican Inquisition. In Spain, Olmos had worked as an extirpator of witchcraft and demonology, skills that he put to use in his work in Mexico.[34] When he arrived in New Spain, he dedicated himself to learning Nahuatl and, according to the Franciscan chronicler Fray Gerónimo de Mendieta, became "the finest translator of the Mexican language in the whole land."[35] He later became professor of Latin and Nahuatl at the Colegio de Santa Cruz Tlatelolco, which afforded him the opportunity to exchange knowledge and information about the Nahua world with his Indigenous pupils, Sahagún, and other Franciscans. He was especially active at the Colegio de Santa Cruz Tlatelolco from 1536 to 1538.[36]

Given Olmos's experience as an extirpator in Spain and his budding skills in Nahuatl, in 1533 Sebastián Ramírez de Fuenleal, president of the Second Audiencia of Mexico, commissioned him to collect as much information as possible about Nahua society.[37] The goals of this ethnographic project were twofold: the extirpation of idolatry and the identification of the good customs of the Nahua world that would facilitate evangelization.[38] Olmos's *Arte* was one of the products of his fieldwork and research among the Nahua during those years. The contents of the grammar went well beyond linguistic description and observations about usage to include examples of Nahuatl high oratory. This was in keeping with the genre of the missionary grammar, which was intended to instruct the parish priest in the art of communication in the Native language. Their prologues and appendixes contained rich historical and ethnographic information concerning Indigenous language, daily life, material culture, gender, and ritual. And sometimes they contained examples of the ceremonial registers of the language. This cultural context was crucial not only for the art of communication but also for packaging the Christian message in a rhetorical form to which a Native audience would be receptive.[39]

Olmos was impressed by the Nahua moral philosophy expressed in the rhetorical form of the huehuetlatolli. He recorded examples of the genre with an eye to providing a model of Nahua ceremonial discourse for use by parish priests in Christian education and conversion. Sahagún also held the huehuetlatolli in high esteem and perceived the genre's utility for the purposes of evangelization. He recorded a number of them in the Florentine Codex, especially Book 6 "Rhetoric and Moral Philosophy" and Book 9 "The Merchants." He also included some in his two-part Nahuatl catechism *Coloquios y doctrina cristiana con que los doce frailes de San Francisco enviados por el papa Adriano VI y por el emperador Carlos V, convirtieron a los indios de la Nueva España*.[40] The first part of the work reproduced a dialogue in the style of the huehuetlatolli between the first Franciscan missionaries sent to the New

World and Antonio Valeriano de Azcapotzalco, Alonso Vegerano de Cuauhtitlan, Martin Jacobita, and Andrés Leonardo. The friars and this group of Nahua nobles engaged in an exchange about the merits of the Christian doctrine and the customs of the elders ("in huehue tlamanitiliztli"). Scholars have argued that this was actually a dialogue of the deaf in which two modes of thinking misaligned.[41] In this view, the Native customs of old embodied a path-oriented moral philosophy in contrast with the truth-oriented objective of Christianity. As such, the Nahuas emphasized *how* to find, make, and transmit a way of life rather than prescribing the end point of the journey.[42]

The huehuetlatolli embodied the mode in which the customs of old were meant to be authoritatively communicated. The purpose of the discourses was to remind community members of their obligations as well as the rules and prohibitions that regulated the Nahua world.[43] Through the high oratory of Nahuatl authoritative speech, the texts expressed codes of comportment, community norms, and proper relations with nature and the sacred.[44] Nobles, rulers, priests, parents, and other authorities used the huehuetlatolli in a wide range of social contexts and for varied purposes. Some of these included official address by the *huey tlatoani* (supreme ruler) to the community, discourses of royal functionaries directed at the huey tlatoani, prayers directed to the gods, didactic moral discourses by parents to children, discourses by parents to children during rites of passage like marriage, orations spoken at birth and death, orations of merchants as they set out for their long-distance journeys, and oratory reserved for court protocol.[45]

Echoes of the huehuetlatolli can be found in other texts of the sixteenth and early seventeenth centuries. Most concretely, they were reproduced by the friars as tools of evangelization in sermons, catechisms, and other didactic genres.[46] Beyond this, scholars surmise that they inspired the "ethnographic" third part of the Codex Mendoza, a mid-sixteenth-century Mexica history and survey of customs.[47] Testimonial evidence from the 1539 Inquisition trial of a Native lord of Tetzcoco, don Carlos Chichimecatecuhtli, suggests that his fiery oratory in defense of pre-Hispanic law and custom, upon which his conviction was based, was delivered in the style of the huehuetlatolli.[48] The Codex Mendoza and the Inquisition trial of don Carlos will be analyzed in greater detail in chapters 3 and 4.

In their zeal to convert, the Franciscan friars of central Mexico engaged Nahua elders and youth to translate Castilian concepts into Nahuatl and produce knowledge about pre-Hispanic Nahua law and custom. The level of detail and amount of information that these efforts yielded were unparalleled in other areas of Mexico. There were many reasons for this, including Spanish perceptions of the centrality of the wealthy and powerful Nahua polities of the Basin of Mexico to the colonial enterprise, the designation of Mexico City as the colonial ecclesiastical and civil administrative center, and the humanist philosophy of the Franciscans, which valued knowledge of all kinds. At the same time, the goal of knowledge production must be kept in view: the destruction of the pre-Hispanic Indigenous order and its rebuilding on the foundations of Christianity and Spanish policía (civilization and good government). This required distinguishing "good customs" from "bad customs" as Spanish law mandated. In this regard, the friars and their counterparts in civil administration found common ground with regard to their attitude toward Native customs: only those that furthered the interests of the evangelical and colonial enterprises could be preserved.

Translating Custom into Mixtec and Zapotec

In central Mexico, the linguistic, ethnographic, and educative work of the Franciscans positioned them as the primary point of contact for the Indigenous population with Spanish colonial administration. This was strategic. Unconvinced of civil authorities' full commitment to the evangelical enterprise, they assiduously built a power base within Native communities, allying themselves with Native authorities who sought to benefit from their presence and persecuting those who resisted Christian norms. At the same time, because of the proximity of Spanish civil institutions like local courts and the Audiencia of Mexico, the Nahuas had some recourse to Spanish authority beyond the missionaries and could take advantage of Spanish infighting.

The moral dialogue between missionaries and Native authorities took on a different cast in New Spain's more remote provinces. In the diocese of Oaxaca, well to the south of central Mexico, missionaries faced less competition from Spanish civil authorities and settlers, who were few in number. But absent the weight of Spanish institutional power, they also faced obstacles to their work, as in the case of the Mixtec town of Yanhuitlan, a pre-Hispanic power center where until the 1540s the Dominican order struggled to gain a foothold due to the resistance of local Native lords and the open hostility of the region's encomendero to the missionary project.[49] In Oaxaca, there was nothing approaching the Colegio de Santa Cruz Tlatelolco, nor were there ethnographic projects like the Florentine Codex. The historian Nancy Farriss notes that the Dominican approach to educating elite Native youth was less ambitious than that of the Franciscans, though they shared the same dedication to developing European literacy among their Indigenous pupils for the purposes of more effective evangelization and church administration. The Native elite of Oaxaca sent their boys to smaller schools and, in some cases, to live in the Dominican monasteries to be raised and educated by the friars. A boarding school for the Native youth of Oaxaca's northern sierra, established by Fray Jordán de Santa Catarina in 1558 in the colonial district seat of Villa Alta, provides an exceptional example of a large-scale Dominican educational institution for Native youth.[50]

Although there is no Oaxacan equivalent to the Florentine Codex, Dominican collaboration with Native authorities did yield copiously descriptive missionary literature, including dictionaries, grammars, catechisms, and confessional manuals. These works provide evidence of how the missionary friars and their Native interlocutors translated the Spanish concept of custom while preserving traces of Indigenous categories of knowledge.

The Dominicans focused their translation efforts on Zapotec (Tíchazàa) and Mixtec (Ñudzahui), the most widely spoken languages, though they produced literature in many other languages of the Oaxaca region as well.[51] Zapotec and Mixtec pertain to the Otomanguean language family and, as such, their tonality and complex structure made them even more difficult for the missionaries to translate than Nahuatl, which belongs to the Uto-Aztecan language family.[52] Due to the later conquest of the region, the slower process of colonization, the paucity of resources in comparison with central Mexico, and the difficulties of translation, the Zapotec and Mixtec dictionaries and grammars were published more than twenty years after Alonso de Molina's Nahuatl dictionary: Fray Juan de Córdova's *Vocabulario en lengua çapoteca* and *Arte en lengua zapoteca* were both published in 1578, and Fray Francisco de Alvarado's *Vocabulario en lengua misteca* and Fray Antonio de los Reyes's *Arte en lengua mixteca* were both published in 1593. As was the case with Molina's dictionary, though, one must remember that the texts were products of intellectual labor begun decades prior to their publication.

Alvarado, Reyes, and Córdova's texts reflect the process of aligning Castilian juridical concepts with the normative orders they encountered in Zapotec and Mixtec communities. As was the case in Molina's dictionary and Olmos's grammar, translations for law and custom drew upon terms for local normative traditions and high rhetorical forms of the Native language. Following Molina, the Dominican friar Francisco de Alvarado listed five entries for law in his Spanish-Mixtec dictionary: law (generally), law of the pueblo, to make law, to remove law, and natural law. The translation for law (generally) was *dzaha huidzo* (lordly speech, word of the ethnic lord) and *huidzo sahu*, a term that the missionaries also used to translate "sermon."[53] Antonio de los Reyes's grammar *Arte en lengua mixteca* illuminates some of the reasoning behind these translation choices. Reyes devotes a section in his grammar to reverential language used by Ñudzahui commoners when addressing their ethnic lords or referring to them. There is an entry for "Law of the Lord" (*huidzo dzahaya*—words of the lord), immediately followed by "Law of the pueblo" (*huidzo sahu*—law or sermon; *dudzuyuvuitaya*—words of the yuhuitayu).[54] Unsurprisingly, some of these translations did not fully hit the mark. For example, the translation "law of the pueblo" fell short of capturing the weight of the Ñudzahui institution of the *yuhuitayu,* sometimes shortened to *tayu,* the superordinate unit of Ñudzahui political organization made up of two communities (*ñuu*) joined through the marital alliance of lords from each.[55] A yuhuitayu, best understood as an ethnic state, was more akin to a European principality than a generic community.

In the grammar's prologue, yet another translation for law appears in reference to a Mixtec origin story, which recounts that their ancestral lords came from a place called Apoala and brought with them the laws and commandments of the land (*yya nisaindidzo huidzo sahu*).[56] The reference to the mythistory of Apoala draws from Indigenous knowledge recorded in the Mixtec pictographic history known as the Codex Vindobonensis (fig. 2.1).[57] The distinctions among these translations for law—Laws of the ancestors, Law of the Lord, and Law of the pueblo—reflected the Spanish idea that there were different sources of law and laws that applied to distinct social groups, while at the same time pointing to specific realms of Indigenous authority.

Following Molina, Alvarado's four entries for custom—custom of the pueblo, life habit, to become accustomed, woman's costume—underscored the idea of custom's locality (the municipality), its quotidian and habitual nature, and its conceptual and linguistical linkage to clothing (costume) in the European tradition.[58] Eight more entries in which custom formed part of a larger phrase—including habit, raising a woman according to custom, corruption of customs, a woman's blouse, to grow up according to good customs, to inflict damage on another's customs, to raise someone with good customs (to habituate), and style and custom of the land—infuse the idea of custom with gendered notions of moral education and proper comportment.[59]

As with Molina's gloss for "costumbre del pueblo" in his Nahuatl dictionary—*tlamanitiliztli*—Alvarado's entry for "custom of the pueblo" most closely approximates the Mixtec idea of custom as a source of law. Alvarado and his Native coauthors translated it using periphrasis in three iterations: "dzavua yu iyo sa naha," "dzavua caa ñuu," and "dzavua caa tayu."[60] The first can be broken down into two parts, the first of which (*dzavua yu iyo*) trans-

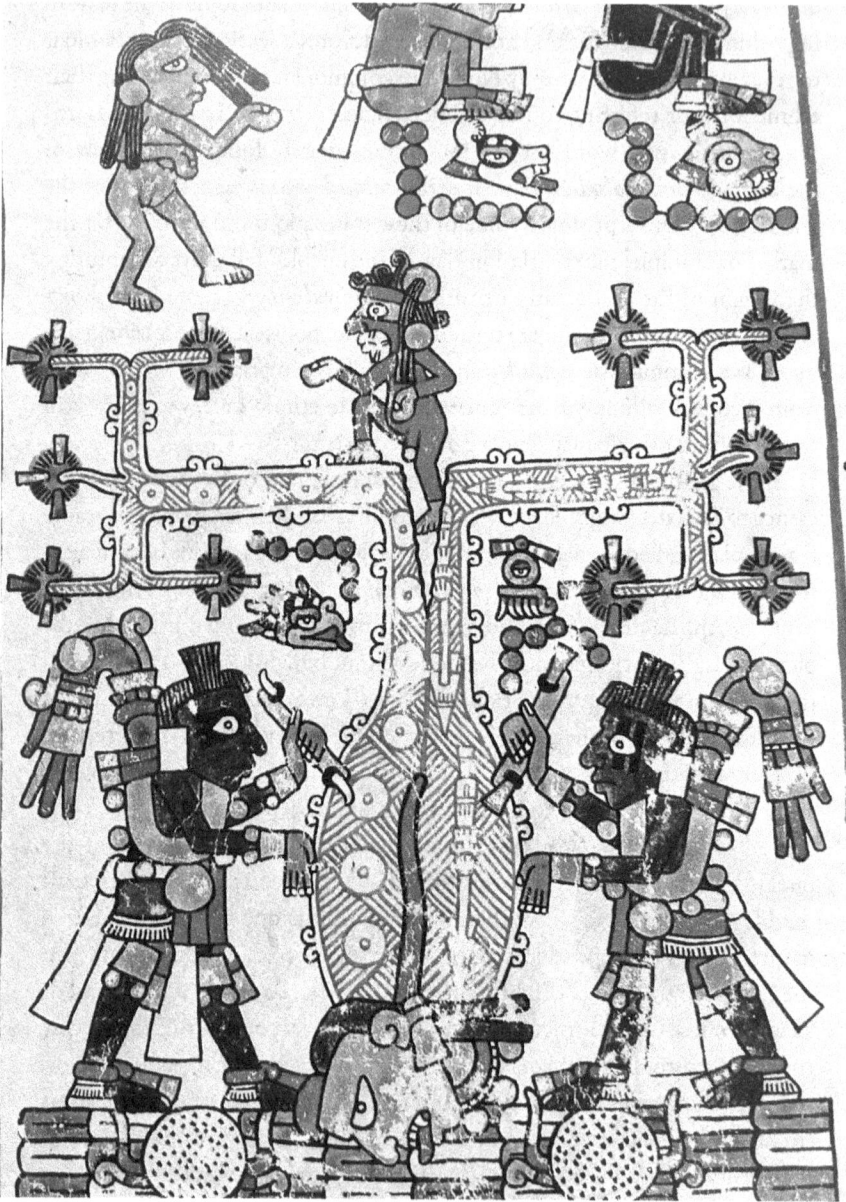

Figure 2.1 Tree birth, Apoala, Codex Vindobonensis. Founding Mixtec ruler, colored red, steps out of the Great Tree of Apoala, depicted with red striations and disks. Two deities, colored black, prepare the tree.

lates as "to use among some or all," "style" (*estilo*), and "custom of the land."[61] The second part (*sa naha*) translates as "in former times" (*antiguamente*), "a long time ago," or "something small or trivial."[62] "Style" and "use" appear as synonyms for custom in many Spanish sources, including the *Siete Partidas*, Nebrija's dictionary, and Covarrubias's *Tesoro*. "Something small or trivial" may have signaled custom's ordinariness and mundaneness, distinguishing it from the laws of the ethnic lords and reinforcing the idea that rulers made laws and the people made custom. "Antiquity" provided the element of time incumbent in custom's ancestral origins. In the eyes of the missionaries, though, Native antiquity was not a neutral marker of time. As we saw with the missionaries' treatment of the tlamanitiliztli and huehuetlatolli in central Mexico, the customary practices and rhetorical forms of old provided a resource for conversion at the same time that they were tainted by what the missionaries considered idolatry.

In the case of the second and third iterations of custom in Mixtec—"dzavua caa ñuu" and "dzavua caa tayu"—the question of the kind of polity to which custom pertained came into play, as did the idea of custom as the nature, essence, and collective identity of the social group. "Dzavua caa" means "style or custom of the land" (*costumbre o estilo de la tierra*) and "inclination, tendency, propensity, or disposition" (*inclinación*).[63] "Ñuu" (community) and "tayu," short for *yuhuitayu* (seat of lordship), the terms that modify custom in both iterations, suggest a hierarchy of custom among the Mixtec, such that the customs of constituent communities that made up the ethnic state could be distinct and independent from that of the seat of lordship. Such a translation was in keeping with the autonomy of the ñuu, which could and did often secede from their yuhuitayu in order to join with other ñuu to form new polities or realign themselves with other yuhuitayu. This translation served to combine the European concept of custom as essential to a community with terms that were specific to Mixtec political organization.

The Dominican friar Juan de Córdova's Zapotec entries for custom in his *Vocabulario en lengua çapoteca* shared many similarities with those in Alvarado's dictionary but were ultimately more numerous and nuanced. This is not surprising since Córdova's *Vocabulario* was the most expansive of its kind in all of the Americas, with entries double the number in Nebrija's Spanish-Latin dictionary and the Spanish-Nahuatl section of Molina's dictionary. With 29,500 Spanish entries and 69,900 Zapotec glosses, Córdova combined the translation strategies of prolific modification of Spanish concepts with detailed Native-language description.[64] Although linguists and ethnohistorians have noted the problematic nature of many of the dictionary's translations, they acknowledge its ethnographic richness, "unmatched by any of the other colonial dictionaries," and characterize it as "more of an encyclopedia than a dictionary."[65]

Córdova provided fourteen entries for law that ran the gamut from natural law (with the most extensive Zapotec glosses), to the law of the Christian God and the pope, to marriage (through a contrast with unmarried sexual relations), to making and abrogating law. The translations for "law generally" (*tíchapéa, tichatàopèa*)—"the essential words, the very essential words"—contrast with the translation for "law of the pueblo or custom" (*xitíchaquéche*), or "our community's words."[66] The use of *ticha* signaled the centrality of rhetoric to authority in both the Spanish and Indigenous traditions, highlighted the connection between custom and language, and linked the concepts of custom and law. At the same time, the modifier *queche* (community) marked a difference between custom and law by modifying custom as a particular form of law, pertaining to the community. It is notable that although *ticha* was used to translate both law and custom, it appeared more frequently in entries for law, whereas custom's glosses leaned toward practice, core being, and essence, a distinction in keeping with custom's meaning according to natural law and Aristotelean philosophy.

Córdova's eleven entries for "costumbre" continued the process of linking the meanings of custom and law while differentiating between them. His first entry for custom includes the Spanish synonym *modo* (mode, style) and is glossed in Zapotec using constructions with the Zapotec terms *péa* (property or essence of something), *làchi* (heart), and *tícha* (word).[67] In his *Arte en lengua zapoteca*, Córdova lists the term *pea* as one of seventy entries in an appendix of important words for effective communication in the language as defined by the missionary enterprise. Unlike the dictionaries, which translated from Spanish to the Native language, appendices of key words in missionary grammars did the reverse, translating from the Indigenous term to Spanish with long explanations of meaning and usage. Under the entry for "pea," Córdova lists the term *costumbre* as well as others in keeping with custom's semantic field, including the Castilian terms for "use," "mode," "manner," and the "nature of something" as well as "law and commandment."[68] Recall that in his dictionary, Córdova used *pea* to modify *ticha* (word) in order to translate both law and custom. He distinguished between the two by using *tíchapéa* as an equivalent for "law" and "speech generally," and *tíchalipéa* for "custom," "mode" and "style of speech," producing the idea of law based in orality.

Lachi, the second core term that Córdova used to translate "custom," is ubiquitous in constructions across many genres of missionary literature and

Native-language notarial writing. *Lachi* was an especially rich and polyvalent term, around which Zapotec speakers and writers built many metaphors, as evident in missionary literature and notarial writing.[69] Its meanings included seed of a fruit or other living thing, seat of intention, interior of a human being, conscience, soul, or a vital force that gives life to a living creature or person. In Zapotec and Mixtec moral philosophy as well as in Christian thought, the heart was the seat of the will and emotions, making it a particularly effective bridge for missionary translation.[70] The use of *lachi* and *pea* to translate Córdova's first entry for custom rendered it as emanating from the will of the people as if from a seed, and as authentic and essential to a people and place.

Córdova's second entry for custom—"custom of the land or pueblo"—reproduces the Zapotec glosses for custom as "mode" and anchors it in space by adding a doublet: *quélahualache* (the essence of the land or country) and *tíchapea hualáache* (the law of the land or country).[71] This translation served to territorialize and essentialize custom by producing the idea of the particular, essential, or popular law of a territorial entity. The term *quela*, with which the first construction is built, has a wide range of meanings, including corn stalk, and the essence, property, or core being of someone or something. As he did for the term *pea*, Córdova included *quela* in the appendix of important words in his grammar. He and his Native coauthors note the polyvalence and exceptional utility of the term and that in addition to its many meanings, it served an important grammatical function. By placing it in front of a verb form, it turned the verb into a noun (a verbal noun), making it a particularly useful tool of translation.[72] When fused together, the semantic meaning and grammatical function of *quela* served to communicate core being and a state of being, contributing yet another dimension to the alignment of the Zapotec meaning of custom with natural law.

Córdova's remaining entries for custom include custom as life habit, human habit, something one does without thinking, custom that one imposes on others, to become habituated to custom, and to instill good customs, all of which drew upon Aristotelian notions of habituation and moral education. Additionally, he provided nine entries in which "custom" formed part of a larger phrase, including habit, custom; abuse, bad custom; corruption of customs; to have good or bad manners; style of speaking; habit of heart; a person's nature; a woman's customary blouse; and menstruation.[73] In these modifications of custom, he expanded well beyond Nebrija's two short entries, while following Nebrija's gendered construction of "custom" as nature by associating it with both the interior (menstruation) and exterior (costume) of women's bodies.

A final entry is worth scrutinizing for the conceptual work it performed in distinguishing between "good" and "bad" customs. In Córdova's entry for "gentile," he includes the modifier "things of the gentiles or their customs."[74] Here, Córdova refers to the customs of the Indigenous before the conquest and their conversion to Christianity. His translation of custom as law hinged upon its distinction from custom as the law of the ancestors. He translated "gentil, cosa de gentiles, o costumbre de ellos" (gentile, gentile things, or their customs) by modifying the terms *ticha* (word), *china* (work, office, and obligation), and *pea* (essence) with the prefix *xi* (our) and the compound suffix *penipezelào*, which he translated as pagan, unbaptized, and non-Christian infidel.[75] *Peni* meant person and *pezelào* likely derives from Pezèelào, which Córdova identified as the deity of the underworld or hereafter.[76] Unsurprisingly, he translated "devil" as Pezelào or *pezèelào*.[77] In this formulation, key aspects of pre-Hispanic social and political life were associated with paganism: words and laws; work, office, and forms of obligation; the lord of the underworld, and the very essence of the ancestors. Crucially, Córdova's primary gloss for idolatry was *quela pezèlào* (the devil's custom).[78]

Córdova used other translation strategies to mark the idea of the Natives' gentility and to associate their laws, customs, and practices of old with the concept of idolatry.[79] In the appendix of important vocabulary in his grammar, he lists the Zapotec term for antiquity: *colaala* (also spelled *colaça*).[80] As the linguist Martina Schrader-Kniffki and I have shown, missionary friars and Native authorities used the term frequently in pastoral literature and notarial writing to frame the spiritual encounter; as a modifier, it sorted ritual practices according to colonial and Christian notions of time—before and after the conquest, and before and after Christian conversion—often with moral implications.[81]

Despite the stark opposition between the laws and customs of Indigenous antiquity and the Christian present in much of the missionary literature, it is important to underscore the ambivalence with which the friars viewed the Native past. This was especially true for the earliest generation of missionaries who produced the sixteenth-century vocabularies, grammars, and catechisms. They recognized that they could not condemn the Native past wholesale; Native antiquity could be used as an analogy with which to explain Christian practice. In the absence of Native equivalents for many Christian terms, they turned to the pre-Hispanic past to provide keys to translating the Christian message in terms that appealed to Indigenous sensibilities and understandings. They also acknowledged, sometimes grudgingly, that in order to succeed they needed to make compromises with Indigenous forms of authority and customary practice. This narrow bridge to the Indigenous past was a fine line to walk and required subtlety of translation. In Fray Francisco de Alvarado's *Vocabulario en lengua mixteca*, he translated the expression "to bless what the Indians ate in former times" as "yodzocondi nuu ñuhu," which means "to offer to god."[82] The translation introduces the Christian concept of "to bless" through reference to the Indigenous practice of making offerings to deities, while locating the Indigenous practice in a past to which there was no return. The missionaries' efforts to distinguish between Native custom generally and customs of the gentile ancestors points to how Indigenous people in the Americas could not share fully in the legitimizing claims of custom's antiquity in the same way that people living in Spain's varied pueblos, towns, and localities could. Only certain practices could persist across the dividing line of the Spanish conquest.

The translation strategy of using Christian and colonial notions of time to assign morality to Native customs was especially evident in the catechisms, which were intended for Christian education. In rural settings where there were fewer colegios dedicated to teaching Native youth, parish priests and their Native assistants taught the Christian doctrine through oral catechesis. Native parishioners were expected to congregate on Sundays in rural communities throughout New Spain to recite by heart the Sunday prayer, Our Father, Ave María, the Credo, the twelve articles of the faith, the Ten Commandments, the five commandments of the church, the seven sacraments, and the seven deadly sins.[83] This practice was designed to train the conscience and the body at the same time with the goal of morally habituating children and neophytes and inculcating them with an understanding of the articles of faith, which was necessary for the administration of the sacraments. The Native-language translations of the catechism were much longer and elaborate than the Spanish-language originals because they incorporated explanations and analogies to Indigenous culture in order to make the message meaningful to Native people. This required the missionaries to tack back and forth between the customs of the pre-Hispanic period and Christian norms as a means of casting the Native past as bad and the Christian present as good. The Dominican friar Pedro de Feria's translation of the "Our Father" in his bilingual Zapotec-Spanish catechism *Doctrina cristiana en lengua castellana y çapoteca* demonstrates that the term *colaça* could be used to mark the Native past as a former regime and as idolatrous: "When you need something, do not go to ask your idols of wood and stone, nor confide in your dead as you did in former times [*colaça*], rather only to God should you tell of your needs."[84] In Francisco Pacheco de Silva's 1687 bilingual Spanish-Zapotec catechism *Doctrina cristiana traducida de la lengua castellana en lengua zapoteca nexitza*, he uses *golaaza* (in the orthography of Nexitzo Zapotec) to modify the term *idols*, as in "the idols of former times," showing how this translation strategy endured across a century and across different geographic regions and linguistic variations of the language.[85] In an *exemplum*—a genre intended for preaching—from the 1666 *Miscelaneo espiritual*, the Dominican friar Cristóbal de Agüero uses *colaaza* (rendered here in yet another orthography) to refer to a depraved time before Christianity.[86]

As Olmos, Sahagún, and other Franciscans did with the huehuetlatolli, Feria incorporated Zapotec ceremonial style known as *libana* to package the Christian message in authoritative Native rhetoric. In his *Doctrina*, he posed a rhetorical question: "Where have the old gods gone since the Christians arrived, where are they hidden, where have they fled, why do they not return through their law and religion? One sees clearly that they were not real gods, but rather all of it was the devil's great lie and trickery."[87] While falsifying Native law and custom by associating them with the devil, bilingual catechisms also served to lift up the laws of the Christian god, the good customs of faithful Christians, and the lives of the saints, thereby providing what in the missionaries' view was a counterexample and antidote to the bad customs of old. In his 1687 catechism, Pacheco combines the Zapotec terms *china* (work, labor, office, obligation) and *tzahui* (good) to communicate the idea of "saintly works," the "deeds of the saints," and "virtue." By using the negative (*acca*), he contrasts these with "bad customs" (*china acca tzahui*).[88] According to this logic, people of good customs followed the law of the Christian god, embodied in the virtuous lives of the saints.

Pacheco's use of *china* in the Zapotec gloss for "saintly works" and "bad customs" expanded its meaning beyond essence, words, and laws, and into the realm of work and obligations. The primary meanings of china—labor (*labor*) and office (*oficio*)—signaled duty, obligation, and reciprocity.[89] "Labor" was a social relation that bound Indigenous commoners to nobility and community members to one another as well as to the community's lands and resources. "Office" encompassed the responsibilities and duties of Native authorities to the community, and to higher authorities like the ethnic lord and the sacred ancestors. The translation of custom through the concept of *china*, then, produced yet another facet of custom: a set of social obligations and a kind of social contract.

Zapotec constructions for custom in sixteenth-century dictionaries, grammars, and catechisms were reproduced and given additional meaning in confessional manuals. Confession was part of the arsenal of Christian education, complementary to the collective experience of catechism or listening to sermons. Through the sacrament of confession, the priest engaged the individual conscience of the penitent, eliciting an account of sins and prescribing concrete actions to allow for reconciliation with the church.[90]

The philosopher Michel Foucault famously argued that confession—predicated on the notion of a self that could sin and a process of revealing the self through truth telling—represented a means by which the modern individualized subject and new forms of power and discipline were produced, beginning in the medieval era.[91] Foucault's argument falls short, however, in the context of colonialism, where priests had to communicate with Indigenous penitents in languages that had no equivalents for many Christian concepts, most crucially that of sin. Important scholarship on colonial Mexico and the Andes analyzes bilingual confessional manuals, the primary tool of the confessor, to reveal the ways in which confession as a strategy of conversion fell prey to the challenges of translation, yielding unanticipated forms of syncretism, or failing utterly to connect the idea of sin with sex or other quotidian practices.[92]

According to Nancy Farriss, the sacrament of confession provided one of the greatest communicative challenges for the missionary enterprise because in contrast to guidelines regarding the teaching of the catechism or delivering sermons, the church strictly prohibited the presence of Indigenous translators during confession. Furthermore, the practice of confession was conversational and improvisational, as the priest probed the conscience of the penitent with follow-up questions based on what he or she revealed to him. This required sophistication of linguistic skills well beyond those demanded by the one-way delivery of a sermon or the stock template of the catechism. To make matters even more difficult, confessional manuals in Indigenous languages were scarce across much of colonial Mexico since the missionaries had prioritized the production of dictionaries, grammars, and catechisms as instruments of conversion. When they did appear, it was relatively later—in the late sixteenth and seventeenth centuries—following on the heels of the Council of Trent when church authorities elevated the sacrament of confession to a position of greater importance.[93]

Farriss notes that only two confessional manuals were published in Native languages of Oaxaca during the colonial period: one in Zapotec by Fray Cristóbal de Agüero in 1665 and another in Mixe by Fray Agustín de Quintana in 1733. However, there were many more unpublished and unedited manuals that were highly abbreviated and directed at clergy with elementary language abilities. Farriss characterizes these as the "confessional counterpart to the basic catechism."[94] She notes that these simple manuals were likely more representative of the practice of confession than the elaborate *confesionarios mayores*, which reflected the concerns of the Council of Trent, conciliar decrees, and theological treatises.[95] In keeping with confessional manuals throughout Europe and the Americas, the abbreviated manuals contained follow-up questions for particular commandments that were tailored to the identities of the penitents and the temptations to sin that were characteristic of their particular contexts and social worlds. In European manuals, special questions were dedicated to the confession of members of different professions, occupations, and guilds and addressed the morally compromising situations (from a Christian perspective) in which different groups of penitents might find themselves. In the Americas, bilingual confessionals aimed at Indigenous penitents were adapted to colonial preoccupations with the customs of the Indigenous population, such as the governing practices of Indigenous elites and town officers, fair prices and honest dealings in marketplaces, the treatment and comportment of Indigenous laborers, Native sexuality, and what ecclesiastical officials perceived to be the ongoing threat of idolatry.[96] Through translation, the abbreviated manuals produced and refined intercultural meanings of Native custom so that priests could query their penitents and at the same time reinforce local norms and practices that aligned with Christianity while combating those that did not.

Fray Alonso Martínez's 1633 Zapotec confessional manual *Manual breve y compendioso para enpesar a aprender lengua zapoteca y administrar en caso de necesidad* provides an example of an abbreviated manual, and during its time it likely served as a field guide for translating colonial concerns about Native custom in the confessional booth and beyond. The first section, designed to familiarize the priest with key phrases for administering confession, includes words and phrases like "how many times?" and "always," and the question "do you have/do this customarily? [Tienes esto de costumbre?]."[97] Martínez translated "custom" in this query as "pea lachilo," combining the Zapotec term for "essence" or "property of" (*pea*) with that of "heart" (*lachi*), two concepts that were crucial to Fray Juan de Córdova's translations of "custom." Tailoring the manual to what he perceived to be the errors of his Native parishioners, Martínez included a separate section titled "Brief and Necessary Additions to this confessional manual regarding the sins into which Indians most ordinarily fall." In this part of the manual, Martínez posed questions regarding what clergy and colonial authorities perceived as the intractable transgressions of the Indigenous population, including drunkenness, eating meat on Fridays, casting spells and curses, not complying with one's marital duties, and for women especially, a question regarding taking herbs to induce abortion.[98] Taken together, the questions about custom and comportment posed in the "Key Phrases" and "Brief and Necessary Additions" served to link notions of Native custom, sin, and Indian identity.

Like most confessional manuals, the meat of Martínez's text was structured around the Ten Commandments. In a follow-up question to the first commandment (not to worship false gods), Fray Martínez linked pre-Hispanic custom with idolatry by translating the question "As creido en idolatria antigua?" (Have you believed in ancient idolatry?) as "Cuyeelii lachilo ticha colaça, xiteni bitoo xihui?" The Zapotec version differs from the Spanish original, glossing "ancient idolatry" as "the ancient custom or law [ticha colaça] of the false god [xiteni bitoo xihui]," thereby reinforcing Spanish notions of the inferiority and illegitimacy of Native custom.[99] As Schrader-Kniffki and I have shown, Martínez was explicit about his translation strategy in an appendix titled "Advertencias" (Warnings), which many confessional guides in New Spain included in order to keep friars from making errors in translation. In Martinez's appendix, he identified two Zapotec words—xihui ("bad/false") and chahui ("good") (a different spelling than "tzahui," discussed earlier)—as a means by which to mark out a Christian semantic field of sin and virtue.[100] By modifying "bitoo" (god) (also spelled "pitoo") with "xihui," he produced the idea of a "false god" and marked ancient custom with the taint of mortal sin.

Martínez's confessional manual also spoke to political concerns in Indigenous communities, such as good governance and social order as defined by Spanish principles. Four separate sets of questions addressed to "Native magistrates [alcaldes] and Leaders [mandones]" move back and forth between the brass tacks of colonial administration—including labor, the use of the community's financial resources, and litigation—and pre-Hispanic practices that linked community leaders and ritual specialists. The first set of questions, subtitled "exceed their authority," asks Native alcaldes whether they exercise their authority cruelly, demand excessive fees, impose levies (derramas) for illicit purposes, or deceive others in illicit dealings. The second set, subtitled "Pleitistas y el Jornal" (Litigiousness and the daily wage), asks Native authorities whether they spearhead frivolous lawsuits and coerce commoners to support them, force commoners to work on Sundays, or demand unpaid labor of commoners. The third set of questions, titled "Hechizeros" (Sorcerers), asks whether the Native alcaldes consult sorcerers who continue to perform the old rituals of Native antiquity, and whether they use herbs or animals to cast spells on others, or form a pact with the devil to do so. The fourth and final set of questions, titled "el tecolote y paxaros" (the owl and birds), asks whether the Native alcaldes believe that the calls of owls and other birds reveal one's good or bad luck, and whether they ingest herbs for purposes of divination and casting spells.[101]

These questions reflected widespread colonial attitudes regarding Indigenous authorities. On the one hand, they evinced colonial assumptions about the "tyranny" of Native leaders, while expressing anxiety about elite Native acculturation by underscoring the ill effects of Native legal consciousness and the propensity of Indigenous leaders to bring disputes to Spanish courts. On the other hand, the questions expressed dismay at the capacity of Native elites to command unpaid labor from Native commoners—glossed in Spanish as "servicio personal" (personal service)—which the Spanish viewed as a holdover of customary elite prerogatives from the pre-Hispanic period. Despite numerous legal prohibitions of personal service by the Crown and decrees that Native laborers should be paid wages for their work, many Native elites and Spanish colonizers continued to require personal service and unpaid labor from Native commoners. Finally, while colonial officials fretted over how quickly Native leaders had learned to bring a case to court, they also wrung their hands over the continuities of Native ritual practice, the role that Native leaders played in its perpetuation, and the way in which it undergirded legitimate authority in Indigenous communities. In short, the confessional manual provides a glimpse at the contradictions of Spanish colonialism and the ambivalence of colonial Native custom and authority in the eyes of Spanish officials and missionary priests.

Fray Martínez's confessional manual makes clear that ecclesiastical officials imagined the confessional as a regulator of local governance through the teaching and enforcement of good customs among the general population in Indigenous communities, but especially among Native leaders. The authority of parish priests and Native officials was deeply intertwined and, as the confessional manual shows, riddled with points of friction. Continuity of pre-Hispanic ritual practice, exceeding the authority and jurisdiction afforded to them by Spanish law, initiating lawsuits on behalf of the community, and overtaxing Native labor figured front and center among priests' concerns regarding the power and comportment of Native officials. As will be shown in chapter 6, these concerns were central to legal disputes regarding custom in Indigenous communities throughout the colonial period.

Conclusion

Missionaries and their Indigenous interlocutors were key agents in the production of colonial legal consciousness. Their collaborative work in four arenas of the evangelical enterprise—translation, ethnography, education, and the extirpation of idolatry—represented an uneven and incomplete process of aligning the social conventions and daily habits of Native parishioners with Christian order. Custom as an abstract concept and a concrete set of practices lay at the heart of this project. As prescribed by colonial law, Native authorities—the friars' primary partners in the theater of evangelization—were instructed to govern according to its norms. This posed a conundrum since the missionaries sought to dismantle the moral and material basis of Native law and custom and rebuild Native communities on a new foundation. At the same time, although they sought to impose a new order, the missionaries recognized that to wield influence, they had to draw upon Indigenous forms of authority and its discourses and moral underpinnings. The twin impulses to preserve and destroy opened a space for the continuity of Indigenous modes of governance and customs that could pass Christianity's repugnancy test.

The translation process that gave rise to the concept of custom in Native languages was nourished by centuries of translation in a Mediterranean-Atlantic context in which meaning accreted and changed according to popular practice and the objectives of rulers, elites, theologians, and a professional class of jurists. Long before the conquest of America, custom served as a tool of empire and a means of managing cultural diversity and jurisdictional complexity throughout Europe. The many cycles of conquest in Iberia produced a context in which diverse legal traditions informed one another and the boundary between custom and law was highly porous. The concept of custom as translated by Nebrija and the missionary friars who emulated his method manifested deep traces of this historical process. Missionary friars and the Native authorities who worked with them aligned concepts derived from the ancient Mediterranean world, natural law, and the medieval Spanish legal tradition with Indigenous categories of knowledge, including modes of political organization, authority, reciprocity, speech, language, interiority, labor, and office holding. This process produced a concept of Native custom that encompassed a set of social obligations and conventions that were Indigenous and Christian, territorially rooted, constitutive of the collective identity of the Native community, and whose relationship to Native antiquity was tenuous.

Native law, custom, and governing institutions provided a foundation for Spanish colonial administration via indirect rule by Native elites and authorities in New Spain. From the perspective of the Spanish Empire, the catch was to maintain those customs commensurate with Spanish law and Christianity and suppress those that were not. As evident in the missionary texts, distinguishing between good and bad customs represented one of the central tasks of evangelization and, by extension, Native governance. The next chapter examines how the framing of pre-Hispanic Native law and custom during two watershed moments of the sixteenth century contributed to this process.

Good & Bad Customs in the Native Past & Present

Part II

SIXTEENTH THROUGH
SEVENTEENTH CENTURIES

Framing Pre-Hispanic   3
Law & Custom

IN A WORKSHOP SOMEWHERE in central Mexico sometime during the
1540s or early 1550s, a group of Native painter-scribes (tlacuiloque) answered
back to Spanish theologians, jurists, and missionaries who disparaged the
customs and civilizational status of Indigenous peoples. Through their anonymous and unsigned work—known today as the Codex Mendoza—they deployed Mesoamerican history, culture, and pictographic conventions to meet
their detractors on a European rhetorical terrain, framing and evaluating the
realm of Indigenous law and custom according to European notions of civility. They and their patron or patrons knew that the stakes were high; they
likely surmised that the position of Native communities in the colonial order depended in some small part on whether their narrative could persuade
a Spanish audience.

The debate over the Indies opened a space for a semiautonomous Native
jurisdiction in which according to imperial law, Native authorities could rule
in keeping with their old laws and customs, provided that they were "good"
and did not contradict Christianity. As the friars evangelized, they provided
Native people with tools with which to make a case for their good customs
and, by extension, semisovereignty in terms intelligible to Spanish authorities: an education in humanist thought. In schools for elite Native youth such
as the Colegio de Santa Cruz Tlatelolco, friars taught not only the Christian
doctrine but also grammar, rhetoric, and Scholastic theology, and required

Indigenous pupils to read ancient and medieval European texts. In the process, young Indigenous men became fluent in Latin, Spanish, and Nahuatl, and well versed in European notions of civility. Upon graduation from the colegios, many became interpreters and authorities in their communities and used the knowledge they acquired to frame their own norms and practices in terms comprehensible and acceptable to Spanish officials. Even outside the hallowed halls of the colegios, the idea of natural law as a measure of the civilizational status of Native people circulated through missionary translation, education, and catechesis, and through the interaction of Native authorities with the church and Spanish institutions.[1]

This chapter analyzes the framing and evaluation of pre-Hispanic law and custom by Native youth, elders, and authorities and their Spanish interlocutors in two iconic colonial texts produced during two watershed moments of Spanish colonial rule, and in two distinct settings. The Codex Mendoza, one of the best-known Native histories of the early colonial era, was created by Nahua painter-scribes sometime during the 1540s or possibly early 1550s, the decades during which the debate over Native civilizational status and sovereignty was raging in Spain. A Spanish interpreter and scribe translated and glossed the images created by the tlacuiloque, which together portrayed pre-Hispanic Mexica history, institutions, customs, and laws as commensurate with European notions of political order, thereby making a case for Mexica semisovereignty. The codex's hybrid style, which juxtaposed Indigenous pictorial writing with Spanish-language text in the format of a European book, made it a consummately colonial text. Just as importantly, its translations of image, text, and language provided a model for making claims that aligned Native custom with natural law.

Produced in response to a Spanish imperial crisis during the late 1560s, the Relaciones geográficas was a royal survey administered in the Native provinces and towns of New Spain and Peru from 1579 to 1585. The survey was designed to gather information about the Crown's American holdings with an eye to reforming its colonial policies. It included questions about land, labor, and resources, the bread and butter of the colonial enterprise. It also yielded a famous set of maps—recently designated by the United Nations Educational, Scientific and Cultural Organization (UNESCO) as the patrimony of humanity—which capture the interpenetration of Native and European conceptions of space and sociopolitical relations.[2] Crucially, the survey also produced knowledge about pre-Hispanic Native customs, laws, and governing institutions, while evaluating them in relation to Spanish law and Christianity. Although some Spanish priests and governors took it upon themselves to author the survey responses, most relied on local Indigenous elders and leaders for the content and substance. In the absence of a document like the Codex Mendoza in the diocese of Oaxaca, the Relaciones geográficas provide evidence of how Indigenous customs and laws, filtered through the tongues of interpreters and the pens of notaries, were framed for a Spanish audience. The survey responses provided a more ambivalent and pessimistic assessment of Oaxaca's pre-Hispanic institutions than that of the Codex Mendoza for the Mexica, making a case for Spanish stewardship of Native jurisdiction.

Custom, Law, and Civility in the Codex Mendoza

The Codex Mendoza is one of the best known and celebrated pictorial manuscripts of early colonial Mexico. It has provided generations of scholars with historical and ethnographic information about pre-Hispanic Tenochtitlan, the Mexica Empire, and the pictographic conventions of sixteenth-century Nahua painter-scribes. Early scholarship on the codex suggests that it was commissioned by Viceroy Antonio de Mendoza (hence the title) for a Spanish audience and created around 1541 by Francisco Gualpuyogualcal, an Indigenous master of painters working in collaboration with Indigenous elders, a Spanish translator well versed in Nahuatl (*nahuatlato*), and a Spanish notary who wrote the accompanying Spanish text.[3] Recent scholarship argues that the codex was not made by a single master painter but by two tlacuiloque in a single workshop.[4] Scholars have also identified the Spanish canon Juan González and Franciscan friar, linguist, and ethnographer Fray Andrés de Olmos as likely authors of the codex's Spanish text.[5] Recently, carbon dating has also expanded the possible dates of the codex's production, positing that it could have been created anytime between the 1530s and 1560s, though the late 1540s to early 1550s are the most likely.[6] New scholarship has also cast doubt that the codex was made by order of Viceroy Mendoza, arguing instead that it may have been commissioned by Indigenous elites for an audience of Spanish officials in order to influence their policies toward the Native population.[7]

We do know for sure that the Codex Mendoza did not end up in Spain as was intended. It was loaded onto a Spanish galleon but lost at sea, most likely at the hands of French privateers. It ended up in the French royal court via André Thevet, a French cleric, cosmographer to the king of France, and collector of manuscripts and books. It then moved through a network of manuscript collectors, in 1587 to Richard Haklyut, in 1616 to Samuel Purchas, and then in 1654 to John Selden. In 1659 it ended up in Oxford's Bodleian Library, and it reappeared in facsimile reproduction in Lord Kingsborough's nine-volume *Antiquities of Mexico* (1831–48), and again in a 1938 facsimile by James Cooper Clark.[8] Frances Berdan and Patricia Anawalt published four volumes dedicated to the codex, including a full-size color facsimile, an interpretive volume, a descriptive volume, and a volume of drawings, transcriptions, and translations in 1992.[9] Mexico's Instituto Nacional de Antropología e Historia (INAH, National Institute of Anthropology and History) digitized it and made it available to the public online in 2014.[10]

The Codex Mendoza consists of seventy-one folios, whose front and reverse sides amount to 142 pages. Seventy-two of the pages are primarily pictorial, sixty-three textual, and seven blank. The pictorial and textual pages are juxtaposed, the text providing an interpretation and commentary in the Spanish language of the pictorial content on the opposite page (fig. G1). Additionally, individual images on the pictorial pages are glossed with Spanish and Nahuatl terms and brief Spanish-language explanations. The final page of the manuscript (fol. 71v), in which the notary who wrote the Spanish text briefly explains how it was made, reveals a complex process of translation in which Indigenous tlacuiloque painted images, Indigenous individuals explained their meaning in Nahuatl, a Spanish interpreter translated their words from Nahuatl to Spanish, and the Spanish notary provided written textual description and glossed the images (fig. G2).[11] In this regard, the codex is both a hybrid text and a work of translation. As such, it is not just a repository of information about pre-Hispanic Mesoamerica but also a "site of cultural negotiation and mediation" that says as much about the colonial world in which it was produced as about the pre-Hispanic world it purported to represent.[12]

Notably, the translation process that gave rise to the Codex Mendoza followed the conventions of translation in legal contexts. This is made clear on the last page of the manuscript (fol. 71v), where the Spanish translator-scribe asks the reader to "excuse the rough style in the interpretation of the drawings in this history, because the interpreter did not take time or work at all slowly; and because it was a matter neither agreed upon nor thought about, it was interpreted according to legal conventions [*a uso de proceso*]" (fig. G2). By "legal conventions," the translator-scribe referred to the context of early colonial Mexican courts in which Indigenous litigants presented pictographic accounts as evidence of their claims and interpreted the images in spoken Nahuatl for a court interpreter who in turn translated them into Spanish, which a notary transcribed into the written record of the court proceedings. The "legal conventions" that yielded the text of the Codex Mendoza were distinct from the missionary context in which other codices and books dedicated to the description of Indigenous history and culture, such as the Florentine Codex, were produced. In the missionary context, learned Indigenous grammarians wrote text in elegant and refined language found in the European chronicles and histories of the time. In legal contexts, an interpreter worked quickly to summarize and gloss the essence of the content he was translating, which the notary transcribed using abbreviations and legal formulae. As the interpreter and notary worked, they created written text that oriented the Spanish reader to the images, thereby producing a Spanish cultural framework for their interpretation.[13]

The Codex Mendoza is divided into three parts that form a coherent narrative arc whose pictorial style and conceptual scaffolding present Mesoamerican content within a European frame. The first section (sixteen folios) chronicles the founding of Tenochtitlan and its ascendency as a regional hegemon through successive conquests of Native polities. In keeping with Mesoamerican conventions, history is periodized according to the rule of individual lords (*huey tlatoque*, pl.; *huey tlatoani*, sing.). In the visual depiction, chronology is rendered according to time glyphs, whereas in the text, the dates are recorded according to Christian time. The second section details the tributary relationships between Tenochtitlan, the Aztec capital, and each conquered community through iconographic representations of the goods paid at regular intervals and their quantities. The third section portrays Indigenous social life from birth, to the education of youth, to marriage, to adult participation in the civic and economic life of Tenochtitlan. It also portrays the role of the city's laws and judicial institutions in maintaining political order.[14]

Part III of the Codex Mendoza is the least studied and most poorly understood of the three sections. The first two sections are clearly modeled on pre-existing Mesoamerican texts: the first, on a dynastic history; and the second, on an extant pre-Hispanic document known in Spanish as the Matrícula de Tributos. The painter-scribes who produced these first two sections served primarily as copyists. Part III, however, is anomalous, with no known model or precedent.[15] Foundational scholarship points to the huehuetlatolli (words of the elders/ancient ones), discussed in chapter 2, as a possible model, as well as European genres, such as the Ars Moriendi and Mirrors for Princes, the first of which provided advice and prescriptions for a good death, and the second, instructions for young rulers regarding proper comportment and advice for effective leadership.[16] The connections are suggestive, however, rather than conclusive or definitive. As Edward Calnek has argued, we should consider part III as an original composition, which situates the tlacuiloque not just as copyists but as authors, or at least coauthors, who may have received some direction from the patron who commissioned the work, and who likely consulted with Indigenous elders regarding the content. Painter-scribes were considered skilled craftsmen (*tolteca*), which positioned them as relatively privileged commoners within Tenochtitlan's social stratum of petty artisans, the largest component of the city's population. The narrative in part III was emblematic of their class position in that it focused on the moral education and career paths of artisans as well as the nobility. Unlike the ethnographic content of the Florentine Codex, which relied on the knowledge of the noble class and represented an elite perspective, part III of the Codex Mendoza provides a commoner perspective on Mexica moral education, law, and custom. And unlike the Florentine Codex, there appears to have been little or no Spanish oversight in its production.[17]

Recent scholarship casts the Codex Mendoza as a Native intervention in the Spanish debate over the Indies. The art historian Jorge Gomez Tejada argues that Indigenous authorities likely commissioned the work with the intention of demonstrating the civility of Mexica society in service to the Indigenist cause. He interprets the codex as a tripartite portrayal of Mexica politics, economy, and society that drew its conceptual architecture from Aristotle's *Nicomachean Ethics* and *Politics*. These texts were central to Bartolomé de Las Casas's framing of Mexica society in his *Apologética Historia Sumaria*, in which he contended that although the Mexica lacked the light of Christian truth, they were civilized because they ruled "according to custom and the law."[18] The Codex Mendoza supports Las Casas's assessment through an Indigenous narrative. Part I of the codex charts an evolutionary trajectory over time of the increasingly virtuous rule of Mexica leaders, culminating in the just and wise government of Moctezuma II. Part II, which details the tributary economy, presents an image of an efficient and well-organized empire, an economic narrative that complements the political narrative of part I. And by detailing the educational, laboral, and legal institutions of Tenochtitlan, part III presents the Mexica as virtuous, disciplined, and hardworking.[19]

In my analysis of part III of the Codex Mendoza, I build upon Gomez Tejada's work by attending to how the dialogue between image and text yielded a vision of Mexica society that aligned with natural law and Aristotelian ideas about the relationship among moral education, custom, and law. Together, the images and text framed Tenochtitlan as a republic, the European ideal of urban civility. Among the three parts of the codex, part III makes the strongest case for Indigenous sovereignty by demonstrating the social depth, ranging from nobles to commoner artisans, of Tenochtitlan's rational political order. It shows how local-level institutions—families, schools, neighbor-hoods, wards, and craft guilds—worked in tandem with the rational laws and formal legal institutions of the city to reproduce good customs and regulate social life. Due to the complexity of the themes elaborated in part III, the translator's annotations and summaries are more fulsome than in parts I and II. In addition to identifying, glossing, and describing the images, the transla-tions provide explanations of the motives and actions of the figures depicted, thereby lending the paintings a narrative coherence and intelligibility for a Spanish audience.[20] In this regard, the translator's work in part III evinced an emerging mode of translating Mesoamerican custom for the eyes of Spanish judges, officials, and administrators.

Teaching Good Customs in Families and Schools

The narrative structure of part III of the Codex Mendoza, which consists of fifteen pages of pictographic illustrations and accompanying text, can be an-alyzed in three discrete sections that form a coherent whole, all focused on different stages of moral development: childhood education in the family, public education in the city's schools, and civic education through the city's laws and customs. The first five folios address the moral education of children from birth to age fifteen. The pictorial narrative and accompanying Spanish text, which focus on the rearing of children in the home by their parents, con-nect education to political order through the habituation of youth to good customs. The images of the first folio and Spanish text illustrate the Mexica "manners and customs" surrounding the birth of a child, the "customs and rites" involved in naming the child, and the central figures responsible for bringing the child into the political community: the mother, father, midwife, and head priest (fig. G3). Each of the four registers of the second pictographic folio details the mode of instruction given by fathers to boys and mothers to girls in ages three, four, five, and six (fig. G4). Ages seven through ten, repre-sented on the third folio, mark an important turning point: at age seven, girls learned how to spin and boys to fish. At the age of eight, children began to be punished physically by their parents for failing to perform the tasks required of them, and by age ten, rebellious children were beaten by their parents (fig. G5). According to the Spanish text, these harsh corporal punishments were intended to encourage children to apply themselves to useful activities and steer them away from "idleness and vice." Notably, in early modern Catholic communities, the age of seven was also a turning point in childhood develop-ment because it marked the age when children were old enough to be held accountable for deadly sins.[21] Ages eleven to fourteen represent the final stage in the training of children by parents at home, featuring a progression from more severe punishments during ages eleven and twelve to a liberation from punishment by age thirteen due to hard-earned conformity with adult expectations. At age fourteen, boys learned to fish and girls to weave (fig. G6).

Boys and girls came of age at fifteen in Tenochtitlan, according to the two registers of folio 61r (fig. G7). In the upper register, a father delivers a fifteen-year-old boy to either the head priest for training for the priesthood, military, and judicial and civil leadership at a rigorous school for this purpose, glossed in Nahuatl as the *calmecac*, or the master of youths at a school glossed in Nahuatl as the *cuicacalli* (house of song). There was a class dimension to these two options for schooling: generally speaking, the sons of the nobility attended the first, and those of the commoners, the second.[22] Up until this point, the side-by-side pictographic representation of the education of girls by their mothers and boys by their fathers reflected Mesoamerican gender parallelism, but in this crucial transition from family to state-run schooling, girls fall out of the story. They return to the scene, however, on the bottom register of folio 61r, which depicts the customs surrounding "legitimate marriage," as glossed in the Spanish text (fig. G7). The elaborate composition depicts the *amanteca* (midwife-healer) carrying a bride on her back to a groom's house, where the groom's parents received her and led her to a patio. There, she sat on a reed mat with the groom, next to a burning hearth, and according to the Spanish text, together, they "offered copal incense to their gods." Then, they and the assembled elders ate, and afterward, the elders instructed them on how to behave, fulfill their responsibilities, and live in peace. The Spanish text makes clear that a "legitimate marriage" was a sacred affair and that parents continued to shape the character development of the young couple through their good advice.

In this first section of part III of the Codex Mendoza, the painter-scribes aligned Mesoamerican and European philosophies of early education by presenting childhood in stages, emphasizing strict gender division in early upbringing, highlighting the role of parents in moral instruction, and lifting up marriage as a crucial step toward participation in the political community. For Plato and Aristotle, whose works informed the education of Native youth in New Spain's colegios, the goal of education was as much about the formation of character as intellect, with emphasis placed on deference, obedience, and modesty. Parents were central figures in children's character development, and gender division marked child rearing. Fathers were responsible for raising boys, and mothers, girls; parents did not raise their children

CHAPTER THREE

together or across gender lines. This training, which Aristotle glossed as *ethismos*, habituated youth to moral virtue through action and punishment of vice in the context of the family.[23]

Marriage was the culmination of this process. The size of the image representing the marriage ceremony and the married couple communicates its importance in the life cycle of individuals and the social and political order of the community. The interpreter's use of the term *legitimate marriage* to characterize the union reflected principles established in canon law about what made a marriage legitimate in the eyes of the Catholic Church and society. According to these principles, marriage had to be contracted "publicly and formally, with full solemnity, not entered into casually or secretly."[24] Ideally, it should also involve the exchange of vows, gifts, a ring, and a priest's blessing, though these were not requirements. The crucial part was its public, ritualized, and solemn nature.[25] The tlacuiloque made it clear that Native marriage customs met this bar. The centrality of the marriage ceremony to this section of the codex spoke to contemporaneous debates among church authorities in colonial Mexico and Spain about whether Native marriages made before the conquest or according to Native custom should be considered legitimate. These debates had enormous bearing on the political and social structure of Native communities and ethnic states in the early colonial context, and will be discussed further in chapter 4.

Through its schools, customs, and laws, the city of Tenochtitlan provided the arena for the civic and political education of youth after age fifteen, according to the four-folio series (fols. 62r–65r) that follows the section on early education. Alternating registers represent the training of noble youth for the priesthood and military, and of commoner youth for military and public service. This series focuses on young men alone; young women have disappeared from the pictorial and textual narrative. The top two registers of folio 62r depict the training of youth in the calmecac (register 1) and telpochcalli (register 2) (fig. G8). In both contexts, they perform services so that in the future they too could instruct and command other youth. The third register details punishments meted out for negligence and excess. As with punishment at home, the Spanish text notes that the goal of corporal punishment was to avoid idleness, laziness, negligence, carelessness, excess, and vagrancy, and to encourage youth to apply themselves to virtuous things ("cosas [sic] de vertud"). In the bottom register, a father offers his son to a courageous warrior (glossed as *tequigua* in Nahuatl, and "que es valiente en guerra" in Spanish) for training in the art of warfare. The Spanish text notes that the fathers placed their sons with masters of the skills or arts that their sons sought to develop.

The training of noble and common youth and examples of good and bad comportment occupy the space of folio 63r (fig. G9). In register 1, novice priests perform services for senior priests engaged in nighttime rituals. Register 2 shows commoner youth going to war bearing provisions and arms for senior warriors alongside the beating of a youth as punishment for living with a woman, as glossed by the Spanish text "in order to deter them from whoring...according to the laws and customs of the lords of Mexico." A head priest sweeps a temple in register 3, an important activity that had sacred meaning, whereas in an adjacent image, a novice priest is punished for having excessive sexual relations with a woman. The term "whoring" appears again in the Spanish gloss. Register 4 shows the punishment of youth who according to the Spanish text "went about in vagabondage and vice." This image of deviance contrasts with an image of another youth in a canoe transporting sod for the repair of the temple.

Service to the altepetl (city-state) leads to public recognition and honor in folio 64r (fig. G10). Register 1 shows a novice priest paddling a canoe to deliver stone for the repair of a temple, and another novice priest going to war, carrying a senior priest's gear. Register 2 shows a youth serving as an "intendant," according to the Spanish gloss, for a judge who oversees repair of roads and bridges, and a youth capturing a warrior in battle. Registers 3 and 4 depict warrior ranks according to the numbers of captives taken in battle, and include corresponding insignia and costumes. Folio 65r depicts the completion of training in the calmecac and telpochcalli, showing how valorous service to the altepetl leads not only to honor but also to office holding and positions of leadership (fig. G11). Registers 1 and 2 emphasize how success in warfare translated into political and military authority. The first shows the hierarchical ranks of priest-warriors, determined by numbers of captives taken in battle and marked by increasingly prestigious insignia and costumes. Register 3, which occupies the bottom half of the page, shows two rows of figures, the first being officers and constables of the lords of Tenochtitlan, and the second, warriors, captains, and generals in the Mexica army. The pictographic images in concert with the Spanish text present public education in Tenochtitlan as the second stage of Aristotle's habituation to virtue, demonstrating the effectiveness of the institutions of the calmecac and telpochcalli in reproducing the good customs of the city. Schools served intertwined ethical and political purposes in that they were meant to prepare youth for virtuous citizenship through training for professions and offices that served the social, economic, and administrative order of the city.[26]

The images and text of this section of part III of the Codex Mendoza work together to argue that individual virtue was a product of the customs of the city and at the same time produced and reinforced them. Courage and temperance, the first two virtues addressed in *Nicomachean Ethics*, play a central role in the narrative of this section of the codex. In the ancient Greek tradition, the battlefield provided the paradigmatic context for displaying courage. Courage in war, which meant courting death, qualified men for the highest honors bestowed by the polis.[27] Success on the Mesoamerican battlefield, defined by captive taking, and the honor and status that such success incurred represent a culmination of youth training in this part of the codex, reinforcing the centrality of courage to Mexica ethics and politics. The warrior-teacher on folio 62r, glossed in Nahuatl as *tequigua* (courageous warrior) and in Spanish as "valiente en guerra" (courageous/brave in warfare), signifies to the reader how courage was reproduced in Tenochtitlan through learning in action. The Spanish word "valiente" (courageous/brave) peppers the bottom two registers of folio 64r and the entirety of folio 65r, which portray courage in battle and the honors attendant to those who displayed it. Temperance, another cardinal virtue, was defined against the vice of self-indulgence, especially excess in food, drink, and sex.[28] In this second section on public education, punishments for "excess" and "whoring" feature centrally as methods for instilling temperance.

Custom Plus Law Equals a Rationally Ordered City and Empire

The narrative arc of part III of the Codex Mendoza culminates with a six-folio section dedicated to an exposition of how the city's schools and social customs habituated youth to moral virtue. At the same time, the section shows how the city's laws played a central role in forming individual moral character and maintaining the political order of the city and the empire as a whole. Folios 66r–67r recount a parable of imperial justice. The fully trained and educated constables and warriors depicted on registers 3 and 4 of the previous page (fol. 65r) spring into action in this cautionary tale about a provincial lord defying the rule of Tenochtitlan (figs. G12, G13). According to the narrative, the subjects of a local ruler (cacique) murdered Aztec merchants who were traveling through the province and stole from them. When the lord of Mexico recalled his ambassadors and officers from the province to Tenochtitlan, the caciques' subjects assaulted them en route in a clear sign of war. The lord of Mexico condemned the cacique to death, waged war on the province, and sent his constables to execute the cacique. The story unfolds backward, beginning with the execution carried out by the Mexican constables and followed by the enslavement of the cacique's wife and son.

The tlacuiloque complemented the parable of imperial justice by focusing on how youth participation in the city's laws and judicial system contributed to the production of virtuous citizens and political order. On folio 68r, which charts the career paths of married youths, four judges appointed by the lord of Mexico to hear civil and criminal cases are pictured facing male and female litigants who seek justice (register 3) (fig. G14). Each judge has a young apprentice seated behind him in order to learn matters of justice with an eye to advancing to the position of judge. Folio 69r follows this trajectory to its logical end (fig. G15). The entirety of the page depicts the layout of Moctezuma's palace complex, featuring at the top and center of the page Moctezuma seated on the dais where he gave audiences and heard cases as Tenochtitlan's supreme judge. Lodging quarters for the lords from the other altepeme of the Triple Alliance—Tetzcoco and Tlacopan—appear in a courtyard to Moctezuma's left, and quarters for other allies, including the lords of Tenayuca, Chiconauhtla, and Colhuacan, appear in a courtyard to Moctezuma's right. Stairs from these upper courtyards lead to the Council Hall of War and the Council Hall, which housed Tenochtitlan's high court. Four judges are pictured inside, in front of whom litigants appeal their cases. The Nahuatl gloss for the court, *tlacxitlan*, which literally means "at the feet," is fitting given that the four litigants appear at the judges' feet. The accompanying Spanish text on folio 68v frames the composition in terms of European notions of civility, noting that due to Moctezuma's "wise and good disposition, of his free will" he was able to impose "order, account, and reason in all things so that the kingdom would be well governed." The text also noted that lack of conformity with these ends resulted in severe punishment, and that before Moctezuma's succession to the lordship, there had been less order in the administration of the "Republic."

Folio 70r juxtaposes examples of virtue and vice (fig. G16). In the upper register, the image and accompanying Spanish gloss portray a father counseling a son to be "virtuous" and avoid vagrancy. On either side of the father-son pair appears a messenger, and singer and musician. According to the Spanish text, youths who achieved virtue were recognized and rewarded by the lords of Mexico with honorable offices such as that of messenger, and singer and musician. A master of public works ordering youths to perform labor occupies the left side of the second register. To the right are juxtaposed images of a vagabond, thief, ball player, and player of *patolli* (a dice game). The Spanish text notes that the youths dedicated to public works are crying because they have been made to do corvée labor. The mayordomo is giving them "good advice," telling them to leave behind their idleness and vagrancy. The bottom register shows artisans teaching their sons their individual trades. These virtuous artisans are juxtaposed on the right with vice-ridden figures: a "person with a vicious tongue, a gossiper," a drunken man, and a drunken woman. The Spanish text notes that the fathers instruct their sons to apply themselves so that when they become men they can dedicate their energies to their professions, occupy themselves with virtuous things, and avoid idleness, which gives rise to vices like gossiping, drunkenness, and theft.

The final pictographic folio, 71r, brings the treatise on law and custom as regulators of virtue and vice to its telos (fig. G17). The top register depicts six youths who were executed for their crimes. Three had committed drunkenness: one man, one woman, and one nobleman, demonstrating that capital punishment for excessive drinking was consistent across gender and social rank. The fourth figure, a thief, had been stoned to death for his crime, as had an adulterous couple. The Spanish glosses above these compositions note that the youths had died for their crimes according to the laws and customs of the lords of Mexico. The second register shows an old man and woman getting drunk, surrounded by their children and grandchildren. The Spanish text notes that according to the "laws and fueros" of the lords of Mexico, old men and women over age seventy were allowed the liberty and privilege to become intoxicated, even though such "excess" in younger people was punishable by death.

This final section of part III dedicated to education through law makes the case that law and judicial institutions played a crucial role in habituating youths to virtue and productive adult life in pre-Hispanic Tenochtitlan, an idea deeply resonant with Aristotle's view of the relationship between ethics and politics. Custom was central to this nexus of law, education, and good government.[29] In *Politics* and *Nicomachean Ethics*, customary laws were defined as the traditions and rituals practiced by the community since antiquity, including "respect for elders, the prohibition of murder and incest, marriage customs, and moral virtues generally."[30] Although both law and custom had a didactic function, custom was more fundamental to political order because unlike laws, which operated through compulsion from above, the locus of custom was bodily and moral habit repeated across generations. Habituation resulted "not just in acting in conformity with the law but also ... of feeling the right way as one acts, for this is the mark of virtue as opposed to mere continence."[31] The role of law, then, was to complement the central function of custom in undergirding the order of the city by compelling obedience since living virtuously often required people to act against their impulses. At the same time, law could not compel without habituation, which oriented individuals to accepting laws as just.[32]

The didactic role of law in Tenochtitlan and the empire more broadly is evident throughout the final section of part III. The parable of the rebellious cacique on folios 66r–67r extends Moctezuma's role as the lawgiver and chief judge of Tenochtitlan to the maintenance of imperial hierarchies and relationships, while contrasting the virtue and rationality of the laws of Tenochtitlan with the local cacique's rule. The images and accompanying Spanish text that follow the story address the process of habituating youth to good customs with a focus on each of Aristotle's four cardinal virtues: courage, justice, prudence (also known as practical wisdom), and temperance. By portraying the apprenticeship of young judges in the same composition as the promotion of honorable youth to the position of courageous warriors, folio 68r introduces justice as another important end, alongside that of courage, to which the education of youth was oriented. The Spanish text that accompanies the image on folio 69r of Moctezuma as supreme judge issuing rulings from his palace emphasizes his wisdom and reason, evident in the laws and institutions that he imposed during his rule. The juxtaposition of virtue and vice on folio 70r demonstrates how youth were habituated to temperance and moral behavior through discipline, law, and custom. In its portrayal of capital punishment of youth who committed crimes, folio 71r shows how law stepped in where inculcation of good customs and temperance failed. The artist-authors contrast the unfortunate ends of the errant youth with the happy lives of the old people who held to a virtuous path.

In sum, part III of the Codex Mendoza charts a coherent narrative of the effectiveness of Tenochtitlan's customs and laws in habituating its citizens to virtue through education, from birth to old age. Domestic order provided the foundation of political order, and, as such, moral education began in the family, progressed outward into the city's schools, and continued beyond them as young adults came to hold positions in the city's civic, military, and judicial institutions. Custom and law provided the curriculum, and their rationality was evident in the product: a city governed according to reason. Such a vision countered Francisco de Vitoria's assertion that "the Indians have neither laws nor magistrates that are adequate; nor are they capable of governing the household satisfactorily."[33] In the Codex Mendoza, Indigenous people were not natural children, as many European defenders of their cause claimed.[34] To the contrary, their society was a fully functioning republic in which nobles and commoners alike had been habituated to virtue and lived in harmony with natural law.

That the Codex Mendoza's case for Native sovereignty aligned with European ideals of political order does not diminish the Indigenous character of the manuscript. The content and style of all three parts draw extensively from Mesoamerican culture, history, and historiography. There are echoes of the huehuetlatolli in part III, especially the orations and admonitions of parents to their children. And as Raul Macuil Martínez demonstrates, many of the customs depicted, especially those of the first section of part III associated with *pilmatiliztli* or *maltiaconetzin* (bath of children), *uapaualiztli* (education), and *namiquitiliztli* (marriage), are still practiced in present-day Nahua communities through the teachings of the *tlamatque* (sages), who transmit knowledge across generations.[35] Rather than undercutting the value of Mesoamerican practice, the arrangement of the content in the codex was meant to engage with European debates about Native sovereign status. This was equally evident in what was selected and presented, and how, as in what was left out of the manuscript. Although training in the calmecac occupied a good portion of the content of part III, with the exception of one or two images, the tlacuiloque remained almost silent on the topic of Native ritual and religious practice, and accordingly, there was little mention of it in the Spanish text. Training for warfare far outweighed content on religious training in the registers dedicated to education in the calmecac. Polygyny, which was central to Indigenous political order, was not touched upon at all in representations of marriage or civic institutions in part III. And although it was addressed in the Spanish text of the dynastic histories of part I, it was done so in a way that centered its importance to Mexica imperial expansion and the authority of individual rulers.[36] It is indeed striking that there was such scant depiction of human sacrifice, or explicit discussion of polygyny, practices that were often singled out by European observers as evidence of Native "barbarity." Such a selective representation of Mexica customs and laws speaks to the political agenda of the codex's patrons and authors: to refute Spanish arguments of Indigenous cultural inferiority and bolster claims to Native sovereignty.

The Codex Mendoza's message regarding the rationality of Mexica laws and customs was enhanced by its packaging as legal testimony: "a uso de proceso." As its creators knew well, the legitimacy of Native custom depended on whether its antiquity and rationality could be demonstrated by authoritative testimony. Native claimants used pictographic texts accompanied by oral interpretation to make customary claims based on pre-Hispanic practice until the late sixteenth century when Spanish officials' and friars' attitudes toward Native peoples began to harden, and they came to question the rationality of customs associated with Native antiquity. The ambivalent results of the evangelical project raised doubts in Spanish officialdom about whether Native people could be habituated to Christian virtue and whether legal truth could be expressed in Native pictorial writing.[37]

The Relaciones geográficas de Antequera: A Survey of Pre-Hispanic Law and Custom

In 1568, a couple of decades after the Codex Mendoza was loaded onto a galleon bound for Spain, King Phillip II convened a high-level council to create new measures to assert royal control over Indigenous labor and natural resources and expand and deepen royal authority in the Americas. He did so in response to a growing imperial crisis. Power struggles—sometimes violent—between civil authorities and encomenderos who were loath to relinquish their iron grip on Indigenous labor as prescribed by the New Laws threatened Spain's hold on the viceroyalties of New Spain and Peru. At the same time, royal officials were growing increasingly concerned that the missionary orders had amassed too much power and influence over Indigenous peoples, to the detriment of royal interests. Three years after the junta magna, Phillip II appointed Juan López de Velasco as royal cosmographer and chronicler and tasked him with producing a historical and geographical atlas of American territories claimed by Spain. Working in concert with the Council of the Indies, Velasco developed the Relaciones geográficas survey, an attempt to catalog the lands, natural resources, history, and customs of the major towns and settlements of Spanish America's Indigenous inhabitants.[38]

The Crown sent the survey's instructions and questions to the viceroy of New Spain, Martín Enríquez de Almanza (1568–89), between 1578 and 1579. The viceroy forwarded them to the Spanish magistrates and governors of each province and district, who oversaw the implementation of the surveys and redaction of the responses between 1579 and 1585. In the larger provinces with many towns and settlements, the magistrates invested local Spaniards, priests, and missionary friars with the authority to execute the surveys. But the production of the Relaciones geográficas went well beyond the purview of these local officials. It was a public and collective enterprise, involving the active participation of Indigenous authorities who served as both informants and witnesses, interpreters who translated the words of the Native participants, and public notaries who transcribed the responses. All present authorized the validity of the texts with their signatures. Many of the Spanish officials entrusted with conducting the survey referred to the Indigenous authorities explicitly as their sources of information, and in several cases the Native authorities drew their knowledge from extant ancient codices.[39]

The Relaciones geográficas yielded hundreds of texts and dozens of maps for regions across the Americas. In the province of Antequera (Oaxaca), the survey resulted in forty-one relaciones, thirty-four of which survive today. Since many of the communities targeted by the surveys were the centers of politically complex polities made up of several dependencies and smaller settlements, many of the individual relaciones included responses not only for the administrative center but also for the multiple localities under its jurisdiction. The responses reflect the diversity of Oaxaca's ethnic and linguistic composition, including Mixtec, Zapotec, Cuicatec, Amuzgo, Chinantec, Chocho, Chontal, Mixe, and Popoluca, among other ethnolinguistic designations.[40]

At first glance, it might seem discordant to juxtapose the Codex Mendoza and Relaciones geográficas de Antequera as intellectual and political projects. Their genres, formats, proveniences, and purposes are distinct. The first focuses on the history of Tenochtitlan and the Mexica Empire in the service of the Indigenist cause, and the second on the diverse peoples of Oaxaca in the service of imperial economic and political power. Yet despite these differences, the two projects share much. Both combine pictorial and textual elements to produce historical accounts of Indigenous politics, economy, and society, though the balance between these is different in each case, as is the relationship between the visual and textual elements. Both were created "a uso de proceso," through a complex process of translation in which Native witnesses provided testimony (in some instances in the Relaciones geográficas relying on pictorial evidence), an interpreter translated their words, and a notary transcribed them into written text. In both cases, the interpreters and notaries framed Indigenous knowledge using Spanish categories informed by imperial political projects.

The common terrain of the Codex Mendoza and the Relaciones geográficas is clearest in the space that both allocate to ethnographic descriptions of Native law and custom. Analyzing them together reveals much about the production of the concept of Native custom in New Spain and its alignment with Spanish expectations. As was true of the Codex Mendoza, the Relaciones geográficas texts were filtered through the lens of natural law. Yet whereas the Codex Mendoza made a clear case for the civility of Mexica laws and institutions, the Relaciones geográficas of all of New Spain portrayed

Native customs in either an ambivalent or pejorative light. Most likely, this has to do with the balance of power in their collective authorship, which in the case of the Codex Mendoza tipped toward the Indigenous side and in the case of the Relaciones geográficas tipped much more toward Spanish authorities who were invested in showing that Spanish rule was more rational and just than that of the pre-Hispanic period.

The darker light cast on Native customs by the Relaciones geográficas was also a product of its historical moment. When Phillip II acceded to the throne of Spain in 1556, he inherited a huge debt from his father, Charles V. In order to bolster the Crown's ailing finances, he instituted policies that undercut the wealth and power of New Spain's Indigenous nobility. In 1564 he mandated that *mayeque*—dependent laborers attached to Indigenous noble estates—had to pay tribute directly to the king, an obligation from which they had been previously exempted. Adding to this burden, beginning in the mid-1560s Phillip II declared that Indian tribute was to be assessed individually rather than collectively, causing deep unrest among Indigenous commoners who expressed their frustration by challenging the authority of their Native officials and the Indigenous nobility. Rotational labor drafts known as the *repartimiento* were firmly institutionalized by the mid-1570s, putting further demand on Indigenous labor. Epidemic disease compounded the squeeze on Native communities; a virulent epidemic from 1576 to 1580 exacerbated the sharp demographic decline that had begun in the 1560s. To put a point on it, the Indigenous population of Mexico had plummeted from a population of 2.65 million in 1568 to 1.9 million in 1585. All these changes meant that by the time of the royal survey, Indigenous nobles and communities had suffered successive blows to their economic solvency and jurisdiction.[41] This nearly untenable situation must have affected the ways in which Native elders and respondents reflected upon their histories and the laws and customs of the past and how they regarded their present.

Shifts in Spanish attitudes toward Indigenous justice accompanied the new policies of the 1560s and 1570s and likely shaped how Native respondents and local Spanish administrators viewed the Native judicial institutions of the past. Whereas New Spain's early administration had allowed relatively open access of the Indigenous population to the colonial legal system, from the late 1560s forward, that access diminished. Viceroy Enríquez de Almanza considered Native people—especially the elite—to be overly litigious, blamed the missionaries for encouraging them to bring lawsuits to the Audiencia, and advocated for limiting Native access to colonial courts. Luis de Velasco (the younger, 1590–95) took concrete steps to reform Indigenous justice and during the 1590s established the Juzgado General de Indios (General Indian Court), dedicated solely to hearing Indigenous disputes. The court was designed to streamline cases through summary justice and provide legal counsel and services for free. A half-real tax funded the operation, and the court remained a crucial forum for Indigenous claimants and litigants for the entirety of the colonial period.[42] At the same time, this forum for Indigenous justice reinforced caste distinctions that were meant to separate Spaniards and Indigenous peoples according to a paternalist and hierarchical logic.

Missionaries also had a role to play in these changing sensibilities and policies. For some, early optimism regarding the potential for Native people to remake and redirect their customs and institutions toward the goal of Christian virtue had turned to disappointment and cynicism regarding the Natives' "dark conscience."[43] The Franciscan order, many of whose members had early on dedicated themselves to the study of Indigenous languages, cultures, and histories, was divided over the place of Native customs and knowledge in the evangelical enterprise. During a meeting of the provincial order in 1570, Fray Bernardino de Sahagún's Florentine Codex project came under fire for the expenses and resources that it required, which ran counter to Franciscan vows of poverty, and more importantly for the ideological ramifications of recording the institutions and lifeways of the Indigenous ancestors. The Franciscan provincial fray Alonso de Escalona ordered Sahagún to disband his team and finish the project alone. He also ordered the books to be confiscated and distributed to other friars so that they could be scrutinized for their content. Soon thereafter, the president of the Council of the Indies, don Juan de Ovando, requested that the books be sent to him so that he could incorporate them into a broader project to record the histories of the Indigenous peoples of the Americas. At the time, Ovando was also overseeing the development of the Relaciones geográficas survey. For Ovando and other royal officials, Indigenous knowledge had to serve the administrative and fiscal needs of the empire.[44]

As was true of the Codex Mendoza, the Relaciones geográficas survey responses regarding the Native laws and customs of the past spoke to the politics of the present. As a whole, they made the case that Spanish ecclesiastical and civil officials needed to exert stronger control over the government, resources, and labor of Indigenous communities in order to make them good Christians and productive subjects of the empire. The theme of idolatry, which was notably absent from the Codex Mendoza, cast a long shadow over the Native laws and customs described in the Relaciones geográficas. In keeping with contemporary European notions that societies passed through stages, moving from barbarism to civilization, the account of Native law and custom in the royal survey situated Native communities less favorably along that spectrum, with a heavier emphasis on barbarism.

Moral Classification, Christian Time, and Aristotelian Paradigms of Political Order

The Instrucción y memoria (instructions and survey questions) of the Relaciones geográficas contained fifty questions and items, many of which, true to the title of the enterprise, focused on geography, albeit the capacious early-modern conception of the term, which blended culture and history with territorial description. Most of the questions focused on climate, features of the landscape, altitude, flora and fauna as well as aspects of political geography, including population, the ecclesiastical jurisdiction to which the communities belonged, and distances to other settlements and administrative centers. The survey also inquired about natural resources like gold, silver, timber, fruit trees, grains, crops, medicinal herbs, and salt, as well as matters pertaining to the local economy, such as trade and the prevalence of industries like mining, and silk and cochineal production. The Crown also used the survey to probe cultural and linguistic knowledge, asking for the name of the community in the Indigenous language and the origins of the name.[45]

Among these wide-ranging survey items, two focused on the intertwined elements of pre-Hispanic religion, governance, law, and custom. Item 14 asked "under whose authority they [the Indigenous] lived during the time of their gentility [*gentilidad*], and the kind of rule their lords exercised over them, what they paid in tribute, and the worship, rites, and customs—good and bad—that they had." Item 15 asked "how they governed, and with whom they waged war, how they fought, the clothing (costume) they wore then and wear now, how they sustained themselves then and now, whether they were healthier in former times [*antiguamente*] and now, and the reasons for it, according to their understanding."[46]

Items 14 and 15 raised thorny issues for the surveyors, such as how they were to recognize Indigenous customs when they saw them, what constituted good and bad customs beyond the most obvious contraventions of Christianity, and what good pre-Hispanic customs meant for the legitimacy of the colonial order. There does not appear to have been firmly established notions of "good" and "bad" that preceded the survey, nor clear parameters, or neat boxes or categories to check in the reporting on Indigenous customs.

Improvisation, at least at the beginning, must have been the order of the day as surveyors identified Native customs and then situated them within the framework of their own worldview. This process is what the historian Anthony Pagden has glossed as the "problem of recognition." He notes that for Spanish chroniclers of Indigenous cultures, "the observer not only has to decide what he is seeing, he also has to find some place for it in his own world. This task is made all the more urgent, and the more difficult, if the observer is possessed ... by a belief in the uniformity of human nature, a belief which required every race to conform, within certain broad limits, to the same 'natural' patterns of behavior."[47] The conviction that there was "a scale of humanity going from the bestial at the one end to the god-like at the other" informed the description, conceptualization, and classification of pre-Hispanic Native practices as civilized and uncivilized.[48] Following the School of Salamanca, Spanish authorities assumed that custom was the key to civilization, but how, precisely, did Native customs need to change in order to achieve a more rational legal and political order? Was it possible to remove those elements of Native custom that did not conform to Christianity without unraveling the entire Indigenous social and political order? And if Indigenous peoples had *buen gobierno* and *policía* (good government and order) before the arrival of Spaniards, how could colonizers justify their civilizing presence in the New World?

The problem of recognition and classification was partially resolved for the surveyors by the use of Christian categories of time to frame the questions regarding Indigenous law and custom. The Spanish concepts of "antiquity" and "gentility" divided the Indigenous respondents from their ancestors by inserting a historical rupture between the time before the Spanish conquest and the Natives' conversion to Christianity. The assumption was that the conquest represented a watershed that divided a barbarous Indigenous past from the civilizing project of the present. In this regard, the concepts of "antiquity" and "gentility" allowed for what the anthropologist Johannes Fabian has coined the "denial of coevalness," a process through which colonizers (and modern anthropologists) situated Indigenous peoples in a different time and at an inferior stage of human evolution, thereby rooting them in a different era.[49] Yet, as seen in the missionary texts analyzed in chapter 2, the concepts of "antiquity" and "gentility" marked this division while allowing for some continuity, and for the possibility of Native people crossing the divide between their gentility and the Christian present. After all, over the course of the lifetime of an individual or group, a gentile could become a Christian. And at a collective level, the rupture with the Indigenous past that colonialism required could be partially repaired by distinguishing between the ancestors' good and bad customs and allowing for the persistence of the "good." By opening a space through which to transcend barbarism, Spanish civilizational discourse provided for the coexistence of Native custom with colonial order.

Alongside Christian moral classification and historical time, Aristotelian typologies of political order informed questions about Native governance in items 14 and 15, such that Native customs, laws, and governing institutions were portrayed along a spectrum with tyrannical barbarism on one end and the rationally ruled republic on the other. As the authors of the Codex Mendoza strove to show for the case of Tenochtitlan, following Aristotle, the polis was the most ideal form of government because its laws and customs habituated its citizens to virtue and its rulers (law givers) were an educated citizenry of equals who governed through deliberative institutions and justice in the interest of the common good. Tyranny, on the other hand, was defined by the arbitrary rule of an individual who governed in his own interest: in short, a state of lawlessness and absence of justice. For Aristotle, those who lived under tyranny were little better than slaves since it was the form of government that most denied freedom.[50]

Survey Responses: The Frame of Barbarism and Civility

The imperative of classification and the ideologies of time and political order that coursed through the language of items 14 and 15 of the Relaciones geográficas strongly shaped the survey responses. Some described customs, laws, and institutions in terms that approximated the civility of the ideal polis, whereas others described Indigenous governance as absent of law or reason, as nothing more than the "will" of the cacique whose arbitrary rule and exploitation reduced commoners to "servitude" and "misery." The notion of Native tyranny reflected in the responses was enshrined in Spanish law. In January 1552, Carlos V mandated the recognition of the rights of caciques (Native lords) and at the same time declared that their "excesses" be moderated. The law cited the oppressive tribute demands imposed on Native commoners by their caciques and ordered Spanish officials to investigate whether the tribute and labor owed to caciques by commoners had roots in Native "antiquity" and the consent of Indigenous commoners or whether it was imposed by the caciques "tyrannically, against reason and justice."[51] If the latter were the case, the demands for goods and labor had to be curbed. The Relaciones geográficas followed in this vein of colonial knowledge production regarding the customary rule of Native lords.

Commentary about Native antiquity in the survey responses therefore concerned the political order of the present, evincing Spanish preoccupations regarding the continued legitimacy of the Native nobility and their laws and customs. The Relación de Atlatlaucca y Malinaltepeque and the Relación de los Pueblos de Tecuicuilco, Atepeque, Zoquiapa, y Xaltianguiz noted in the exact same language that despite the benefits of Spanish-style municipal governance, the "lawless barbaric government" of pre-Hispanic ethnic lords carried through to the present, as evident in the "respect" that the commoners still held for their caciques.[52] The repetitive language may have been a product of duplication of responses by Spanish authorities. Plagiarism across the responses was common in the case of Yucatán but not for those of the diocese of Antequera. The Relación de Tecuicuilco is the only one in which certain passages appear to have been copied from other relaciones, in this case from that of Atlatlaucca y Malinaltepeque.[53] The patterned nature of the language on this topic reinforces how commonplace the idea of Native tyranny was for Spanish authorities.

Following Las Casas and other European chroniclers with varying degrees of paternalist sympathy toward the Indigenous population, many of the responses situated Native laws and customs somewhere on an evolutionary scale between the poles of tyranny and republican civility. According to the European evolutionary model of history prevalent at the time, barbaric societies had the potential to become more civilized when habituated toward reason. For Spanish ecclesiastical and civil authorities, Christianity and Spanish governance provided the key to Native progress along this evolutionary scale, an idea on full display in the Relación de Xalapa, Cintla, y Acatlán. When asked "if the Indians of said province were more barbaric than now, and if they knew as much as now, and what they were inclined to do in the time before the conquest," the respondents noted that "they were more barbarous at the time of the conquest; that now they have use of reason, and that they were always inclined to drunkenness and vice, and that they were never as far from vice as they are now."[54]

According to European thinking, law in barbaric societies focused narrowly on the punishment of crime, a rubric that encapsulates many of the descriptions of Native law in the survey responses. In the Relación de Teutitlán, respondents noted that "they governed with laws that they had to punish crimes: for each matter, its law and punishment."[55] The relaciones portrayed Native punishments for crimes as absolute and harsh, positioning Spanish law as more just and civilized. Many relaciones identified theft and adultery as some of the most serious of crimes, resulting in severe corporal punishment and disfigurement, and sometimes slavery or death. In some cases, the victims of theft were compensated with the confiscated goods and belongings of the thief, and in other cases, the belongings of thieves and adulterers went to the lordly estate. The Relación de Justlahuaca identified insoluble debt as a crime, noting that depending on the amount that they owed, debtors were punished with slavery or death.[56] In other relaciones, the commentary on Native law and punishment was more explicitly negative. In the Relación de Atlatlaucca y Malinaltepeque, the respondents noted that they "punished adultery and theft with great rigor" and that the "investigations were barbaric, and accordingly, many who were not guilty died."[57] Despite this negative assessment, some of the responses noted the positive effects of a purportedly harsh Native law: little theft or adultery. Ultimately the evaluation of Native laws regarding crime and punishment reflected an idea based in Aristotelean political theory that the imposition of order through fear and force was an inferior mode of governance, characteristic of barbaric societies, in contrast with well-governed states in which habituation to virtue, driven by the free will and innate disposition of the individual, led to happiness and the common good.

The Relaciones geográficas reflected not only Spanish interest in the punishment of crimes like theft and adultery but also Spanish concern about deviant behaviors within a Christian context. The Relación de Ixcatlan, Quiotepec, y Tecomahuaca noted that although there were punishments for all "vices," there was none for "sodomy."[58] Whereas male homosexuality was accepted in certain contexts in Native society, Spanish law classified it as a crime and punished it severely. Following Thomas Aquinas in his *Summa Theologiae*, Spanish ecclesiastical and civil officials considered sodomy as a "sin against nature," in which the natural order was violated and injury was done to God, who sets nature in order.[59] The idea that Native law did not punish sodomy was evidence for Spaniards that Native societies did not conform to natural law and were therefore barbaric.

Although many of the responses to items 14 and 15 situated Native communities closer to barbaric tyranny, some portrayed Native communities as civilized according to European standards, with well-functioning institutions such as governing councils of elders who elected and advised the lord, and clearly defined laws and legal fora. For example, the Relación de Nexapa claimed that the Indigenous lords governed with such "rectitude" that if any "preserved and used justice, it was they," and that government was so "well ordered" that from the time they were children, the Natives "grew up in conformity with the laws of the realm."[60] This short description evokes the narrative of part III of the Codex Mendoza in which the laws and customs of Tenochtitlan habituated the city's children and youth to virtue and rational political order. Other respondents used comparison with their neighbors to accentuate their own civility. In the Relación del pueblo de Ocelotepeque (Chichicapa), the respondents noted that the Natives of the region waged war with "Native communities of a different language called mijes ... and others who were chontales, barbarous people, who still are, even today."[61]

Justice, wisdom, and rationality, cornerstones of Aristotelian ethical and political theory, provided a litmus test for Native civility in the Relaciones geográficas as they did in part III of the Codex Mendoza. The Relación de Tilantongo underscored the orderly fashion in which legal cases were heard and adjudicated, describing how the Native lord of the town had four aldermen who governed the kingdom, received all complaints and disputes, and consulted with the lord in order to make decisions of a judicial nature. The aldermen served as an advisory council to the lord, and the "wisest" among them acted as head of the council. They addressed questions of commerce, ritual, and warfare, activities that evidenced a well-ordered society according to European norms.[62] The Relación de Tetiquapa and Cozauhtepec detailed how the Native lord delegated authority for tribute collection and other matters to lesser nobility (*principales*) who oversaw the different wards of the town.[63] In the Relación de Guaxilotitlan, the authors noted that the Native lord governed according to Spanish principles of justice, resolving conflicts, punishing crimes, and settling land disputes. He also ruled through clearly discernible institutions and offices, assigning a *tequitlato* (tribute collector) to govern each ward, manage labor requirements, and bring legal disputes to his attention. The relación equated the tequitlato with the justices of the peace (*jurados*) who attended to public matters in the wards of Spanish towns.[64]

The act of drawing analogies between Mesoamerican and Spanish institutions, a practice that repeated itself across the Relaciones geográficas and in Spanish commentary on Native societies more broadly, served to evaluate Native political order in relation to that of Spain. The ubiquity of the term *linea recta* (straight line) to describe dynastic inheritance in many of the relaciones provides one example in which respondents, interpreters, and notaries signaled an alignment of Native and Spanish practice.[65] In the early years following the conquest, Mesoamerican customs of royal succession in which lateral kin—brothers, sisters, cousins, nephews, and nieces—were eligible for rulership clashed with Spanish norms of straight-line succession, preferably to a direct male descendant. Changes in Mixtec codices over time reflected this conflict, with pre-Hispanic codices portraying genealogical complexities

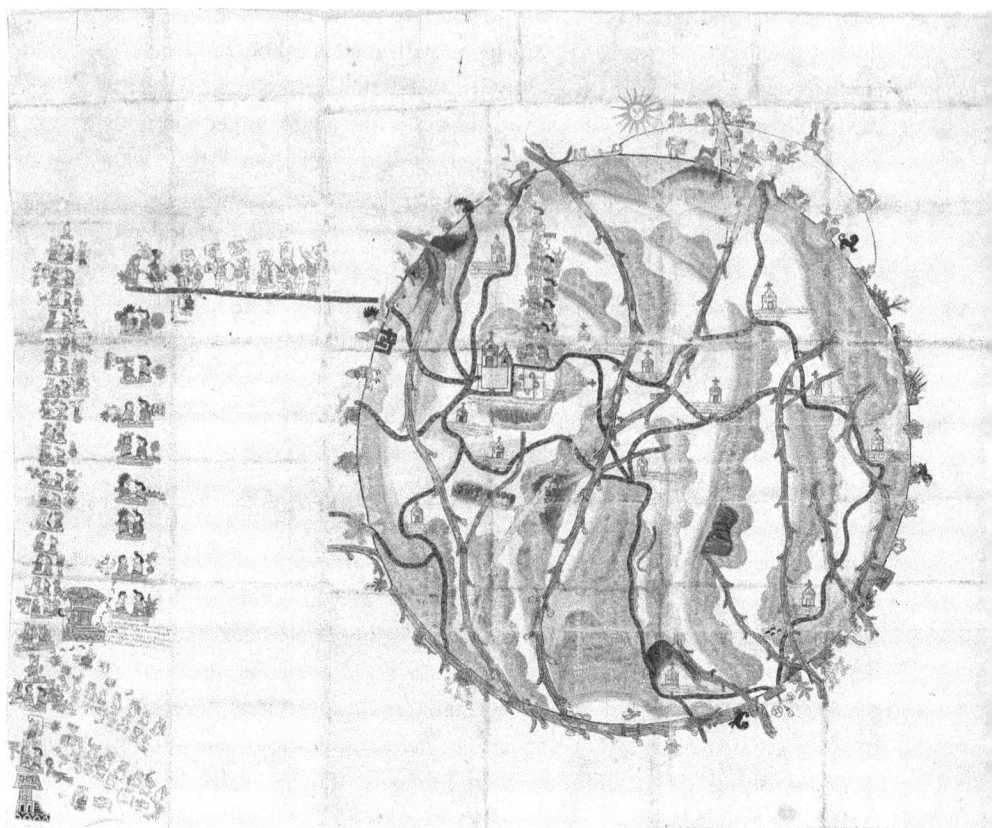

Figure 3.1 "Mapa de Teozacoalco," *Relaciones geográficas de Antequera*, 1580. Courtesy of Benson Latin American Collection, LLILAS Benson Latin American Studies and Collections, the University of Texas at Austin.

and colonial-era codices depicting a linear "king list," featuring only inheriting rulers and their spouses.[66]

The Relación geográfica map of Teozacoalco (known as Chiyocanu in Mixtec) provides a clear example of the linear king list format (fig. 3.1).[67] The map, a circular projection of community space typical of Mesoamerican mapping conventions, has been celebrated for its intricate rendering of territorial boundaries through logographic place-names. As the art historian Barbara Mundy puts it, "what better way to express boundaries than to show them lending a community a perfect form, creating around it a sealed enclosure?"[68]

As was characteristic also of Mesoamerican cartographic conventions, the map's producer incorporated genealogical information into the representation of space. Three vertical, straight-line genealogies painted onto the map convey the dynastic history and marital alliances of the ruling lineage of Teozacoalco (figs. 3.2, 3.3).

At the far left of the map appear the four dynasties of Tilantongo, a powerful yuhuitayu celebrated in Mixtec pictorial histories. The column to the right depicts the last ruling pair of Tilantongo's first dynasty, which produced a daughter who married into the Tilantongo line, initiating the second Tilantongo dynasty. The ruling lineage that emerged from this pair ended with the seventh couple, which failed to produce a male heir. A maternal grandson stepped in to found the third dynastic line, depicted inside the radial map of the community, which endured until the sixth generation failed to produce a male heir. A man from Tilantongo's ruling lineage stepped in to marry a woman from the ruling lineage of Teozacoalco whose son—the last of the line—appears to have been the ruler at the time that the map was produced in 1580 (fig. 3.4).[69]

Indigenous claims to succession through "linea recta" as expressed in the map of Teozacoalco and other colonial pictographic records reflected Spanish expectations while convincing Spanish officials that this was indeed Indigenous custom. In 1614 Felipe III issued legislation requiring viceroys, Audiencias, and Spanish governors to maintain the "ancient law and custom" of succession by linear descent in cacicazgos.[70]

Public occasions that displayed and reinforced the authority of ruling lineages represented another convergence of Spanish and Mesoamerican customs highlighted by the Relaciones geográficas.[71] In the Relación de Ixcatlan, Quiotepec, y Tecomahuaca, respondents described in detail the pageantry that accompanied the death of a lord and that secured the perpetuation of the dynastic line. Rather than denigrating the mortuary ritual, the language of the relación recognizes the importance of funereal pageantry, legitimized by the presence of the lord's "vassals," as an important means of securing stable succession.[72] In the same relación, the custom of bequest, rendered as "el modo de testar," pointed to an effort to align the ways that Natives and Spaniards secured upon their deaths the passing of material wealth to family members and religious institutions.[73] Not surprisingly, the Christian last will and testament quickly became part of colonial Indigenous custom, allowing community and family members to attend to the spiritual passage of the soul to the afterlife and property to the next generation.[74]

Sartorial distinctions according to status, which occupied significant space in the Relaciones geográficas, provided another opportunity for evaluating custom through analogy. In the Relación de Tilantongo, the respondents

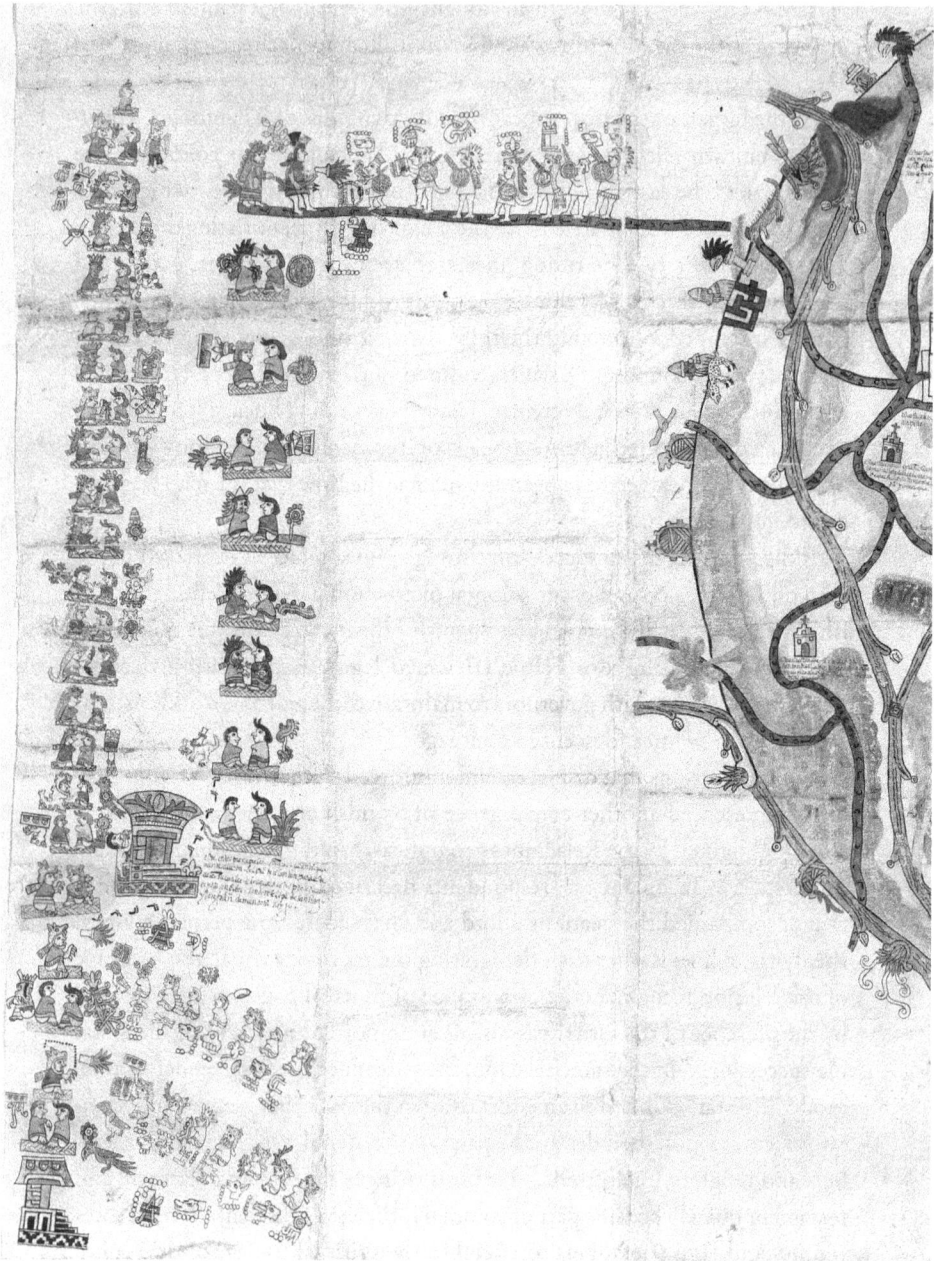

Figure 3.2 Detail of Relación geográfica map of Teozacoalco, with linear genealogies of Tilantongo and Teozacoalco. Courtesy of Benson Latin American Collection, LLILAS Benson Latin American Studies and Collections, the University of Texas at Austin.

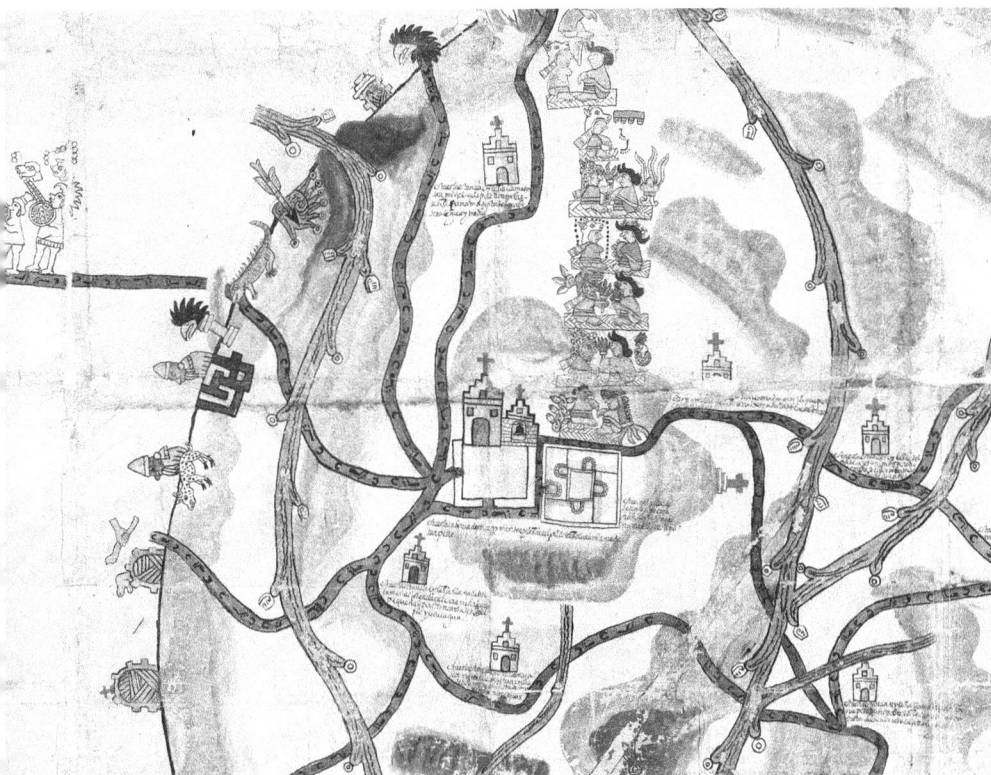

Figure 3.3 Detail of Relación geográfica map of Teozacoalco, with linear genealogy of Teozacoalco inside radial map. Courtesy of Benson Latin American Collection, LLILAS Benson Latin American Studies and Collections, the University of Texas at Austin.

noted that in the pre-Hispanic period, the aldermen who acted as judges and constituted the advisory council to the lord marked their status with long cotton capes, which were painted "in the manner of university graduates" ("a manera de capas de licenciados"). They also remarked that on days of ritual sacrifice, the priest dressed in much featherwork with an elaborate painted cape, and "on his head, he wore a miter, like a Bishop" ("en la Cabeza se ponía una mitra, a manera de Obispo").[75] The editorial flourishes—perhaps inserted by the interpreter, notary, or the respondents themselves—show how Native customs were sorted and reconfigured through a mirroring process in which participants recognized elements of Spanish practice in Native guise, with the effect of underscoring Native civility.

Figure 3.4 Detail of Relación geográfica map of Teozacoalco, ruling pair. Courtesy of Benson Latin American Collection, LLILAS Benson Latin American Studies and Collections, the University of Texas at Austin. Transcription and translation of gloss: "Estos son los principales e señores que antiguamente salieron del pueblo de Tilanton[go] para este de Teosacualco e lo que de estos prosedieron e oy día son bibos. Son don felipe de Santiago y don Francisco de Mendoza su hijo" (These are the notables and lords who long ago left the town of Tilantongo for this town of Teozacoalco and those who issued forth from them, and today are living. They are don Felipe de Santiago and don Francisco de Mendoza, his son).

The historical relationship of Oaxaca's communities to the Mexica Triple Alliance was of primary concern in the Relaciones geográficas de Antequera. Many of the Oaxacan communities surveyed had been conquered tributaries of the Triple Alliance and as such were portrayed as culturally inferior to the Mexica. The implantation of Tenochtitlan's institutions of law and justice and the imposition of tributary requirements therefore came through as positively valued elements of Mexica rule across many of the survey responses. They were clear evidence of a well-ordered empire in Spanish eyes. The survey pointedly asked what each community paid in tribute, to whom, and whether they were subject to Moctezuma's rule. In this regard, they represented the inverse of part II of the Codex Mendoza, which detailed the tributary relationships of Tenochtitlan with its subject communities, including those of many regions of Oaxaca. They also followed the mandate of the 1552 law discussed previously that required investigation of the customary origins of tribute and labor demanded by caciques.

In the Relación de Tecuicuilco, the respondents identified Moctezuma as the "universal lord"—a gloss that appears repeatedly across the relaciones—who ruled them under a regime of tribute and warfare.[76] The authors of the Relación del Pueblo de Atlatlaucca y Malinaltepeque noted that although they paid tribute to Moctezuma, in all other affairs of government, local lords were left alone to rule according to their own strictures, pointing to a system of indirect rule.[77] In the Relación de Chinantla, the respondents reported that Moctezuma administered justice in all the communities of the region through the appointment of two magistrates (alcaldes) who visited the towns, heard cases, and protected the commoners from the abuse of local lords, suggesting that the lords of Mexico were bulwarks against provincial tyranny.[78] This idea resonates with the parable of the rebellious cacique in part III of the Codex Mendoza. Notably, Berdan and Anawalt hypothesize that the story was based on a rebellion against the Triple Alliance directed by a provincial lord from Coixtlahuaca, Oaxaca.[79] For the most important matters of justice, the Natives of the Chinantla region requested an audience with judges in an impressive court at Moctezuma's garrison in Tuxtepeque.[80] The Relación de Ucila noted that "the law that they had during those times, and that Moctezuma gave them," concerned priestly abstinence in anticipation of biannual rites.[81] Although some elements of Mexica rule pertaining to judicial institutions and governance were portrayed in a positive light, other Mexica impositions were framed as pernicious. Chief among these were religious rituals and sacrifice, which were evidence, according to Spanish officials, of the barbarism and tyranny of Mesoamerican peoples as a whole.

"Bad" Customs: Sacrifice, Idolatry, and Polygyny

No matter where the responses to items 14 and 15 of the Instrucción y memoria of the Relaciones geográficas landed a particular community on the scale of European civility, the penumbra of idolatry and associated practices of sacrifice and polygyny hovered over most of the responses, clear marks against Oaxaca's Native peoples in Spanish eyes. In this regard, the responses produced in Oaxaca were not unique. Across the entire corpus of New Spain's Relaciones geográficas, from Michoacán to Nueva Galicia, to the elaborate Relación de Tlaxcala authored by the mestizo chronicler and interpreter Diego Muñoz Camargo, the language of idols and demons framed the customs and rites of diverse Indigenous peoples.[82] Although the responses were supposed to catalog religious practices and customs of the pre-Hispanic past, Spanish and Indigenous respondents acknowledged that these practices persisted across the watershed of conquest. Early extirpation efforts that swept the Diocese of Oaxaca dovetailed with the highly publicized Inquisition trials of Native lords in Tehuantepec and Yanhuitlan during the sixteenth century to place concerns over idolatry front and center in the minds of Spanish and Native authorities.[83] In the Relación de los Pueblos de Tecuicuilco, the respondents noted that their painted histories had been confiscated because "it was understood that because of them, they had the same rites and ceremonies as before."[84] As was the case with characterizations of Native governance, commentary on the religious customs of the past could quickly slide into suspicions about ritual practice in the present. In the eyes of colonial authorities, the links between pre-Hispanic and colonial-era customs were dangerous and the process of redacting the responses brought them to the fore.

Among the varied customs described in the relaciones, across dozens of Oaxaca's diverse communities, the content of Native religious practice was portrayed almost uniformly. Respondents detailed ritual acts such as taking herbs and hallucinogens, fasting, practicing sexual abstinence, dancing, playing music, and drinking alcoholic beverages such as pulque. They often referred to the ritual calendar as a means of lending order to the ritual cycle. And in all the responses, ritual sacrifice occupied center stage. Filtered through the words of interpreters and the pens of notaries, respondents describe heart excision of small dogs, quail, slaves, men, women, and children as a means of satisfying the "gods" and "idols" of wood and stone. Ritual cannibalism often shared space in these descriptions.

In addition to the specific content of Native ritual, its framing was consistent across the dozens of responses. Since the conquest, missionary priests had developed a very specific language with which to denigrate Native ritual, which made its way into the responses. Through the tongues of Native interpreters, many of whom were trained by priests, and priests themselves, who sometimes served as interpreters or authors of the responses, Native informants and Spanish scribes rendered images of ancestors as "idols" and "demons." In some cases, respondents characterized the practices as "general custom" across the entire territory, which presumably meant the Diocese of

Oaxaca, and possibly all of New Spain. Despite their diverse languages and geographies, what unified the Native people in the frame of the responses was their idolatry. Through the writings of many missionary friars and chroniclers, idolatry became the core of Indian identity, the shroud that "darkened the conscience" of Native people, and the pernicious custom that lurked beneath the colonial social order.[85]

As they directed, translated, and transcribed, Spanish and Native authorities and interpreters undoubtedly steered respondents in certain directions and engaged in a process of inclusion and exclusion of content. As they probed the Native elders and leaders about the Native past, Native priests, portrayed as guardians of custom, appeared as figures of special interest. In the Relación de Teozacualco, the Indigenous respondents described the training of priests, who entered the temples as boys and whose material needs were sustained by the cacique. They were prohibited from leaving for any reason, and if they did leave or engage in sex with a woman, they were put to death.[86] In this response and in others, Native informants underscored priests' high status, which was either equivalent or superior to that of Native lords.

From a colonial perspective, Native priests were especially dangerous figures, which is undoubtedly why they figured so centrally in the Relaciones geográficas and also why they were mercilessly persecuted after the conquest. According to the responses, they governed alongside caciques and oversaw many aspects of communal life, whether affairs of state or the rites of passage of community members. Discussion of the place of Native ritual specialists in the complex of Native authority reflected the ongoing concerns of Spanish officials about the viability of Native customs and institutions. How could Native ritual practice, which persisted despite missionary efforts at evangelization, be excised from Native society? These questions and doubts figured into debates about Native authority and indirect rule in some regions of Oaxaca well into the eighteenth century.

Like religious ritual, polygyny was a custom that was both central to Native authority and contrary to Christianity, and therefore of intense interest to Spanish officials. According to the Relación del pueblo de Atlatlaucca y Malinaltepeque, the respondents noted that caciques could have as many wives as they wanted, though only one was considered the primary wife and only her children could inherit the position of lord. If she had no children, then the closest relative inherited the rulership and supported the remaining children of the cacique, who were considered "bastards." They also noted that the primary wife had to be of noble lineage, and much effort and attention were placed on arranging noble marriages that could produce a "straight line" of rulership over generations.[87] Rulers sought husbands or wives outside the ethnic state, making marriage a key form of diplomacy and alliance. The criminalization of polygyny and ritual practice—the fulcra of Native custom at the state level—was a crucial step in the sixteenth century process of aligning Native law and social order with that of the Spanish Empire.[88]

Although polygyny was clearly at odds with Christian custom, the contractual and solemn nature of Native marriage customs as portrayed in the responses aligned with canon law. The Relación de Guaxilotitlan noted that when a noble couple sought to marry off their son, they appointed a marriage broker who approached the prospective bride's parents with gifts, negotiated the terms of the union, and brought the bride to the home of the groom, where the couple were seated together on a reed mat with their cloaks tied together and given pulque to drink in order to seal their union.[89] In this instance, the relación resonates with the depiction of Native marriage in part III of the Codex Mendoza and met the standards of "legitimate marriage" in Spanish eyes.

Conclusion

Like the Codex Mendoza, the Relaciones geográficas de Antequera constitute a palimpsest of Indigenous and imperial knowledge about pre-Hispanic law and custom that had bearing on the colonial present. Both projects show how Native custom came to be defined in a process of translation, comparison, and alignment with Spanish norms that distinguished "good" and "bad" customs. A crucial distinction between the two works was the strong overlay of the discourse of civility in the Codex Mendoza and that of tyranny and barbarity in the Relaciones geográficas. The framing of Native custom to meet Spanish expectations was clear in the absence of Native ritual and polygyny in the Codex Mendoza and in the consistent framing of Native ritual and polygyny as the heart of Native custom in the Relaciones geográficas.

The diverse arenas in which this knowledge was created—in the workshops of Indigenous tlacuiloque in the viceregal capital and the rudimentary administrative buildings of Native towns in the farthest reaches of the mountains of Oaxaca—demonstrate how ideas and knowledge about law and custom percolated beyond universities and courts, within cross-cultural networks of Indigenous and Spanish authorities. The production of colonial legal consciousness in these settings shaped how Native people made customary claims, through recourse to the past and "a uso de proceso," and the way that Spanish judges evaluated the legitimacy of those claims. Across all these contexts, natural law represented the measure by which the legitimacy of Native customs was assessed.

Antiquity was central to the portrayal of customs in the Codex Mendoza and Relaciones geográficas de Antequera. While both texts made a case for the "good" customs of the pre-Hispanic period that Native authorities could use to govern their colonial communities, the Relaciones geográficas in particular highlighted the "bad" customs associated with Indigenous religion and state building, some of which persisted into the present. The evaluative and sorting function of custom made it a tool of imperial domination and control. Spanish authorities pointed to the continuity of "bad" customs as evidence of the need for vigilance in the evangelical project and the strengthening of Spanish municipal-style governance and judicial institutions in Native towns. Whereas the Nahua elite of Mexico City adapted quickly to colonial expectations, securing legitimacy for themselves in the process, in Oaxaca accommodation to colonial rule was slower and uneven across the great diversity of the Native population. Dominican missionaries in particular were intent on rooting out the "bad customs" of Oaxaca's Indigenous communities, and they persisted in their efforts until the early decades of the eighteenth century. It is toward the criminalization of these customs— especially polygyny—in central Mexico and Oaxaca that we turn in the next chapter.

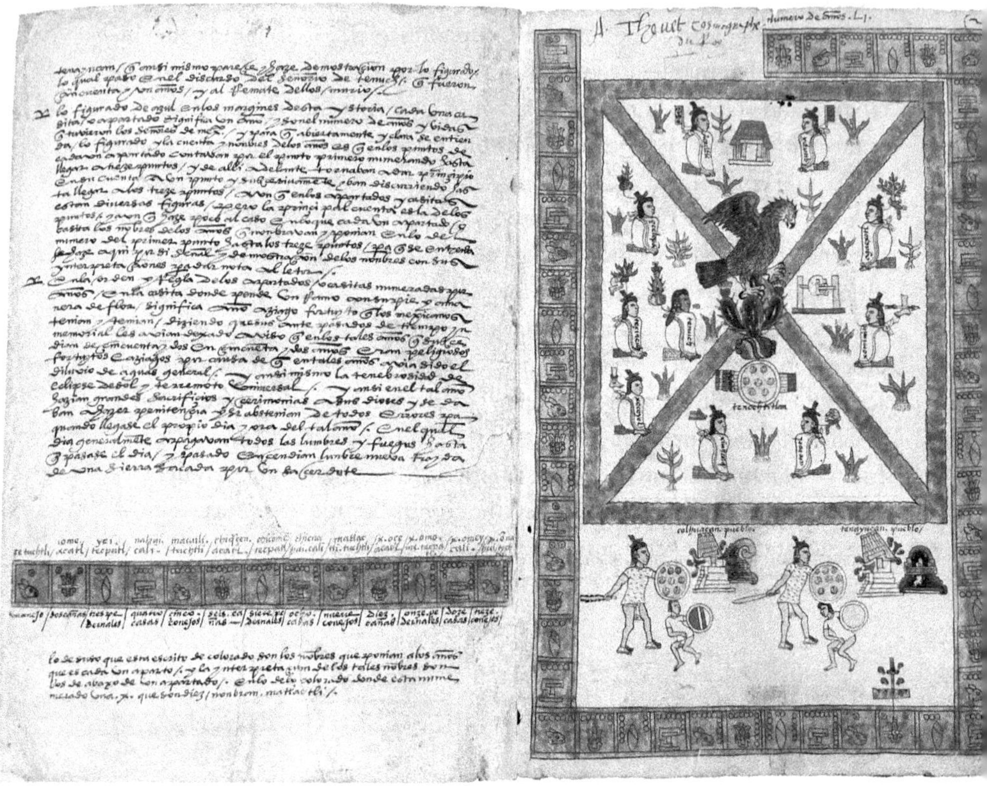

Figure G1 First pages of the Codex Mendoza: city of Tenochtitlan on the right, featuring an eagle on a nopal cactus (the symbol of the city), seated rulers, warriors, and blue lines representing Lake Tetzcoco. The translation-interpretation of the image appears on the left.

El estilo grosero e ynterpretaçion delo figurado en
esta ystoria suple el letor, por que no se dio lugar
al ynterpretador de myngun longar, y como cosa
no acordada ni pensada se ynterpreto a cabo de
proçeso. Ansi mysmo en donde van nonbrados
alfaqui mayor, y alfaqui noviçio, fue y nadvertençia
del ynterpretador poner tales nonbres que
son moryscos, ase de entender por el alfaqui
mayor, saçerdote mayor, y por el noviçio, saçerdote noviçio, y donde van nobrados mezquitas
ase de entender por templos. Diez dias antes
dela partyda dela flota se dio al ynterpretador
esta ystoria ya que la ynterpretase, el qual
descuydo fue delos yndyos que acordaron tarde
y como cosa de corrida no se tuvo punto enel estilo que convenia ynterpretarse, ni se dio lugar para
que se sacara en limpio limando los vocablos
y orden que convenia, y avn que las ynterpreta-
çiones van toscas no se a de tener nota syno ala
sustançia delas aclaraçiones lo que signifcan las
figuras, las quales van bien declaradas por ser
como es el ynterpretador dellas buena lengua
mexicana

A. Thenetus.
1553

Figure G3 Codex Mendoza, fol. 57r. On the top third of the page are the mother and newborn (on the left), and the midwife bathing and naming the child (on the right). On the bottom two-thirds of the page are the father and mother (on the left), and the head priest and master of youths (on the right), with the child in the center. All four adult figures are seated and pictured with speech glyphs.

Figure G4 Codex Mendoza, fol. 58r. The page is divided into four registers in which the father instructs the boy (on the left) and the mother instructs the girl (on the right). Blue disks represent the child's age, and ovals with black dots represent the child's tortilla ration.

Figure G5 Codex Mendoza, fol. 59r. In the first register, the father instructs the boy with a fishnet (on the left) and the mother instructs the girl with a weaver's spinning bowl and work basket (on the right). The next three registers show the parents disciplining their children when they fail to perform their assigned tasks.

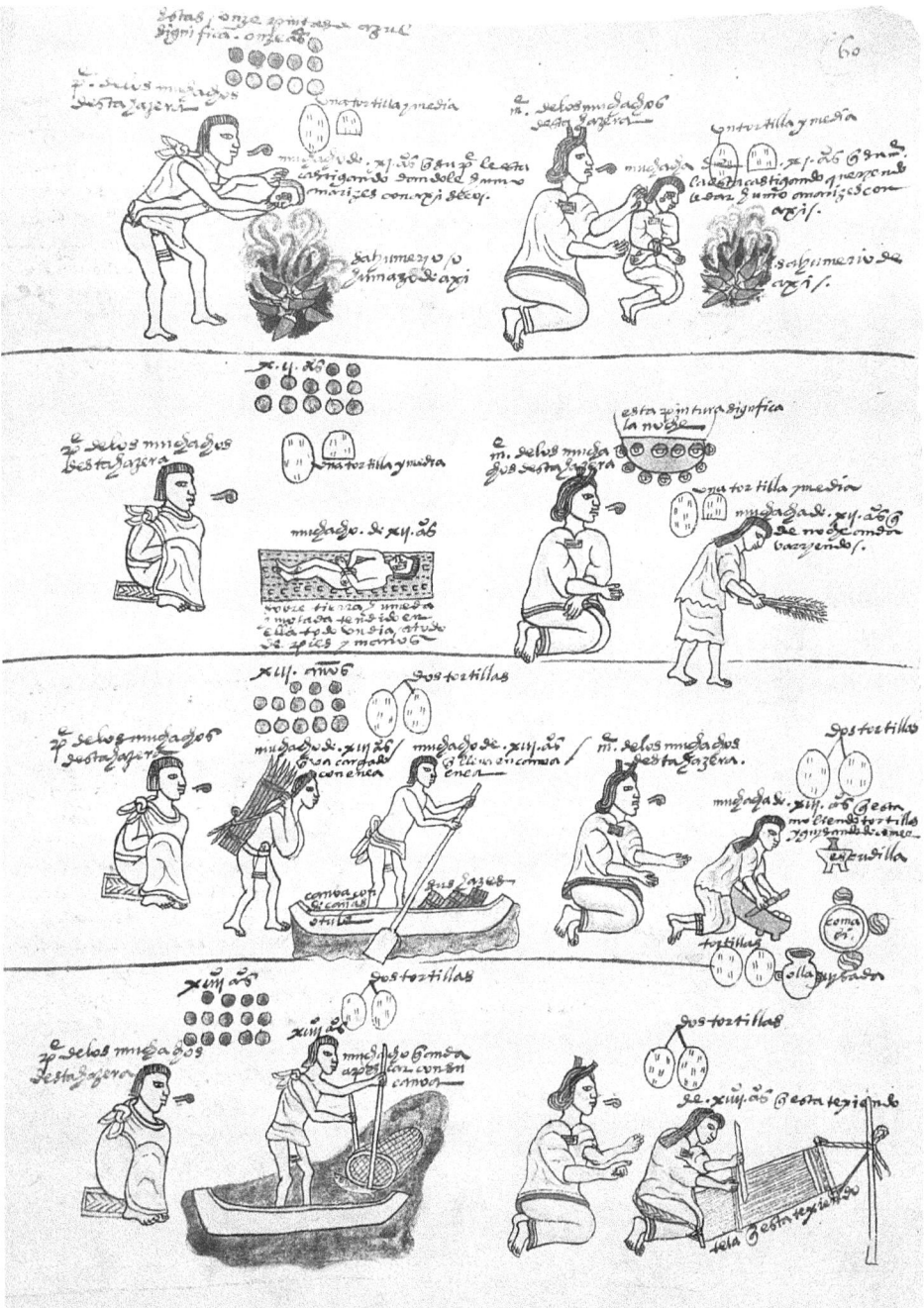

Figure G6 Codex Mendoza, fol. 60r. The four registers show parental discipline and instruction as the children age. Moving through the registers, parents hold children over chile smoke; the father binds the boy as a punishment (on the left); the mother instructs the girl who sweeps (on the right); the boy transports reeds on his back and in a canoe (on the left); the girl grinds maize (on the right); the boy fishes (on the left), and the girl weaves (on the right).

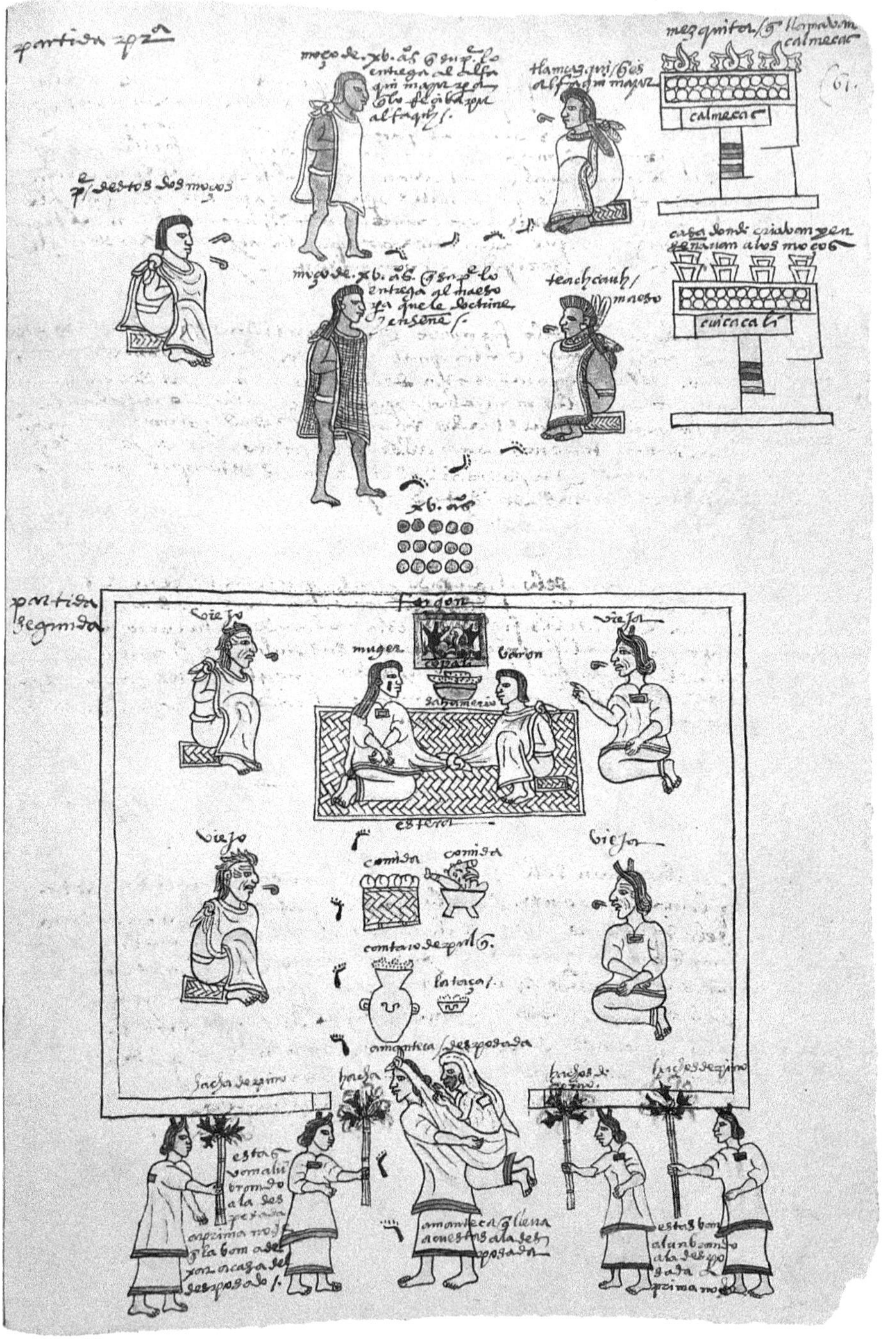

Figure G7 Codex Mendoza, fol. 61r. In the top half of the image are a father, a male youth, a head priest, a temple, another male youth, a master of youths, and a house of song. In the bottom half are the wedding ceremony, with the parents and married couple on a reed mat, and, below, the matchmaker with the bride on her back accompanied by four women bearing torches.

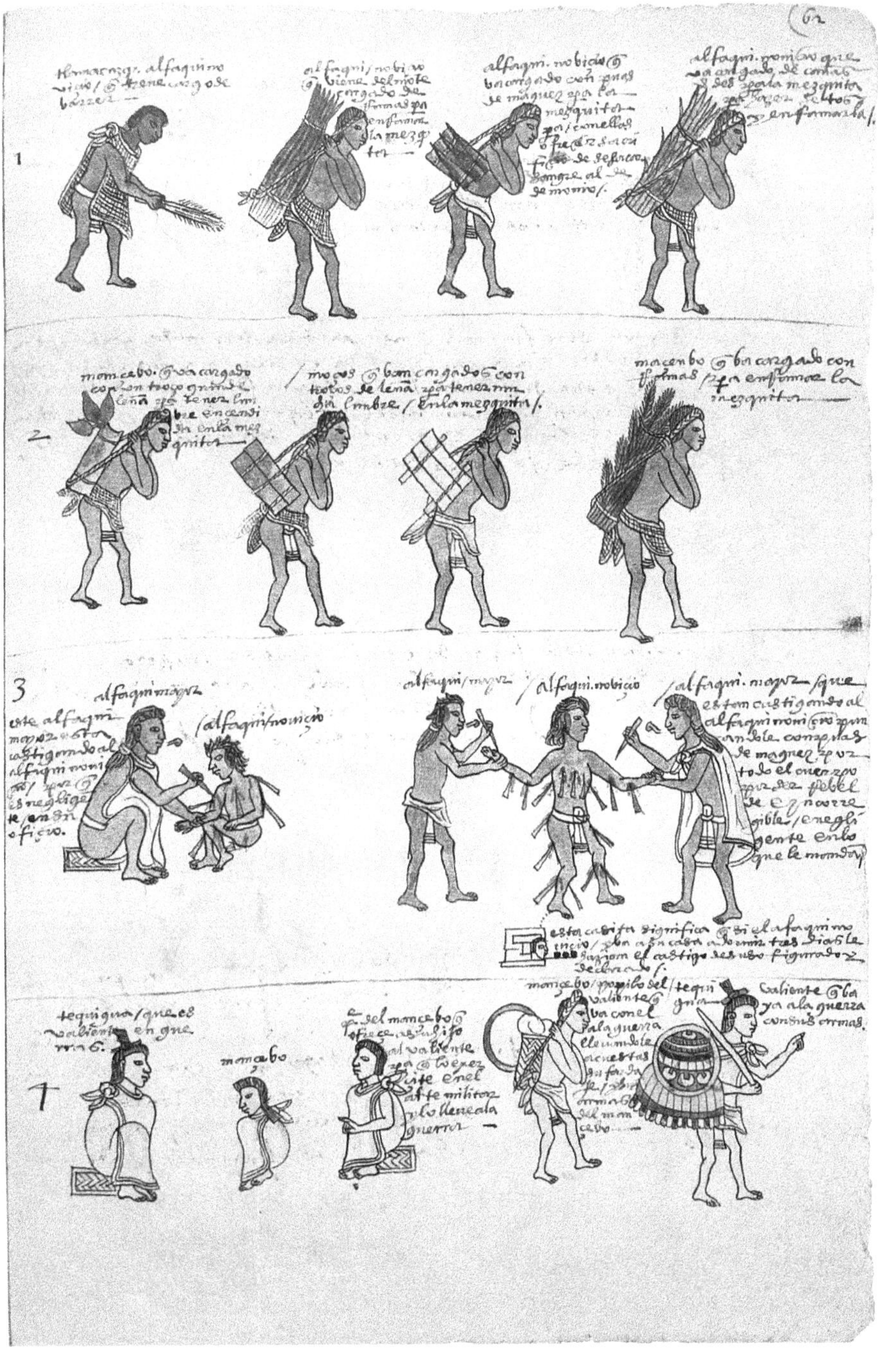

Figure G8 Codex Mendoza, fol. 62r. In the top two registers, male youths sweep and carry loads. In the third register, teachers punish male youths. In the bottom register, a father offers his son to be educated as a warrior.

Figure G9 Codex Mendoza, fol. 63r. The top register depicts training for the priesthood featuring priests using incense and a drum, and observing the stars. The second register depicts warrior training and two figures punishing a youth. The third register returns to priestly training, depicting a youth sweeping and another being punished. The fourth register depicts two figures punishing a youth, and a youth paddling a canoe with a temple in the background.

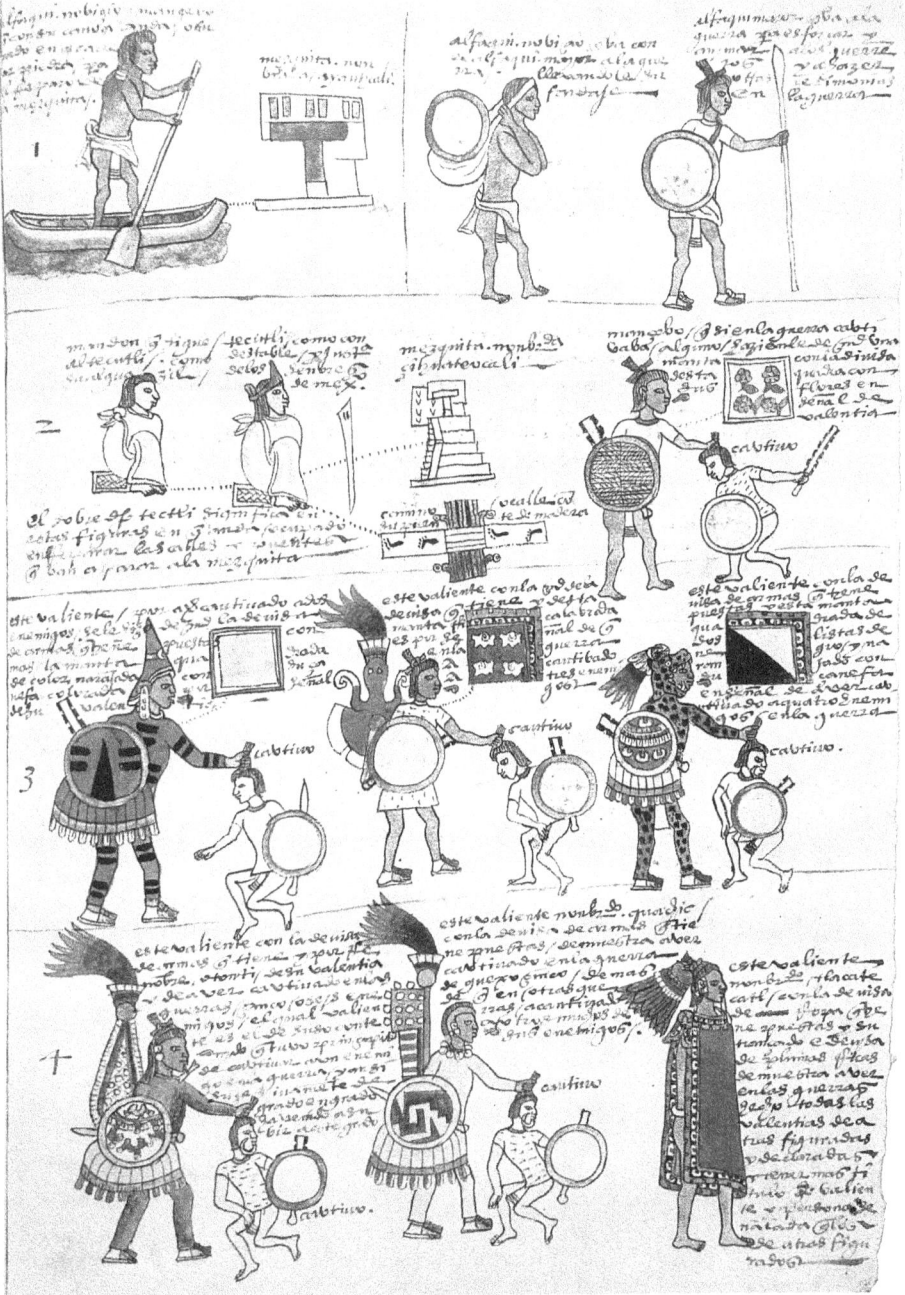

Figure G10 Codex Mendoza, fol. 64r. The first register shows a youth in a canoe with a temple in the background, and two youths carrying weaponry. The second register shows a seated lord and his assistant facing a temple, road, and bridge (on the left) and a warrior taking a captive (on the right). The third and fourth registers show warriors in regalia taking captives, and in the bottom register, in the right corner, is a high-ranking warrior.

Figure G11 Codex Mendoza, fol. 65r. The first two registers depict six priest-warriors (four in elaborate regalia) with captives. The third register shows four constables in undecorated cloaks and, below, four generals with hair ornaments in decorated cloaks.

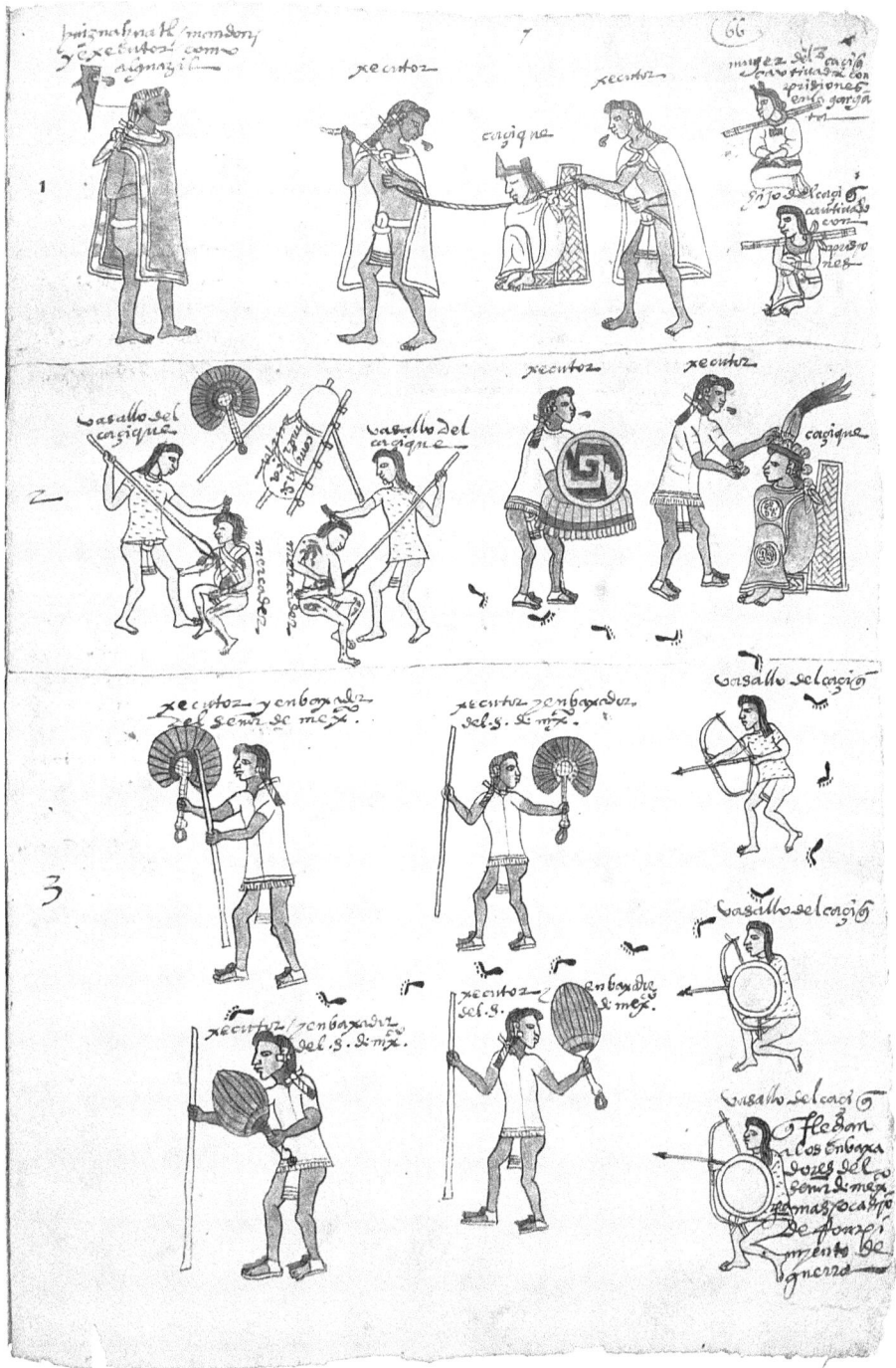

Figure G12 Codex Mendoza, fol. 66r. The first register depicts the constables with the strangled cacique and the cacique's wife and son. The second depicts the murder of Aztec merchants (on the left) and two constables with the seated ruler (on the right). The bottom register shows three warriors (on the right) attacking four constables (on the left).

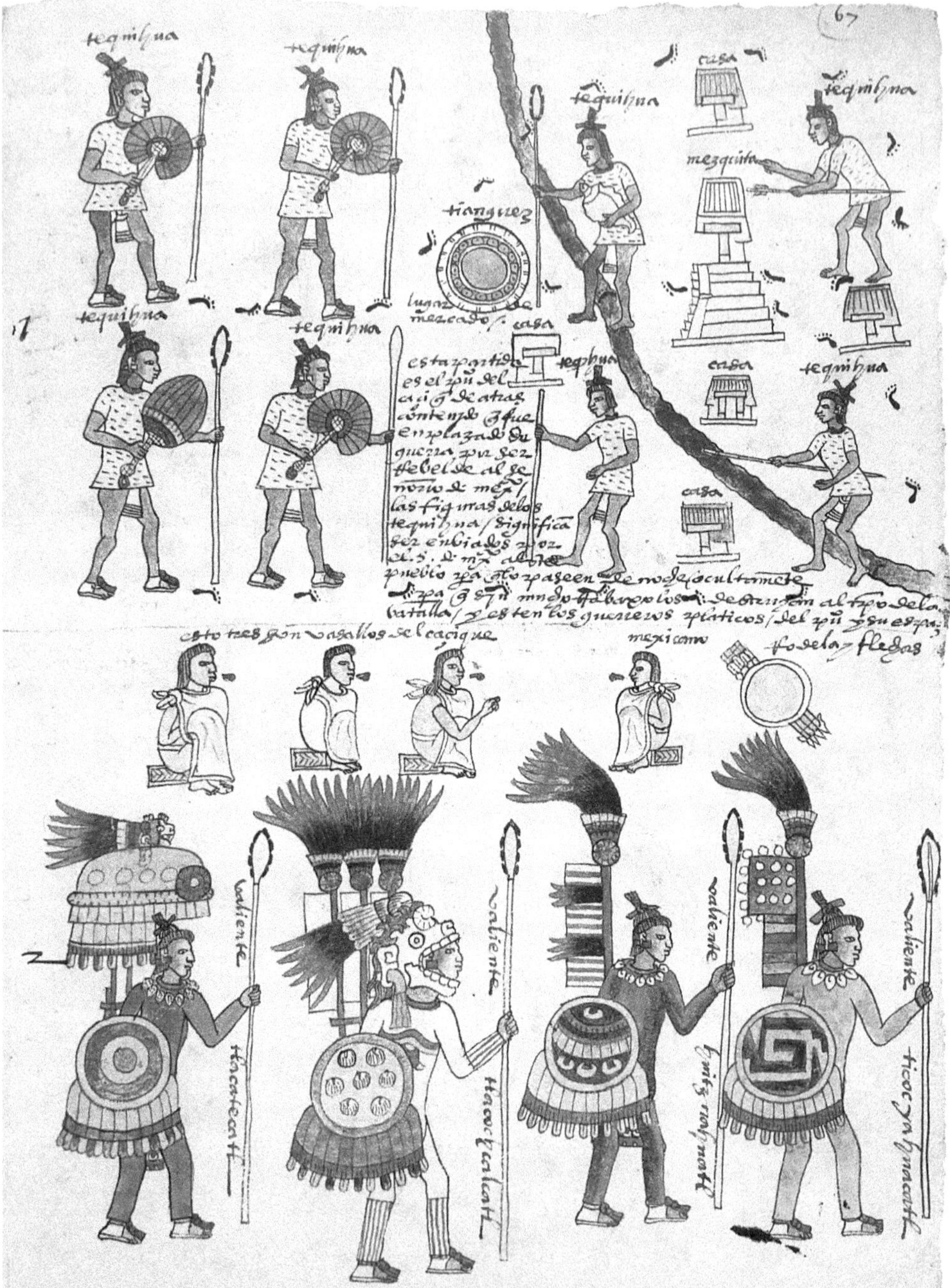

Figure G13 Codex Mendoza, fol. 67r. The top register shows eight warriors in cotton armor with weaponry and a river, temple, and houses (on the right). The bottom register shows three seated rulers facing another one with speech glyphs emanating from their mouths. Below them are four warriors in elaborate regalia.

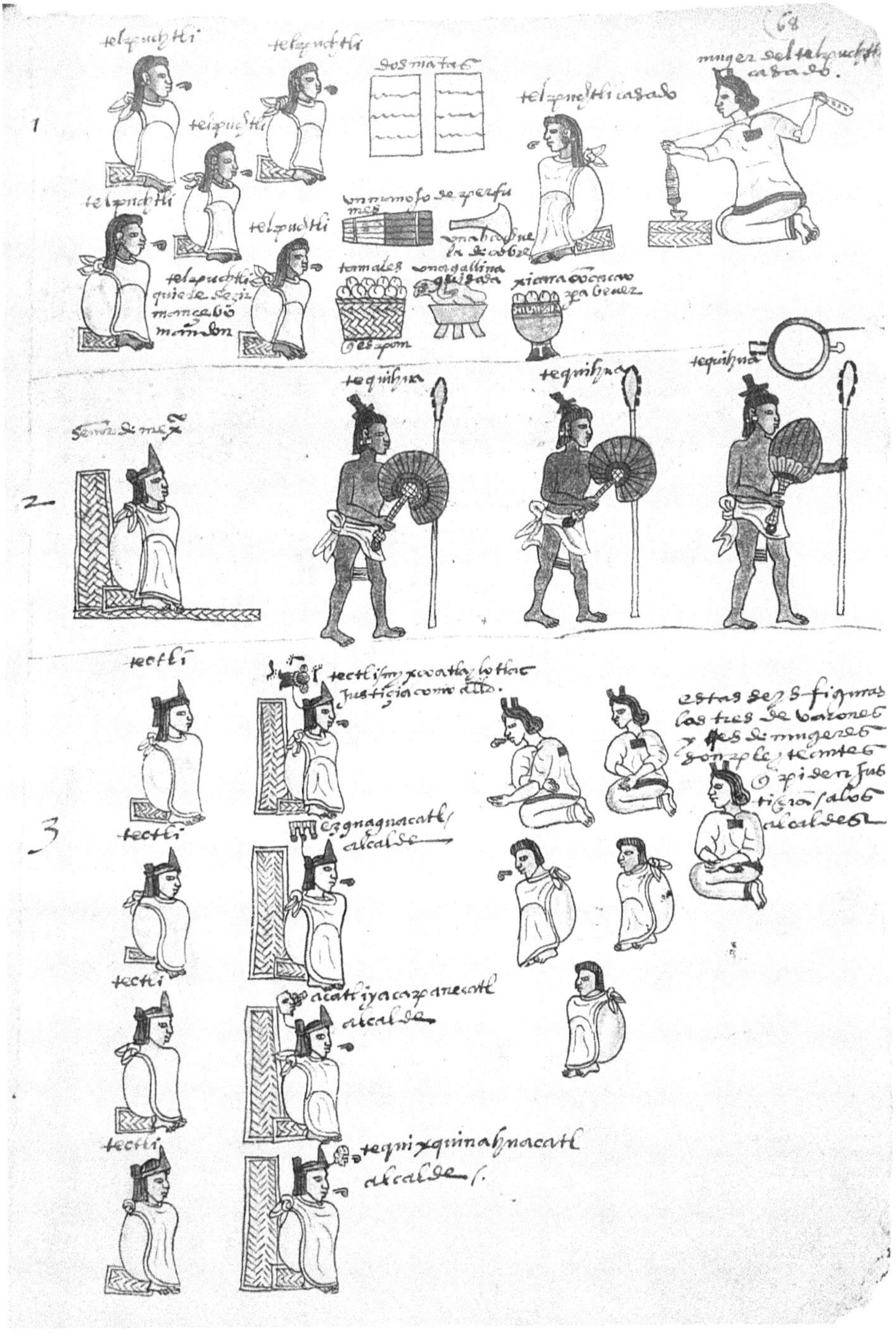

Figure G14 Codex Mendoza, fol. 68r. In the first register is a male youth with a woman spinning behind him (on the right), and facing five other youths (on the left). Between them are capes, tamales, turkey, and cacao beans. In the second register are a ruler and three warrior emissaries. In the bottom register on the right are litigants (three of whom are women), judges in the center, and apprentices behind them (on the left of the page).

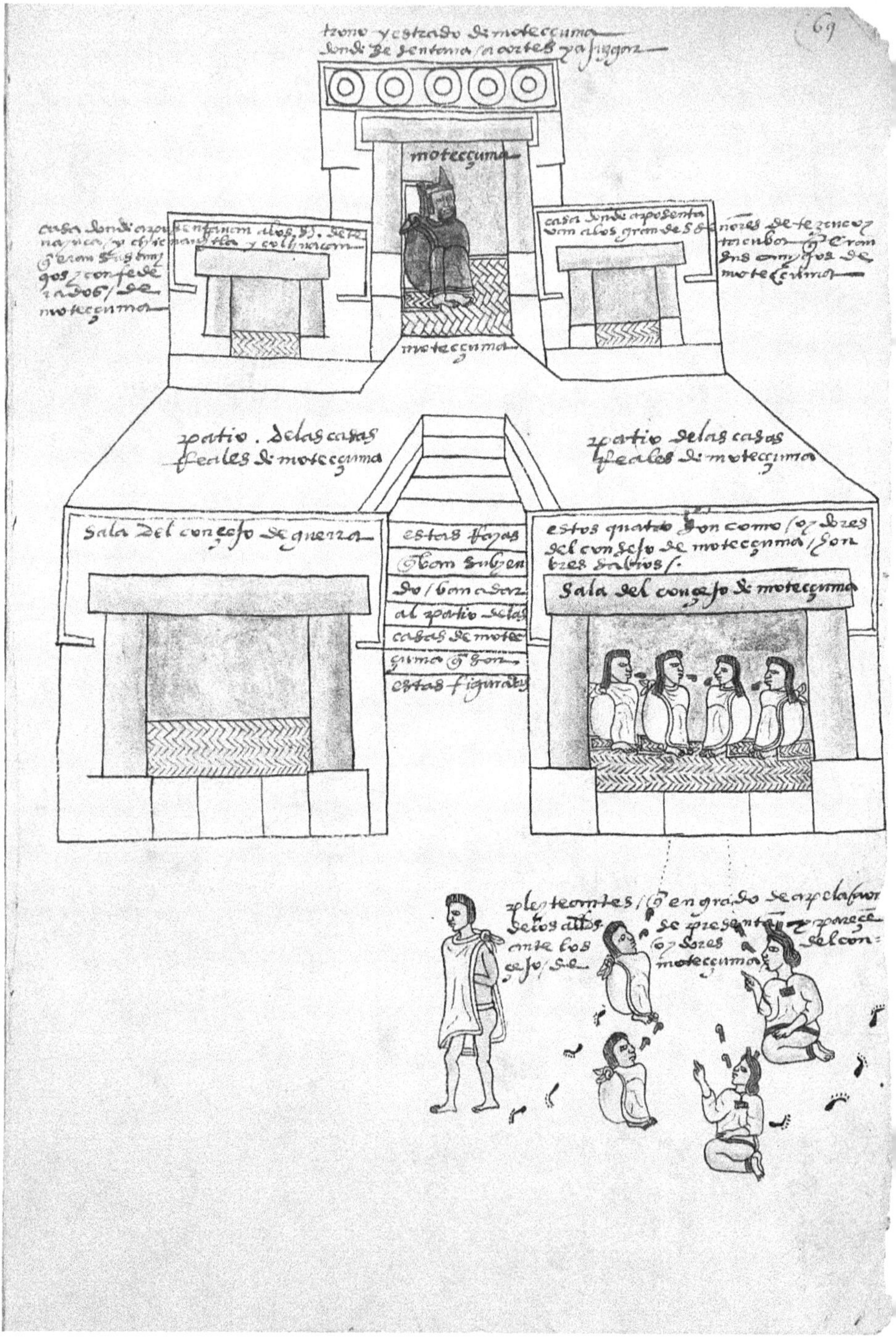

Figure G15 Codex Mendoza, fol. 69r. This page depicts Moctezuma's palace. There are two rooms and four seated councilmen on the bottom story, and three rooms with Moctezuma seated at the center on the top story. Litigants (two of whom are women) appear outside.

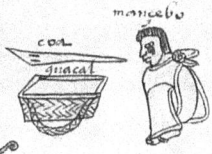

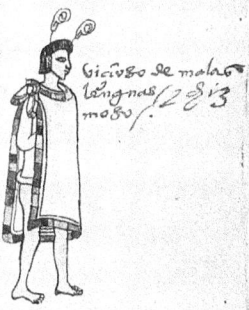

Figure G16 Codex Mendoza, fol. 70r. This page depicts a father counseling his son (top center), four male figures exhibiting bad behaviors, five artisans teaching their sons their crafts, a gossip, and a drunk man and woman.

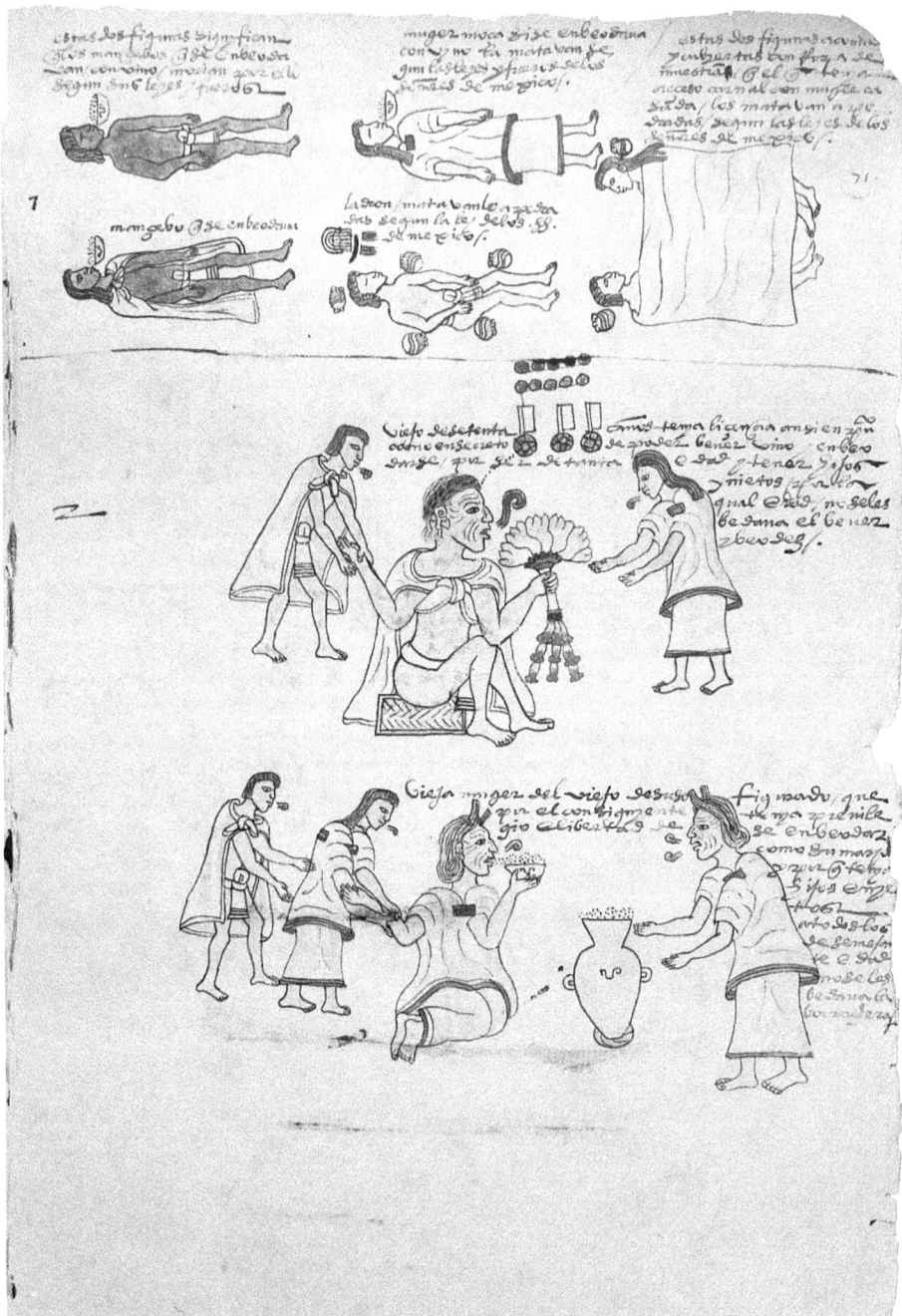

Figure G17 Codex Mendoza, fol. 71r. The first register depicts three young men and women, lying prone with pulque bowls near their mouths; a fourth young man, prone and surrounded by five stones; and a couple under a blanket with stones next to their heads. The bottom register depicts a man and woman drinking and enjoying their old age.

The Old Law, Polygyny & the Customs of the Ancestors

ON JULY II, 1539, Francisco Maldonado, a young Nahua Christian, gave damning testimony in the Inquisition trial against don Carlos Ometochtli Chichimecateuctli, an Indigenous nobleman and claimant to the lordship of the powerful central Mexican altepetl of Tetzcoco. Maldonado, a former student at the Colegio de Santa Cruz Tlatelolco and a Native of Chiconautla, a subject town of Tetzcoco, had officially denounced don Carlos three weeks earlier for engaging in bigamy, pagan worship, and heretical dogmatism. In his testimony, Maldonado attributed to don Carlos a searing discourse that he allegedly gave while visiting Chiconautla that indicted the missionary friars for practicing a double standard in their effort to suppress Native customs.

> Look, the friars and clergy each have their own manner of penance; look, those of Saint Francis have a manner of teaching, a manner of living, a manner of dress, a manner of prayer; and those of Saint Augustine have another, and those of Saint Dominic have another; and other clergy, as we all see, and it was this way also among those who kept our gods, that the Mexicans had a manner of dress, a manner of prayer, offering, and fasting, and in other towns, other manners; in each town they had their manner of sacrifices, their manner of prayer and offering, and this is what the friars and clerics do such that none agree; let's follow that which our ancestors had and followed, and let's live as they lived, and so it should be under-

stood; as the friars teach us and preach to us, as they make us understand; that each of his own will should follow the law, customs, and ceremonies that he wants.[1]

The high oratory voiced by Maldonado suggesting that don Carlos had equated the status of Christian and Indigenous custom was striking on many levels. According to Maldonado, not only did don Carlos create an analogy between the variability of customs among the missionary orders and those of the different communities of central Mexico; he also suggested that the friars' teachings had left the matter of which laws and customs to follow up to the will of the individual. In the eyes of Spanish authorities, this particular invocation of Christian teachings and the assertion that the missionaries set an example for cultural relativism contributed to the view that don Carlos not only had committed crimes against the faith but had also crossed the line into sedition.

The Inquisition trial of don Carlos focused on his public denunciation of Christianity, including his express disgust at the Chiconautlans' use of Christian rather than Indigenous ceremonies to pray for the end of a devastating drought. It also focused on his polygynous, consanguineous, and sometimes coercive relationships with Native women. The testimony of Indigenous witnesses framed don Carlos's comportment as a Native nobleman through a juxtaposition of pre-Hispanic and Christian law and custom. According to one witness, don Carlos initiated his discourse "as in the old custom," which recent scholarship suggests was a reference to the huehuetlatolli.[2] The contrast between the old law and the new was therefore reinforced by don Carlos's style of speech, which Francisco Maldonado reproduced in his testimony. What better way to make the case that don Carlos posed a threat to colonial order than to point out that he had delivered his defense of the old law in the authoritative discourse of the ancestors?

Maldonado's testimony and that of other witnesses must be read in the context of intense generational and cultural conflicts in central Mexican Native towns during these years. The Franciscans sent young Native Christians, many of whom were alumni of the Colegio de Santa Cruz Tlatelolco, back to their home communities to promote a new ritual order, serve as their eyes and ears, and denounce those members of the Native elite who continued to follow the practices of old. The Inquisition served as an arena for this confrontation and a platform for the clergy and their Native allies to stigmatize and discredit Native law and custom through the production of a discourse of the "old law" and "customs of the ancestors." These conflicts did not end with the sixteenth century and the removal of Native people from the Inquisition's jurisdiction in 1571. The struggle between the old and new laws and customs persisted into the seventeenth and even early eighteenth centuries in more remote reaches of the empire, like the northern sierra of Oaxaca.

This chapter analyzes how the legal and social process of dismantling polygyny—a core tenet of the "old law"—shaped politics and gender relations in Native communities, allowed for accommodation between Native elites and Spanish ecclesiastical and civil officials, and helped define the ambit of legitimate Native custom in central Mexico and Oaxaca. As enforcers of moral and social discipline, the Inquisition and Indigenous courts of first instance feature centrally in the narrative. Whereas important work has shown how the Inquisition's war on idolatry undermined Indigenous social order during the sixteenth century, only recently have scholars honed in on its role in dismantling polygyny.[3] Methodologically speaking, ethnohistorians have tended to treat Inquisition cases as sources for Indigenous ritual practice.[4] When read alongside first-instance legal cases from later periods, however, they reveal continuities in the production of legal meaning and the boundaries of legitimate Native authority. Through conflictive and bitter litigation over polygyny, which Spanish civil and ecclesiastical law defined as bigamy and concubinage, Spanish officials and Native litigants, witnesses, and judges gave new meaning to the transatlantic concept of the "old law," inflecting it with gendered significance particular to the Indigenous world. The "old law of the ancestors" defined "good customs" through antithesis, by aligning Native practice with colonial law and producing an ever-narrowing ambit of licit Native custom.

The Inquisition Case against Don Carlos Chichimecateuctli

Francisco Maldonado's framing of don Carlos's comportment under the rubric of the "old law" and "customs of the ancestors" drew from discourses produced by the transatlantic Inquisition. In Spain, Jews who converted to Christianity (conversos) after the forced expulsion and conversions of the 1490s and Muslims who converted to Christianity (moriscos) often referred to their respective former faiths as the "old law" in the testimonies they provided to the Inquisitors. When hauled before the Inquisition for backsliding or expressing adherence to the customs and rites of old, some even adopted a culturally relative stance, radical for its time, arguing that all could be saved according to their own law.[5] Like the conversos and moriscos of the Iberian Peninsula, Mexico's Indigenous peoples found themselves caught between an evangelizing church and their own traditions of authority and morality. Indeed, during the sixteenth and seventeenth centuries, Spanish ecclesiastical officials made comparisons between the Jews and Indigenous peoples of the Americas in an effort to determine how to categorize and treat Native converts. Some officials argued that Indigenous peoples and Jews were profoundly dissimilar as converts since the Indigenous did not live according to a religion or law, as did the Jews; rather, they had lived according to natural law, which made it easier for them to embrace Christianity. Others firmly equated Indigenous peoples with Jews, arguing that like the Jews, they were idolaters who held on to their old law while pretending to accept Christianity.[6]

Don Carlos's case was quite different, though, from that of the artisans, milliners, rural laborers, or even higher-status merchants and urban notables across the Atlantic who found themselves in the Spanish Inquisition's crosshairs. He was a member of the Native nobility of a newly conquered territory whose alleged defiance of Christian norms and public pronouncements against them threatened the moral and legal order that colonial officials sought to impose. The timing of don Carlos's alleged sedition was crucial. In 1539, the same year as don Carlos's trial, the citizens of Ghent rose in rebellion against the Spanish king and Holy Roman emperor Charles V in protest of a tax hike to fund Spanish imperial wars. As discussed in chapter 1, it was also the year that Francisco de Vitoria challenged the legitimacy of Spanish dominion in the Americas, provoking Charles V to censor him. All these events took place in the fall of 1539, creating a tense political environment. For these reasons, don Carlos's case took on an outsized importance and provoked such a harsh, exemplary punishment.[7]

The notoriety of don Carlos's case has attracted the attention of generations of historians. Most studies analyze the case in terms of the extirpation of idolatry and the conflict between Christian and Indigenous religious norms and forms of authority in the colonial context.[8] More recently, the historian Patricia Lopes Don has focused on the centrality of gender to the case, arguing that don Carlos's polygyny proved a more contentious issue than his idolatry. She highlights the role of Native women witnesses in pushing back against the traditional sexual prerogatives of elite Native men and argues that the case allowed for a renegotiation of the terms of noble masculine privilege.[9] Finally, scholars have interpreted the case through the lens of Tetzcoco's factional politics, viewing the denunciation of don Carlos and the testimony against him by his kin and peers as a product of a struggle over succession to the position of tlatoani.[10] My analysis contributes to this scholarship by approaching the case through the lens of legal history. I situate the case as part of a broader centuries-long effort on the part of Spanish authorities to criminalize Native sexual customs and instantiate Christian norms of marriage, inheritance, and property through laws and the courts. Part of that effort required the ongoing production of legal meaning in Native communities, a process in which Spanish officials and Native people actively participated.

As Lopes Don asserts, even though the case against don Carlos involved public denunciation of Christianity, there was substantial testimonial evidence for only one of the three formal charges brought against him: bigamy.[11] This came primarily from women witnesses: his niece, doña Inés; his sister, doña María; his sister-in-law, who was the widow of his deceased brother don Pedro, also named doña María, and her servants; and a third doña María, who was don Carlos's Christian wife. According to their testimony, don Carlos had a long-standing relationship with his niece doña Inés, the daughter of his full-blooded sister.[12] He had two children with her, one of whom survived. His brothers, who were eager to conform at least outwardly to Christian norms, disapproved of his relationship with Inés and pushed him to marry doña María, a distant relative and noblewoman of the dependent town of Huexotla.[13] Doña Maria claimed that the marriage was harmonious for about two years, until he moved doña Inés into their home. At that point, doña Inés became the primary wife and began to run the household, at doña María's expense.[14] Finally, don Carlos's sister-in-law, doña María, claimed that after her husband, don Pedro—who was don Carlos's brother and former lord of Tetzcoco—died, don Carlos attempted to force her into a sexual relationship with him.[15] The testimony of these women painted him as a man who in his refusal to give up polygyny was living in the "old law."

They were certainly correct on this count. By Christian standards, don Carlos's sexual behavior was scandalous and violated the law, but according to pre-Hispanic law and custom, he was exercising his noble, masculine privilege. In pre-Hispanic Mesoamerica, polygyny was a sign of high status, an engine of noble wealth, and a determinant of royal succession. In central Mexican lordly households, wives occupied varied statuses depending on their birth and the type of marriage they contracted. High-status wives came from royal lineages and married their noble partners through a process of petitioning that culminated in a public ceremony. When they moved into the palace complex, they brought with them entourages of kin and servants, some of whom became lesser wives and concubines. Men's noble status depended on the status of their mothers, a situation that fostered competition among matrilineal cohorts of varying statuses and, on occasion, jockeying for power when succession was unclear following the death of a tlatoani. To complicate matters further, the status of "primary wife"—the woman of highest rank whose sons were poised to inherit the chieftainship—was vulnerable to change. If a rival lineage superseded that of the primary wife through warfare or political alliance, then her sons would take a back seat to those of a new primary wife who belonged to the newly ascendant lineage.[16] These conflicts could incite internecine violence. Prior to the Spanish conquest, polygyny generated almost one hundred years of warfare in Tetzcoco among rival claimants to the chieftainship and their siblings.[17]

One of the most important functions of polygyny in Mesoamerica more broadly was to allow for the creation of complex and multiple political alliances among Native polities of unequal status. In central Mexico, this worked in two primary ways. The lords of Tenochtitlan and Tetzcoco married their daughters to the lords of subject altepeme in order to cement political ties. These high-status royal women brought impressive wealth to the royal estate, including land, slaves, rights to commoner labor, and luxury goods. Since succession to the position of tlatoani was determined by the mother's status, the sons of Mexica or Tetzcocan noblewomen often acceded to lordship in subject altepeme, thereby tightening the relationship with the ruling polity. In other cases, Mexica and Tetzcocan rulers appointed their sons as rulers in subject altepeme, where they married local noblewomen. Their children became joint members of the local and Mexica or Tetzcocan royal families.[18]

Polygyny played a vital economic role in central Mexican society by determining inheritance customs and property rights among the nobility and producing multiple ownership by kin groups. During the pre-Hispanic period, several categories of landed property existed, including land of the ruler, palace land, corporately held temple lands, corporately held land of the town (altepetl) or ward (calpulli), privately held land of the minor lords, and land acquired through warfare. Commoners did not own land but enjoyed inheritable usufruct rights to land allocated to them by rulers, nobles, and local authorities.[19]

Whereas private property was partible in Mexica society, corporate lands and the royal estate were not. Polygyny ensured the continuity of wealth and land within royal bloodlines across generations by producing multiple potential royal heirs with collective rights to land and allowing for the provision of land for noble kin and progeny of lesser status. Within polygynous unions, women had property rights roughly equal to those of men. They could inherit houses, land, and movables—the three broad categories of Mexica property—in equal measure to their male counterparts. Women's inheritance rights, especially to land, may have been mitigated by the custom of eldest males in sibling cohorts acting as guardians and by the scarcity of land. Even if their inheritance rights were residual, women could pass them on to lateral relatives or their children. Further bolstering women's economic power and autonomy, the property that they brought into polygynous marriages remained theirs, separate from that of their husbands.[20]

Property rights bolstered women's position in polygynous households, but lesser wives without significant property found themselves exploited within the domestic economy. They prepared food and engaged in other chores for the benefit of higher-status kin and co-wives. They also wove textiles, a prized form of tribute, currency, and wealth.[21] The Franciscan friar Toribio de Benavente (Motolinía) surmised that women's productive labor provided one of the reasons that Indigenous men were reluctant to give up polygyny.[22]

After the military conquest of central Mexico, the missionary friars targeted Native polygyny for destruction. They did this in their pastoral work in Indigenous towns and communities and with recourse to ecclesiastical law. Gratian, an architect of canon law during the twelfth century, held that the joining of man and woman in marriage was part of natural law, practiced by all peoples on earth and ordained by God.[23] According to natural law, marriages performed with solemn rites were legitimate, sanctified by a natural contract, and could only be undone by judicial decision. Following this logic, many missionaries held that Native elite marriage, even if not sanctified by Christian ceremony, was equivalent to a sacramental contract, which could not be simply dissolved. On the other hand, sexual unions made without ceremony could be broken through mutual consent. The missionaries used these benchmarks to evaluate which Native unions were undergirded by natural contract and which in their view could be classified as concubinage. Practically speaking, they often identified as legitimate marriages those between a Native nobleman and his first wife. He would have to give up all the others and marry her *in facie ecclesiae*, in keeping with the Christian sacrament.[24]

Tetzcocan nobles were the first to be married according to Christian custom. On October 14, 1526, don Hernando Pimentiel, brother of the Native lord of Tetzcoco, and seven other Native nobles were married with the pomp and circumstance befitting the marriage of Spanish nobility. Prominent figures of New Spanish society, including conquistadors and Mexico City municipal officials Alonso de Avila and Pedro Sánchez Farfán, attended the solemn mass and elaborate banquet and ball that followed. Hernán Cortés sent lavish gifts.[25] It is not surprising that the Tetzcocan lords were the first to publicly embrace Christian marriage customs. In a climactic moment of the Spanish conquest during the battle for the Aztec capital of Tenochtit-lan, a faction of the Tetzcocan nobility led by Ixtlilxochitl split from his compatriots and allied with Cortés. Following the conquest, the Tetzcocans were viewed with favor by the new Spanish overlords.[26] A crucial mecha-nism of the alliances between Spanish conquerors and the Native rulers of central Mexico was the incorporation of the Catholic mission and mission-ary priests into the structure of Native political authority.[27] These alliances cut both ways, enhancing the legitimacy of the Christian enterprise in In-digenous eyes. To the benefit of missionary priests and Spanish officials, the public celebration and spectacle of the marriage of Tetzcocan lords set an example for the rest of Native society. From this point forward, Native no-blemen were to renounce the pre-Hispanic custom of polygyny in favor of Christian monogamy.

In the years that followed, the Crown, the pope, and religious orders rolled out legislation and rules concerning Native marriage. Carlos V in 1530 prohibited both polygyny and polyandry among the Indigenous. Native men and women who had become Christian and married again while the first spouse was still living would be warned to separate, and if they continued cohabitating after two warnings, they would be punished publicly as an ex-ample for others.[28] Rules promulgated by the religious orders make it clear that legal prohibition of polygyny was ineffective. In 1534 the Augustinian order required that Indigenous people practice monogamy as a prerequisite for baptism.[29] In the years that followed, some tension emerged as to the se-verity of punishment for Indigenous polygynists. In 1536 the Crown issued a royal cédula that prohibited branding of Natives who practiced concubinage, a customary punishment in Spain. The law justified greater leniency for New Spain's Indigenous on the grounds that they were new converts to the faith and that it was customary for Native men to have many wives.[30] This decree reflects the special status held by Indigenous people in the Spanish legal sys-tem; they were accorded a degree of leniency due to their status as newcom-ers to the Christian faith.

The question of which wife Indigenous men in polygynous unions should marry also came to the fore in royal, ecclesiastical, and papal decrees of the early postconquest period. In 1537 Pope Paul III issued a Papal Bull declar-ing that Native men should marry the first wife and that those who engaged in serial marriage—cohabitating with one woman at a time—should remain with the one they lived with at the time of their conversion to Christianity, a position that Pope Pius V confirmed in 1571.[31] Also in 1537, the bishops of New Spain complained that Natives married in the church in order to publicly comply with Christian rules, while practicing Native customs, including polygyny, in secret.[32]

The ongoing pronouncements about the need to impose Christian marriage and stamp out polygyny reveal that it continued to be the norm in many communities, among nobility and commoners alike.[33] The historian Sarah Cline's classic study of Nahuatl-language household censuses from the Morelos region from roughly 1535 to 1540 reveals the infrequency of Christian marriage and the continuity of polygyny, even among those who were baptized.[34] Cline points to the sparsely staffed mission churches in the region as part of the reason for these continuities, but even in Mexico City, traces of polygyny appear in wills and legal records. The historian Susan Kellogg has shown that as late as the 1570s, Native litigants brought to the Real Audiencia cases concerning multiple ownership of land and house compounds. She argues that these property arrangements arose from polygyny and that litigants attempted to disguise multiple, consanguineous, and affinal sexual relationships in an effort to present property claims based on Christian marriage and Spanish laws of inheritance.[35] She further notes that pre-Hispanic multifamily residence patterns that absorbed married couples into larger household and kin units persisted through the sixteenth century, as did inheritance patterns based on lateral relations such as aunts, uncles, nephews, nieces, and cousins. These practices point to the continued imprint of polygyny on Native residential and inheritance customs in the five decades that followed the conquest. By the late sixteenth century, however, the norms of Christian marriage expanded residence patterns based on the monogamous nuclear family, as well as inheritance patterns that prioritized monogamous spouses and offspring.[36]

In addition to the trial against don Carlos, several sixteenth-century Inquisition cases against Native men for crimes against the faith, including polygyny and Native marriage customs, contributed to this legal and social transformation. A 1536 case of idolatry against two Indigenous men named Tacatetl and Tanixtetl featured charges of polygyny, consanguinity (in this instance, taking a daughter as a wife), and sexual coercion.[37] In a 1537 case against Martín Ocelotl for idolatry and sorcery, witnesses claimed that he advocated having sex with "our neighbors' wives" and that he implied that the "law of the Christians" was temporary and the Natives could return to practicing their customs since "we were born for nothing else."[38] Eight more cases between 1537 and 1548 involved either primary or secondary charges of polygyny, glossed by Inquisitors as "bigamy" and "concubinage."[39] Four of these included allegations of consanguinity and three included sexual coercion.[40]

Among the cases brought by the Inquisition against Indigenous men for sexual crimes, don Carlos's was certainly the most highly politicized and pivotal. Don Carlos's kin and peers who denounced him were motivated not only by the division between the Native elite who publicly embraced Christianity and those who did not but also by politics of succession internal to Tetzcoco. Don Carlos was the son of Nezahualpilli, a revered pre-Hispanic lord of Tetzcoco, and brother of don Pedro Tetlahuehuetzquititzin, a postconquest tlatoani of Tetzcoco. When don Pedro died, don Carlos made a bid to succeed him through the pre-Hispanic practice of taking don Pedro's primary wife as one of his own. He needed to do this to boost the legitimacy of his claim to the Tetzcocan lordship. Though he was the son and brother of a lord, his mother was not a Mexica noblewoman but one of Nezahualpilli's lesser wives. As such, don Carlos hovered at the margins of the Tetzcocan nobility, and his efforts to claim the lordship of Tetzcoco drew the ire of powerful figures. His public repudiation of Christianity did not help matters, alienating the Native nobility who had allied themselves with the missionary friars and who opposed his accession to the chieftainship.[41] In this regard, the Inquisition case represented a turning point in Tetzcocan politics, characterized by a renewed alliance among the Tetzcocan nobility, missionary friars, and Spanish authorities.

The case against don Carlos also opened a space for conflict over customary gender norms in Tetzcoco, providing an opportunity for elite women to challenge noble masculine privilege, influence colonial politics, and shape the meaning of Native custom. Crucially, the testimony of women witnesses, including don Carlos's wives and women kin who had publicly embraced Christianity, cemented the case against him. Their words reflected Native custom as it would have been seen through Christian eyes, assigning negative meaning to the traditional sexual prerogatives of elite Native men. The allegedly coercive and exploitative nature of don Carlos's sexual relationships was a common theme throughout their testimony. Don Carlos's sister, doña María, claimed that he treated his Christian wife (also named doña María) as a "slave," forcing her to serve doña Inés, his niece, whom he had brought to his house to live as his second wife. She also claimed that he attempted to force his sister-in-law (also named doña María) against her will into concubinage, in keeping with the ancestral practice of the brother and successor of a deceased lord taking his brother's widow as his wife.[42] The claim of sexual coercion was damning because it drew a distinction between the ideal of Christian marriage, which was supposed to be a voluntary union between two people exercising the free will granted to them by God, and the practice of polygyny, which Europeans considered characteristic of barbaric peoples. By glossing don Carlos's polygyny in this way, the women's testimony portrayed him not only as someone who lived according to the old law but as a tyrant who ruled by force, responsive only to his personal whims and, in this particular case, sexual desires. As discussed in chapter 3, according to the evolutionary view of political and social order undergirded by natural law, tyranny was a form of government—often assigned to Native lords—that through the civilizing force of Spanish colonialism would soon be consigned to the past. A powerful element of the women's testimony was that it associated tyranny with the customary sexual privileges of Indigenous noblemen, thereby bolstering the Spanish case against Native forms of authority and hierarchy.

The political transition sparked by don Carlos's defense of the old law and rejection of Christianity was evident in the stance toward colonial authority taken by the lords of Tetzcoco in the years that followed. Upon don Carlos's death, his half-brother don Antonio Pimentel Tlahuitoltzin became tlatoani, ruling from 1540 to 1545. In stark contrast with don Carlos's resistance to Christian norms, don Antonio embraced Christianity, committed resources to building churches in the towns within Tetzcoco's jurisdiction, and forged alliances with missionaries and church leaders like Fray Toribio de Benavente (Motolinía). He also used the Spanish legal system to resist encroachment onto Tetzcocan lands, while at the same time shoring up the status of the traditional ruling elite by naming a successor rather than allowing for the infighting that often accompanied the death of a ruler. His rulership was emblematic of the accommodation to Christianity and Spanish law and custom that a new generation of Native leadership embodied.[43]

Don Carlos's public and scandalous trial and execution brought many tensions in New Spanish colonial society to the fore. One of its enduring legacies was to incorporate Native Christian men and women into the production of a discourse of the "old law" and "customs of the ancestors" that marked long-standing norms and practices related to Native authority, gender relations, political alliances, and inheritance as criminal and contrary to natural law. Polygyny became bigamy and concubinage, and rituals of elite power became idolatry. This process was crucial to the meaning of colonial Native custom more broadly; pre-Hispanic custom had to be conquered and purged of much of its core content before it could be inserted into an imperial legal order.

The Inquisition Trial of the Lords of Yanhuitlan

The public and politicized production of the "old law" played out in other regions of New Spain during the sixteenth century, though the dynamics varied according to the degree of Spanish influence and the local particularities of Native customary practice. In the diocese of Oaxaca, the Dominicans—the missionary order that oversaw the evangelization of the region—had a much more tenuous presence than did the Franciscans in central Mexico. This, combined with a smaller Spanish population than existed in central Mexico and a more atomized pattern of Native settlement, allowed for greater continuity of Native custom and traditional forms of authority in the early years of the colony. Nevertheless, by the 1540s, the Dominicans had begun to make some inroads, and the pressure on Native elites to make alliances with the missionary friars and follow Christian norms increased. The 1544 Inquisition case against don Francisco and don Domingo, the Ñudzahui lords of the large, wealthy, and powerful yuhuitayu of Yanhuitlan, resulted from these pressures (figs. 4.1, 4.2).

The arrest and trial of these men were the culmination of years of conflict between don Francisco de Las Casas, the Spanish encomendero of Yanhuitlan, and the Dominican friars who sought to evangelize the Native population who paid tribute to and labored for the encomendero. Las Casas jealously guarded his authority over the community and adopted an antagonistic stance toward the Dominican and secular clergy. The situation had become so tense that by 1541, Fray Pedro Delgado, the Dominican provincial, ordered the friars to abandon Yanhuitlan and regroup in the Dominican doctrina of Teposcolula, another large and powerful Ñudzahui town. Don Francisco and don Domingo had forged a political alliance with their encomendero. They made sure to organize labor and tribute payments for Las Casas in exchange for autonomy in other matters, including local governance, the organization of religious ritual, and the continuation of Native marriage customs. The Yanhuitlan nobility's adherence to Indigenous norms clashed with the public adoption of Christianity by the Native authorities of neighboring communities, such as Etlatongo, Nochixtlan, Xaltepeque (Jaltepec), and Suchitepec. Layered on top of this were legal disputes between the lords of Yanhuitlan and these same communities over lands and the control of a local market (*tianguis*).[44]

The conflicts came to a head in 1544 when don Francisco's son scuffled with an entourage of Natives from Etlatongo over a number of enslaved Indigenous people they had allegedly taken from don Francisco. The authorities of

Etlatongo denounced the violent encounter to the Audiencia of Mexico, who ordered Esteban Marbán, the royal notary, to arrest Gonzalo (don Francisco's son). Marbán arrived in Yanhuitlan, accompanied by Bachiller Pedro Gómez de Maraver, dean of the Cathedral of Oaxaca, and Martín de la Mesquita, corregidor of Texupa. They insisted on searching the house of don Francisco, which resulted in the confiscation of a cloth covered with bloody feathers and "small idols." Bachiller Maraver denounced don Francisco and don Domingo to Francisco Tello Sandoval, who had become head of the Inquisition in New Spain following Juan de Zumárraga's removal for the excessive punishment that he imposed on don Carlos Chichimecateuctli. Throughout the Inquisition trial, don Francisco sustained that he was the casualty of a power struggle between the encomendero and the Dominicans.[45]

The Inquisition case against the Lords of Yanhuitlan has been analyzed primarily for its ethnohistorical content regarding Native ritual practice.[46] More recently, greater attention has been paid to what the case has to say about gender relations and how charges of idolatry figured into power struggles among Dominican friars, the encomendero of Yanhuitlan, and the town's Native elite.[47] As was true of the case of don Carlos, the trial represented a pivotal moment in legal, social, and political terms, reshaping the local balance of power. In my analysis, I pay special attention to how charges of and testimony about polygyny and Native marriage gave meaning to the concept of Native custom during a period of ongoing alignment and accommodation of Native and Spanish legal norms.

Much of the substance of the trial concerned charges of idolatry. But as the trial progressed, polygyny came to occupy an important place in the testimony. According to the cacique of Etlatongo, don Domingo had married according to Christian sacrament. Shortly thereafter, he married his niece in keeping with "the rites and ceremonies of the ancestors."[48] The governor of Etlatongo added that don Domingo had married his niece "according to the law of the devil, as they did in times past."[49] He noted that the niece was the daughter of don Domingo's brother, who was cacique of Tiltepeque. A Native interpreter and assistant to the friars in Yanhuitlan claimed that don Domingo and his first wife, whom he married in the church, no longer lived together because he did not treat her as a wife.[50]

As for the case against don Francisco, witnesses claimed that he had married an unbaptized woman according to "his law" twenty-two years prior—about five years before he was baptized—and that he had a son with her named Gonzalo, who at the time of the trial was about twenty years old. Her name was Cacañe, and she was the wife of don Francisco's deceased

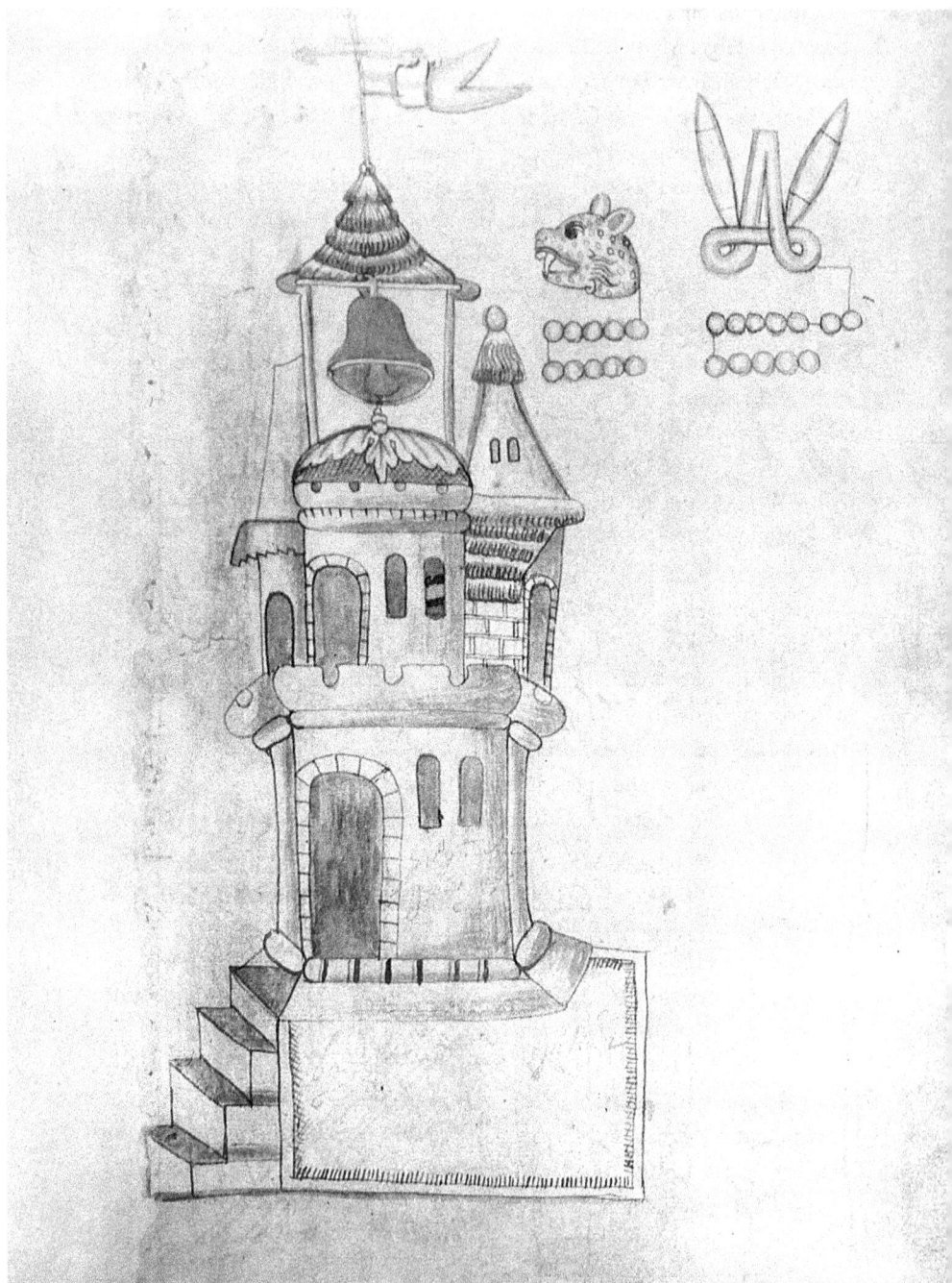

Figure 4.1 Church in Yanhuitlan. Codex of Yanhuitlan. To the right of the church are two calendar glyphs: jaguar (ocelotl) with ten circles, and obsidian blade (tecpatl) with twelve circles.

Figure 4.2 Don Domingo, cacique de Yanhuitlan, with ecclesiastical official holding rosary. Codex of Yanhuitlan.

brother. According to testimony, don Francisco then went on to marry an enslaved Native woman in facie ecclesiae apparently to appease the friars, though witnesses claimed that he did it to mock the church. At the same time, he kept Cacañe and Gonzalo hidden in Tula, a nearby community, and maintained them as his family. The encomendero don Francisco de Las Casas discovered the ruse and had the son baptized. Cacañe remained unbaptized and the encomendero kept the secret to himself.[51]

Noble polygyny in the Mixteca was distinct from that of central Mexico in notable ways. First there was the issue of scale. Codices recounting royal genealogies from the pre-Hispanic and early colonial periods make clear that rulers had fewer wives compared with missionary reports reaching dozens among the nobility of central Mexico. And although marriage in the Mixteca served to create political alliances, as it did in central Mexico, the status of women in those alliances and the place of polygyny in the determination of royal succession were quite different.

In the Mixteca, the yuhuitayu was a dynastic alliance formed through marriage that joined two lordly establishments—royal lands, palaces, and dependents—of two autonomous communities (ñuu). Legitimate royal marriages had to be caste endogamous (only royals could marry royals) and publicly recognized. The children of these unions also had to be publicly recognized and acknowledged and reared by their parents in order to be legitimate successors to the title.[52] Direct descent took precedence over collateral or affinal relations in matters of inheritance.[53] By definition, the yuhuitayu required marriage; a single unmarried ruler could not legitimately claim title to it. The male and female partners in the yuhuitayu maintained the individuality of their estates and designated different heirs among their children, male and female, for inheritance. Bilateral inheritance and the independence of male and female wealth, combined with the fact that women could continue to rule after the death of their husbands, afforded noblewomen in the Mixteca considerable power.[54] The nobility practiced polygyny as a means of forming multiple and simultaneous alliances, sometimes between dynasties of unequal status.[55] No matter the case, only the children of the primary wife were considered legitimate, and as such only they could inherit royal title and the property and privileges that accompanied it. Secondary wives were tied to the royal estate, served the primary wife, and performed household labor. Their children often married into the lesser nobility and merchant class.[56] This meant that the power struggles among matrilineal cohorts and the instability of the status of primary wives that characterized central Mexico were not issues in royal succession in the Mixteca. Lesser nobles and merchants also practiced polygyny, though the number of women depended on the affluence of the man in question given the expense of supporting a large household.

In both Spanish and Native legal traditions, the legitimacy of marriage determined inheritance and, in the case of noble marriages, succession to rulership. A central issue in the interrogatories and testimonies in the cases against both don Francisco and don Domingo was the question of which of their two wives—the one married in facie ecclesiae or the one married according to Native custom—was the "legitimate wife." For the case of don Francisco, the interrogatory asked whether he had married a second time in the church while his "legitimate wife," who was not baptized, was still living. In the case of don Domingo, the interrogatory asked whether having been married in the church, he went on to marry his niece according to Indigenous rites, while his "legitimate wife" was still living.[57] In keeping with Christian and colonial law, the order of the marriages determined their legitimacy, despite the fact that in don Francisco's case, his first marriage was performed according to Native custom, and his second in the church. The case also made clear that according to Christian law, the consanguinity and affinity of don Francisco's and don Domingo's Native marriages were a grave offense against the faith. There were no prohibitions to consanguineous marriage according to Mixtec law. To the contrary, consanguinity was an integral part of noble marriage and the formation of yuhuitayu throughout the Mixteca.[58]

Don Francisco and don Domingo married according to Mixtec custom, building alliances with high-born women in other communities, as did their forebears. As public figures in an important Mixtec polity and contested territory for the Dominican order, they also married other women in facie ecclesiae, much as don Carlos had done, to deflect the attention of the friars. Although they concealed their Native marriages from the friars, all the Indigenous witnesses were well aware of them, claiming that knowledge of them was "public and notorious." For these reasons, the case represented an inflection point in the relationship between the Dominicans and the Indigenous elite of Yanhuitlan, much the way that don Carlos's case was for the relationship between the Tetzcocan elite and the Franciscans and church authorities more broadly. To what extent was the Native nobility willing to accommodate the friars, and how much could they actually resist the imposition of Christian norms?

These questions were crucial in the years that followed the Inquisition case against the lords of Yanhuitlan. Unlike don Carlos and other central Mexican lords, the lords of Yanhuitlan were not found guilty of their alleged crimes. The case record ends in 1547 with no resolution or sentence. Don

Domingo returned to Yanhuitlan in 1548, by which time the Dominicans had reentered the town and asserted themselves as major local authorities. When don Gabriel de Guzmán, don Domingo's son, became cacique upon his father's death in 1558, a new regime of public alliance between the caciques of Yanhuitlan and the Dominican order emerged. Don Gabriel, educated by the friars, embraced Christianity and Spanish authority and deftly mediated between Ñudzahui and Spanish interests, embodying the role of the *indio ladino*, or Hispanized Native.[59]

The Inquisition cases against the lords of Yanhuitlan and of central Mexico made clear to the Native population that public performance of monogamous Christian marriage was a nonnegotiable aspect of Spanish colonial rule. Additional colonial legislation reinforced this point. In 1551 Carlos V mandated that not even unbaptized Indians, whether caciques or commoners, could marry more than one woman.[60] Closing this final loophole meant that the "old law" could no longer produce multiple or legitimate marriages even among those who had not yet entered the Christian faith.

As the alliance between Mixtec elites and the church deepened, the "old law" became shorthand for illicit Native custom. However, beyond the public accommodations made by Native elites to the dictates of colonial rule, some Native customs regarding marriage and legitimate noble succession remained remarkably durable in the Mixteca. Caste endogamy in noble marriage persisted through at least the end of the sixteenth century: Mixtec lords had to marry noblewomen, and only the children of this union could inherit the cacicazgo. Children born of concubines had no rights to inheritance. During the pre-Hispanic period, a ruling couple determined the order of succession among their children, most likely through consultation with a council of local nobles. This practice appears to have persisted into the early colonial period, though by the late eighteenth century, European primogeniture shaped succession order in some cases, though in keeping with Native custom, parents endeavored to protect the rights of secondary heirs.[61]

The alignment of Christian and Native notions of legitimate marriage was central to the incorporation of Native communities into the mature colonial order, though as the cases of the Mixteca and Tetzcoco make clear, the pace and timing of this process varied across localities. The Inquisition, abetted by elite Native men and women who viewed accommodation to Christianity as advantageous in a colonial world, played a central role in criminalizing pre-Hispanic Native practice and incorporating Christian marriage into Native structures of authority. In the wake of the Inquisition cases against don Carlos and the lords of Yanhuitlan, the Council of Trent (1545–63) adopted a more orthodox and rigid stance regarding Christian marriage, underscoring that it was a sacrament of the church that had to be performed publicly and was indissoluble.[62] It also condemned concubinage and declared sinful any sex outside marriage and for purposes other than procreation.[63] When the Native peoples of New Spain were removed from the jurisdiction of the Inquisition in 1571, Native polygyny, serial marriage, consanguinity, and affinal unions fell under the jurisdiction of ecclesiastical and civil courts and were more often prosecuted under the rubrics of incest, concubinage, adultery, and fornication. Following up on the course charted by the Tridentine Council, in 1585 the Third Mexican Provincial Council proscribed concubinage and adultery as violations of the faith and of the holy sacrament of marriage.[64]

The Native population met these doctrinal proscriptions with uneven compliance, and church authorities often afforded Native peoples some leeway. The historian Ana de Zaballa notes that in the sixteenth century the Holy See granted the Indigenous population certain privileges related to marriage in light of their status as neophytes to the Christian faith, including less stringent consanguinity requirements. These and other practices persisted through the colonial period, and were often accepted by local religious and civil authorities as "Indian custom" in an effort to accommodate Spanish and Christian norms to local realities.[65] During the seventeenth and eighteenth centuries in regions where ecclesiastical authorities and parish priests were thin on the ground, Indigenous nobles and commoners continued to form polygynous unions, far beyond the boundaries of acceptable Indian marriage custom, thereby continuing to give meaning to the "old law."

From the Inquisition to the Native Tribunal and Court of First Instance

Early colonial public battles over pre-Hispanic custom diminished over time in their frequency and intensity after the sixteenth century in areas of high contact between Spanish clergy and Native communities like central Mexico and even in communities at a greater remove from Spanish centers like Yanhuitlan in the Mixteca Alta. Although these practices were increasingly relegated to the most remote regions of New Spain, the Indigenous authorities who mediated between Spanish officials and their communities understood the political and economic benefits of publicly aligning themselves with Christianity. Spanish officials increasingly entrusted Indigenous authorities with the task of policing their own communities and ensuring their compliance with Christian norms.

As discussed in chapter 1, during the sixteenth century, the Spanish Crown granted semiautonomous jurisdiction to Native lords, directing them to rule Native towns according to their good laws and customs. Indirect rule by the Native elite made sense on a number of levels; Spain could not support a bureaucracy large enough to rule Mesoamerica's vast conglomeration of Native polities, and the Native nobility had the added benefit of enjoying political legitimacy. In addition to recognizing the semisovereignty of Native lords, the Crown installed cabildos (town councils) in Native communities, a process that will be discussed in further detail in chapter 6. The cabildo was staffed by Native nobility and lesser nobility; it became a vehicle for social mobility and an arena for political rivalry as the balance of power shifted from Native lordship to the jurisdiction of the Native cabildo, though in many cases the Native hereditary nobility continued to exercise considerable influence and power as a shadow government.[66] The cabildo oversaw civil administration, including the collection of taxes and tribute, the orderly transfer of inherited property, and the organization of Native labor.[67]

The Native cabildo was also designed to maintain social order through the exercise of first-instance civil and criminal jurisdiction. A 1618 royal decree stated that Indian magistrates (alcaldes) had the authority to investigate, arrest, and temporarily detain criminals for one day in their own jails before turning them over to the Spanish authorities in the district seat. Native magistrates could also punish their subjects for minor crimes such as missing Mass and religious celebrations, and for other petty transgressions. Repeated drunkenness merited especially rigorous punishment, though the law did not specify penalties. Native judges had to keep physical punishment "moderate," limiting it to six or eight lashes.[68] In short, the law made the cabildo a Native tribunal, overseen by Native magistrates acting as judges of first instance.[69]

As was true of Spanish imperial authority more broadly, the civil authority of the Native cabildo was reinforced by the parallel and overlapping authority of the ecclesiastical jurisdiction in Native communities. Parish priests acted as ecclesiastical judges and punished villagers who did not comply with Christian norms. But not all Native communities had parish priests; indeed, the scarcity of priests increased with distance from central Mexico. In the absence of a parish priest, social discipline was reinforced by a parallel body of Native church officials, including lay catechists, choirmasters, sacristans, and priests' assistants who served as the eyes and ears of the Catholic Church. Drunkenness and failure to attend Mass were punished by public lashings ordered and administered by Native municipal and church officials. In this way, Christian discipline in Native communities became the purview of Native authorities.[70]

Outside central Mexico, in geographically peripheral regions characterized by large Indigenous populations and few Spanish civil or religious authorities, missionary priests and Native communities continued to struggle over the respective roles of Christianity and Native ritual and the relative authority of Native Christians and Native ritual specialists, though these two categories were often overlapping rather than mutually exclusive. The mountainous district of Villa Alta, Oaxaca, was one of these peripheral regions. In contrast to the larger Native polities of central Mexico and the midsize polities of the Mixteca Alta, small communities characterized by less wealth and social hierarchy and greater linguistic diversity occupied a rugged landscape. Whereas the conversion of a few highly visible nobles in central Mexico and the Mixteca facilitated the legitimation of colonial rule, Villa Alta's dispersed settlements posed challenges to the understaffed Dominican order, which struggled to attract resources and manpower.

Ecclesiastical and civil authorities maintained that Villa Alta's Indigenous population was especially reluctant to give up the ways of their ancestors. Part of the problem, the friars and secular hierarchy insisted, had to do with the region's rugged mountainous geography, which impeded the expansion of the Dominican mission into the region and provided a disincentive to Spanish settlement. Until 1700, fewer than 10 percent of the district's Native communities had a resident priest.[71] Linguistic diversity also posed a challenge; there were five languages spoken in the region. The relative absence of Spanish settlers meant that a small handful of Spanish officials and missionary priests had to rely heavily on Native authorities to uphold Christian norms and colonial rule. The dearth of colonial officials also provided a space for Native autonomy and the persistence of Native ritual.[72]

Dominican and secular officials responded to the persistence of "idolatry" in Villa Alta with sporadic extirpation efforts, which entailed the active support of Native Christians who served as lay catechists and priest's assistants. Their strategies were diverse, ranging broadly from coercion to persuasion. After 1660, these efforts escalated into a wholesale campaign, culminating in the Cajonos Rebellion of 1700 in which Native people in the Cajonos region of Villa Alta rose up violently against Dominican friars, Spanish officials, and their Native allies. Repression followed in the wake of the rebellion. Thirty-four Indigenous leaders were tried and convicted for the murder of the priest's assistants of the Native town of San Francisco Cajonos and for instigating the rebellion. Fifteen of them were executed. Parish inspections ensued, during which Native villagers turned over their ritual objects and texts to Spanish authorities, denounced their ritual specialists, and led church and civil officials to their sacred sites.[73]

During the cycle of extirpation that endured in Villa Alta from the 1660s to the 1720s, the conflict between Christian marriage and polygyny emerged as a flash point. This time the primary antagonists were not Inquisitors and wealthy Native lords but Native municipal authorities acting as judges of first instance and the villagers of a remote mountain district. A cache of Zapotec-language criminal records produced by the region's Native cabildos provide evidence of nonconformity with Christian marital norms. These records belong to a larger corpus of seventeen Zapotec-language criminal proceedings and an even broader corpus of thirty-one letters, reports, petitions, investigations, and testimonies related to crime, which the linguist Martina Schrader-Kniffki and I have analyzed in a number of coauthored publications.[74] Criminal proceedings (*procesos*) in Indigenous languages are rare for all regions of Spanish America. There are three Ñudzahui-language procesos in the judicial archive of Teposcolula, one of which includes charges of concubinage.[75] There are additional crime-related documents in Ñudzahui, including a Mixtec murder note, deftly analyzed by Kevin Terraciano.[76] Beyond the case of Oaxaca, Cristina Monzón has published and analyzed procesos in the Tarascan language from the years 1565 and 1602.[77]

Although small in number, Native-language criminal records provide important evidence of how custom, criminality, and other legal concepts were translated from a Spanish and Christian context into an Indigenous one. In the Zapotec-language records concerned with sexual crimes, accusations by village authorities against prominent men in the community featured multiple sexual relationships outside the bounds of Christian marriage, often with female kin or affines, like a stepmother, sister-in-law, or first or second cousin. Some of these relationships appear to have been serial, that is, moving on from one relationship to another, and others simultaneous.[78] Linguistic evidence points to ongoing dissonance between Christian marriage and Indigenous norms. As Schrader-Kniffki and I have shown, in criminal records and other genres of Zapotec-language notarial records, *nigolla quie* (woman of) appears as a calque for the Spanish expression for wife (mujer de), pointing to the ways in which Zapotec speakers adapted the language to accommodate the proprietary notion of Christian marriage.[79]

A 1661 Nexitzo Zapotec-language case of concubinage brought by the Native officials of the town of San Juan Yatzona against Juan Ramos provides a fine-grained picture of how Native judges, defendants, and witnesses wove Christian norms into their authoritative discourse in order to define good customs of local colonial governance against the bad customs of the pre-Hispanic past.[80] Unlike don Carlos Chichimecateuctli or don Francisco and don Domingo of Yanhuitlan, Juan Ramos was not a great lord from a long-standing Indigenous noble lineage but rather a *principal*, one of a select group of village notables, or lesser nobility, who rotated in and out of municipal office holding. At the time of the Spanish conquest, the Zapotec region of the Sierra Norte had only been settled one hundred years prior by migrants from the Valley of Oaxaca. Sierra Zapotec communities were formed by clans and extended families, some of which were more powerful than others.[81] By comparison with the Indigenous nobility of central Mexico, the Valley of Oaxaca, and the Oaxacan Mixteca, northern sierra Zapotec nobles were relatively poor in land and dependents, and the social distance between nobles and commoners was short.[82] Those of highest status memorialized their lineages in pictorial genealogies painted on cloth to support claims to land and noble privileges. As in other regions of New Spain, Spanish officials referred to these men as caciques and principales, denoting higher and lesser noble status, respectively.[83] Principales from different clans often competed with one another to control the Native municipal government and the interests of their extended kin group.[84]

The Native authorities who prosecuted Juan Ramos and authored the criminal case against him were allies of the region's Dominican friars. In particular, don Pablo de Vargas, the governor of San Juan Yatzona, whose signature appears at the end of the case alongside that of the Native priest's assistant (*fiscal*) and other town officers, had publicly and ostentatiously served the interests of the missionaries by supporting church construction and bringing criminal cases against villagers who ran afoul of Christian norms, many of whom happened to be his political rivals.[85]

The criminal record of Juan Ramos's case of concubinage combined Spanish and Indigenous norms of notarial writing and legal procedure. After the standard opening of the criminal case in which Vargas and the Native judges recorded the date and identified themselves as the officials of the community gathered in the "court of the king," they recounted in explicit detail Ramos's sexual relations with multiple women, who were cited by name or identified as the wife of a community member. It is notable that the sexual crimes cited encompassed a wide range of relationships, which in Christian terms included fornication and adultery. All these acts were prosecuted under the rubric of concubinage, under whose umbrella New Spain's ecclesiastical authorities included all "temporary and permanent unions not legitimated by the sacrament of marriage."[86]

The criminal record provided much detail about Ramos's sexual encounters, including information about where, when, and how many times Ramos and his partners were caught. Of the four women who were named in the case, two were his sisters-in-law, which went against multiple Christian proscriptions. The women who allegedly had sexual relations with Juan Ramos took an active role in the narrative; none of them was portrayed as a passive victim. In one instance, a woman left her husband for Ramos for one month, suggesting that she practiced polyandry. In another instance, a woman who alleged that Ramos raped her took her case against him to the Spanish magistrate. As with the case against don Carlos Chichimecateuctli, women also played a key role as witnesses, pushing back against what they portrayed as Juan Ramos's masculine privilege, thereby gendering the meaning of Native custom and the "old law."

As Schrader-Kniffki and I have shown in a close reading of this record, Native authorities framed the case against Juan Ramos in terms of an opposition between the "old law" of the Indigenous past and Christian law. In the opening passage of the document, the Native judges stated, "We the judges say that he is not a Christian, that he does not know the holy Doctrine, he is like a man of former times/antiquity, he lives in the old law of antiquity."[87] The Native judges used the Zapotec term *golaza* (former times/antiquity) and a modified Spanish loanword for law (*ley*)—*leo*—to create the construction *leo golaza*, which expresses the idea of someone living according to the regime of Native antiquity, in the "old law." In a later passage in the case, the expression "old law" appears again, but this time through the voice of Marta de la Cruz, a witness in the case who Juan Ramos allegedly raped. The Native judges wrote: "Marta de la Cruz said, 'Why did you take me by force, there is no God, there is no king, you are still in the time of the old law, you live according to the old law.'"[88]

As Schrader-Kniffki and I argue, the negative meaning of *leo golaza* (the old law) in the case against Juan Ramos drew strongly from Zapotec-language missionary discourse regarding idolatry and the pre-Christian past. The idea of Native antiquity played a central role in the bilingual texts that Dominican missionaries and their Native elite allies produced for pastoral education, confession, sermons, and other activities, as shown in chapter 2. Dominican missionaries made frequent use of the term *golaza/coláça* (in sierra Zapotec and valley Zapotec, respectively) in order to put Christian doctrine and the "old law" into moral dialogue. In some instances, they used *colaça* in constructions that took on positive or neutral meaning, but in others, the notion of Indigenous antiquity took on a negative connotation, associated with idolatry. When the Native judges of San Juan Yatzona accused Juan Ramos of living in the "old law," they marked a moral distinction between the law of the ancestors and the Christian present.[89]

Throughout the narrative of the case, the Native authorities reproduced the idea of good customs by detailing how Juan Ramos, a village notable, defied them. They stated that he was not a good Christian, that he lived like the Zapotecs of old, and that he did not conform to the expectations of the Indian republic, including Catholic education, hard work, and service to the church, and that he did not obey God or the king. Instead, he drank and fornicated. In this way, the Native judges showed how Juan Ramos did not comply with the community's social contract or the colonial pact between Indigenous communities and the church and the Crown. As they built their case against Juan Ramos, they highlighted their own good governance.[90]

Yatzona's Native authorities handed down a harsh sentence, reflecting the severe penalties imposed by Native tribunals in cases of adultery and concubinage in the Villa Alta district and in other regions of eighteenth-century Mexico.[91] They forbade Juan Ramos from ever holding office, entering the municipal hall, or claiming status as a village notable; essentially, they demoted him to commoner status. They ordered that if he did not conform to the sentence, he should be whipped fifty times, jailed for one month, and charged a twenty-peso fine. He should also be mounted on a horse, whipped on every corner of the village, and exiled for three months. They also ordered that if any other village notable were to unite with him or help him attain village office, they, too, would be considered a commoner. Finally, they ordered that the written record of his transgressions be taken to the Spanish magistrate so that he could be aware of Juan Ramos's crimes. Beyond its severity, Juan Ramos's punishment is notable for its effects on local politics: it essentially removed him from eligibility for local office. In this regard, the case was emblematic of the factionalism in San Juan Yatzona and other Native towns of the district of Villa Alta during this period, as competing groups of principales attempted to dominate village government.[92] In an echo of the conflicts in sixteenth-century Tetzcoco and Yanhuitlan, the groups conflicted over the place of Christianity in village life and the relationship of the cabildo with Spanish Church and civil officials as they jockeyed for position in the colonial order.

The "old law" as wielded by Native judges and witnesses in the district of Villa Alta referenced not only polygyny but also other behaviors associated with the norms of the pre-Hispanic Indigenous past or the Spanish category of idolatry. In a 1683 Zapotec-language criminal case brought by the Native judges of San Juan Tanetze against Joseph de Yllescas, they accused him of crimes against Spanish law and local custom. According to the record, when Yllescas was *alcalde* (judge and magistrate) he failed to organize the communal labor necessary for the clearing of a communal cornfield, as was mandated according to "custom." He also denounced a fellow villager to the parish priest for practicing the "customs of old," such as bathing in the river at night, presumably for the purposes of ritual purification prior to an important rite of passage such as the investiture of new community authorities.[93] Notably, the custom that aligned with Spanish law—organizing communal labor—was expressed with the Spanish loanword, written as "costombre." The old custom that did not align with Spanish law—ritual purification through bathing—was expressed in Zapotec as *china golaaza*, which translates literally as "obligation of former times" and figuratively as "old custom."[94]

The discourse of the "old law" and "customs of the ancestors" figured centrally as well in Spanish administrative and legal proceedings concerning idolatry in Native communities at the turn of the eighteenth century. In 1703 Pascual García, the Native governor of San Juan Tabaá and ally of Spanish ecclesiastical and civil authorities, denounced the cabildo officers of Tabaá as idolaters. He claimed that "because of me, their old teachers have fled, because I had accused them, because I wanted them to lose the old law of their grandfathers, and to forget their gods."[95] From November through December 1704, Spanish judge and inspector general Lic. Don Joseph Aragón y Alcántara took the confessions of the Native authorities of Villa Alta's one hundred pueblos regarding the identities of their ritual specialists, the location of their ceremonial spaces, and the nature of the rites they performed. Native authorities were also required to yield their ritual implements to the parish inspectors and explain how they paid for the small dogs, chickens, cacao, and other ritual materials. The confessions, which conformed to a template, cast Native custom as an inheritance of "the ancestors," "rooted in antiquity," "in the time of their gentility," and which was allowed to survive because no one had bothered to "pull out the root."[96] In an admission that must have horrified Spanish officials, the officials of Yovego confessed that they conducted some of the ceremonies in the town hall, glossed as the "house of justice," a space that represented royal authority.[97]

As noted at the opening of the chapter, the discourse of the "old law," which originated in the Iberian Peninsula, positioned Jewish and Muslim customs outside Christian order by situating them in the past. Among New

Spain's clergy, there were influential voices who equated the clandestine persistence of Indigenous customs and rites with that of the Jews of Spain who had converted to Christianity. Don Isidro de Sariñana y Cuenca, bishop of Oaxaca from 1683 to 1696, and Diego Jaimes Ricardo Villavicencio, a secular priest and zealous extirpator who worked in Tlaxcala and Oaxaca, viewed Indigenous people through the lens of the backsliding converso. Sariñana was a prime mover of the extirpation of idolatry in late seventeenth-century Oaxaca. Villavicencio, an acolyte of Sariñana, published in 1692 an extirpation manual, *Luz y methodo de confesar idolatras, y destierro de idolatrias, debajo del tratado siguiente: Tratado de avisos y puntos importantes, de la abominable seta [sic; secta] de la idolatria*, in which he made frequent and disparaging parallels between the Native population and Jews.[98] The production of the idea of the "old law" through the mixed Spanish-Zapotec construction of "leo golaza" embodied these layers of meaning and inserted Native custom into a centuries-long transatlantic process of marking non-Christian peoples as unreliable imperial subjects, in unending need of discipline and tutelage.

Conclusion

The Inquisition trials of don Carlos and the lords of Yanhuitlan and the criminal trial of Juan Ramos by the Native authorities of San Juan Yatzona show how living in the old law represented a crime not only against the faith but also against civil order. Polygyny, a vital element of pre-Hispanic Native politics and society, constituted a core element of the old law, whose negative connotation gave meaning to "good customs" that met Spanish expectations of Christian civility and colonial governance. The dismantling of polygyny implied profound changes in Native norms of marriage, gender and sexuality, property holding, inheritance, residence, succession, and political alliance. In this regard, the Inquisition and the Native tribunal were key sites for the ongoing creation of the idea of colonial Native custom and its gendered dimensions. Native women, in their capacity as witnesses in select high-profile cases, were central to this process.

In Tetzcoco and Yanhuitlan, the 1530s and 1540s marked pivotal moments. Spanish and papal laws imposing monogamy and defining what constituted legitimate marriage for a Native society in transition to Spanish colonial rule set the table for conflict with Native lords who were keen to maintain pre-Hispanic norms. The trials of don Carlos and the lords of Yanhuitlan gave voice to political fissures within and between powerful Native polities and their subject communities, producing realignments of Native and Spanish authority. In both cases, the Native regimes that emerged from the ashes of the trials adopted a wholly different posture toward the missionaries and Spanish authority more broadly, publicly pronouncing their Christian bona fides and cooperating with Spanish administrative and economic impera- tives. At a much later moment and at a great distance from the colonial cen- ter, Native authorities of Oaxaca's rugged northern sierra demonstrated their fidelity to Dominican friars and Christian norms during the late seventeenth and early eighteenth centuries by persecuting Native villagers for adherence to the old law. Their public effort to align Native and Christian norms left traces in Zapotec notarial language.

The idea of marriage as a Christian sacrament and contractual obligation replaced the polygynous unions of old as the model of legitimate marriage. This process was bolstered by the Council of Trent and the Third Mexican Provincial Council, which took a rigid stand against practices that deviated from Christian monogamy, including concubinage and bigamy. It is worth noting that the contractual notion of marriage informed Native custom- ary practice during the centuries that followed. For example, last wills and testaments—a crucial element of Christian and European custom intro- duced to Native communities by the friars and incorporated into the practice of Indigenous self-governance—reveal a pattern established by the late six- teenth century in many regions of Mexico of bequeathing property to Chris- tian spouses in keeping with Spanish customs of inheritance. The wills show the persistence of crucial aspects of Indigenous material culture and social life as well as the transformative effect of Christian marriage on Native customs and their conceptual and practical foundations.[99] It is toward this contractual notion of custom and social obligation in the realms of Native landholding, self-governance, and labor—the primary categories for disputes over custom in the seventeenth and eighteenth centuries—that I turn in the following three chapters.

Custom in Oaxaca's Courts of First Instance

SEVENTEENTH THROUGH
EIGHTEENTH CENTURIES

Part III

Custom, Possession & Jurisdiction in the Boundary Lands   5

LAND REPRESENTED A NEXUS for Native customary claims in Mexico's colonial courts across three centuries of Spanish rule. The Crown recognized the lands of the Native nobility, who were considered Mexico's "natural lords" and known as caciques, as entailed estates under the designation of cacicazgo. The question of which noble lineages controlled what lands provoked much controversy, as did the use rights of commoners. From the 1530s through the 1570s, in response to challenges mounted by Native rivals or Spanish colonists, Native people appeared in front of the Real Audiencia to claim and dispute ownership or use rights based on pre-Hispanic custom. They often substantiated their claims with recourse to painted histories and maps. Drawing from Mesoamerican pictorial genres and conventions, and tailored for a Spanish audience, Native tlacuiloque (painter-scribes) produced these "juridical codices" specifically for use in colonial courts. The texts ranged from simple renditions of community boundaries to narratives of exquisite complexity.[1] Due to the moral authority that Spanish judges accorded to pre-Hispanic institutions and the practicality of maintaining aspects of Indigenous land tenure and labor, they often affirmed Native claims based on custom.[2] In doing so, though, they did not simply affirm old Native rights; they produced new ones by incorporating Native custom into a Spanish normative order.[3]

Native customary claims to land fell off considerably by the end of the sixteenth century, in part because of Spanish officials' changing attitudes toward the pre-Hispanic past and Indigenous forms of knowledge and also because of the exploitative economic demands of Spanish officials and colonists as well as the ravages of epidemic disease. In response to a precipitous decline in the Indigenous population, and with the ambition of nucleating the survivors into concentrated settlements to facilitate evangelization, corvée labor, and tribute collection, the missionaries spearheaded a program of forced resettlement, known as *congregación* or *reducción*, depending on the region. This took place in two waves, the first in the mid-sixteenth century from 1550 to 1564 and the second from the 1590s through the first decade of the seventeenth century.[4] Congregación and population decline displaced Native people from their ancestral land and left much of it vacated, opening Native communities to expropriation by Spanish colonists.[5] In order to stem the chaotic expansion of Spanish property and harness land distribution and titling to royal power, Philip II issued a royal cédula in 1591 requiring Spanish colonists to present their land claims and titles so that they could be validated by Spanish law. If they possessed land but had no title, they could acquire one for a fee. Any vacant lands without proper title—known as *tierras baldías*, or simply *baldíos*—would escheat to the Crown so that they could be used, sold, or distributed at royal discretion.[6] The fees would go into the royal treasury to ameliorate the Crown's ailing finances. The royal land titling program, known as the *composiciones de tierras*, persisted through the seventeenth century, allowing for a massive transfer of lands from Indigenous to Spanish control.[7]

Native authorities went to court to defend communal lands, and they presented varied forms of evidence to prove possession and make customary claims to land use and tenure, including Spanish legal instruments that recognized Native possession. Native authorities also resorted to Indigenous knowledge and forms of representation to support their claims, despite Spanish disinclination to take such evidence seriously. These included maps that blended European and Indigenous styles, and a genre of painted histories and genealogies known as the Techialoyan codices (figs. 5.1, 5.2).[8]

Native towns also generated a written genre of Native-language documents known as primordial titles that recounted the migration of the community's founding ancestors, the marking of territorial boundaries, the consecration of the community's church, and the establishment of the Native cabildo (municipal council).[9] Across these encapsulations of Indigenous memory, Native writers and painters reimagined antiquity, the anchor of custom, by blending pre-Hispanic and colonial symbols, histories, and chronologies.[10] Despite Native efforts to stem the tide of dispossession, however, the composiciones de tierras continued to transform Indigenous lands into Spanish haciendas and ranches in many regions of New Spain and across Spanish America.[11]

The recovery of the Indigenous population at the end of the seventeenth century combined with the Crown's desperate need to generate revenue to pay for its expensive imperial wars created a shift in land policy, which in turn reinvigorated Native claims to land. Until 1691, the policy of composición applied to Spanish and mestizo colonists, but from 1692 forward, the Crown widened its net to require Native towns to title their lands. In order to do so, they needed to prove possession since time immemorial and pay a "voluntary donation" to the Crown to have their lands surveyed and their boundaries marked. Royal regulations required that communal lands, known in Spanish as *fundo legal* or *bienes de comunidad*, should measure at minimum six hundred *varas* in diameter, from the village church or the center of the pueblo outward. Any territory beyond the limits of officially designated communal land lacking documentation of ownership had to be titled for a fee. If not, it could be declared royal land and subject to confiscation and public auction.[12]

Native participation in the composiciones of the 1692–96, 1707–9, 1717–18, and the composiciones that followed in the rest of the eighteenth century produced a range of results, including Native land titles, the reduction of the extent of Native communal lands, and official recognition of customary and "irregular" forms of land tenure that sat at the margins of the law.[13] Prior to the eighteenth century, most Native communities possessed land rather than owned it, since securing or producing title of ownership was more difficult than claiming possession in Spanish courts.[14] Possession constituted a primary means by which individuals and communities held land in the Spanish Empire, and the Mediterranean-Atlantic world more broadly.[15] The *Siete Partidas* defined possession as lawfully entering, occupying, and holding a piece of land, a concept that was distinct from ownership, which required legal title. Central to this definition was the absence of force or coercion, which made a claim to possession unlawful and unjust. Evidence of possession included long-standing use and cultivation, manifested by crops or structures.[16] The community's judgment often determined the legitimacy of claims to possession in courts of law, expressed by the stock phrase "since time immemorial," which often served as a "category of proof, rather than a measure of time."[17] Immemoriality usually signaled that there was no tangible proof to substantiate the claim, and the presumption of continuous practice as attested to by high-status and respectable witnesses often sufficed to

Figure 5.1
Mexican noble
genealogy,
Techialoyan
Codex García
Granados.

Figure 5.2 Hapsburg Heraldic Shield, Techialoyan Codex García Granados.

legitimize possession. Judges' rulings in favor of immemoriality were in keeping with Spanish juridical culture, which construed law not as a structured application of rules or norms but as "a continuously open process of normative production in which primacy was given to existing states of affairs."[18] Whereas titles carried heavy weight as evidence of ownership, so too did local practice and the status quo as accepted and recognized by the community. In this regard, possession shared many of the same underlying warrants as custom in the European ius commune and the Spanish imperial context.

This chapter analyzes Native claims to customary land tenure and possession since time immemorial in response to the composiciones de tierras and other challenges to communal territory in the Mixteca region of Oaxaca. The land titling program dovetailed with the expansion of the livestock economy, population growth, and an increase in tribute and taxes during the late seventeenth and eighteenth centuries. In a context of increasing scarcity and pressure to normalize landholding, many Native communities went to court with competing claims to land. But conflict and litigation were not the only strategies deployed by Native authorities to address the need for subsistence and income. Indigenous communities also came together to create plural ownership that allowed them to pool resources and share territorial jurisdiction. Partnership contracts—the form in which plural ownership was legally instantiated—were more legible to Spanish authorities than codices, maps, and primordial titles and had practical benefits since they were much less costly than litigation. Through partnership contracts, Native authorities preserved or extended the territorial expanses of their communities, challenged or whittled away at the property of powerful caciques, and transformed customary claims into new legal rights with an eye to securing the territorial integrity of their communities for the future.

Ñudzahui Territory, Land Tenure, and a 1690 Partnership Contract

Oaxaca provides a counternarrative to Native dispossession during the early rounds of composiciones de tierras of the sixteenth and seventeenth centuries. In fact, most Native nobles and communities in Oaxaca maintained their landholdings from the conquest until the end of the colonial period. Oaxaca's economy, which was dominated by commerce and fueled by Indigenous production rather than mining and Spanish-controlled haciendas, provides a central explanation for this trend.[19] In the case of the Mixteca region, the few Spaniards who settled there rented land from Native nobles and communities and focused their energies on trading in the valuable products of Native labor, most notably cochineal dyestuff, wheat, cattle, leather, and cloth.[20]

The persistence of Native landholding meant that community land tenure remained deeply informed by Indigenous notions of territory, which did not conform to clearly delineated boundaries. In the Mixteca, this fungible relationship was expressed by the Ñudzahui institution of the yuhuitayu, sometimes shortened to tayu, a political entity made up of two communities (ñuu) joined through the marital alliance of lords from each, as discussed in chapters 2 and 4. The yuhuitayu was not a geographical designation, as was a European kingdom or señorial estate, but rather a shifting mosaic of constituent communities and subunits, known as *ñuu*, that periodically realigned depending on elite intermarriage and the tributary claims of their lords. Often, they were not contiguous territories, nor evenly distributed geographically. A small settlement in close proximity to the palace complex of one yuhuitayu might have been subject to or affiliated with another yuhuitayu. Autonomy often defined the relations of the ñuu within the yuhuitayu and between individual ñuu and the seat of the yuhuitayu. Although lordly marriage served to combine the resources of the constituent ñuu, it did not compromise the autonomy of either. Sometimes ñuu seceded from yuhuitayu and shifted allegiances to others.[21]

The yuhuitayu as a form of territorial and political organization endured well into the eighteenth century, though it had been modified somewhat by the late sixteenth- and early seventeenth-century process of congregación, spearheaded by Dominican missionaries. The effort to impose the Spanish administrative arrangement of the cabecera (administrative and parish seat, literally "head town") and its *sujetos* ("subjects"), which were geographically proximate and politically subordinate villages or dependencies and whose residents owed tribute and labor to the authorities of the cabecera, met with only modest success. Dispersed settlement patterns persisted, and many ñuu maintained their identities, locations, and lands. The territorial imprint of the yuhuitayu persisted through the colonial period, as did its political meaning, as evidenced by the pervasive use of the term in Ñudzahui-language documentation.[22]

Although it did not affect territorial organization as much as Spanish officials had intended, the imposition of the cabecera-sujeto model had important political implications for intercommunity relationships. Spanish officials designated some yuhuitayu, and not others, as cabeceras, and recognized some lords (*yya*) as caciques by granting them title to cacicazgos, while discounting the claims of others. The yuhuitayu that were assigned the lesser status of subject towns resisted the imposition of new hierarchies strongly, bringing legal cases to the Audiencia of Mexico from the 1550s forward in which they argued for the right to secede from their cabeceras. In their petitions, they railed against paying tribute and performing services for cabeceras and caciques, and they were aggrieved that their neighbors, as parish seats, had become the centers for sacred rituals.[23] For their part, caciques and cabeceras took advantage of their status, and competition between yuhuitayu took new forms, including legal disputes over the boundary lands that separated communities, which, according to Ñudzahui *lienzos* (Indigenous cartographic histories painted on cloth), included sacred sites.[24] These conflicts heated up at the end of the seventeenth century as the Indigenous population recovered from its devastating decline during the previous century and as the livestock economy expanded. Both developments put new pressures on land.[25]

Royal legislation at the end of seventeenth century contributed to the tensions. In 1687 the Crown issued a cédula that granted subject communities the same expanse of lands that had previously been reserved for cabeceras: six hundred varas radiating outward from the town church. The idea was to provide expanding settlements with the territorial foundation necessary for subsistence agriculture and pastureland. Consequently, many subject communities built churches, had their land surveyed, and declared themselves independent cabeceras in their own right, to the chagrin of the authorities of their former cabeceras.[26]

Litigation in Spanish courts provided one answer to these conflicts, though not a desirable one because it was expensive and time consuming. Native authorities turned to other means to address land disputes, pivoting away from Spanish courts and attempting to resolve conflict within the ambit of Native jurisdiction. A 1690 Ñudzahui-language notarial record documenting a land-use agreement between the communities of San Juan Sayultepec and San Andrés Sinaxtla provides an example. As occurred with many Native-language legal records, the 1690 agreement was sewn into a voluminous 438-page land dispute between the two communities, adjudicated in a Spanish court across three and a half decades, between 1713 and 1749.[27]

The 1690 Ñudzahui-language record was a genre of contract, whose origins can be traced to the concept of partnership (*societas*) in Roman law. In contrast to commercial contracts, which were reciprocal in nature (one party does something to receive something else from another party) and presumed an opposition of interests, the purpose of partnership contracts was to pool resources, such as property or labor, for a common purpose, and sometimes

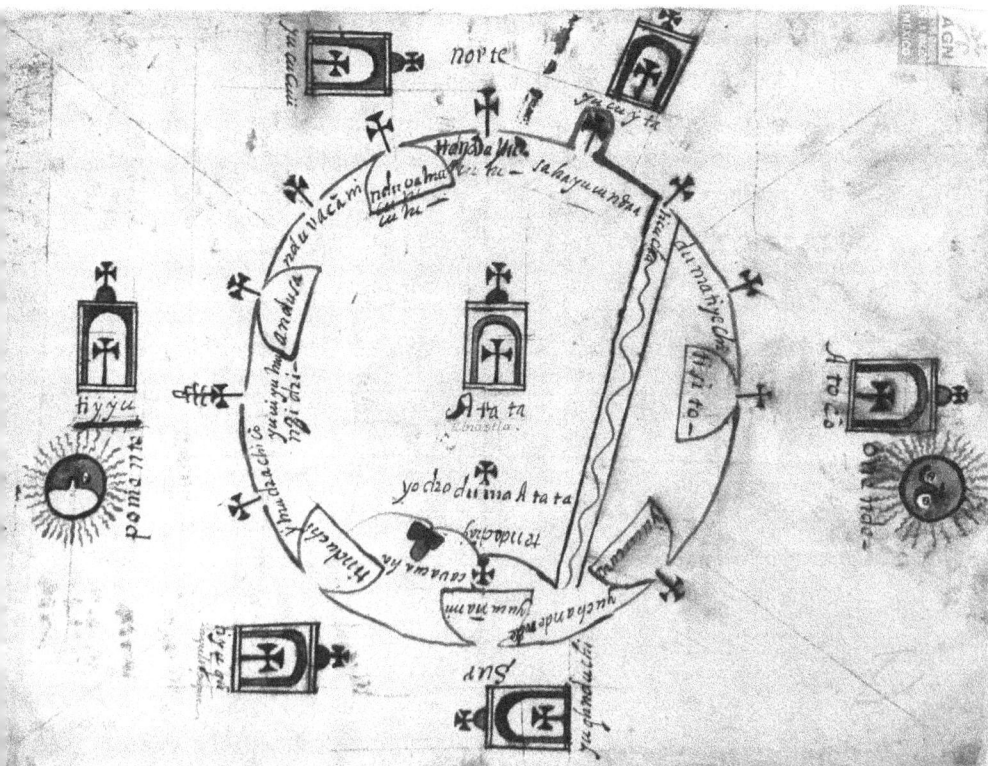

Figure 5.3 Radial map of San Andrés Sinaxtla (Atata) showing Indigenous conception of territory. AGN, Tierras, 1690, no. 0670, vol. 308, exp. 4, fol. 29, Fondo Hermanos Mayo, concentrados, sobre 363.

against the interests of a third party. Partners in *societas* were friends and allies rather than antagonists.[28]

Through the Ñudzahui-language contract, the Native authorities of San Juan Sayultepec and San Andrés Sinaxtla aligned the relationship among *yuhuitayu* into the Spanish relation of partnership. In the text of the contract, they referred to their communities as "chayu" (a variation of "tayu," short for *yuhuitayu*) instead of using the Spanish designations of *cabecera* and *sujeto*. For place-names, they used Christian-Ñudzahui hybrids rather than the Christian-Nahuatl names imposed on their communities by Spanish and Mexica conquerors: San Juan Sayultepec was written as "Sa Juan tiyuqh" and San Andrés Sinaxtla as "San Andrés atata" (fig. 5.3).

The Native authorities stated that the purpose of the contract was to protect the agricultural lands of the two communities against the territorial predations of a third community, Santa María Asunción Nochixtlan, an important pre-Hispanic and colonial-era commercial and political center. In the 1680s, Nochixtlan, which had been part of the Spanish province of Teposcolula-Yanhuitlan, became a Spanish administrative seat, with jurisdiction over the pueblos of Tilantongo, Chachoapan, Etlatongo, Huaclilla, Tejutepec, Tiltepec, and Jaltepec.[29] The concentration of Spanish and Indigenous political power in Nochixtlan produced tensions with Sinaxtla and Sayultepec, powerful Native communities in their own right. Perhaps emboldened by newfound status, the Native authorities of Nochixtlan saw an opportunity for territorial expansion. In the text of the contract, the officials of Sayultepec and Sinaxtla expressed their common outrage that the Natives of Nochixtlan sought to expropriate valuable irrigated land where cornfields cultivated by each community came together at the boundary among all three towns.

Through their partnership, the officials of Sayultepec and Sinaxtla joined together in common cause against another mutual antagonist: the cacique don Domingo de San Pablo. The narrative of the agreement devoted significant space to a shared past in which the communities united in "friendship" against the cacique and the authorities of the town of San Mateo Yucucuhui who made heavy demands of them, presumably in labor and tribute. The authorities of Sayultepec and Sinaxtla stated that they would no longer recognize don Domingo or any other Native lord as their cacique and that "only the lord God and lord King are our lords."[30] Their refusal to recognize the cacique's customary authority tracked with broader trends of declining cacique power across the Mixteca and in other regions of New Spain and the Andes.[31] Economic and cultural transformations spurred by colonialism created greater social distance between caciques and Indigenous commoners and prompted legal disputes that intensified during the eighteenth century.

In the Mixteca, Spanish entailment of cacicazgos in the early colonial period transformed don Domingo de San Pablo and other Native lords into a powerful rentier class who earned significant income from the lease of their lands to Spaniards, mestizos, and other Natives. Don Domingo and other Ñudzahui caciques like him were often wealthier than the region's Spanish merchants, and they had the goods to show it: luxurious European clothing, horses, high-quality wooden and silver home furnishings, and elaborate Christian art. Their easy assimilation to Christianity and migration to urban centers where they could live comfortably off their earnings expanded the cultural gap between themselves and Ñudzahui commoners. Caciques' detachment from their pueblos loosened the reciprocal obligations that bound them to their communities, stoked resentments, and led to what one historian has called the eighteenth-century "revolt against the caciques." The revolt was expressed in the courts, where pueblos sued caciques to protest unjust demands and abuses of authority.[32]

Disavowal of don Domingo in the contract may have had something to do with the land under dispute, in that it could have pertained to his cacicazgo. By claiming that they did not recognize don Domingo as their cacique, the authorities of Sinaxtla and Sayultepec cleared the way to claim possession of the land for their communities, which if it had belonged to don Domingo, they might have worked through usufruct in the past. The remainder of the contract recounted legal procedures typical for recognizing possession, including a boundary survey and placement of boundary markers in order to preclude controversy in the future. The fact that the Native authorities of the two communities conducted a land survey and produced a legal agreement on their own, without the presence of a Spanish court functionary, points to an autonomous Native forum and set of procedures for addressing conflicts over boundary lands.

The agreement closed with a reassertion of friendship and partnership. Behind the aspiration of social harmony, however, lingered some doubt. The contract closed with the stipulation that if any member of either community were to disturb the peace, the officials of either pueblo could appeal to the Real Audiencia, the highest colonial court in the land, which would ensure the maintenance of the agreement. With this clause, the signatories concurred that only the king's justice could enforce the partnership between the communities.[33]

This legal instrument was written, then, with an eye to preventing conflict in the future, not only with Nochixtlan but also between its authors, the communities of Sinaxtla and Sayultepec. Although it was written in the Ñudzahui language and archived in the town halls of the signatories, the Native authorities produced it with an eye to presenting it to a Spanish judge as evidence of possession in the boundary lands, the most liminal and vulnerable part of a community's territorial grant, and where friends of the moment could become enemies in the future. This indeed came to pass. As discussed previously, the officials of San Juan Sayultepec submitted the agreement as evidence in a land dispute with Sinaxtla in 1713, arguing that the Natives of Sinaxtla had broken its terms by claiming the land as their own.

The 1690 partnership contract written and signed by the Native authorities of Sayultepec and Sinaxtla embodies core elements of Indigenous territorial and political organization. At the same time, it reveals how the European legal category of possession shaped intercommunal relations in the boundary lands between Ñudzahui communities and how customary claims to land could be used to instantiate new rights through written agreements. The ephemerality of the agreement and its incorporation into a future land dispute point to an important dynamic in Oaxaca's agrarian history during the late seventeenth and eighteenth centuries. Partnership contracts were but one component in *longue durée* struggles over land. Although they were supposed to endure, they often did not. Rather than etching the contours and conditions of communal land in stone, they represented a reprieve from open conflict and a space for the renegotiation of political and territorial relationships.

This process of territorialization and reterritorialization through legal disputing over boundary lands was not unique to colonial Mexico or Spanish America but occurred throughout the Atlantic World. In her landmark work comparing land disputes on the Portuguese and Spanish frontiers in Europe and the Americas, the historian Tamar Herzog chronicles a long-term conflict among the neighboring communities of Aroche, Encinasola, Moura, Noudar, Barrancos, and Serpa on the boundary between Andalucía (Spain) and Alentejo (Portugal) that began at the end of the thirteenth century and ended sometime in the nineteenth. The disputed land sat between the communities, and residents from opposing sides burned crops, sequestered animals, and even resorted to occasional murder to drive one another off the land and claim it for themselves. In 1542 representatives of the Spanish and Portuguese Crowns insisted that the communities sign an agreement that instantiated common use of the land and shared Spanish-Portuguese jurisdiction overseen locally by the towns of Aroche and Moura. The document, which served as a kind of local treaty, became foundational to making claims to customary land rights in the centuries that followed. Its very existence and continued relevance through the centuries underscore the points that like their Indigenous counterparts in the Americas, Iberian rural communities did not conform to clearly delineated boundaries. They shared boundary lands, fought bitterly over them, and enshrined customary claims in written agreements to produce new kinds of rights.[34] In a recent study of late seventeenth- and eighteenth-century rural France, the historian Rafe Blaufarb shows how peasants sued their lords over land rights and signed partnership contracts with them as a means of securing access to land and ensuring social peace. Often, these agreements held temporarily, ushering in a new wave of legal negotiations over land tenure and use, resulting in an ongoing reformulation of the agrarian order.[35] As these examples demonstrate, partnership contracts constituted a transatlantic strategy used by rural communities to negotiate land rights. In this regard, the authorities of Sayultepec and Sinaxtla were actively contributing to an Atlantic world legal culture as they forged their Ñudzahui-language agreement in their rural town hall in the Mixteca.

Partnership and Plural Ownership in the Eighteenth-Century Composiciones de Tierras

The eighteenth-century composiciones de tierras provided an opportunity for Ñudzahui communities to reaffirm customary landholding patterns in their boundary lands, while creating new legal norms. Whereas the communities of Sayultepec and Sinaxtla achieved this temporarily within the ambit of Indian jurisdiction, the special court of land titling constituted a higher-order legal forum in which Native officials could negotiate customary access to boundary lands. In July 1717, the Native authorities of the Ñudzahui communities of Tecomatlan and Magdalena Zahuatlan appeared before don Félix Chacón, Spanish magistrate of Teposcolula-Yanhuitlan, with such a petition. The land bureau tasked with overseeing the composiciones de tierras—the Superintendencia del Beneficio y Composición de Tierras—had appointed Chacón as judge to the royal commission of claims, titling, and sale of land and water in the district of Teposcolula-Yanhuitlan. In this role, he was tasked with overseeing agrarian matters, especially payment for the composiciones de tierras.[36] The court that he administered for this purpose was known as the Juzgado Privativo de Tierras.[37]

The Native authorities' petition requested a license to form a partnership contract regarding possession of some land that lay in between their communities, much like the written agreements produced by Sayultepec and Sinaxtla, and the Iberian towns of Aroche, Moura, and others. In the recent past, the Natives of each town had claimed the land as their own. With forensic detail, the officials related the Ñudzahui place-names that the land encompassed, citing the river that contoured it and the location of three crosses that served as boundary markers (fig. 5.4).

The problem was that although both towns had asserted possession, in actuality, farmers from both communities planted corn on it, such that their crops were interspersed. According to Spanish law, occupation manifested by cultivation proved legal possession, so barring the existence of legal title to the land, this dispute would be difficult to resolve in court, a point that the Native authorities understood well. In order to preclude competing le-

Figure 5.4 Crosses as present-day boundary markers in Sierra Norte of Oaxaca. Photograph by author.

gal claims to the land and costly litigation in the future, the two towns had arrived at an agreement to share the land and preserve the custom of interwoven cultivation. Apparently, though, the agreement between the two communities was not enough, which is why they petitioned Judge Chacón to intervene and authorize their agreement. Through the flourish of the Spanish judge's pen, the agreement would produce a relationship of joint possession over the land, valid for all time, equal in force to a decision rendered by a civil judge. In short, the contract would fix the towns' customary use of the boundary lands unless a third party produced a title to the land.[38]

By 1717, the year that the officials of Tecomatlan and Zahuatlan petitioned Judge Felix Chacón to form the partnership, the population of the core region of the Mixteca Alta had jumped from twenty-eight thousand in 1660 to forty-two thousand in 1720, on an upward trajectory that increased to seventy-six thousand by 1803.[39] In the meantime, two rounds of composiciones de tierras had taken place, from 1692 to 1696 and 1707 to 1709, with a third underway from 1717 to 1718, sending Native caciques and communities to Spanish courts to obtain titles to land and firm up their territorial boundaries. The trends that had pushed the communities of Sayultepec and Sinaxtla to form their partnership contract in 1690 had intensified: population growth, commercialization of agriculture, expansion of the livestock industry, increased pressure on land and resources, and an explosion of litigation over land.

As spelled out in their petition, the Native officials of Tecomatlan and Zahuatlan did not seek to clarify their boundaries in order to produce land titles for their pueblos. Rather, they hoped to maintain the custom of interwoven cultivation in their borderlands. As evident in their petition to Chacón, the Native officials surveyed the boundary lands and consulted with one another to hammer out some of the fundamental terms of the agreement. The composiciones de tierras provided them with a unique opportunity to give agrarian custom the force of law and protect landholdings from the predations of third parties, like caciques or larger pueblos.

Judge Felix Chacón was persuaded by the petition and granted the towns of Tecomatlan and Zahuatlan the license they sought to draw up the partnership contract.[40] From where he stood, peaceful relations between pueblos were always preferable to rancor and the threat of violence over boundary lands. Furthermore, whereas a primary goal of the composiciones was to make boundaries and titles, another goal, far more pragmatic—and opportunistic since it implied a fee—was to codify customary uses of land that sat on the margins of the law.

Partnership contracts regarding land tenure were as much an agreement about the nature of the partnership—the ties that bound Native communities to one another—as about the relationship of the communities to the land. This was evident in the 1690 Ñudzahui-language contract between Sayultepec and Sinaxtla, in which the political purpose of the partnership was intertwined with the integrity of each community's landed possessions at the boundaries. The partnership proposed by Tecomatlan and Zahuatlan was different in that the two communities had asked for recognition of an arrangement that did not align with the Spanish ideal of a territorially bounded community. Since the communities would be farming the lands together, the question of who would be responsible for material losses if one party did not uphold the agreement—in short, questions of harm, injury, liability, restitution, and enforcement—had to be taken into account. This required the intervention of a Spanish judge.

According to the Spanish laws of obligation, the nature of partnership depended on how liability and damages for breaking an agreement should be distributed among the partners. Roman law, a foundation of Castilian law, distinguished between joint obligation and proportionate obligation, that is, between the idea that all signatories were fully liable for a debt in its entirety versus the idea that each signatory was responsible for his share. Proportionate liability provided the default assumption in Roman contract law. If the partners or co-owners preferred joint liability, it had to be specially signaled in the language of the contract or through some sort of legal provision.[41]

In its provisions for co-ownership of property, the *Siete Partidas* adopted from Roman law the preference for proportionate liability. Partida V, which treats the laws of obligation, states that the property and profits of partners bound to one another by a contract should be shared, as should all damages and losses.[42] Early modern Spanish law followed suit. In Title XVI of the *Novissima Recopilación de las Leyes del Reino* (the compilation of early modern Spanish legislation), "On Contracts, Obligations, credit, debt, and debt payment," the first law stipulates that if two parties entered jointly into a contract as debtors, each was responsible for half of the debt unless they stated expressly that they were both liable for the debt in its entirety.[43] The idea of proportionate obligation was expressed in Spanish as "mancomunidad" (literally "common hand," figuratively, commonly held through partnership), whereas the idea of joint obligation was expressed by a combination of Spanish and Latin terms, "de mancomún, in solidum."

Although Roman law preferred proportionate liability, joint liability provided a perfectly reasonable alternative within a Roman legal culture that privileged individualism. However, it troubled many medieval Castilian jurists and theologians who were strongly influenced by Christian ideas of community. In their eyes, the scholastic principle of equity, which informed Spanish legal philosophy and ideas of justice, did not square with the notion that if one partner to a contract did not pay his share of debt, the creditor could go after the other partner for the amount in full. It seemed neither fair nor just. Joint obligation should therefore be used in special circumstances and serve as the exception rather than the rule. Moral discomfort led Spanish jurists to fold joint obligation into canon and civil laws concerning suretyship (*fianza*), a relationship in which someone guaranteed the debt or obligation of another.[44]

As global commerce expanded, concerns about equity began to give way to concerns about utility and profit, a shift that could be seen as early as the seventeenth century in Spanish judges' views of Indigenous landholding.[45] A change to the Spanish laws of obligation in the mid-seventeenth century reflected this shift, tipping the scales toward joint liability through *in solidum* partnerships as a more common norm. In an increasingly complex and risky world of trade, merchants and lawyers felt that if one partner defaulted on a debt, creditors should have the right to go after the other for payment in full. According to Pedro de Sigüenza's popular 1663 notarial manual, in order to enforce this more rigorous mode of obligation, the signatories to a partnership contract had to renounce the laws of "duobus Reis debendite el autentica prescorte cobdice del fide jusoribus," the clauses of the Justinian Code that prescribed partial liability.[46] The laws of "duobus Reis" were known in Spanish as the *leyes de mancomunidad*.[47] The next step was for the partners to enter into a relationship of "mancomún, in solidum," signaling joint liability, in which each was responsible for the debt in its entirety.[48]

The laws of obligation—contract law—in the Americas were essentially those of Spain.[49] So when Spanish and Native authorities brokered agreements and wrote up contracts, they drew upon the principles laid out in the *Siete Partidas* and *Novissima Recopilación* and incorporated joint liability into the framework of partnerships. In their 1717 contract of joint jurisdiction and possession, the authorities of Tecomatlan and Zahuatlan entered into a partnership of joint liability, in which the Native authorities of both pueblos renounced the laws of "duobus Reis" and "mancomunidad" in favor of the obligation of "mancomún in solidum." This notarial formula appears with frequency in contracts of varied sorts entered into by Native officials, such as letters of attorney that gave power of attorney to an individual to conduct legal business on behalf of the pueblo for a fee and rental contracts in which Native officials leased communal lands to an individual or another pueblo for the benefit of the municipal treasury.[50] Partnership contracts were different from rental agreements and letters of attorney in that they did not involve the exchange of money or services but rather the delineation of the terms of a mutually beneficial relationship. In the case of partnership contracts between Indigenous communities, joint liability meant that every member of the pueblo had to comply fully with the contracts' stipulations, even though the document was signed only by the Native officers. And any member of the pueblo who broke the agreement had to pay the stipulated damages in full.

The partnership contract signed by the authorities of Tecomatlan and Zahuatlan entailed a promise to one another to uphold special rules and mutual obligations regarding land use. Preservation of customary agrarian practice, harmonious relations between the two communities, and collective possession of the land provided the contract's stated purpose. The first of its five clauses indicated that the lands that the Natives of each pueblo cultivated would be the lands that they continued to cultivate without alteration. The language used to express this—"*sin ynnovar* en cosa alguna"—was also part of the medieval Spanish discourse of custom, which was double-edged: it preserved long-standing, continuous practice but at the same time could be altered and established anew, as discussed in chapter 1. Custom's flexibility allowed for change and adaptation, but in this case the Native authorities adopted a staunchly conservative posture toward it in their attempt to preclude any innovation. Part of the fifth clause underscored the imperative to preserve custom by stipulating that if the Natives of one pueblo or the other had more of fewer crops in the commonly held lands, they should not try to sow them equally; instead, each pueblo should sow what they presently sowed even if some of the lands remained baldíos (uncultivated lands). The importance of maintaining the status quo "in order to avoid disputes" was accentuated by the risk implied in leaving untitled lands uncultivated. The policy of the composiciones program held that untitled and uncultivated land could be confiscated by the Crown via invocation of eminent domain, to be redistributed according to royal discretion. Despite the risk, the second clause held that the land would remain untitled: neither pueblo nor Natives therein could claim legal title to it. The Native authorities appear to have counted on the contract as a form of insurance against expropriation, a process that could be triggered by an *amparo*, or judicial stay based on legal documents that provided evidence of possession. The objective of maintaining good relations between the pueblos and avoiding litigation was telegraphed clearly through the contract's fourth clause, which maintained that the pueblos "must conserve and continue always the peace, union, and law-abiding manner in which they have lived without disputes." The remainder of the fifth clause sought to preserve the peace by precluding the land invasions that were increasingly common in the region: each pueblo would possess and continue to possess its parcels without entering into one another's lands.

At the same time that it aimed to shore up horizontal and equitable relations between the pueblos, the contract reinforced the hierarchies of status and power that structured Ñudzahui communities. The final clause prescribed punishment for any member of the pueblo who broke the agreement. The punishments varied according to social status, reproducing the distinction between commoners and principales. Unlike caciques, principales were not recognized as "natural lords" or granted landed estates (cacicazgos) by the Spanish administration in the years following the conquest. Instead, they hailed from the lesser ranks of the Indigenous nobility and, as such, were distinguished from commoners by their wealth and inherited status, often manifested by generations of office holding. They were the middling stratum of Indigenous society, held high offices in the Native cabildo, and when they did not hold office, served as informal advisors to the cabildo. Their special status was reflected in the contract: if a principal were to break the agreement, he would be fined 100 pesos common gold (*oro común*), half destined for the judge of the Real Camara and half for the compliant party. If the perpetrator were a *macehual* (commoner), the punishment would be two hundred lashes. The penalty of two hundred lashes was serious business; it constituted the common punishment for highway robbery, murder, and sedition, and could easily lead to the death of the person to whom it was applied. The disparity in punishment was in keeping with Spanish criminal law, which applied punishment unequally according to social rank and advised harsher punishment for commoners.[51] In this case as in many, Spanish law served a conservative function in Indigenous communities, reinforcing Native social hierarchy.

The contract was meant to be iron clad, legally speaking. The Native authorities left no open loopholes in their legal effort to "conserve" the land and labor arrangement and the peace that the two pueblos had enjoyed "since time immemorial." Pointedly, it stated that not only would breaking the contract result in punishment for the individual perpetrators; breaking part or all of the contract would result in its revalidation and authorization, even if new contingencies were introduced. At the end of the contract, both pueblos renounced the right to dissolve it based on claims of a fraudulent exchange, explicitly citing the pertinent law in the medieval Spanish code of the Ordenamiento de Alcalá.[52] By renouncing the law, they ensured that "no one could speak or move against the agreement because of this law or any other reason." Although commercial contracts authorized by Spanish notaries were supposed to be valid for a designated period of time after which they had to be renewed or discontinued, this contract was written so as to be legally valid in perpetuity, as if "it were a decision [*sentencia*] rendered by a civil judge." The contract stipulated that those who opposed it would not be heard by a judge and would be punished. If challenged in court, the agreement would be revalidated and authorized anew, giving it renewed judicial force.

Perhaps most importantly, the contract required each pueblo to renounce its own jurisdiction over the land and transfer jurisdiction to one another in order to produce joint jurisdiction. Additionally, each pueblo had to renounce legal claim to the lands and transfer possession to one another to produce joint ownership and remain "equal pueblos." Property and jurisdiction were separate but related legal categories as applied to Indigenous communities. Property pertained to the community land base and jurisdiction to authority over the people and territory of the community. Joint ownership meant that both communities possessed the land. Joint jurisdiction implied authority over the land, the capacity to determine its use, and the power to punish those who transgressed the laws that applied to it. The clause about joint jurisdiction was in keeping with transatlantic developments in legal agreements regarding collective land tenure in which the emphasis was as much on the right to administer common lands and resources as a means of conserving and defending them from encroachment by third parties as it was on possession and ownership.[53]

A final aspect of the contract bears scrutiny in its special treatment of what both Spaniards and Natives referred to as the "business of Indians." The contract stipulated that if the equilibrium between the pueblos created through joint ownership were to tip out of balance such that one pueblo owed money to the other for labor or production, the debtor should give it freely as a gift—"donación graciosa" or "intervivo"—as the law provided. *Inter vivos* donations represented a pillar of customary exchange in medieval and early modern Europe.[54] According to the *Novissima Recopilación*, a *donación* (gift) at its most basic level was the irrevocable transference of the right to an object or good by one person to another. Gifts were given most frequently among family members and in two modes: the first, when the giver was living (in Latin, *inter vivos*), and the second, through a last will and testament, upon the giver's death.[55] Recompense for breach of contract through a mode of exchange reserved primarily for transference of property and goods among family members reflected the idea, rooted in Roman law, that the obligations that governed a family should govern a republic and that family law provided the foundation of civil law.[56] The partnership contract between Tecomatlan and Zahuatlan manifested this idea in a form particular to the Spanish colonial context: each Indigenous community was a republic—a family writ large—in the eyes of civil law.

Don Félix Chacón authorized a second partnership contract during the 1717–18 composiciones de tierras to which Tecomatlan was a signatory. Tecomatlan and the pueblo of San Francisco Jaltepetongo, one of its subject towns, petitioned Chacón to authorize a written agreement that would allow both towns to cultivate contested lands in which their cornfields were interspersed and graze their cattle on the land. The fields sown and cultivated by each pueblo would remain in the possession of each, and the Natives of the other pueblo should not enter them. The grazing lands would remain common, and no rent could be charged for grazing.[57]

The decision to share cropland and pastureland, each in close proximity to the other, ran counter to regional trends to commoditize uncultivated land for grazing, pit cultivation against pastoralism, and litigate over boundary lands. The dramatic expansion of the livestock economy of the Mixteca during the late seventeenth and early eighteenth centuries transformed agrarian relations, in particular the ways in which Indigenous people perceived and used the fluid borderlands between ñuu. Borderlands tended to encompass forested lands on high ridges where the people of adjacent communities could collect firewood, berries, plants, and small game without disturbing the cropland of their neighbors. The destructiveness of wandering sheep and goats, which were pastured on these tierras baldías (uncultivated lands), became a lightning rod for intercommunal conflict and a primary cause of litigation.[58] In the case of Tecomatlan and Jaltepetongo, rather than taking one another to court, the two communities found a way to accommodate competing pressures while maintaining the customary agricultural practice of interwoven cultivation. The contract stipulated that neither pueblo could claim the boundary lands as their exclusive property, and the pueblo of San Francisco would possess two parcels that lay between lands possessed by Tecomatlan, a pattern of land tenure that likely had its roots in the yuhuitayu. As with the contract celebrated between Tecomatlan and Zahuatlan, the horizontal bonds between ñuu were counterbalanced by social hierarchy articulated by unequal punishment for breaking the terms of the agreement: payment of fifty pesos of oro común to the parish church of the other community for principales and two hundred lashes for commoners.

The partnership contracts for collective land tenure celebrated by Tecomatlan and its neighboring subject towns expressed a growing class division between elites and commoners manifested by the unequal burden of compliance based on status. At the dawn of the eighteenth century, commoners' access to land was limited to the communal holdings (*bienes comunales*) of pueblos, and as a result, many of them worked as tenant farmers on cacique lands. To be sure, unequal distribution of resources and social stratification marked pre-Hispanic and early colonial Ñudzahui society, but bonds of reciprocity mitigated social divisions. The legal regime of property combined with the commercialization of agriculture in the region, which accelerated during the eighteenth century, transformed traditional Native social hierarchies into starker class divisions.[59]

At the same time, in the customary pattern of interwoven cultivation and the horizontal bonds of reciprocity and equality between pueblos that it upheld, the contracts reproduced intercommunal relations characteristic of the yuhuitayu. Tecomatlan had been a yuhuitayu prior to the Spanish conquest, and after the first congregaciones, it became a subject town of Yanhuitlan, which the Spaniards designated as cabecera. The nobility of Tecomatlan chafed against the town's newly subordinate status and attempted to secede from Yanhuitlan in the 1580s by appealing to the Real Audiencia of Mexico. Tecomatlan lost this case but a century later achieved cabecera status in the courts.[60] As the population grew and commoners looked to expand their limited access to land, the composiciones de tierras of 1717 provided an opportunity for Tecomatlan's subject communities to order their relationships in a way that reinstated the equitable bonds among the ñuu of a yuhuitayu while creating a legal mechanism for social discipline of commoners.

For their part, Tecomatlan's Native authorities, who benefited from the community's status as cabecera, likely saw the writing on the wall: better to share borderlands and resources as "equal pueblos" than face the scourge of litigation and secession by its subject pueblos. The diffuse settlement pattern in the Mixteca meant that many communities with small populations that cultivated widely dispersed lands could claim that they possessed the minimum territory required to obtain a bona fide title—600 varas measured from the town church—which put them on legitimate footing to secede from their administrative seats and become cabeceras, a process that accelerated through the eighteenth century with the composiciones. Contracts of joint possession and cooperative use of land provided a strategy for Native officials of large communities to share land and power and avoid territorial and political fragmentation.

Spanish judges authorized other contracts during the 1717–18 composiciones de tierras that followed the logic of the contracts celebrated by Tecomatlan and its neighbors: in order to preserve intercommunal peace and avoid the expense and rancor of litigation, the authorities of the signatory pueblos bound themselves to one another for the mutually beneficial use of land and to exercise joint jurisdiction over it. In another contract authorized by Judge Chacón, the cabecera (yuhuitayu) and Spanish administrative seat of Nochixtlan and one of its subject towns, Santa María Añuma, agreed to end litigation over a parcel of boundary land so that the livestock from both communities could pass freely through it and have access to salt licks. Each pueblo renounced its dominion over the land and agreed to joint ownership and jurisdiction. If the livestock of one community destroyed the crops of the other, the offending community would compensate for damages. Once again, the expansion of the livestock industry shaped possession and jurisdiction over land as contested territory at the boundaries of communities turned into jointly possessed pasture.[61]

In another contract authorized by Judge Chacón, the communities of Nejapilla and Topiltepec agreed to allow one another to enter their uncultivated lands to cut wood, greenery, and flowers for religious festivities and to let their livestock graze freely, without impediment. However, they could not sow crops on one another's lands. In effect, the contract modified an earlier composición initiated by San Pedro Topiltepec that delineated its boundaries with the communities of Santiago Tillo, Tiltepeque, Texapilla, Santo Domingo Tlachitongo, San Francisco Chundua, and San Andrés Tlacosahuala. The great plurality of pueblos with whom Topiltepec shared boundaries suggests a complicated patchwork of land tenure. It is unclear why Topiltepec chose to create an alliance with Nejapilla rather than its other neighbors. The quality of grazing land at their boundaries may have had something to do with it. As with the other agreements authorized by Chacón, breach of contract resulted in the harsh penalties seen in the other contracts: 50 to 100 pesos of oro común for principales and one hundred to two hundred lashes for commoners.[62]

In a 1718 contract authorized by don Gaspar de Yrigoyen, Chacón's lieutenant who served in his stead, the Chocholtec pueblos of Nuestra Señora la Concepción (a subject town of Coixtlahuaca), San Antonio Abad, and Santiago de las Plumas agreed that rather than continuing a dispute over a contested parcel of land at the boundaries of all three pueblos, they would share the lands as one pueblo, though the Natives from each would cultivate the lands separately. According to the petition submitted by their authorities, due to unspecified hardships—perhaps depopulation due to disease or crop failure due to poor lands—residents of San Antonio Abad had moved from the site of their pueblo to live on lands that the Real Audiencia had ruled were in the possession of La Concepción. The squatting provoked the legal dispute among the three pueblos. Upon consideration of the costs of pursuing the case, and the summoning of Christian "charity," the authorities of La Concepción decided that sharing the lands with the refugees made more sense. They also conceded that becoming one pueblo would facilitate the celebration of the sacraments. According to the agreement, all three pueblos would join together as one, no pueblo would be subject to another, and they would go to court to request a single title.[63]

A 1733 contract authorized by don Joseph de Bestia, lieutenant to the alcalde mayor, rectified a failed attempt to produce a partnership contract during the composiciones de tierras. The cabecera of San Mateo del Peñasco and its subject town San Agustín agreed to end a dispute over a contested parcel of land that housed a corral for livestock belonging to the Christian confraternity (*cofradía*) of the Excelentísimo Sacramento.[64] According to Spanish law, Native authorities could designate communal lands for use by the religious confraternities of their communities. During the eighteenth century, many Ñudzahui town councils entrusted communal herds to cofradías as a means of protecting this valuable collective property from growing demands for taxes and tribute. Since the resources of cofradías fell under the ecclesiastical jurisdiction, they were shielded from the predations of civil authorities. The problem was that as the population grew, land for livestock butted up against expanding cropland.[65]

The contract stated that the Indigenous people of San Agustín wanted to sow crops on the land designated for the cofradía's corral. The Native officials of Peñasco, the parish seat, complained to the Spanish magistrate, who in turn attempted to intervene by determining which community legally possessed the land. The officials of both towns maintained that two troublemakers from San Agustín frustrated the Spanish judge's efforts to settle the dispute. This may have been so, but it was also a convenient way to assert that troublemaking disrupters rather than the officials of either community were to blame. Rather than pursue costly litigation, the Native authorities decided to settle the dispute via a partnership contract. They agreed that they would share the land and designate some of it for cultivation by the farmers of San Agustín and the rest for the confraternity's livestock, thereby satisfying the needs of both pueblos. Notably, the contract stipulated that the agreement would serve as a composición for the two pueblos unless either could pro-

CHAPTER FIVE

duce a title, at which point the title would take precedence over the contract. Unlike the other contracts, punishment was not determined by social status; anyone who broke its terms would be fined 100 pesos to be paid to the other pueblo and would serve four months in jail. For Native farmers, whipping was often preferable to jail time, which kept them away from their fields, livestock, and other responsibilities. Village and district jails were dank, dirty, and unsanitary places whose conditions sometimes mortally sickened their inmates.[66] As with the contracts celebrated fifteen years earlier, internal discipline marked the production of partnership.

The interpueblo partnership contracts created during the composición program represented attempts by Native authorities to short-circuit conflict and litigation over land as well as expropriation by the Crown and third parties, like caciques or more powerful pueblos. They also served to maintain aspects of customary agrarian practice rooted in the yuhuitayu, while accommodating the expansion of the livestock economy. At the same time, the contracts instantiated a logic of debt—particularly individual responsibility for joint liability—into local relations of land tenure, which reproduced social inequality between Native principales, who often held the highest town offices, and commoners via distribution of unequal penalties. Through the threat of corporal punishment or jail time, commoners were subject to "obligatio" as defined by archaic Roman law, in which the person who was liable was literally laid in bonds, insuring his debt or promise with his body.[67] Justinian's Digest maintained the language of bondage by defining "obligatio" as "binding another person to give us something to do, or perform something."[68] For the Spanish judges, lawyers, and colonial subjects who inherited the Roman tradition, the concept of obligation retained some of the meaning of an "invisible rope around the neck."[69] The rigor of "in solidum" obligation tightened the rope further. In this light, partnerships of co-ownership did not represent an assertion of egalitarian communalism against powerful local landholders and state actors but a means by which Native authorities strengthened their power to control and manage common land and resources.

Partnership, Plural Ownership, and Cacicazgos

Native authorities also used partnership contracts to transform customary use rights of cacique lands into joint possession, thereby expanding and securing their land base at the expense of cacicazgos. As the historian Margarita Menegus Bornemann has shown, almost all communal land in the Mixteca fell under the designation of *propio*, lands used to sustain the cabildo and the tax and tribute obligations of the community. The pueblos of the region do not appear to have held *tierras del común repartimiento*, which in other parts of Oaxaca and New Spain were distributed to individual families for subsistence. Instead, Native commoners often enjoyed usufruct rights on cacique lands, which they cultivated for their own use in exchange for rent paid in specie or labor to the cacique. These relationships were not written down or contractual but regulated according to custom. During the composiciones de tierras, some of these pueblos claimed that they possessed the land since time immemorial and should therefore be given title. They insisted that they did not recognize the authority of any caciques, only that of the Spanish king. Claiming land in this way was strategic since usufruct rights were distinct from possession. According to Spanish law, usufruct encapsulated the right granted by a proprietor to someone to work his or her land usually in exchange for labor or fees. Even if dependent laborers (*terrazgueros*) had worked the land for decades or even centuries, they could not claim it through possession because it belonged to someone else. Nevertheless, communities of terrazgueros seized upon the opportunity of the composiciones to claim the land through immemorial possession. By disavowing their caciques, they rejected the basis of the cacique's right to their labor and the land. Through this legal sleight of hand, they transformed customary usufruct rights into ownership, making the cacique's land their own.[70]

Two partnership contracts from the Mixteca Alta district of Tlaxiaco show how communities and caciques disputed and resolved their competing claims to land outside the confines of the composición program, and in a region in which land rights were especially layered and complex. During the pre-Hispanic period, Tlaxiaco was one of the largest and most powerful yuhuitayu of the Mixteca. Its territory encompassed lands in different ecological niches, including cold, temperate, and tropical, allowing for agricultural complementarity and the production of diverse trade goods. It was also a multiethnic polity, composed of a majority Mixtec population, with Triqui and Nahua minorities. Compound lordship defined its political organization, with many yya (lords) controlling specific territories through shared or confederated authority.[71]

After the congregaciones of the late sixteenth century, Tlaxiaco became a cabecera with multiple subject communities, some of which were cabeceras in their own right, making its jurisdiction layered and at times conflictive. Due to its strategic location, it became a center for trade, and its fertile lands, especially a territory known as the cañada de Yosotiche, made it a center for sugar production, livestock grazing, and agricultural production more broadly. During the eighteenth century, the cabecera of Tlaxiaco rented the rich agricultural lands of Yosotiche to Spanish sugar producers, positioning it as one of the most important proprietors in the Mixteca region.[72] Tlaxiaco's commercial success can be explained not only by its location and the quality of its lands but also by its relationship with its subject communities, which was more cooperative and complementary and less hierarchical than that of other yuhuitayu of the Mixteca region. Each community managed grazing and agricultural lands to the benefit of the whole, contributing to a generalized prosperity.[73]

Tlaxiaco's strength was counterbalanced by the multiple cacicazgos of the region, which concentrated power and wealth and created additional layers of authority. The compound lordship of the pre-Hispanic period may explain this phenomenon of plural cacicazgos. In some cases, subject pueblos of Tlaxiaco and other cabeceras were embedded within the territorial limits of cacicazgos. Notably, San Pedro Mártir Yucuxaco, San Juan Ñumi, San Antonino, San Sebastián Almoloya, and Santo Domingo, all subject towns of Tlaxiaco, were located within the cacicazgo of don Pedro de Chávez y Guzmán, making them subject to the authority of both the cabildo of Tlaxiaco and the Chávez family. During the sixteenth and seventeenth centuries, various members of the Chávez family served in the cabildo of Tlaxiaco, making the body an instrument of lordly power.[74]

In the eighteenth century, the Chávez family's hold on regional power began to wane, as the cabecera of Tlaxiaco and many of its subject communities came to define their interests against those of the caciques. As discussed earlier in the chapter, this local trend tracked with a broader regional pattern in which cacicazgos across the Mixteca found themselves in crisis by mid-century due to challenges from Spaniards and Native commoners. As the livestock economy expanded, caciques leased their land to other caciques, Native commoners, mestizos, and even religious orders, some for cultivation but most for grazing. The rent of cacique lands increased fourfold from 1671 to 1730, with a marked increase from 1700 to 1730. Many of the most significant renters were Spanish ranchers, who often sought to turn the land they leased from caciques into their own property by making dubious claims in court. For the most part, the caciques successfully defended their cacicazgos, but at the high price of endless legal fees. By 1740, almost all the Mixtecan cacicazgos were embroiled in some form of litigation over land, a process that seriously undermined their economic solvency.[75] Not only did they face challenges from Spaniards; they also faced challenges from communities of terrazgueros and subject communities located on their lands. Sometimes caciques rented the boundary lands of their subject communities, sending Native authorities to the courts to cry foul.

The caciques of Tlaxiaco played their part in this process. Between 1714 and 1742, don Pedro Martín Chávez de Guzmán entered into seven rental agreements.[76] One of them, signed in 1723, authorized the rent of lands named Yosoñama to Leonor de Aguirre, a wealthy resident of Tlaxiaco, so that she could use it to establish a ranch for cattle, sheep, and goats. Yosoñama sat within the limits of the pueblo of San Juan Ñumi, whose territory was embedded in Chávez's cacicazgo. In addition to an annual fee of twenty pesos, she was expected to pay for all the improvements to the land required for the founding of the ranch. Like most rental agreements, it was valid for a period of nine years, in this case, until 1732.[77]

Doña Leonor's ranch disappeared from notarial records after the 1730s, and its fate remains unclear. It does appear, though, that ownership of the lands called Yosoñama, nested within the concentric circles of San Juan Ñumi, Chávez's cacicazgo, and the cabecera of Tlaxiaco, was muddy enough that the municipal authorities of Tlaxiaco attempted to rent the lands in 1741 to don Juan Antonio de Ladesa, the lieutenant of the Spanish magistrate of Teozacoalco, for nine years at the rate of seventeen pesos per year.[78] This set off a land dispute among the municipal authorities of Tlaxiaco, San Juan Ñumi, and don Pedro Chávez. In 1742 the dispute gave rise to a partnership contract in which the municipal authorities of Tlaxiaco and San Juan Ñumi claimed joint possession of the land for cooperative use, against current and future claims of the Chávez family.[79]

Tlaxiaco and Ñumi had not always enjoyed a cooperative relationship. In their petition for a license to form the contract, the authorities of both towns recounted how since August 1742, the two pueblos had been engaged in litigation over Yosoñama. The officials of Ñumi asserted that under pressure from don Pedro Chávez, they entered a claim to Yosoñama in court, implying that Chávez was angling for a land grab from Tlaxiaco. For their part, the cabildo of Tlaxiaco defended what they claimed was their right to Yosoñama. To put an end to the dispute, Tlaxiaco agreed to give Yosoñama to San Juan Ñumi, but only under the condition that villagers from Tlaxiaco could continue to enjoy the fruits of the land through usufruct, not rent. In fact, they insisted that the land could not be rented at all. In short, the partnership contract would transform lands that the cacique don Pedro Chávez had formerly claimed as his own to lease out for ranching to agricultural land jointly held by Tlaxiaco and Ñumi.

The problem was that the authorities of Tlaxiaco had already tried to claim the land as their own and rent it to don Juan Antonio de Ladesa. To address this problem, the contract stipulated that Ladesa would have to remove his livestock by June 1743. By ceding the land to Ñumi, a community that did not have a rental contract with the Spanish rancher Ladesa, the cabildo of Tlaxiaco did not have to break its contract, and Ladesa and his animals could be sent packing. Once the land was free of livestock, the two pueblos could strengthen their claim to possession by putting the land under cultivation for the necessities of each community, one of the stated purposes of the partnership and a surefire way to protect the land from expropriation by the Crown.

The other crucial part of the agreement was that neither pueblo would recognize any of the Chávez family as their caciques. As discussed previously, disavowal of cacique authority represented a strategy used by communities to claim cacical lands through the composiciones. At the same time, relations among Tlaxiaco and its subject communities and the Chávez family had been souring for decades. From 1715 to 1734, Tlaxiaco and some of its subject communities, including San Juan Ñumi, formed a partnership to rent pasture land to the Compañía de Jesús del Colegio de la Nueva Veracruz. In the 1715 contract, don Pedro de Chávez de Guzmán and his brother Miguel Chávez formed part of the partnership. Afterward, they did not.[80] It appears that Tlaxiaco and Ñumi had either cut the Chávez brothers out of the agreement or claimed the land as their own. And in 1723 the pueblo of San Martín, which like San Pedro Ñumi was embedded within Chávez's cacicazgo, sought an *amparo* (writ of protection, or judicial stay) to protect communal lands in their possession from Chávez's claims.[81] One year later, Chávez agreed to "donate" the lands under dispute to San Martín and allowed the pueblo to maintain its writ of amparo, ensuring that its possession of the lands would be respected in the future.[82] The resolution of the dispute raises questions. If the pueblo of San Martín possessed the lands, why did Chávez need to donate them? Perhaps Chávez preferred this extrajudicial arrangement to the costly litigation that a full-blown land dispute entailed. Indeed, Chávez appeared to be facing pressures from many sides. During the same year, the cabildo of Tlaxiaco gave power of attorney to an alcalde and principal of their community to represent them in the Real Audiencia in a land dispute against Chávez.[83]

The 1742 partnership contract between Tlaxiaco and Ñumi represents a moment, then, in this long conflict between pueblos and caciques. Perhaps the power sharing among the multiple cabeceras of the region and the more cooperative relations among subject communities facilitated a collective stance against the cacique. This spirit of cooperation for mutual benefit came through in the conclusion of the contract, which summed up its purpose: to end their legal dispute over Yosoñama, farm the land together for their common necessities, never rent the land, and not recognize *any* cacique.[84] Unlike the partnership contracts drawn up during the 1717–18 composiciones, the contract between Tlaxiaco and Ñumi did not invoke joint or partial liability, or liability of any sort, and contained no punitive measures with which to enforce its provisions.

The cabildo of Tlaxiaco formed another partnership in 1742, this time for joint possession of boundary lands with Chilapa, a cabecera that fell under the jurisdiction of Tlaxiaco, and four of its subject communities. The contract put an end to ongoing litigation and allowed all the signatories to enjoy the right to water, palm, maguey, and timber, all customary uses of boundary lands. Each of the signatories had equal claim to the land and would give up any prior or future legal claims to it. Any debts incurred among the pueblos arising from the use of the land would be repaid through an inter vivo donation. Unlike the partnership with Ñumi, this partnership was structured according to joint liability, perhaps because of the added risk of conflict due to the plurality of signatories. Anyone who broke the agreement would have to pay 100 pesos to the partner communities. There were no clauses about corporal punishment or imprisonment, an important difference from some of the earlier agreements.[85] Once again, a partnership contract reproduced customary rights to communal lands at the boundaries and served as insurance against competing claims in the future.

The partnership contracts formed by Tlaxiaco and its subject communities illuminate different faces of the laws of mancomunidad (partnership) as a means of strengthening customary agrarian relations or transforming them into new rights to land. In the first, between Tlaxiaco and San Juan Ñumi, which confirmed Ñumi's possession and Tlaxiaco's usufruct rights, the communities joined together to expand and protect their holdings against the claims of the cacique don Pedro de Chávez. In the second, the partnership secured joint possession in boundary lands, allowing for customary access to water and forest goods, while protecting the land against antagonistic claims from either the signatories themselves or powerful outsiders. In both contracts, Ñudzahui authorities tailored partnerships to local conditions by interpreting and applying the laws of partnership across their full spectrum.

Conclusion

In late seventeenth- and eighteenth-century Oaxaca, where Native landholding and forms of territorial organization endured to a much greater extent
than in other regions of colonial Mexico, legal claims to customary land tenure, use, and possession produced a broad range of new agrarian relationships. Although many Native communities acquired title to their lands
during this period through the composiciones de tierras, others resisted
drawing firm boundaries around their communities, opting instead to share
land through cooperative agreements. In some instances, they resorted to
custom to legitimize claims to joint possession and joint jurisdiction, and in
others they claimed possession in order to transform customary relations of
usufruct. Partnership contracts provided an alternative to the bitter, expensive, and lengthy processes of litigation and land titling, at least temporarily. They also represented a strategy to pool land and natural resources and
to join forces against powerful outsiders, whether Spanish ranchers, officials,
or caciques. In this regard, although claims to custom pointed to the preservation of traditional agrarian order, when incorporated into the partnership contract they became a potent mechanism for challenging that order
and generating new rights and, crucially, strengthening the position of Native
officials as administrators of communal land and resources.

Partnership contracts expand our view of the legal repertoire available to
and developed by Native people to make customary claims and not only preserve but also produce common land. Partnership contracts were distinct
from other forms of Mesoamerican claim making—like maps, primordial titles, and codices—in significant ways. The contracts framed Native territori-
ality and social order in forms that appealed to Spanish norms of ownership,
town administration, and collective and individual responsibility. In addition
to providing evidence of customary practice and possession, the contracts also
produced new legal effects, like liability. By petitioning Spanish judges to put
into law customary arrangements that sat at the margins of legality, a rising
class of legally literate Native officials strengthened their authority over people and land, while ceding some of their limited sovereignty to Spanish judges.
The laws of medieval Spain allowed them to move strategically between agreement and conflict, and social harmony and exploitation. The fruits of their efforts demonstrate that Native custom and communal land in Mexico were not
primordial or static but works in progress, conditioned by laws, Native legal
strategies, and political, economic, and demographic transformations.

Partnerships that entailed joint ownership and joint jurisdiction over land had a lasting legacy in Mexico that stretched beyond the composiciones de tierras. During the nineteenth century and up until the Mexican Revolution, co-ownership (*condueñazgo*) provided a strategy for Mexico's peasant communities—some Indigenous, and some of mixed ethnicity—to respond to state-led efforts to fiscalize, privatize, and legalize communal landholding. The leaders of rural communities turned to local courts to create relationships of condueñazgo over land for a spectrum of purposes, including to reproduce communal land tenure and manage access to natural resources; shore up control over boundary lands between communities; reduce fiscal burdens associated with the maintenance of agricultural lands; and comply with official mandates to produce titles for, privatize, or subdivide communal lands.[86] In these ways, condueñazgo allowed rural communities to reformulate communal territory, thereby challenging and complicating the state-driven process coined by historians as the "desamortización de tierras" (disentailment of communal lands), which began in earnest during the Bourbon Reforms and reached its zenith during the Porfiriato.[87] The partnership contracts produced in the Mixteca Alta during the late seventeenth century and first half of the eighteenth century extend the timeline backward for the history of condueñazgo and form an important part of the centuries-long story of the generation and regeneration of forms of collective land tenure by rural communities—glossed as custom—in response to changes in law and agrarian policy.

Custom as Social Contract   **6**

NATIVE SELF-GOVERNANCE AND LABOR

THE INDIAN CABILDO, the body of Indigenous municipal government based on the Spanish institution of the same name, provided the Spanish Empire with a fulcrum for indirect rule by preserving a space for Native semi-autonomy and self-governance as well as a mechanism for the administration of Indigenous communal lands and the organization of Indigenous labor. In 1525 Hernán Cortés designated members of the Indigenous elite of Milpa Alta, Oaxaca, as cabildo officers of their community, and by 1530 Indigenous nobles served as colonial governor, magistrates, and aldermen in the Nahua town of San Marcos Tlayacac in the Cuernavaca region. By 1535 Viceroy Antonio de Mendoza was actively naming Native elites to cabildo posts, and in 1538 a royal cédula put an end to the early colonial policy of recognizing members of Indigenous ruling lineages as "natural lords," mandating that they should be named as governors of Native towns.[1]

These early traces of the Indian cabildo signal its importance as a ruling strategy for Spanish conquistadors and administrators. Some historians have argued that by the end of the sixteenth century, the transformation from the traditional rule of ethnic lords to colonial rule by Indian cabildos was complete, abetted by the reorganization of Indigenous territory due to population decline, forced resettlement, and the imposition of the Spanish regime of property.[2] Others argue that despite the implantation of the cabildo, the Native nobility exercised authority over their communities well into the colonial period by occupying cabildo posts and serving as a shadow government and informal council when they did not formally hold office. Their influence preserved customs of Indigenous governance, collective labor, and land tenure, some of which harkened back to the pre-Hispanic period.[3] The balance between continuity and change in these studies depends in part on regional specificity and the historian's source base. Generally speaking, the Indian cabildo should be understood as a hybrid institution whose governing logic blended pre-Hispanic customs of semiautonomous local rule grounded in unequal reciprocity among status groups with Spanish-style municipal governance oriented toward fulfillment of colonial demands for the product of Indigenous labor.

Labor lay at the heart of the relationship between Indigenous rulers and commoners in pre-Hispanic Mesoamerica: Native lords distributed land to Native commoners in exchange for tribute. The functioning of the tributary pact hinged upon the lesser nobility who governed subject communities. These local rulers apportioned land and collected tribute for the Native lord and organized labor for public works within the community.

The core economic responsibilities of local Native leadership and the commoners they ruled transcended the watershed of the Spanish conquest, with some important modifications. Tribute formed the heart of the Spanish crown's vassalage pact with its Indigenous subjects, and the organization of labor for public works remained a central task for the Native cabildo. Commoners were expected to provide labor, goods, and specie for social superiors— Indigenous and Spanish—within and beyond their communities, and for public works. Indigenous cabildo officers were expected to organize and oversee commoner labor, collect its product, and either channel it to Spanish officials and settlers or Native lords or redistribute it within the community through construction projects, agricultural labor, or ritual celebrations organized around the Christian calendar. Native officers also had to maintain the community treasury and account books that recorded income and expenditures, according to Spanish norms.[4] The legitimacy of Native officers depended on their ability to perform these tasks and deliver tribute and the fruits of commoner labor to royal authorities, while maintaining social peace in their communities. The prestige and influence of lesser elites (principales) increased over time as many high-status Native lords (caciques) assimilated to elite Spanish culture, leaving the administration of their communities and the staffing of the Indian cabildo to this middling stratum.

The centrality of tribute and community-oriented labor to Native colonial governance appeared early in New Spain's Native colonial documentary record. From 1545 to 1627, the Indian cabildo of Tlaxcala produced one of the largest surviving archives of colonial Indigenous-language municipal records. The Tlaxcalan Actas, as they are known by modern historians, contain the minutes of municipal council meetings and provide a clear view of the most pressing issues facing the Native authorities of a large and powerful altepetl, (in)famous for its military alliance with Cortés, and the recognition of its colonial descendants as "Indian Conquistadors" by the Spanish Crown.[5]

The organization of commoner labor emerges as the primary responsibility of Tlaxcala's Indian cabildo in the Actas. Tributary labor in Tlaxcala, which mirrored that of Mesoamerica more broadly, was organized according to a system of rotating labor drafts, glossed in Nahuatl as *coatequitl* (reciprocal work, turn work). Labor drafts for public works within the community, glossed as *yeilhuitequitl* (three-day duty), occupied even greater space in the Actas.[6] The exploitation of commoner labor so crucial to the functioning of pre-Hispanic and early colonial Mesoamerican communities was legitimized through long-standing notions of reciprocity and obligation to the collective. After the Spanish conquest, the channeling of Indigenous labor power toward the interests of Spanish colonists and the colonial Native nobility transformed the terms of that reciprocal pact.[7]

In regions with large Indigenous populations like Oaxaca where Spanish settlement and administration were skeletal, and where Native towns were smaller and more numerous than in central Mexico, Native custom served as a framework for local rule and the administration of Indigenous labor until Spanish independence, though its content and meaning changed considerably over time. During the second half of the seventeenth century and throughout the eighteenth, new referents and warrants for Native customary claims emerged, in which customs of an older vintage (glossed as "ancient custom") vied with customs established in the recent past (glossed as "new," "modern," or "innovated customs"), a practice that the seventeenth-century Spanish jurist Juan de Solórzano Pereira, who held a conservative view of custom, advised against.[8]

Legal disputes over old and new customs related to self-governance and labor reveal how the reciprocal pact between status groups and the meaning of community itself changed over time in colonial Oaxaca. This chapter analyzes a sample of eighty-three claims and references to custom—glossed explicitly as "costumbre"—during the late seventeenth and eighteenth centuries from Oaxaca's colonial archives. The common language mobilized by Native authorities, elites, and commoners to make their cases clustered around concepts central to natural law, including tyranny, force, and servitude; consensus, consent, and free will; and the common good. These concepts undergirded Native legal claims in earlier periods, but they took on new meaning in the eighteenth century. Through their legal arguments, Native litigants reoriented the terms through which the balance between exploitation and protection was legitimized, away from relations of unequal reciprocity rooted in antiquity and the privileges of the Native elite toward new forms of mutual obligation based on economic utility and defense of communal interests through litigation. Over the course of the eighteenth century, as Indigenous commoners and notables competed for high offices in the Native cabildo, they framed customs of self-governance and labor as contractual rather than primordial obligations to the community, incorporating Enlightenment ideas into the norms of local rule.[9]

Reciprocity and Communal Obligation as Translated in Oaxaca's Native Languages

The idea and practice of reciprocity bound Indigenous nobility and commoners together to produce social cohesion and the political entity of the colonial Indigenous community. Casting the mutual obligations of different status groups as custom legitimatized the reciprocal pact by anchoring it in time and tradition. The strong semantic link between self-governance (performed by nobility and notables) and communal labor (performed by commoners) during the colonial period is evident in Oaxaca's Indigenous-language notarial and legal records, as are the changing meanings over time of customary obligation and community. The Zapotec term *guelaguetza*, a system of mutual aid and exchange of pre-Hispanic origin, encompassed a wide array of collective duties and responsibilities, including communal labor for public works, office holding, and contributions for religious and ritual feast days. The term appears in a handful of Zapotec-language wills and legal documents from 1576 to 1675, pointing to the ongoing relevance of these associated practices well after the Spanish conquest. In one case, a Zapotec witness referred to the practice of guelaguetza as "uso y costumbre."[10] As the colonial period wore on, guelaguetza centered around the organization and exploitation of communal property and labor, including the allocation of corporately held land, the maintenance of the town hall, church construction, and the generation and accumulation of funds to pay the salaries of schoolmasters and the costs of communal litigation.[11] In this regard, the term linked the idea of mutual obligation with communal economy, even as such obligations and economies changed over time.

Like the term *guelaguetza*, the Zapotec concept *china* encompassed ideas that included work, office, obligation, and duty. It appears more frequently than guelaguetza in colonial Zapotec-language records. As seen in chapter 2, the missionary friars used the term in bilingual catechisms to refer to the good customs of the saints. In chapter 4, I described how Native authorities paired the term *china* with *golaza* (ancient, pertaining to antiquity, of former times) in a Zapotec-language criminal record to produce the idea of old obligations (*china golaza*)—in this particular case, ritual bathing and purification in rivers expected of Native office holders in the late seventeenth century. *Tniño*, the Ñudzahui-language analog for *china*, also encompassed meanings that included office holding, work, and obligation.[12]

Spanish and Native authorities also used the Nahuatl term *tequio* (that which owes tribute), a modifier related to the noun *tequitl* (tribute, duty), and the verb *tequiti* (to perform tribute duty, pay tribute) as a gloss for communal labor in court records from colonial Oaxaca, just as the Native officers of Tlaxcala did in their town council records.[13] This linguistic borrowing may have been a holdover from the tributary relationship of Oaxaca's Indigenous communities to the Mexica Triple Alliance, or the application of the term by Spaniards who grafted their own tributary regime onto that of the Mexica, incorporated Mexica institutions and concepts into their colonial administration, and used Nahuatl as an intermediary language of empire.[14]

Two eighteenth-century disputes from the district of Villa Alta further our understanding of how Indigenous concepts for office holding, work, and obligation informed the changing meanings of custom during the eighteenth century. The first dispute erupted in the Spanish court of Villa Alta in 1717 when a number of principales from the Zapotec town of Lachichina complained in a Spanish-language petition to the Spanish magistrate of Villa Alta that the town's Native authorities were breaking with custom by forcing them to participate in collective labor—glossed with the Zapotec loanword *chinalagues*—customarily performed by the commoners of the pueblo.[15] The Zapotec term *lague* (or *lahui*, a different spelling), which appears frequently in Zapotec-language notarial records as a gloss for community (in Spanish, *el común*), modified the term *china* to produce the idea of work as an obligation to the community.

The principales claimed that the Native authorities of Lachichina had recently made an agreement with Spanish officials that all community members regardless of status had to provide labor, service, and fees to support the parish priest. From the Native authorities' point of view, the logic was that the priest ministered to all community members equally, and as such, all community members should support the priest's needs equally. The principales shot back that according to custom, they should be exempt from communal labor based on their social status. In short, their inherited privilege should override any impulse toward a more evenly distributed burden of labor in the community's reciprocal relationship with the parish priest. They decried the imposition of a "new custom" that ignored their ancient privileges and equalized communal obligations.

If principales did not perform collective labor, how were their obligations to the community defined? And if the old custom of exemption based on hereditary status no longer held, what was the basis of new custom? A 1750 dispute from Santiago Lalopa heard in the Spanish court of Villa Alta provides some clues. In 1750 don Miguel Martínez de Velasco, a cacique of Santiago Lalopa, complained in a petition to the Spanish magistrate of Villa Alta of the "tyranny" of the current alcaldes (Native magistrates) of his town who he claimed were doling out an excessive punishment of fifty lashes to the elite men in the pueblo who refused to accompany the town council to the district seat to pursue a lawsuit. The alcaldes responded by claiming that any men of high standing who did not participate in town council meetings—glossed with the Zapotec loanword *chinalahui* (a different spelling, but the same word as the term *chinalague*)—had to report to the town hall and pay a fine of four reales, a penalty that was customary and rooted in the "consent of the community."[16] In this case, *chinalahui* referenced the work for the community—town leadership and governance—performed by municipal officers and town notables rather than manual labor performed by commoners. These distinct forms of "work for the community," separated according to class and status, were expressed by the same Zapotec-language concept and linked by the idea of reciprocal obligation. In this instance, the town officials claimed that don Miguel Martín de Velasco's protest against these customary obligations was emblematic of an "older generation of troublemakers" who resisted the new objectives—the pursuit of communal interests through litigation—to which the Native authorities were bending village custom.

These contests over custom—new customs instantiated by commoner municipal officers versus old prerogatives and privileges claimed by principales and caciques—intensified in tandem with the rise of the discourse of *el común* (community) as popular, collective legal voice and political subject.[17] The Spanish concept *el común*, which comprised the intertwined ideas of the community as a political entity, a collectivity of people, and commonly held lands and wealth was ubiquitous in Indigenous petitions, legal cases, and notarial records from Oaxaca and, more broadly, throughout Spanish America during the eighteenth century. El común took on an explicitly class character in this period as commoners entered the ranks of cabildo offices, jostling for power with principales and defining their interests against those of the hereditary elite. Through these social and political transformations, the idea of el común increasingly came to refer to a shared commoner status, to the exclusion of the Native elite.[18] Accordingly, the eighteenth-century discourse of custom developed along two opposing lines: customs tied to hereditary privilege, and customs linked to what Native authorities claimed were the common interests of the community.

In the two disputes analyzed above, eighteenth-century transformations in the meanings of custom and el común came to the fore. Native litigants pitted the privileges of caciques and principales against new ideas about work and obligation in the name of the common good of a community run by commoners. Whereas Native principales and caciques claimed exemption from communal activities based on hereditary status, commoner Native authorities appealed to an ethos of mutual obligation that ignored distinctions of status and privilege. The high born based their claims on customs that were old, and the commoner Native authorities on new customs that sought to maximize labor power and direct community resources toward litigation in defense of commonly defined goals. As shown in the testimony of litigants and witnesses, the meanings and practices associated with the tightly linked concepts of custom, community, and reciprocity were not static but rather a dynamic set of contested relations subject to change. Native town officers, who served as intermediaries between their communities and colonial officials in both cases, participated in the colonial balancing act of exploitation and protection, adapting and aligning the work and obligations of all status groups to changing community needs, class interests, and colonial imperatives.

Laboring for the Community, Laboring for the Powerful

Through intra- and intercommunal disputes, the mutual obligations that defined china, tniño, and tequio in colonial Oaxaca aligned partially over time with the Spanish ideal of the common good, a guiding principle of colonial justice and administration. As was the case with custom in the Spanish Empire more generally from the mid-seventeenth century forward, its legitimacy in New Spain's Indigenous communities came to rest on its public utility, meaning that it should benefit the entire community rather than a private individual or powerful few, and produce a harmonious balance in which all members fulfilled their obligations to community, God, and king. Since commoner labor and the organization and distribution of its product provided the sinews of the reciprocal compact in Oaxaca's Indigenous communities and between those communities and the Spanish Crown, it is not surprising that of the eighty-three disputes over customs surveyed, forty-five concerned commoner labor directly and another twelve concerned fees and head taxes, which were products of commoner labor. The remaining twenty-six cases concerned municipal office holding, which will be discussed later in the chapter (table 6.1).

In many of the cases concerning labor, fees, and taxes, the tension between the ideal of el común and the practice of colonial exploitation emerged. Commoners challenged the customs that governed the provision of labor, while Native authorities sought new ways to justify and enforce collective labor. This dynamic marked disputes over the custom that commoners had to generate tribute or informal payments in labor, goods, or specie for powerful figures, including Spanish magistrates, Spanish *vecinos* (prominent residents of larger towns), priests, and caciques.[19] For example, in Villa Alta, commoners provided hens and fish to the Spanish magistrate's lieutenant on a monthly basis, a practice that in one case, elite Native officers supported and commoners challenged.[20] Native authorities often pocketed for themselves a portion of tribute, such as cotton mantles or specie destined for Spanish authorities, justifying the practice as customary. In addition to producing tribute, commoners labored on public works projects that benefited the community, such as clearing roads, building hammock bridges over rivers and streams, and constructing temporary shelters with which to receive Spanish officials performing legal, administrative, or ecclesiastical business.[21] Commoners also performed labor that benefited the *culto divino* (divine cult) of Christianity within the community. This included work dedicated to the preparations for village celebrations of the Christian calendar such as feast days for the patron saint and church repair.[22] Disputes over commoner labor often revolved around claims on the part of Native authorities that the labor demands that they made were customary, versus the assertions by commoners that Native authorities abused commoner labor through usurpation, harassment, and tyranny.

Class conflict marked disputes over customary labor, as the question of who should perform labor for the community took center stage in legal disputes. Four of the cases over communal labor concerned claims to exemption by principales and caciques. Principales brought complaints of abuse of

Table 6.1 Selected disputes and decrees regarding custom in late seventeenth- and eighteenth-century Oaxaca

Customs of Indigenous labor

Commoner labor	45
Public works (generally)	*10*
Divine cult (within the community)	*3*
Tribute	*9*
Personal service	*9*
Owed to parish seat by dependency	
(cabecera-sujeto)	*14*
Fees and derramas (illicit levies on households)	12
TOTAL CASES	57

Customs of Indigenous self-governance

Obligations pertaining to officeholding	12
Electoral rules and procedures	14
TOTAL CASES	26
OVERALL TOTAL CASES	83

authority against Native officers who compelled them to work in tasks that they argued were the purview of male commoners of working age, and from which principales and caciques were customarily exempt. The legal argumentation in these cases was remarkably consistent. The Native nobles appealed to custom to support their claims to exemption, arguing that they descended from high-born families whose privileges and exemptions had been respected in the past, "since time immemorial," signaling that they likely had no written proof attesting to their status. They argued that the Native authorities who expected them to perform work beneath their social station were haughty and tyrannical, and that they did not respect local custom. For their part, Native authorities argued back that the principales did not comply with their obligations as members of the community, which were rooted in custom.[23] In a context in which the empire was looking to maximize revenue from Indigenous communities, Native officers often asserted that communal labor obligations should apply to all. Their appeal to custom was both moral and pragmatic: all should work for the common good no matter their social station.

Disputes over communal labor often threw the legitimacy of Native authorities into question. Commoners sometimes refused to participate in labor drafts imposed by Native authorities, who they viewed as falling short of their responsibilities, which they understood in moral and reciprocal terms. Commoner resistance to labor drafts sometimes appeared in cases of complaints that Native officials abused their authority by whipping villagers for failure to perform tequio (Nahuatl, "communal labor"). Native litigants often decried the bad government of their Native authorities and the unjust nature of the labor requirements, using the language of tyranny. The Crown's increased demand for revenue from Native communities during the eighteenth century may have pressured Indigenous authorities to compel labor through coercion, a practice that ultimately undermined their legitimacy in the eyes of commoners who expected them to make labor demands that were just.[24]

Labor disputes sometimes spilled out beyond the boundaries of the community. In separate cases, the Native authorities of two neighboring villages argued over the terms of a customary rotational labor draft through which each community in its turn built a hammock over a rushing river that divided the territory of the two villages and cleared the road that ran between them. In each of these cases, arguments about whose turn it was to do the work were folded into broader intercommunal disputes, one concerning conflict over land, the other concerning violence between members of neighboring communities. Legal and violent animus between the communities threatened to undermine the custom that bound the two communities together, which depended on peaceful relations.[25] As intercommunity disputes multiplied across eighteenth century Oaxaca, intercommunal and supracommunal custom fragmented and splintered.

Commoners labored not only for their own community's or even their immediate neighbor's benefit but also according to custom, for the benefit of the administrative unit of the cabecera. Unequal reciprocity within communities based on status groups was reproduced within the cabecera-sujeto relationship. As parish seats, cabeceras had the power to demand "contributions" of labor and goods from their subject communities for the purposes of sustaining the parish priest who resided in the cabecera and also for parish celebrations, which were notoriously lavish, costly, and labor intensive.

Over the course of the eighteenth century, demographic growth, pressure on land, scarcity of resources, and the declining prestige of the Native nobility undermined the reciprocal bonds between cabeceras and sujetos, leading Native commoners and dependent communities to challenge the foundations of customary labor.[26] In fourteen cases, cabeceras and sujetos contested the terms of labor owed by subject communities, including the provision and preparation of food, construction of ceremonial arches, church repair, and contributions of cotton mantles, which served as a kind of currency. Cabeceras often cited custom as the root of such labor arrangements, grounding their arguments in moral principles such as reciprocity, friendship, obligation, service, contribution, and the common good. Subject communities, on the other hand, emphasized the disadvantageousness of the agreements for themselves based on the onerousness of the labor demands. Their arguments combined old and new conceptions of "utility" and the "common good" in which local practice and justice had to serve the benefit of all (in this case the subject communities) rather than the interests of the powerful, the few, or the individual (the cabecera). They also drew on eighteenth-century notions of "utility" that cast the baroque practices of the Native cult of the saints as unnecessarily elaborate and wasteful.[27]

Custom also regulated the production of fees in specie or in kind via communal labor. Fees were directed toward a variety of outcomes: religious celebrations and church-related public works, such as financing an altarpiece or purchasing wax or adornments for the church; fees paid to officials for legal services such as translation or power of attorney; and religious alms. In six cases, custom came into play when the justice and legality of these fees were either upheld or called into question.[28] In instances in which litigants characterized fees as just, custom exerted a moderating force on Spanish authorities' impulse to overcharge Indigenous people for administrative services or contributions to the church. For example, the viceroy issued an order in 1721 to the officials of Teposcolula who were charged with collecting the alms for the confraternity of the Benditas Animas del Monte Santo, warning them not to charge any amount more from the Indians than was customary.[29] In 1751 Native litigants from Talea complained that the court interpreter of Villa Alta was charging them one peso for their services, when the customary fee was the considerably lesser sum of two reales.[30]

The principle of utility guided the policies of the Bourbon dynasty that ruled Spain from 1700 forward. As the eighteenth century progressed, there was an increased effort on the part of Spanish officials to regulate customary fees, which they viewed negatively since they tended to deplete the coffers of Indigenous communities and households, hurting the town treasury and by extension colonial interests. Spanish authorities' negative view of customary fees contributed to an imperial discourse that condemned custom more broadly in terms of its inutility. This synergy of attitudes and policies was evident in a royal provision issued in 1731 in Villa Alta that mandated that the fees paid to parish priests should correspond to those stipulated in the Real Arancel (fee schedule).[31] Seven years later, in 1738, the Spanish magistrate of Teposcolula circulated a royal decree that abolished the "antiquated, abominable, pernicious, and noxious custom" of charging Indian vendors a half real for their stalls in the market of Yanhuitlan, a practice deemed "abominable and against justice." The decree stated that Indian vendors should only pay the royal tax (*el real derecho de alcabala*).[32] The Bourbon reformers of the late eighteenth century, who sought to squeeze even more revenue out of Spain's American colonies, instituted tighter controls on Indigenous town treasuries, which the Crown felt could provide a more robust source of royal income.[33] In an effort to keep Indigenous town treasuries solvent, Bourbon officials further regulated the fees and taxes that local officials imposed on Native people. The royal fee schedule published in 1791 explicitly targeted the "noxious customs" of charging excessive fees from the Indians for legal services.[34]

In many disputes, royal policies controlling and limiting how Native authorities managed communal labor and their municipal treasuries confronted Indigenous ideas about how to make the best use of communal resources. There were divisions within Indigenous communities about this issue, depending on the purposes to which the resources were directed. In 1743, following a devastating epidemic when community resources were stretched to the breaking point, the Spanish magistrate of Villa Alta conducted a *visita* (district inspection) in which he reviewed the municipal treasuries and accounts of the towns in his district and the towns' general state of affairs. The magistrate was particularly critical of the practice on the part of Native officials of charging a supplementary levy (derrama) from the community's households in order to pay for village fiestas. He made it a point to distinguish between giving freely for a fiesta versus what he viewed as the coercive custom of the derrama.[35]

Derramas were frequent flash points in disputes over custom. In 1563 the Spanish king, don Felipe II mandated that no one could impose a derrama without license authorized by the king, and in 1582 he exempted Indigenous people from derramas.[36] Nevertheless, Native authorities imposed derramas to collect sufficient goods and specie to provide tribute to the parish priest and court officials like the Spanish magistrate's lieutenant (*teniente*) and chief constable (*alguacil mayor*). They also used derramas to pay for the increasingly common lawsuits that engulfed the region, as communities litigated with one another over land and other matters. In six disputes, Native litigants bitterly denounced their Native authorities to the Spanish magistrate for imposing derramas, which they cast as "mala costumbre." Paying these levies required significant labor on top of the many labor obligations they already owed to community, church, and Crown, not to mention their own subsistence. For their part, Native authorities insisted that instituting and collecting derramas for the purposes of litigation were becoming part of the customary obligations of office holding.[37]

The opposition between coercion and free will provided a common refrain in disputes over customary labor in eighteenth-century litigation more broadly. Nowhere was this clearer than in legal disputes over personal service (*servicio personal*). Although it was illegal according to Spanish legislation, Native authorities in eighteenth-century Oaxaca commandeered the labor of Native commoners in order to provide a wide variety of unpaid services and goods for Spanish officials, parish priests, and Native governors and caciques, including construction and building, domestic labor, food, water, wood, cloth, and other staples. Native and Spanish authorities who benefited from the labor skirted the issue of its legality by locating it in the realm of custom. Some commoners challenged the validity of such customary labor demands with reference to laws that maintained that Indigenous labor of all kinds should be voluntary.[38]

These tensions around personal service reached back to the early postconquest period. As noted previously, the custom of providing commoner labor and service to nobles was part of the reciprocal pact that linked distinct status groups in pre-Hispanic Mesoamerica. A class of dependent laborers, who were landless and exempt from tribute, were bound to the nobility of the larger ethnic states, working on their lands or in their palaces either through assignment by local leaders or based on heredity. After the conquest, encomenderos, Spanish officials, and priests expanded this practice to make excessive and onerous demands for the uncompensated labor of Indigenous commoners for their own benefit. The abuses that resulted from the institution of personal service immediately generated controversy in Spain and the Americas and called into question the justice and legality of Spain's American empire. The Crown adopted the role of protector of the Indians against the colonists' rapacity through the promulgation of the New Laws (1542), which among other things outlawed Indigenous slavery and put an end to the rights of succession of the encomienda. Chapter XXII of the New Laws specifically targeted personal service by prohibiting anyone from demanding involuntary, unpaid Indigenous labor.[39] Although illegal, personal service persisted well into the eighteenth century, especially in regions that were marginal to New Spain's market economy, including Oaxaca.[40] Over time, it was folded into local practice and became intertwined with norms of hierarchical reciprocity. During the eighteenth century, when ideas about free wage labor and liberty came to stand as a foil to servitude, personal service figured centrally in legal conflicts over custom.

Self-Governance

As evident in disputes over the customs that regulated communal labor, Native litigants often threw the roles, expectations, and obligations of Native authorities into the spotlight. As the fulcrum of the colonial tributary pact, Native municipal officers fulfilled their obligations to Crown and church by commanding the labor of their community members. They offset this exploitation by appealing to custom and an ideology of good government characterized by a commitment to utility and the common good. Protecting the well-being and interests of the community while adhering to colonial demands was a practical and moral obligation, and failure to perform it could land them in court, through complaints from below or above.

Of my sampling of eighty-three legal disputes over custom, twenty-six concerned municipal office holding. Of these, obligations pertaining to office made up twelve, and electoral rules and procedures fourteen.[41] The cases point to the various functions of the Native cabildo, such as the maintenance of the accounts of the communal treasury, the provision of tribute to Spanish authorities, the management of the repartimiento that produced cotton mantles and cochineal (and other goods), care of communal lands, maintenance of the church, and organization of the labor and resources necessary to put on village fiestas. Disputes over the customs of office holding also revealed the norms that regulated Indigenous governance. Many Native litigants argued that governing decisions should be communal and based on consensus, and all officers and nobles should participate in decision making. Sometimes lesser-known customs of office holding bled into the disputes, such as the practice of the Native authorities of a bride's village preparing chocolate for the authorities of a groom's village in preparation for a wedding that joined a couple from different communities.[42] Ritual exchanges like this one reproduced horizontal, reciprocal bonds within and between communities that tempered vertical and unequal relations of reciprocity.

A crucial function of Indigenous municipal government was to ensure its own perpetuation through proper election procedure. During the eighteenth century, electoral custom was often challenged by rival political factions within communities, and in the case of the Mixteca by subject communities who participated in elections of high officers in the cabecera. The issues raised in these cases included whether the entire community or a set of electors should elect high officers, such as governors or the alcaldes. More broadly, litigants called into question the role of caciques and principales in elections and whether they should have a disproportionate influence on the outcome. Relatedly, Native authorities sometimes contested the electoral interference of priests and their assistants, who often witnessed elections and approved results. Disputes about where caciques and principales should enter into the ladder of office holding also arose, especially during the late eighteenth century. Village notables often argued that according to custom, they should only hold high office, whereas commoners argued that merit should trump hereditary privilege in determining one's fitness to govern. Such disputes led to spirited discussions concerning the qualities and qualifications of a good officer. Spanish-language skills and familiarity with the law became increasingly important criteria during the late eighteenth century.

As legal knowledge and Spanish-language skills took center stage as criteria for office holding, the successful pursuit of litigation in defense of communal interests came to define the obligations of Native officers. Recall that in the 1750 case from Santiago Lalopa discussed earlier in the chapter, the cacique don Miguel Martínez de Velasco denounced his local authorities for whipping village notables who refused to participate in a council meeting regarding a community lawsuit. The alcaldes had countered that according to custom, these council meetings, glossed in Zapotec as *chinalahui*, were obligatory for all town officers and notables. Martínez de Velasco and his sons objected to the reframing of governance in the communal interest in terms of the pursuit of what they characterized as costly and frivolous litigation. In short, the custom of obligatory attendance at council meetings was not the problem but the purpose of the meetings was. This argument was replayed numerous times over the eighteenth century, spurring shifts in how the customary obligations of Native nobles and authorities were understood by those who held office and by those they governed, purportedly in the interest of the common good.

The disputes over chinalahui—work for the community—discussed earlier in this chapter were emblematic of a broad refiguring of custom, which reflected a shift during the eighteenth century in the relationship between the Spanish Crown and its Indigenous subjects. To serve the common good, Indigenous people had to be not only loyal vassals, good Christians, and faithful payers of tribute; they also had to be economically useful. This meant that from the perspective of colonial officials, the management of the communal treasury and common lands—the commons—had to serve the economic needs of empire rather than communally defined objectives. This transactional and instrumental understanding of reciprocity inflected not only the relationship between Spanish officials and Native subjects but also that of Native authorities, nobles, and commoners. Customs based on claims to antiquity and inherited privilege were challenged or displaced by new customs based on utility and advantage. By the middle of the eighteenth century, many Native authorities agreed that the most expeditious way to secure the advantage of one's community was to channel community resources toward litigation.

Challenges to old customs were also mounted in a language of will (*voluntad*), and sometimes during the eighteenth century, free will (*libre voluntad*). The relationship of the concept of will to religion, law, and politics had a long trajectory in European thought. In Christianity, will was considered a property of the soul, and God's will, the ultimate source of law. In the early modern period, the legal theory of voluntarism, which undergirded absolute monarchy, held that the will of the lawgiver—the king—gave law its binding force.[43] One has only to peruse early modern Spanish legislation and laws proclaimed in the name of "nuestra voluntad"—the king's will—to discern their source of legitimacy. Sixteenth-century Spanish colonial legislation used the concept of "voluntad" in relation to Indigenous people primarily to underscore their right as free Christians to refuse to labor against their will. Until the end of the eighteenth century, Native litigants in Oaxaca regularly invoked their freedom and will against the custom of involuntary labor. They also invoked the concept of voluntad in collective terms, as the will of the community.

In the eighteenth century, voluntarist theories of the state, originating in Europe, held that consent of the individual subject legitimized political authority. During the eighteenth century, Native litigants invoked the idea of individual free will against customs that demanded consensus and upheld tyranny, expanding the idea of Indians' free will beyond the realm of labor and into the sphere of political authority, and beyond the collective toward the individual. In short, Native litigants were articulating Enlightenment notions of political subjecthood. Their arguments, based in utility, advantage, and free will, redefined ideas of reciprocal obligation and reformulated the social contract of their communities. In fact, as we shall see in the following three case studies about the changing customs surrounding self-governance and communal labor, in the eighteenth century, custom was beginning to look more like a contract than a primordial obligation.

From Consensus to Free Will

On December 1, 1707, the Native officers and notables of the town of Teposcolula and its subject communities gathered to elect their governor and two alcaldes (local magistrates).[44] Teposcolula was a large Indigenous town that served as an administrative and ecclesiastical center for its eleven subject communities and at the same time was a Spanish administrative seat with a sizable population of Spanish vecinos (citizen-residents). The town had multiple and overlapping administrative and legal bodies: a Native cabildo, a Spanish cabildo, and a Spanish provincial administration and district court. These layers of governance made for jurisdictional contests in matters concerning the local Indigenous population.[45]

Each of Teposcolula's Indigenous subject communities elected their own aldermen (regidores), who oversaw their local civil administration. These men, in addition to select principales and elders, served as electors who annually congregated in Teposcolula to choose cabildo officers and every two years to choose the governor. These elected officials could come from any of the subject communities, but the governors tended to be Indigenous nobles from the cabecera.[46] In keeping with electoral procedure, the electors documented the election results in a short Ñudzahui-language text that used Mixtec concepts to refer to social status, office holding, and intercommunity hierarchy. The officers were to be chosen from a pool of lords (yya) and lesser nobility (*toho*), and they were to perform the duty of office holding (tniño). The eleven subject communities were referred to as *ndaha ñuu* (tributary communities), and Teposcolula was referred to as a yuhuitayu, and with its Ñudzahui name, Yuncundaa. The document then listed the names of the elected governor and sixteen cabildo members. The signatures of the thirty-five electors—all written in the same hand by the Native notary—appear at the bottom of the list, authorizing the election's outcome.[47]

According to the record, don Pedro García, the governor of the previous year, had been reelected. Although it was forbidden by Spanish law in a 1622 decree, reelection of governors, who tended to be lords, was commonplace in the Mixteca and in many parts of central Mexico during the colonial period. Reelection served as a mechanism through which colonial office holding could be made to align with the pre-Hispanic custom of lifelong hereditary rule and at the same time with Spanish interests. Reelection also served as a strategy for litigation. As communities engaged in long-term lawsuits to pursue collective interests, with governors often serving as legal agents and coordinating legal strategies, continuity of the governorship bolstered chances for success.[48] Sometimes Spaniards and Native officials abetted the reelection of governors. Continuity of Native lords in high office allowed for the creation of alliances and economic arrangements that benefited the powerful, including Spanish merchants and landlords, parish priests, and members of a middling stratum of Native notables made up of principales and, increasingly during the eighteenth century, commoners who had obtained cabildo offices, wealth, Spanish literacy, and legal skills. But this middling stratum did not consistently align itself with Native caciques or Spanish administrators. Their heterogeneous origins and interests fueled tensions and conflicts over village elections.

Once the record of the election had been made and signed, the next step in the electoral procedure was to bring the results to the Spanish magistrate for his approval, as was customary and required by law. Although Spanish magistrates almost always approved Native elections, on this occasion don Alonso de Soto Guevara, Spanish magistrate of Teposcolula, balked. In the margins of the Ñudzahui-language election results, he noted that legally speaking, don Pedro García could not be reelected because of a royal decree that forbade the reelection of Native officers. These grounds for objection were disingenuous given that Spanish law regarding reelection of Native governors was customarily ignored by Native electors and Spanish officials alike. A more plausible cause for Soto's opposition appeared in the left-hand margin, where he noted that don Pedro García had fallen behind on the previous two tribute payments owed to the Crown. Don Pedro García's failure to pay tribute was serious, and the Spanish magistrate noted that he did not anticipate that García would fulfill the upcoming March tribute payment and that the royal tribute collector would be displeased. He concluded his marginalia by noting that one of the alcaldes of Teposcolula had said in front of two Spaniards that don Pedro should not be reelected until he paid the tribute.[49]

Don Pedro García's reelection also faced opposition from the Native authorities of Teposcolula's subject communities. On December 9, 1707, Pascual de la Cruz, regidor of the pueblo of Santa Catarina; Domingo Marcial, regidor of the pueblo of Santo Tomás; and four principales from the two pueblos presented alcalde mayor Soto with a petition denouncing the election results. According to Cruz and Marcial's criminal complaint, they had voted against don Pedro García and in favor of another candidate, Juan de Tapia, citing a royal decree that forbade the reelection of governors and Native officers. They claimed that when they presented their vote to the electors from Teposcolula, they were thrown out of the cabildo. They requested that the alcalde mayor either annul the election or allow their communities to separate themselves from the cabecera of Teposcolula and grant them the right to elect their own alcaldes in order to "throw off their servitude to said cabecera."[50]

The plaintiffs followed up with a second, more detailed petition a few days later, making a case for the annulment of the election based on procedural grounds and on don Pedro García's failure to fulfill his responsibilities as governor. They argued that a handful of electors from Teposcolula had rigged the results and overruled the majority to secure García's reelection. Then they pivoted to argue that as governor García failed to uphold good government, serve the common good, and promote utility. He had not delivered the royal tribute or provided to Spanish officials a full accounting of the communal treasury or levies (derramas) that he had imposed on the community, as was his duty. To make matters worse, he had brokered an arrangement in which community members provided barley, which was valuable feed for livestock, to Spanish residents of Teposcolula who funneled payment for it through García. Instead of paying the Native farmers, he had pocketed the money for himself. The plaintiffs claimed that the electors of Teposcolula who were responsible for García's reelection profited from this scheme and voted for him so that they could continue to enjoy the benefits. By contrast, Juan de Tapia, a principal from the subject town of San Felipe who had served as alcalde in Teposcolula during the administration of governor don Pedro de la Cruz, had treated community members well, maintained social peace, and kept immaculate accounts of the community treasury. They felt that he should be governor instead.[51]

García's defenders, who included the officers of the cabecera and those of Teposcolula's other nine subject communities, deflected the accusations and responded to the plaintiffs' claims with an appeal to custom. They argued that as they always had, they gathered in the town hall of the cabecera and elected their governor and alcaldes consensually, in "total unanimity," as evident in the signatures at the bottom of the document that recorded the results of the election. When a reelection was unanimous, according to the will of all, then it had to be approved by the Spanish magistrate. They pointed to the recent reelection of officers in the cabeceras of Tamazulapan, Tejupa, Tlaxiaco, and Achiutla, all approved by De Soto himself. If the Spanish magistrate had allowed custom to override royal law in these other instances, why would he not do so in this case?[52]

By flagging the principles of consensus and unanimity of collective will, the defendants appealed to an electoral custom that aligned elements of pre-Hispanic procedure and Spanish law. Generally speaking, Indigenous electors applied Spanish law selectively, ignoring the prescribed practice of individual balloting in favor of the pre-Hispanic method of discussion, deliberation, and consensus, a practice that Spanish officials generally accepted. Consensus was quite narrowly defined, however, since the group of electors who determined the outcome was restricted to community members of noble status and high standing, and sometimes an even smaller, elite group within the electorate body.[53] Spanish electoral law did not require consensus but did stipulate that elections should be free from coercion and result from the voluntary participation and liberty of the electors.[54] The electors' signatures at the bottom of election records attested to the free nature of the electoral process, thereby legitimizing its results.[55]

The ideals of consensus and unanimity in Native elections were often betrayed by factionalism and manipulation of results, a pattern reflected in the electoral dispute in Teposcolula. On December 22, new challenges to García's reelection emerged based on claims to a contested, coerced, and illegal electoral process. Don Joseph de Tapia and Pasqual de Feria, the aldermen of Santa María Nduayacu and San Joseph, two more subject communities of Teposcolula, complained to the Spanish magistrate that, like their peers in Santa Catarina and Santo Tomás, they and the majority of electors voted against the reelection of García because it was contrary to royal law. When they voiced their opposition, they were thrown out of the election, leaving the decision to a small minority. They claimed that they were then forced to sign the election results. The Spanish magistrate filed the petition with the other testimony. The case file concludes at this point, suggesting that the case was either unresolved or the final judgment unrecorded.[56]

The dispute over García's reelection might seem at first glance a straightforward case of Indigenous factionalism abetted by Spanish interference in the Native electoral process. However, the discursive terrain upon which the proponents and detractors argued over electoral custom demands attention. Both sides asserted that will (voluntad) should undergird electoral custom. García's detractors claimed that they had voted for the other candidate, Juan de Tapia, out of their own free will (libre voluntad) and had been thrown out of the cabildo for doing so. García's supporters, on the other hand, framed will in terms of consensus: reelection by virtue of a union of votes and the will of all (unión de votos y voluntad de todos), unanimous and in agreement (unánimes y conformes).

According to the plaintiffs, unanimity and conformity were a fiction upheld by the powerful. They sustained that if the Spanish judge viewed them as possessing insufficient reason or aptitude to vote in the cabecera's cabildo elections, then they should have the right to free themselves of their "servitude" to the cabecera of Teposcolula and create their own municipality governed by their own alcaldes. Their proposal to secede from Teposcolula followed a pattern of fragmentation of Indigenous states (yuhuitayu), which Spanish officials had attempted to reconfigure along the lines of Spanish cabecera-sujeto relations. Although subject communities in the Mixteca had sought to break away from cabeceras from the sixteenth century forward and used their desire for liberty from servitude to the cabecera as an argument for doing so, the process accelerated during the eighteenth century and the arguments were framed in new ways. In this case, the plaintiffs confronted claims about ancient, reciprocal obligations based on consensus with ideas about popular sovereignty grounded in free will.

In Native petitions and litigation, the will of Native people—and liberty, its close corollary—was almost always conceived of in collective terms. The formulation of Indigenous will as collective was undoubtedly a result of the corporate nature of Native rights, exemptions, and privileges according to Spanish law. The idea of collective will also corresponded with medieval Spanish notions of custom, founded on communal practice and legitimized by a collective, popular will. By the seventeenth century, Spanish formulations of individual liberty and free will began to challenge the legitimacy of collective obligations. As it applied to Indigenous people, however, will and liberty were almost always presented in their corporate guise, as the will and liberty of the community (el común) or, as in the case described here, the unanimous will of all, and the liberty of the subject town from its cabecera.[57] The notion of individual free will put forth by don Pedro García's detractors stands out, then, as a harbinger of something new.

From Personal Service to Collective Advantage

In 1784 Gabriel Phelipe, a regidor (alderman) from San Vicente, petitioned Pedro de Quevedo, the Spanish magistrate of Teposcolula, to put an end to the custom of providing a *topil*—the lowest rung on the ladder of municipal office—for the personal service of the Native governor of Teposcolula. In his petition, Phelipe emphasized that as a "father and head of the republic" of San Vicente to whose "defense" he was dedicated, he was "stimulated" to write his petition by the "plebeian sons" (*hijos plebeios*) of the pueblo who had grown tired of the custom of conscripting a topil for the personal service of the Native governor. Phelipe supported his opposition to the custom with reference to a recent royal order that prohibited the sons of the pueblo from providing involuntary personal service, as had been customary. He asked the alcalde mayor to stop this "abuse" and notify the current Native governor of Teposcolula, Ignacio de la Cruz, that he was not to demand personal service from the commoners of San Vicente for this or any other purpose.[58]

Upon receiving the petition, the Spanish magistrate praised the legal basis upon which it rested and ordered that Ignacio de la Cruz cease to avail himself of the topil's labor, even though it was custom. In acceding to the request made in the petition, the Spanish magistrate was careful to note the involuntary nature of the labor. When Cruz was notified of the alcalde mayor's order, he elaborately proclaimed his willingness to dutifully obey, but before he could—and the caveat was very important—he had to confer first with the principales of Teposcolula, under whose jurisdiction the case fell because it pertained to a first-instance matter of one of its subject communities. He asked for eight days. The Spanish magistrate granted them.[59]

Ignacio de la Cruz returned with a well-armed counterargument, laced with a strong dose of derision. Against what he acerbically referred to as Gabriel Phelipe's "juridically" based petition, he threw the weight of time, jurisdiction, utility, and reciprocity. He claimed that the custom of providing the Native governor of Teposcolula with a topil for his personal service was "ancient" and that all the pueblos within the parish of Teposcolula willingly adhered to it without contradiction or exemption. Furthermore, the principales of Teposcolula who governed not only the Natives of the cabecera but also its subject communities were in full support of the custom, arguing that whoever served as governor abandoned his own interests and pursuits for the purpose of single-mindedly serving the Spanish magistrate. Having a topil to help with menial tasks such as collecting water and firewood would help the governor to better serve the colonial government, an argument that appealed to the idea of utility. In an effort to dodge the charge that the topil provided involuntary personal service and cast the arrangement in terms of reciprocity, Cruz referred to the topil's labor as a "small gift" (corto obsequio), or courtesy.[60]

According to Cruz's writ, the reciprocal relationship was legitimate due to custom and law. In return for the gift of the topil's services, the principales of the cabecera provided the community of San Vicente with a good piece of land, which they were free to use and cultivate as they saw fit. Cruz noted that this agreement was codified in a legal document in 1768, a copy of which sat in the district's notarial archive, threatening to undercut Phelipe's claim regarding the coercive nature of the custom. How could a practice be coercive if both parties had willingly agreed to it by signing a legal document? If the authorities of San Vicente chose to break with the agreement and withdraw the topil's services, the principales of Teposcolula would see fit to repay their "ingratitude" by repossessing the land.

Having achieved the upper hand, Cruz positioned himself as a generous and rational broker. He surmised that since Gabriel Phelipe and the rest of San Vicente's cabildo probably hoped to maintain the use of the land, they might be open to an alternative proposal that he had devised. Rather than providing a topil for personal service, the community would send a regidor (alderman). Unlike the office of topil, which occupied the bottom rung of the cargo system of office holding and entailed relatively menial tasks, the office of regidor was a weighty one that entailed matters of local governance. According to electoral custom, regidores from subject communities stood the chance of serving as Teposcolula's governor in relatively short order, after working their way through the hierarchy of offices in their hometowns. Cruz proposed a reconfiguration of reciprocity in this case, then: the benefit of potentially serving as Native governor in the future required the sacrifice of serving the current governor. In this way, Cruz argued, the custom of personal service could be "advantageous and adaptable" rather than "nocuous or prejudicial law" (*lei nociva*). But if the officials of San Vicente did not like it, then they would have to give up the land. Gabriel Phelipe and the rest of the officials of San Vicente lost little time in dropping the case.

Cruz's successful strategy scuttled Phelipe's effort to pit the custom of involuntary labor against laws that supported free wage labor. From the perspective of Phelipe and his fellow village officials, the benefits of the land provided in return for the labor outweighed the harm done to the liberty of the unlucky topiles who were sent to serve the governor. The young or humble topil had to figure out how to sustain his crops and uphold his household responsibilities while in the service of another. He might have to hire a field hand and go into debt. But without the land, the community would have less acreage in production and therefore fewer resources with which to pay tribute or put on the feast for the celebration of their patron saint. As for the proposal to replace the topil with a regidor, the officials likely thought "better the topil than me." These were the prerogatives of colonial administrative power enjoyed by Native officials. The choice was clear: best to end the litigation and allow custom to prevail.

What made custom so thorny in this case was that it was based in long-standing relations of unequal reciprocity and at the same time had been codified in a contract, allowing Cruz to argue in support of custom from two angles. In his statement to the court, Cruz located the custom of providing a topil in the distant past with the term *antiguo*. A few lines down the page, he noted that the provision of land in exchange for the topil's labor was something relatively new, cemented into law and practice with a legal document signed and archived in the district court. Custom had evolved over time in its content and form, likely due to resistance to the practice on the part of the authorities of San Vicente. And although the new custom was now codified in writing, Cruz allowed that it could be altered yet again through his proposal to replace a topil with a regidor. Such innovation would make the custom "advantageous and adaptable" rather than nocuous (*nociva*). The use of the term *nociva* to refer to the custom was not accidental but representative of the legal language that during the second half of the eighteenth century, Spanish officials, lawyers, legal agents, and, increasingly, Native litigants applied to the customs that diminished the capacity of Native peoples to generate labor and resources for the Crown. These included involuntary service, the production of fiestas, and charging excessive fees for a range of services.

Changes regarding the status and perception of custom came to the fore in Phelipe's petition as well. The Enlightenment had reinvigorated sixteenth-century arguments against involuntary labor on moral grounds and on a reformulated understanding of utility, according to whose logic involuntary labor was considered economically unsound. The Spanish Crown put Enlightenment ideas into practice with considerable contradiction, railing against the pernicious continuity of the Natives' involuntary personal service, while at the same time renewing the repartimiento and *mita* (Indigenous labor drafts) in an effort to resuscitate the mines of northern Mexico and the Andes. Cruz's reliance on the contract, which required consent based on the free will of the signatories—and at the same time the principle of utility— circumvented the Crown's opposition in principle to involuntary labor. His innovation turned a "nocuous" custom into a legally binding and mutually (if unequally) advantageous one.

From Fiestas to Litigation

In 1798 the town of Santa María Asunción Lachixila Vijanos in the northwestern corner of the Sierra Norte of the Villa Alta district stood bitterly divided over the labor and resources that went into the celebration of the two most important feast days in the pueblo's ritual calendar: those of the Virgin of the Assumption (August 15) and the Virgin of the Conception (December 8). Sitting at the border of the Chinantla lowlands and the Zapotec Sierra, the multiethnic community was divided into two barrios, one Zapotec and one Chinantec. On November 3, 1798, at least two dozen men, claiming to represent a large group from both the Zapotec and Chinantec barrios, denounced their authorities to the presiding judge of first instance—the lieutenant of the subdelegate of Villa Alta—for reinstituting the customary labor for the fiestas, which they claimed had been abolished by both the civil and the ecclesiastical courts. Their complaint followed on the heels of a letter written one month earlier by the intendant of Oaxaca to the subdelegate of Villa Alta confirming that he had ruled against the continuation of these customs, which he argued prevented the officials and villagers from meeting their fiscal obligations to the Crown. He presumed that the current authorities of Lachixila had reinstated them despite his orders because they thought that in order to be good members of the community (*buenos hijos del pueblo*), they had to follow ancient custom. He ordered the subdelegate to notify the authorities of Santa María Lachixila that they must comply with his decision. According to Narciso de la Cruz, who spearheaded the legal case against the officials, they had failed to do so.[61]

In their petition, Cruz and his associates argued that the intendant and the bishop had rightfully classified the customs associated with the preparations for the fiestas as "corrupt" and that they had justifiably "abolished" and "cut them at the root." The Spanish term for corruption—"corruptela"—was also a synonym for "mala costumbre" (bad custom), characterized as "abuse" and "introduced contrary to law."[62] In some cases, it also signified petty corruption.[63] In this case, according to the claimants, these bad customs consisted of excessive and involuntary labor performed by the pueblo in the name of producing an extravagant celebration, consisting of elaborate dances, including the Danza de la Pluma—a dramatic reenactment of the conquest—and an elaborate feast. In order to pull this off, the governor, alcaldes, and regidores had to spend from their own household funds such that they remained in debt for three to four years, buying food, renting clothes, and paying parochial fees. In order to offset costs, they instituted a levy (derrama) of four to five pesos per household and half as much for widowers. They also delegated labor by appointing officers to oversee the fiestas and requiring a mayordomo to work with his wife in the parish priest's kitchen. The unfortunate couple burdened with this task spent the entire year working and preparing, uncompensated for their labor. In 1795 the ecclesiastical and civil courts had determined this to be excessive and abolished the dances and feast, the derrama, and the involuntary service that went along with it, requiring only payment of the parochial fees. The Native authorities had complied until this year. But now, the new authorities, for whatever reason—perhaps due to a desire to show devotion to the priest—reinstituted the abolished custom. The claimants argued that to do so went against the king's desire that his Indian subjects enjoy liberty and relief from such burdens.[64]

The Native officials countered back that when they entered office, as was customary in the pueblo, they called the entire community together to inform them of their expectations for the year, which included a range of communal labor and obligations. They claimed that Narciso de la Cruz and his co-claimants showed up to express their discontent, hurling insults at them and refusing to recognize them as legitimate authorities. In response, the Native officers hauled Cruz and his associates off to jail for the night and then released them, at which point they began to sow discord in the pueblo, threatening to bring litigation against them and the parish priest. The Native officers insisted that the customary labor and fees that they required from the villagers were moderate. They used the language of free will, free labor, and reciprocity to characterize the custom: "we provide our parish priest with this small ration and light service according to the pleasure and will of all of the pueblo, as a sign of our gratitude and reciprocity." They insisted that the elaborate Danza de la Pluma that they put on during the pueblo's titular feast day resulted from the pleasure, will, and vote (*gusto, voluntad y voto*) of the entire community. They concluded that if anyone was bleeding the pueblo dry, it was their opponents who had spent more than 200 pesos on a trip to Oaxaca to bring the case in front of the intendant.[65]

In his decision, the Spanish judge agreed with Cruz and associates that the labor and levies associated with the fiestas were "bad customs" (corruptelas) and that the officials needed to comply with the intendant's orders to put an end to them. But he also condemned Cruz and company as troublemakers and fomenters of dispute. He warned them that they needed to drop the case against their officials that they had brought to the court of the intendant of Oaxaca or he would bring criminal charges against them and impose the fine reserved for "seducers and ringleaders of riotous sounds."[66] He found their impulse to litigate as dangerous as the officials' impulse to put on elaborate religious celebrations. Both diverted the productive resources of the pueblos away from the Crown.

While the conflict in Lachixila provides insight into how Spanish judges and officials viewed Native custom at the turn of the nineteenth century, it also captures changing notions of work for the community—composed of collective labor and office holding—within Oaxaca's Indigenous towns. How did Native officials and commoners define reciprocity and obligation? What was Native self-governance and communal labor for? Fiestas or litigation?

Cruz and company sought to divert Native labor, in the form of derramas, toward legal defense of what they deemed were the community's interests. They had a different vision from that of the Native and Spanish officials in this case of the ends to which communal resources should be directed.

Conclusion

From the late seventeenth century forward, Native litigants and Spanish authorities produced transformations in the meaning of Native custom as it applied to self-governance, collective labor, and communal obligation. Through first-instance legal disputes and responses to royal legislation, Native officials of commoner and principal status, whose interests were diverging during this period, pitted new customs against old ones in an effort to change or maintain the terms of electoral procedure and eligibility for office and tear down or protect hereditary privileges and exemptions from collective labor. In the process, they redefined relationships of reciprocity within their communities and between their communities and powerful individuals. Economic utility came to stand in as a primary measure of the common good and a means by which to evaluate whether a custom was good or bad, a process that accelerated during the second half of the eighteenth century. In short, economics had become a gauge of custom's morality.

Native authorities and Spanish officials alike cast the customary labor required to produce elaborate religious celebrations as wasteful. Native authorities of commoner status and Spanish judges also denounced personal service—long justified through recourse to custom—as illegal and contrary to the economic health of the community. Native authorities also demanded that men who claimed hereditary privilege perform labor that had previously been relegated to commoners, maximizing manpower to meet heightened tribute and fiscal obligations to the Crown. And they demanded that highborn men participate in town council activities oriented toward litigation in defense of the common good, reflecting the growing power of commoners in the Native cabildo and the ways in which custom came to be defined according to class interests. While Native authorities appealed to custom to justify coercive measures toward those who failed to comply with communal obligations that benefited an economic and instrumentalist view of the common good, some Native litigants appealed to the right of individuals to opt out of participation when they perceived custom as unjust and to the benefit of a few rather than the broader collective. When there was no custom to justify such a stance, they sometimes invented a new one.

Custom had always been a contested legal terrain in Native legal disputes, from the moment that Native litigants first appeared bearing their codices that documented long-standing practices of land tenure or collective labor. The eighteenth century produced a multiplier effect, however, in the proliferation of meanings and practices attached to custom, many of which reflected a widening gap in the interests of different status groups within Indigenous communities. For these reasons, Native authorities found it beneficial to write down their version of custom, as evident in the 1784 dispute over personal service in Teposcolula. If they could acquire the consent of those they governed—signaled by the signatures of community members on written agreements—they could use the paper as proof of custom's legitimacy. The next chapter examines in detail laboral customs enshrined in simple contracts in eighteenth-century Oaxaca.

Prescriptive Custom 7

WRITTEN LABOR AGREEMENTS IN
NATIVE AND SPANISH JURISDICTIONS

THE ORGANIZATION AND PROVISION of labor constituted a core obligation of Native communities and a key tenet of Native custom, as made
clear in the disputes in Spanish courts of first instance discussed in the previous chapter. The internal workings of customary labor, administered and
negotiated within the jurisdiction of Native towns, provides another perspective on the remaking of the social contract in Oaxaca's Native communities
during the eighteenth century. In Native town halls across the mountainous
expanses of the region, Indigenous scribes wrote short and simple documents
that enshrined their community's customary labor obligations on paper. The
documents were written in the Native languages of Oaxaca's rural communities and archived in the town hall. Native authorities retrieved them from
safekeeping when disputes over who should do labor and for whom erupted.
If they could not resolve the conflict within the confines of their community or administrative unit, they folded the documents carefully in a piece of
cloth or a reed mat and brought them to the court of the Spanish magistrate.
There, they initiated a legal suit and submitted the contracts as evidence in
the case. The objective was to force commoners and dependent, subject communities to comply with custom and perform their labor. Sometimes decades
elapsed between the production of the original contract and the end of the
suit in the Spanish court.

The contracts and the litigation that unfolded around them provide a longitudinal view of how custom was produced, contested, and transformed through the dynamic interplay of Native and Spanish jurisdictions on the one hand, and social memory and paper records on the other. The documentary trail illuminates the legal arguments that commoners and subject communities used to challenge onerous customs of communal labor that benefited the Native elite or larger, more powerful communities as well as the strategies that Native authorities used to impose, maintain, or challenge them. The juxtaposition of the Native language of the contracts and their translations into Spanish provides further insight into the production of cross-cultural ideas about customary labor, communal obligations according to class and status, and the common good.

It might seem counterintuitive that Native people wrote custom down in eighteenth-century Mexico. Romantic conceptions of Native custom—and of local custom in the Mediterranean-Atlantic world more broadly—construe it as oral tradition, grounded in popular memory and the will of the community. These assumptions have more to do with essentialist notions of community and identity than they do with historical reality. Historians of medieval and early modern Europe have shown that custom was in fact recorded in writing, beginning with the legal revolution of the twelfth century. As discussed in chapter 1, European kings enlisted jurists to redact custom as part of a long process of centralizing legal authority. As the historian Susan Reynolds notes, these written compilations of custom "were themselves products of the new, professional law, fossilizing custom, and adapting it to the new world of bureaucratic government."[1] The impulse to put custom in writing went beyond the purview of emerging states. Local-level authorities in the Iberian Peninsula and other parts of Europe also wrote custom down in response to quotidian disputes, contests over its meaning, and as a hedge against the impositions of royal power and future conflict of all kinds. In the process, old customary rights were reinforced and new ones instated.[2]

Colonial Mexico's Spanish administration took a different stance toward Native custom and writing than did their counterparts in Europe, based in part on their attitude toward Indigenous knowledge. As discussed in chapter 5, whereas in the early colonial period Spanish judges accepted Indigenous codices as testament to pre-Hispanic norms and often ruled to uphold the customs for which they provided evidence, after the 1580s Spanish authorities grew increasingly skeptical of codices and other forms of Indigenous memory. On top of this, according to colonial law, Native communal justice, based in custom, was supposed to be administered summarily and orally

CHAPTER SEVEN

within the ambit of Native pueblos. Scholars have assumed, therefore, that judges, lawyers, and litigants restricted Native customary claims primarily to the realm of orality. Rich studies of Indigenous custom in colonial Mexico and other regions of Spanish America, which rely on oral testimonies of Native witnesses whom Spanish officials called upon to testify to custom's content and origins in civil lawsuits, reinforce this assumption.[3]

It turns out, however, that Native authorities did write custom down, in their own languages, in Spanish genres of written agreements. These short texts, often buried among the dozens and sometimes hundreds of pages of civil proceedings that constituted Indigenous lawsuits, are easy to overlook. When analyzed closely, they tell a different story about the relationship of Native custom to writing and of Native custom to colonial law. As authors of these records, Native officials showed themselves to be not only petitioners, litigants, and subjects of imperial law but also its authors, producers, and enactors. They wrote custom down in contractual form in order to impose social discipline and avail themselves of Spanish legal enforcement of local norms at a time when Native commoners, litigants, and Spanish authorities were contesting the meaning and legitimacy of Native custom. In the narrative that follows, I focus on two long-term disputes over custom, one in San Juan Tabaá from 1709 to 1766 and the other in Teposcolula from 1723 to 1776. Both disputes were initiated under the umbrella of village justice and then moved to the Spanish courts of Villa Alta and Teposcolula, respectively. These cases provide an encapsulation of the process through which custom's unwritten code could become a binding contract and, ultimately, a provisional form of local law that served the interests of the powerful in Native communities.

The Case of San Juan Tabaá, 1709–1765: Who Should Build the Fences?

THE CONTRACTS: 1709, 1729, 1730

On August 12, 1709, the heads of household of the Zapotec town of San Juan Tabaá—133 men, including caciques, principales, commoners, and unmarried youth—gathered at the municipal hall to put a labor agreement into writing.[4] It was customary for the male community members to gather together to conduct important town business; it lent legitimacy to communal politics. If village authorities made big decisions or acted without the consent of the community, then it could be contested or called out as invalid.

The Native governor presided over the gathering along with the town's municipal officers. As was true in many regions of colonial Mesoamerica, the labor of Indigenous commoners was intimately entangled with the use of the pueblo's collectively held lands, which served multiple purposes. The town council administered communal lands by allotting individual plots to families who held them in usufruct and farmed them to sustain their families. These lands were known as *tierras de común repartimiento*.[5] Other plots, known in Spanish as *propios* and *arbitrios*, were dedicated lands of the municipal council that supported village officers and their families, activities of the town council, and taxes. The village's Christian confraternities administered another portion, working or leasing the land in order to sustain the local cult of the saints.[6] Forests and grasslands at the edges of Native communal holdings, known as tierras baldías, supplied the community with resources such as wood, herbs, berries, medicinal plants, and pasture land but could not be cultivated.[7] Other plots of communal land could serve as pasture. In the case of San Juan Tabaá, some of the town's powerful and prosperous men, identified as principales, owned oxen and mules, which they grazed in the commons. Unsurprisingly, if left untended, the animals made a mess, trampling and eating their way through villagers' crops. But from the principales' point of view, this was not their problem. They insisted that the commoners who farmed in the adjacent fields should build a paddock for the livestock and fences around their crops to keep the livestock out.[8]

No matter that the fencing duties fell to men who did not own oxen or mules. Even though this seemed unfair, the principales later maintained that the arrangement was actually a reciprocal one. After all, the whole community benefited from the use of mules and oxen to transport the produce of communal and confraternity lands and to transport the bishop, Spanish magistrate, and other judges during their visits and parish inspections. The principales noted that they provided their animals for such purposes without charge. They further maintained that the commoners should fence their fields rather than principales building paddocks for the livestock on their private lands. In this way, if the livestock were to escape and trample the commoners' crops, it would be the commoners' own fault for having built weak fencing. It would also prevent the commoners from suing the principales since the law allowed for civil suits against the livestock owners if the paddock were built on their private lands. According to the principales, the entire arrangement—from the requirement that farmers build fences around their fields, to the assumption of damages by the farmers if their crops were destroyed by wandering livestock, to the use of privately owned livestock for communal economic and ceremonial purposes—was legitimate because it benefited the common good. And just as importantly, it was legitimate because it was ancient custom.[9]

The short half-page document penned on common paper in the Zapotec language was a simple written agreement stating that the commoners had to build the paddock for the principales' livestock and fences around their own fields. The text of the document adheres to the norms of Indigenous colonial notarial writing, with an opening that notes the date and location of the document's production and authorities and persons present, followed by the meat of the text, a ceremonial formula for closing, and the signatures of those who authorized the document. The formulae and the signatures demonstrate the close relationship between orality and writing in the face-to-face context of village administration and justice and its performative nature (figs. 7.1, 7.2).

The language of the text itself points toward the ongoing process of producing intercultural notions of authority, law, obligation, and custom. As was typical of Indigenous notarial writing, the text combined Zapotec concepts of order, hierarchy, and reciprocity with Spanish legal terms and concepts expressed through loanwords. To express the idea of the town hall in the opening, the Native officials used the mixed construction *yoho lahui Audiencia lichi Rey* (the community and court, house of the king), which connected the Native officials' civil and legal authority directly with that of the Spanish king.[10] The body of the agreement centers on the interrelated concepts of labor, land, and custom. The Native officials used the Zapotec term *china*, which, as discussed in previous chapters, combines the ideas of labor, obligation, and office holding to frame the commoners' work as a duty to the community defined by their social position and as part of a web of reciprocal social relations. They used the hybrid construction *yoo testamento* to express the idea of privately held land and land held in usufruct, passed down through families via last wills and testaments. In the absence of expensive legal titles, Native-language testaments were the primary evidence of individual land tenure in Indigenous communities. Distinguishing between individual and communal land was crucial to the agreement, since the principales claimed that liability for damages did not apply on common lands. Custom, an idea central to the legal claim in the agreement, appears as a hybrid formulation, combining the Spanish loanword *costumbre* with the Zapotec terms for forebears (*xosi*) and antiquity (*golaza*): "the ancient custom of our fathers and grandfathers."[11] Reference to custom's antiquity met Spanish legal expectations that in order for custom to be legitimate, it required longevity. The invocation of the community's forebears anchored custom in the authorita-

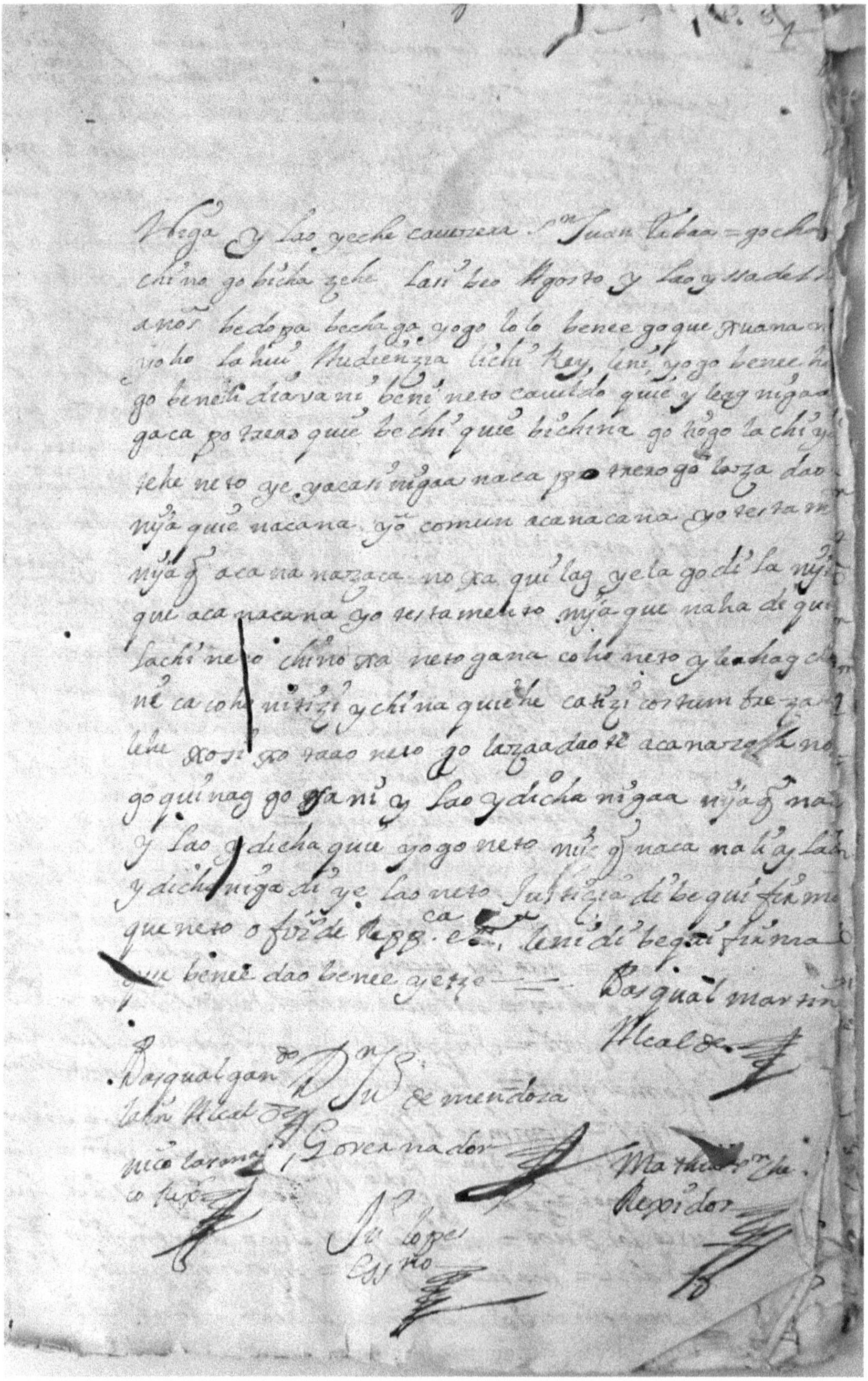

Figure 7.1 Convenio de San Juan Tabaá. Courtesy of the Archivo Histórico Judicial de Oaxaca.

Figure 7.2 Signatures of the común of San Juan Tabaá. Courtesy of the Archivo Histórico Judicial de Oaxaca.

tive role of ancestors in Zapotec society. At the same time, reference to blood lineage evoked the centrality of family and community to custom in the Mesoamerican and Iberian worlds.

The document closes with the solemnities typical of Spanish legal writing, stating that no one could break the agreement because it was grounded in the community's collective, true judgment and legal reasoning. The closing text also makes claims to its legal force by stating that no one could thwart the agreement because it was legally binding and agreed to by all. The signatures of the town officials, their governor, and 133 heads of household, all written in the hand of the town scribe, follow the closing text. The signatures take up an entire page, dwarfing the short text of the contract and producing an illusion of consensus.[12]

The agreement's format and language mattered. Even though it was written on common paper in an Indigenous language, it was a notarized record with the power to create real-world effects. According to the *Siete Partidas*, a written agreement qualified as a promise, defined as "words granted by men to one another with the intention of binding themselves to one another, coming together about a particular thing that they must give or do."[13] Promises—written or unwritten—were binding in the eyes of God and, according to many theologians and jurists of the time, in the eyes of civil law.

Written promises could become custom if they applied to community norms. Newer customs, of more recent provenience, lent themselves well to written form, in part because they could not be legitimized by claims to antiquity. According to the *Siete Partidas* (as discussed in chapter 1), customs could be established if they were reasonable, born of the will and consent of the majority, and practiced for ten to twenty years. Establishing customs required substantial deliberation by the community and a public, standardized process for their founding. Popular consent had to be given freely; coercion, fear, ignorance, and error made the establishment of a custom invalid. A newer custom also had to survive a judicial test. During the ten to twenty years required for its institutionalization, it had to be upheld at least twice by a judge or authority without objection, and if a judge ruled against a legal challenge to it after hearing testimony from both parties, then custom could stand.[14]

Francisco Suárez, a Spanish theologian who wrote prolifically about custom in his widely circulated 1612 treatise *Tractatus de legibus ac Deo legislatore* (*On the Laws and God the Legislator*), elaborated on the question of how to establish a custom. He reinforced the principles set forth in the *Siete Partidas* that the process of introducing newer customs must manifest popular consent, arguing that a minority could not establish a custom binding on the entire community, though the consent of the majority could be taken to stand in for that of the whole corporate body. Equally important, he argued, acts introducing customs had to demonstrate the will and intention that the custom "become a law for posterity."[15] Intention was therefore crucial to establishing custom's legitimacy. Mere repetition over long periods of time could not establish custom as a source of law if intention was absent. Suárez also noted that customs could only be established by communities that had the authority to create laws for themselves and that possessed "the power of being bound by their own laws."[16] He quibbled with the idea that the judicial decision of a magistrate was necessary to validate a custom. A magistrate could only confirm its existence.[17]

The Native authorities of San Juan Tabaá appear to have understood the principles for establishing customs set out in colonial legislation, the *Siete Partidas*, and Suárez's treatise. Colonial law held that Indigenous communities could rule themselves according to their old customs or those that they established anew after their conversion to Christianity; in short, they held the power of being bound by their own laws, provided that those laws did not contravene Christianity or Spanish law. The signatures on the written agreement provided evidence of the consent of the community's heads of household, and the signatures of the Native authorities showed that it had been authorized by a local judge (the Native alcalde). The formal proceedings in the town hall that accompanied the production of the document fulfilled the need for a public, standardized, and deliberative process, captured by the solemnities of the ceremonial language that closed the document. The written agreement itself, designed to formalize the custom, was proof of the will and intention that the custom serve as local law for posterity. The assertion that the custom was actually old lent it added legitimacy.

By presenting local custom in the language and format of a written promise, the Native authorities of San Juan Tabaá designed a document that would stand up in a Spanish court as valid proof of prescriptive custom. But its content raises important questions regarding its pretensions to representing the popular will and consent of the majority. After all, the agreement enshrined a custom that benefited the principales while cutting a raw deal for the commoner farmers. Why, then, did the commoners sign it? Did they fully understand its provisions or were they deceived? Did they acquiesce because of the moral authority of the village officials and principales? Did the village scribe simply add their signatures without their knowledge?

Not only was the labor arrangement a raw deal, but so too were the other terms of the contract. Despite its ostentatious claims of reciprocity, the contract saddled the commoners with risk and immunized the principales from legal liability. If the commoners neglected to build good fences, then the livestock owners would not be liable for damages to crops; the farmers would have to absorb the loss and effectively lose their work. The only explanation for the commoners' consent, if they in fact provided it, was the weight of their social superiors' authority, perhaps reinforced with the threat of coercion. In fact, the agreement was likely drawn up in the first place because the farmers were not building the fences as the principales wanted them to do, and the principales sought a legal means to force them into line. Through the agreement, then, the principales and the Native authorities attempted to mold social reality to their interests. The power that the Spanish legal system invested in written agreements lent the document itself a weighty significance, independent of the negotiation that produced it and the labor relations it represented. In this way, it acquired a social value and reality all its own, a "papereality" that produced two interrelated levels of conflict in San Juan Tabaá over the ensuing decades: people were fighting about laboral custom and the paper on which it was recorded all at once.[18]

In 1729 and 1730, the Native governor, cabildo, principales, and commoners of Tabaá gathered once again to replay the solemn ceremony they had enacted two decades earlier and re-enshrine the custom in a new contract. Why did they do so? Were the commoners falling down on their end of the bargain by refusing to build the fences? Were the Native authorities at the urging of the principales attempting to fulfill the requirements set out in the *Siete Partidas* for the establishment of a new custom, in which said custom had to be upheld by a judge twice within ten to twenty years? It is likely that a combination of commoner resistance and legal procedure motivated the rewriting of the agreements. The principales' desire to add new provisions to the agreement may have also motivated a redrafting. According to the new versions, commoners could farm nopal cactus on communal lands, but they would have to fence their cactus fields (*nopaleras*). If their crops were by chance damaged by livestock, they would not be entitled to seek damages. According to Spanish law, Indigenous commoners were legal minors and, as such, they could demand restitution if harmed.[19] This new agreement undercut the legal protections afforded to Indigenous commoners by forfeiting their right to claim damages for labor lost.

Economic and demographic changes provide some explanation for these new provisions. Cochineal, a coveted red dye-stuff produced by a parasitic insect that lived and reproduced on the paddles of nopal cactuses, dominated the colonial economy of Villa Alta during the eighteenth century. Its gorgeous red-purple hues—created by drying the insects, crushing them into a powder, and mixing the powder with water—colored the attire of Europe's royalty and nobility. Indigenous farmers cultivated nopales, and collected and dried the insects (known as *grana de cochinilla*) through the system of corvée labor known as the repartimiento. The Spanish magistrate of Villa Alta, who held an official monopoly on cochineal trade, provided periodic cash advances to the region's Native authorities who oversaw local production. In some cases, though, the Spanish magistrate contracted repartimiento debts directly with individual families or with principales. At the end of a stipulated period, Spanish officials returned to collect the grana. The profits to be made from grana de cochinilla were massive and, as a result, the administrative post of Spanish magistrate of Villa Alta was one of the most sought after and expensive saleable offices in the colony.[20]

Although the broad mechanisms of the repartimiento of grana de cochinilla are well known, the specific means by which communities organized household production varied and in many cases remain murky. In Villa Alta, individual households sometimes cultivated small plots of nopales on their house lots so that women and children could tend to the insects. When larger pieces of land were devoted to nopales, it appears that local customs of land tenure reigned supreme. In the case of San Juan Tabaá, midcentury documentation regarding land use shows that individual families worked two small cactus fields presumably to pay for individual repartimiento debts. The community directly administered two additional cactus fields on communal lands, presumably to pay for repartimiento debts contracted by the community.[21] The 1729 and 1730 written agreements introduced a new element, then, into customary land tenure and labor relations in San Juan Tabaá. Native authorities were not worried about the principales' livestock trampling just any crop planted on communal lands; the communal nopal cactus plots were of paramount concern because they ensured the community's ability to make good on their repartimiento debts.

THE CIVIL SUIT

The inequities built into the new terms of the labor agreement in San Juan Tabaá did not hold. Barely a year after the ink on the paper had dried, the commoners balked by refusing to build fences. This time, rather than dealing with the matter within the confines of the community, the municipal authorities and a number of principales of Tabaá went to the Spanish magistrate to complain that some villagers had not complied with their obligations and damage was being done to the fields. They brought the written agreements with them as evidence of village custom. Following legal procedure, the Spanish magistrate don Antonio Blanco de Sandoval received their instruments of justice and ordered the court interpreter to translate them into Spanish.[22] Once they were translated, the alcalde mayor categorized them according to Spanish genres of notarial writing, deciding that they were *convenios*, the simplest form of contract between parties concerning property, right, or obligation. Convenios, which grew out of the wide terrain of medieval European *convenientiae* (written agreements), represented a common format for the establishment of custom in writing. Convenientiae did not conform precisely to a prescribed template or to the rigorous obligation of a formal commercial contract. Rather, it was a flexible genre that could be molded to the customary usages of diverse places and times.[23] Good faith, unanimity of opinion, the consent of the signatories, absence of outside interference or disturbance, and the goals of good government and social peace lent these written customary agreements legitimacy in the eyes of a judge.[24] In seventeenth- and eighteenth-century Oaxaca, convenios represented a means by which customary labor arrangements within pueblos and between multiple pueblos regarding the construction of hammock bridges, formation of highway patrols, and, most commonly, support of the Christian cult were formalized.[25]

Tabaá's officials requested that the Spanish magistrate validate the agreements, thereby lending them the weight of royal authority. They argued that they needed to enforce the protection of the crops grown on communal lands because the grana and other goods they produced supported Spanish ecclesiastical and civil interests and served the common good. Notably, they defined the common good in terms of economic utility, in keeping with eighteenth-century trends discussed in chapter 6. The Spanish magistrate supported their argument and confirmed and validated the agreement with a judicial decree. He stated that no one could break the agreement and that anyone who did would suffer the appropriate penalty. He also added a rider to the agreement: those who had nopal cactus fields should fence them in, and those who did not should not damage them on purpose. He also noted that the agreement applied only to the community of Tabaá; the custom was not valid elsewhere.[26]

Three aspects of the alcalde mayor's judgment on the matter merit attention. First, in ratifying the agreement, he introduced the application of a penalty for anyone who broke it. The Zapotec-language agreements forged in Tabaá's municipal hall made no mention of penalties. This makes sense since Native authorities were prohibited by law from imposing penal fines on community members; this was the provenience of Spanish jurisdiction. Clearly, the town's Native authorities felt they needed the coercive power of Spanish legal authority to enforce custom. Second, the stipulation that the agreement should apply only to the community of Tabaá and was not generalizable to other towns in the district reinforced the local character of the custom and validated the idea that the Spanish magistrate would weigh each community's claims to custom according to unique political and economic circumstances. The judge's position reflected the contingent value of local custom, which depended on its relation to colonial interests. Third, the Spanish judge flagged the special necessity of fencing fields of nopal cactus and admonished those who did not have them not to damage the cactus fields on purpose, perhaps suggesting that the commoners had been sabotaging nopal cactus fields as a form of resistance.

With the Spanish magistrate's support behind them, the authorities of Tabaá returned to their community to draw up a *compromiso*, a different kind of legal instrument that had more teeth than a convenio. A compromiso was a contractual agreement between parties that gave power of arbitration to an outside party, essentially authorizing him to resolve or decide the dispute and impose damages.[27] The content of the compromiso, which was written in Zapotec, signed, and witnessed on October 11, 1731, more or less mirrored that of the earlier written agreements and cited custom as its source. But this time, the agreement's binding power did not reside in mutual promise. The signatories gave power of arbitration to the Spanish magistrate and stipulated corporal punishment—whipping—for the commoners who broke it.

The signatories were many, in fact, more than had signed the 1709 agreement: a new governor, municipal officers, and town scribe, and 173 male villagers—40 more and a 30 percent increase over those who signed in 1709. The expansion of signatories reflected population growth in San Juan Tabaá, which jumped from 699 in 1703 to 1,019 in 1742, a 45 percent increase consistent with a demographic boom across the district.[28] The rise in population combined with surging demand for grana de cochinilla heightened the stakes in the dispute, as the community sought to expand cultivation of nopal cactus. More land devoted to nopales meant less land available for subsistence crops. In this context, allotting communal lands for pasture and expending labor to build protective fences placed an increasingly heavy burden on the commoners of San Juan Tabaá.

Two additional signatories added to the weight of the 1731 compromiso: the parish priest, don Joseph Gutiérrez Girón; and a resident Spaniard, don Juan Martín de Escapa, who the alcalde mayor had requested serve as witnesses to the agreement. As local authorities and notables, these men's signatures guaranteed the legitimacy of the process and agreement's content. The priest confirmed in a written statement at the bottom of the compromiso that the Native authorities, town notables, and male members unanimously agreed that the compromiso was in the best interest of the peace and calm of the community. On October 23, the Native authorities of Tabaá sent the compromiso back to the Spanish court, where the Spanish magistrate authorized and validated it.[29]

The transformation of the convenio into a compromiso signaled a shift in power by moving the arbitration of custom from the ambit of Native jurisdiction to Spanish jurisdiction. In the process, the agreement's binding authority, which had been based in the consent of the signatories, transferred to legal authority outside the community, in this case, the Spanish magistrate. The signatories of the compromiso also granted the Spanish magistrate the authority to punish those who transgressed it. The process of moving custom from a Native-language record to an instrument of Spanish law reveals the dynamic co-creation of custom and provisional law enforceable by the coercive power of a Spanish judge.

Despite the fact that the 1731 compromiso bore the weight of Spanish authority and threat of punishment, commoner farmers of Tabaá continued to flout their obligations. In May 1765, sixteen principales from San Juan Tabaá, none of whom were office holders, presented a petition to the Spanish magistrate, complaining that some villagers who did not have oxen or mules refused to fence their crops, to the detriment of the community. Their lament was familiar, as was their reasoning. The wandering livestock were ruining the communal cornfields and those dedicated to the confraternities. Although it seemed unfair that those who did not own livestock should build the fences, the custom was reciprocal because the principales allowed the community to use their animals for a variety of purposes without charge. In addition to rehashing the dispute, the principales requested that the Spanish magistrate require villagers from the neighboring community of Lachirioag whose lands bordered those of Tabaá's to fence their crops. They ended by citing the support of their municipal authorities; the alcaldes of San Juan Tabaá had agreed to appear in the Spanish court to support their petition should the Spanish judge require it.[30]

The Spanish magistrate did not lose much time in ruling to uphold the terms of the 1731 compromiso. He reasoned that whether villagers owned livestock or not, they had to fence the paddocks, their cactus fields, and croplands. He also went above and beyond the stipulations of the 1731 agreement by ruling that those who lost their work—and the community's crops—due to roaming livestock not only had no right to claim damages but also had to pay damages for the losses incurred by the community. Furthermore, it was not enough to build fences; they had to be well made, and if not, and livestock broke through, villagers could not claim damages in Spanish court. He concluded his response to the petition by an admonition to the villagers of Tabaá to be "diligent and not negligent in caring for and attending to their own interests and the things that sustain themselves and their families."[31] In other words, building fences served the common good.

The commoners were unmoved by the Spanish magistrate's legal decision and refused to comply with custom. Tabaá's municipal authorities responded by informing the Spanish magistrate of their disobedience and notifying him that they were planning a visit to the Spanish court to make their case to uphold custom and the terms of the written agreement. The commoners mobilized too and showed up en masse at the district court to make their case. On May 22, 1765, the Spanish magistrate wrote that a "copious number of Indians" from San Juan Tabaá came before him to request exemption from fencing in their fields given that they were in the middle of sowing season and could not afford to divert their labor from the task at hand. The parish priest sent a letter to the Spanish magistrate to support their request, arguing that it required significant labor for each individual to fence in his fields and that such an obligation was particularly onerous during planting season. He also suggested that the custom was unfair: shouldn't those who have livestock fence the paddock?[32]

The priest's appeal appears to have hit a chord with the Spanish judge. Not only was the principle of equity central to the ideology of Spanish justice, but Spanish law also upheld the right of all the Crown's subjects and vassals, including enslaved peoples, to subsistence. The Spanish magistrate conceded that given that the petitioners needed to attend to their fields, they did not have to fence their cropland until after they finished planting. But once the sowing season was over, he would vigorously enforce the 1731 compromiso and the terms that he had added to it: the villagers who planted on communal lands had to build sturdy fences around their cactus fields and croplands, and it was up to the authorities of Tabaá to ensure that the fences were strong and well made. In addition to building fences around their own crops, they had to build a paddock for the livestock.[33]

With the passage of eighteen months and the election of new municipal authorities, the case took a turn. The municipal government, which had supported the claims of the principales regarding the validity of local custom, switched sides and supported the commoners' resistance to the principales, a very meaningful turn of events. Now, the Native cabildo represented the interests of the commoners rather than serving as a tool of the powerful. In the legal instruments produced during this new phase of the case, the union of cabildo, community, and commoner interests was expressed by the concept of el común, which as discussed in chapter 6 was a juridical term that embodied the idea of community as popular, collective legal voice and political subject, to the exclusion of the hereditary nobility. The shift in meaning of el común was in keeping with general trends in the second half of the eighteenth century in which Native authorities increasingly counted commoners within the ranks of high offices and challenged the customary privileges of principales and caciques.[34]

In November 1766, Tabaá's governor, municipal officers, and lawyer presented a petition to the Spanish magistrate on behalf of 219 heads of household. The petition called into question the validity of the Zapotec-language agreements, arguing that they did not have the force of law as would a transactional legal agreement (*instrumento de transacción*) or a compromiso.[35] Their reasoning raised the question of what made an agreement binding, a topic that inspired long-standing legal and moral-theological debates. In the medieval and early modern Spanish legal tradition, there were many forms of binding agreements and contracts, which fell under the broad category of pacts. Pacts came in different forms. According to Pedro Murillo Velarde's *Cursus Iuris Canonici Hispani et Indici* (*Curso de derecho canónico hispano e indiano*), an eighteenth-century compendium of Spanish civil law, canon law, and colonial legislation, a pact was an agreement between two or more parties born of mutual consent based on the convergence or coincidence of the wills of the participants.[36]

In the 1765 dispute over custom brought before the Spanish magistrate, the nature of the written pacts presented by the opposing parties in Tabaá was paramount, and the legal representatives on both sides drew from long-standing European debates about what made a written agreement binding. Early modern jurists and moral theologians used the metaphor of clothing to categorize pacts. A naked or simple pact rested on the consent of the parties to the agreement, and conscience bound the parties to comply with the natural obligations to one another agreed to in the pact. A pact was dressed, however, if written in the language and genres of the law. Such clothing produced a civil obligation enforceable by a legal authority. According to Leonardus Lessius's 1605 treatise *On Justice and Law*, pacts could be clothed in many ways, including formal wording, writing, an oath, or performance of the agreement by one party. Pacts could also be dressed by designation as nominate contracts, meaning contracts named by virtue of their particular purpose, such as purchase and sale.[37] According to the *Siete Partidas*, there were four types of innominate contracts, the first two concerning property transactions and the second two, services and labor.[38] The Zapotec-language agreements between the principales and commoners of Tabaá clearly hewed to the latter. If one party abided by his side of the agreement, he could demand that the other party comply with his obligation and require him to pay any damages and losses sustained through failure to comply.[39] The powerful men of San Juan Tabaá understood these intricacies well and produced their written agreements with an eye to conformity with the Spanish laws of obligation.

The question provoked by these distinctions, which had significant bearing on the civil dispute in Tabaá, was whether simple pacts and innominate contracts were binding in civil courts. This question did not have an easy answer either, and it had inspired long debate among European jurists and theologians. According to Roman law, naked pacts were not binding or enforceable in civil courts. They needed legal formalities, or the clothing of positive law, to be actionable. Adherents of natural law disagreed, arguing that naked pacts were binding because they were formed by mutual consent, which bound the parties to the agreement to one another through the natural law of obligation.[40] As discussed earlier in the chapter, the *Siete Partidas* upheld the validity of simple agreements, claiming that even verbal promises were legally binding. Canon law also recognized the legitimacy of naked pacts, which were binding in ecclesiastical courts because the parties to the agreement were bound by conscience. According to Lessius's treatise, the parties to nominate contracts often had specified rights and obligations prescribed by civil law. Innominate contracts, by contrast, had no specified purpose, and civil law provided no terms, rights, or obligations to make them binding or enforceable. Consensus alone bound the parties to the terms of the contract.[41] Since the early modern Spanish legal tradition drew from all these sources of law—Roman law, the *Siete Partidas*, natural law, and canon law—jurists and moral theologians were divided on whether naked pacts should be recognized as legitimate in civil courts. Although they remained divided on the question of how to determine the extent of promissory obligation exactly, they tended to agree that what distinguished contracts properly speaking from social agreements was the creation of juridically enforceable rights and obligations.[42]

The común of Tabaá and their legal representatives drew upon these distinctions among contracts, thereby inserting their claims within this longstanding legal debate. They centered their case on the Zapotec-language convenios produced by the town's Native authorities. They did not even mention the 1731 compromiso produced in the court of the Spanish magistrate, which carried the weight of provisional civil law. In doing so, they towed the dispute back into the realm of Native jurisdiction, signaled that custom belonged to the realm of communal justice, and asserted that the enforceability of the agreement should be determined by the community.[43]

According to the petition of the común, the Zapotec-language convenio was an innominate contract, which although based on mutual consent was not binding in a court of law. On the other hand, they acknowledged that the agreement was more than a nonbinding naked pact because it included mutual and reciprocal stipulations enforceable by law, specifically the clause that stated that the commoners agreed not to claim damages in Spanish courts. By making these distinctions, the petitioners argued that the rider not to seek damages was binding but the agreement to build fences was not. The law could compel them to pay for value lost according to the clothing of the agreement (its specific clauses) but not to build fences, the naked part of the agreement. The part of the contract that addressed labor—custom—remained enforceable by conscience only.[44]

Alongside this technical argument about the nature of the written agreement, the común argued against the validity of Tabaá's laboral custom by pointing to custom in a neighboring pueblo. They referenced a recent ruling by the Spanish magistrate's lieutenant that upheld the opposite arrangement in the neighboring community of San Francisco Yatee, where the commoners were not required to fence their crops. They effectively asked why should we, the commoners of Tabaá, be compelled to build fences when our neighbors are not? Spanish law held that custom varied from pueblo to pueblo. But the común of Tabaá argued for a reading of custom that was more geographically capacious and that went beyond the jurisdiction of a single pueblo. The petitioners argued that Spanish authorities were inconsistent in upholding distinct customary labor relations in neighboring pueblos and that one custom was just whereas another was not.[45]

Finally, the común of Tabaá appealed to the Spanish legal principle of equity to make their case. They pointed out that in addition to the losses they suffered by not being able to claim damages, "the immense labor and time lost in the construction of the fences is worth nothing." Their loss was to "the total advantage and utility" of the principales. They argued that an entire community "should not be taxed for the utility of eleven individuals." The economic advantage of a few should not outweigh the economic hurt of many.[46]

The appeal to equity and utility for the common good aligned with early modern contract theory, which derived from a symbiosis of law and morality rather than the separation of the two that was characteristic of modern contract theory, and that informed nineteenth-century European private law.[47] From the perspective of early modern moral theologians, whether or not pacts and contracts were enforceable in civil courts, they were binding in the court of conscience, whose primary objective was the salvation of souls and the restitution of what rightfully belonged to another. In this view, equity mattered centrally and pacts needed to be reciprocal and beneficial to both parties. Every form of unjust enrichment constituted an offence against divine law.[48] The común used this notion of equity to argue that although they had entered into the pact voluntarily, its unjust terms undercut its validity. Custom should benefit all—or, practically speaking, most—since benefiting all was impossible.

The commoners' opponents—the principales who owned livestock—addressed the same questions as the commoners did in their own petition to the Spanish judge: what made an agreement morally and legally binding? What was the relationship between custom and the common good? Their answers erred more toward positive law. They claimed the laboral arrangement was legitimate and lawful because the Spanish magistrate issued a decree to that effect, and the entire pueblo had agreed to it with their signatures in the 1731 compromiso. Failure to abide by the contract went against utility and common good. They warned further that the commoner's legal claim would result in a lawsuit that could take up the entire year, incurring excessive costs to the municipal treasury. Meanwhile the fields would remain unfenced, which would compound the hurt to the communal economy.[49]

One of the stumbling blocks to their argument concerned the question of the perpetuity or longevity of the agreement, an issue raised by the legal representatives of the común. Could 212 heads of household and the municipal authorities of a community be bound to an agreement signed thirty-five years prior? What was considered beneficial for the common good then might not be so now. Spanish law made provisions that custom could be changed or abrogated if it was no longer advantageous.

The principales' legal representatives responded with an argument that took this problem of time and transcendence into account. They claimed that the común of Tabaá as a corporate entity (*cuerpo común* or *formal común*) was in quasi possession of the right to have the pastures fenced.[50] The principle of quasi possession derived from Roman law and over time became part of the European ius commune and canon law. The concept rested upon a dis-

tinction between possession of corporeal things—material objects, including moveable and immovable goods—and incorporeal things, which were
immaterial and existed in law, such as usufruct and obligation.[51] Their claim
implied that the right of the común transcended the interests of its individual
members and achieved force of law through continuous practice over time.
In this regard, the principales mobilized the discourse of "el común" for their
own purposes, including themselves within the purview of the community
and commons. They argued that no matter the commoner's complaints concerning equity, the republic and community of Tabaá possessed the right to
have the fences built according to the written agreement.[52] In a 1764 suit that
the López Flores brothers brought against the Native officials of San Juan
Yaeé, another Zapotec community in Villa Alta, for failing to recognize their
privileges as Native caciques, the presiding judge decided that the plaintiffs
would retain "quasi possession" of their noble titles.[53] The claim to quasi possession thus reflected the idea common in late medieval and early modern
Europe that custom constituted a form of communal property.[54]

The principales' case presented the Spanish magistrate with a conundrum.
The custom of fencing fields and paddocks no longer rested upon the consent of the community—if it ever did—but rather on the legal technicalities
presented by a handful of powerful men. This was too much for him to decide. So he sent the case to a *juez asesor* (a judge serving as consultant or legal
expert) of the Real Audiencia.[55]

On July 27, 1767, the juez asesor provided his ruling. He dismissed the legal
argument made by the común of Tabaá that the convenio was not binding in
civil law because it was an innominate contract. He cited reforms to the *Ordenamiento de Alcalá*—a body of medieval Spanish law that incorporated the
Siete Partidas, discussed in chapter 1—that claimed that signatories to a contract could not repent, or back out of, their part in simple agreements because
agreements of this type produced "rigorous, effective, and tight obligations, as
if they were named contracts."[56] Furthermore, the contract could not be dissolved without the consensus of the entire community, which included the
principales. He concluded that the commoners had to build the fences, and
if planting or harvest impeded their work, they could complete it afterward.
If they wanted to contest the perpetuity of their obligation, they were within
their rights to seek an exception to the law through the proper legal channels.[57]

In the end, the legitimacy of the laboral arrangement for building fences
in San Juan Tabaá's communal lands was determined not by the custom's equity or justice but by the qualities of the written agreement that delineated its
terms. No matter that it was produced on common paper in the Zapotec lan-

guage almost sixty years earlier in the community's town hall. The bulk of the civil suit over the custom's validity drew upon medieval Spanish and ecclesiastical ideas and laws about the obligations produced by written agreements. The case underscores the ongoing centrality of the *Siete Partidas* and canon law to matters of contractual obligation in the eighteenth century and their importance to Native legal repertoires. The case also highlights how the idea of contractual obligation defined Native custom during this period. The principales and Native authorities of San Juan Tabaá had good reason on that August day in 1709 to write down their version of custom. With the simple contract, its subsequent iterations, and the support of Spanish judges, they bound the commoners of their community to build fences for a half century and beyond.

The Case of Yolotepec, Yxcatlan, Tacahua, and Ytnuyucu, 1723–1776: Who Should Serve the Parish Priest?

THE CONTRACT

On June 27, 1723, in the Spanish district of Teposcolula, the principales and Native authorities of the parish and administrative seat (cabecera) of Santa María Yolotepec and its three subject towns or dependencies (sujetos)— Santo Domingo Yxcatlan, Santa Cruz Tacahua, and San Miguel Ytnuyucu— assembled for a formal consultative process. A new parish priest had just taken his post in Yolotepec, and the four town councils needed to determine how to support him.[58] Parish priests depended on the support of Native cabildos and especially the assistance of Native church officers to help them carry out their pastoral duties. Native communities viewed the roles played by these "church people," as they were known in various Native languages, with esteem, and the fiscal (priest's assistant) was a powerful and prestigious figure in village governance.[59]

Parish priests also depended on the goods and services—food, water, wood, maintenance of living quarters, and domestic labor—provided by the communities in which they lived for their survival. Customarily, Native officials organized the labor of commoners in order to provide these services—unpaid—playing their part in the unequal and complex set of obligations that sustained community and intercommunity hierarchy and the paternalist relationship between priests and parishioners. As was true of many tenacious customs, though, this one was contrary to Spanish law. According to a 1608 royal decree, priests were entitled to Indigenous labor to support the functions and operations of the church. Native church officers of high and low rank, from the fiscal who helped with catechesis to the topil who served as a watchman for the church and priest's living quarters, performed these services as part of their duties as Native authorities. As demanding or bothersome as this work might have been, there was no expectation that they should be paid for these officially sanctioned services. The law made very clear, however, that priests could not require personal service of commoner Native laborers—including for their subsistence needs—without pay.[60] This royal cédula was one of a series of laws through the seventeenth and eighteenth centuries that sought to abolish the practice of parish priests demanding personal service of Native parishioners and the widespread practice of involuntary, unpaid personal service more broadly.[61] As noted in chapter 6, personal service was a category of labor that sat between slavery and free wage labor. Indigenous slavery had been abolished by the New Laws in 1542, but colonists' demand for Native labor for the functioning of the colonial economy persisted, leading to the rotational labor drafts known as the repartimiento.[62] The legal justification for this form of coerced labor was that it had to serve the "common good" and "utility" of the empire and not the personal needs or interests of Spanish officials, colonists, priests, or Native lords. By cloaking personal service in the guise of custom, Spanish and Native authorities had a means by which to legitimize its continuity.

As the Native authorities and principales of the four pueblos deliberated about how to apportion the administrative support and labor for the priest, they did so within a framework of hierarchical relations in which Yolotepec as cabecera had the right to demand tribute and labor from its subject communities in order to support the church. In this regard, the labor agreement that the four towns produced compounded social hierarchy within individual communities as well as intercommunity hierarchy. Throughout the eighteenth century, Native parishes in Oaxaca drew up written agreements (convenios) that clarified the responsibilities of each town to the divine cult, couched in the language of "old custom," "friendship," "reciprocity," and "utility."[63] The rhetoric of voluntary, horizontal relations masked the onerous labor that maintenance of the parish priest, church building, and the fiesta cycle entailed. The convenios were likely produced because the old hierarchies that had sustained these relationships were fraying, as evident in a wave of secession of subject communities from their cabeceras during the eighteenth century.[64] Native authorities of cabeceras conceived of the contracts as an antidote to this process and sought to shore up long-standing and unequal bonds of obligation through recourse to judicial authority.

The written agreement produced by Yolotepec and its subject communities obscured the hierarchies of the cabecera-sujeto relationship by dividing services and labor equally among the signatory communities. At the same time, it made clear that it would be the commoners in each of the communities who would bear the brunt of the unpaid personal service. The half-page document written on common paper in the Ñudzahui language framed the labor to be provided by the four pueblos as personal service, using the Spanish loanword *serhuicio* (*servicio*). The signatures on the agreement, which represented the free will and consent of the parties, provided a hedge against the law prohibiting involuntary service (fig. 7.3).[65]

The agreement stipulated that each of the four pueblos would take their turn of service on a weekly, rotational basis. The labor and services would be provided by two married couples, indicated in the text of the agreement with the Spanish loanword *casado*; a priest's assistant, indicated by the loanword *fiscal*; and another Native official, indicated by the Ñudzahui-language term *tatno* (usually spelled "tatnu"), which means "staff of office."[66] This was likely shorthand for *tay tatnu* (staff person), referring to a person who holds office. *Tay tatnu* was used in Ñudzahui-language notarial writing as an equivalent to the Nahuatl word *topile* (holder of a staff), a term employed throughout New Spain to refer to the lowest-rung officer of the Native cabildo who often served as a watchman and messenger, among other functions.[67]

The use of the term *tatnu* instead of *topil* signals a broader pattern in colonial Mexico in which the transition from pre-Hispanic institutions of Native governance to the Spanish-style cabildo was often incomplete. While colonial Native authorities adopted the administrative functions commensurate with cabildo offices, they also maintained some of the functions of pre-Hispanic offices. In Ñudzahui-language notarial records, Indigenous scribes used Spanish-language terminology like gobernador, alcalde, regidor, escribano, and fiscal to refer to higher offices within the Native cabildo and Native church offices. However, they used Ñudzahui-language terminology to refer to lower offices like that of alguacil (constable, or *tay yonay tatnu*), alcaide de la carcel (jailor, or *tay yondaa huahicaa*), and topil (*tay tatnu*). Linguistic continuity might have corresponded to some functional continuity with pre-Hispanic offices.[68] It may have been the case, then, that the tatnu assigned to serve the priest fulfilled a broader or slightly different range of functions than those typically expected of topiles.

The tatnu and the fiscal were both Native officeholders whose role it was to help the priest with his pastoral responsibilities and church operations, which was in keeping with the law. The casados, on the other hand, were

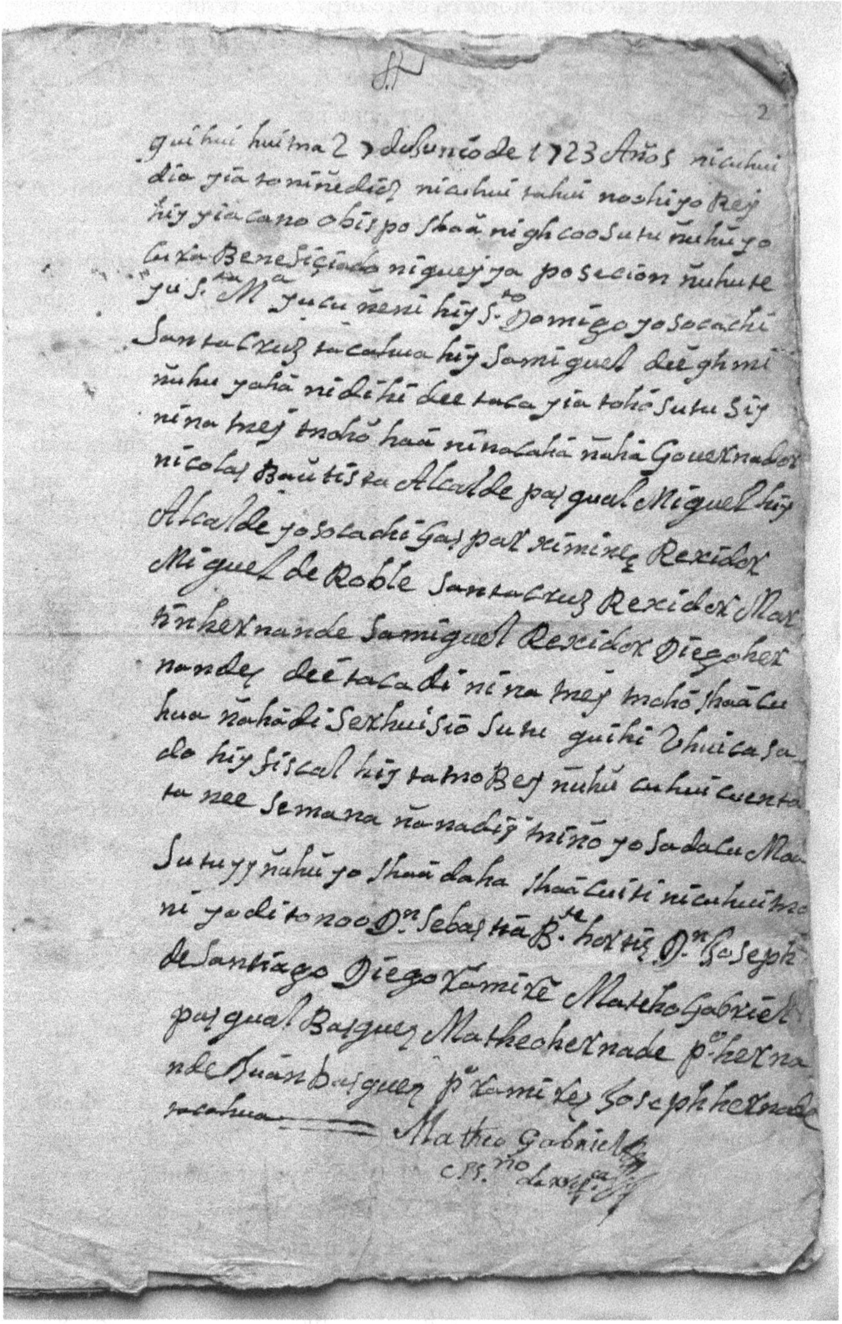

Figure 7.3 Obligación simple de Teposcolula. Courtesy of the Archivo Histórico Judicial de Oaxaca.

Figure 7.4 A couple supplying labor and goods. Codex of Yanhuitlan. On the left, a barefoot woman carries a *metate* (grinding stone) using a head strap. On the right, a barefoot man carries corn kernels in a basket, also using a head strap.

likely intended to perform a range of labor that blurred the boundary between serving essential church functions and the priest's personal needs. The custom of sending married couples to perform personal service for powerful Spaniards can be traced to the sixteenth century. The Codex Yanhuitlan shows a married couple providing food and labor for an encomendero, pointing to a precedent for this particular form of gender-based work (fig. 7.4).[69] It is likely that the women performed domestic duties like cooking and cleaning and the men performed heavier manual labor like gathering firewood and water and maintaining church buildings.

Although the contract provided few details about the specific duties of the Native officers and commoners sent to serve the priest, it did stipulate that the labor, goods, and services were not to be given without limits. In order to ensure this and guarantee that each pueblo supported the priest equitably, the tatnu was to maintain an account of what the Native officers and laborers provided during their weekly turn of service. In the contract, the Ñudzahui term *tniño* (labor, obligation, duty)—a concept that encompassed both the labor of commoners and the administrative responsibilities of Native officials—expressed the obligation to maintain the account. The Ñudzahui term *daha* (tribute in kind) expressed what the villagers who were sent to serve the priest were obligated to provide.[70] The use of the concepts tniño and daha cast the laboral relationship between priest and parishioners within a Ñudzahui framework of tributary labor and communal obligations, mediated by toho (lesser nobility), who were known in Spanish as principales and who served as Native office holders.[71] The document closes with the signatures of all the officials and principales present.

The Civil Suit

As in the case of the labor dispute in San Juan Tabaá, this Native-language labor agreement became the focus of a civil suit in the court of the Spanish magistrate of Teposcolula decades after it was written and signed. In March 1776, the officials of Yolotepec complained to the Spanish judge that according to their "ancient custom," ratified through the Ñudzahui-language contract, all four communities that were signatories had to provide the parish priest with the personal service stipulated in the written agreement (glossed as *obligación simple*).[72] Although the claim to antiquity might appear to have been a stretch for a labor arrangement produced only fifty-four years prior, according to the *Siete Partidas*, in order for a local norm to be recognized as custom, it had to be practiced continuously, without interruption, for twenty years. The authorities of Yolotepec claimed that although they continued to adhere to their "custom and obligation" as indicated in the contract, the three subject communities had not. They asked the Spanish judge to compel the officials of the three subject communities to appear in court, acknowledge the validity of the contract, and comply with it punctually unless they could present an order to the contrary from a superior court. The Spanish judge acquiesced and called the Native authorities of the three subject towns to the district seat.[73]

In their testimony to the court, the Native authorities of the subject towns challenged the claims of Yolotepec on four grounds: the validity of the contract as a legal instrument, the customary nature of the arrangement that it underwrote, the reciprocity that it implied, and the illegality of the personal service that it required. To answer back to Yolotepec's claims that the labor arrangement was legally valid according to custom, they acknowledged that their ancestors did in fact agree to the contract but that the community never actually fulfilled its provisions to provide labor and services to the parish priest. They denied ever having provided a fiscal or topil to serve the priest—only a domestic servant and two commoner laborers, who took water and wood to the priest on a weekly basis. They claimed to have stopped providing these services in 1753 because of the repeated complaints of the laborers, who said they were mistreated by the fiscales and topiles of Yolotepec. The thrust of this line of argumentation was that if the arrangement detailed in the contract was never put into practice, it could not be customary. Furthermore, the stripped-down services they provided ended exactly thirty years after the contract was signed, around the threshold of time required for a practice to become custom.[74]

In an effort to dispel the notion that reciprocity among the four towns lent legitimacy to the agreement, the officials of the three subject towns claimed that according to practice and custom, when the parish priest or his vicar came to their pueblos, they required nothing in the way of labor, service, or goods from the community of Yolotepec to support the priest's activities, and the community of Yolotepec provided nothing. They also claimed that in no way could the authorities of Yolotepec oblige them to provide the services as stated in the contract because they were involuntary, and therefore illegal, and they had won a legal decision from a higher court that said so. Finally, they argued that even though their past lords and rulers might have agreed to the contract's provisions and signed it, they did so out of ignorance, without thinking about the grave wrongs that could flow from it. Having experienced such wrongs, they refused to comply with the written agreement.[75]

In April 1776, the subject communities presented the superior legal decisions that they had cited in their testimony. The officials of Santo Domingo Yxcatlan and Santa Cruz Tacahua submitted a ruling from the Real Audiencia dated May 28, 1773, ordering priests and vicars of Yolotepec to respect the laws of the realm that stated that Indians could not be compelled to provide involuntary personal service and that if they did provide service, it had to be voluntary and paid. For their part, the officials of San Miguelito Ytnuyucu submitted a ruling from the viceroy dated December 24, 1766, declaring the separation and independence of the community from the parish and administrative seat, releasing them from any prior obligations to the parish priest.

In doing so, they participated in the wave of secession of subject communities from their cabeceras. With these legal instruments in play, the Spanish magistrate felt that the case was cut and dry. In his decision in favor of the subject communities, he wrote that the superior rulings "destroyed the force of the communities' obligations authorized by their authorities" in the 1723 contract.[76] Native custom had been thwarted by a higher authority.

As with the civil suit over customary labor in San Juan Tabaá, the legal dispute between Yolotepec and its subject communities hinged on the binding power of the written agreement and the legitimacy and equity of the custom that it promulgated and preserved. The difference in the outcome had to do with the fact that the subject communities had the law and timing on their side. After 1763, Bourbon reformers rekindled debate regarding the involuntary labor of Native people and the right of parish priests to demand payment for their services in kind. They considered both practices contrary to the economic utility of the colony since they diverted Indigenous labor and resources away from the Crown. This shift in policy likely informed the decisions of the superior judges to whom the subject communities appealed their case and whose rulings ultimately determined its conclusion.

Conclusion

In eighteenth-century Oaxaca, Native authorities recorded custom in written agreements in their own languages and in their own town halls. Doing so represented a move to shore up customary rights to commoner labor and the labor of subject communities in response to challenges from below. As they prescribed custom, they did so with awareness of the function and weight of simple contracts according to medieval Spanish law. They also did so cognizant of the legal requirements to create a new custom, especially related to the provisions of time, popular consent, and judicial validation. The contracts that they produced formed part of a diverse Native legal repertoire and indicate the depth and breadth of colonial legal consciousness, even in remote reaches of the Spanish Empire.

The disputes over custom in both case studies featured in this chapter addressed ongoing debates about the morality and legality of different forms of Indigenous labor and servitude. They did so in a context in which eighteenth-century colonial policies were realigning the Spanish moral-legal concepts of equity, reciprocity, and the common good with economic utility. The timeline of the disputes, which began in 1709 and 1723 and concluded in 1765 and 1776, respectively, provide a longitudinal view of how struggles over custom moved between Native and Spanish jurisdictions, drew upon and contributed to eighteenth-century moral and economic debates, and reflected and shaped the relationship among Native commoners, elites, and authorities, and powerful Native centers and their dependencies. The long timeline also points to an eighteenth-century process of localizing custom within individual pueblos as Spanish judges upheld customs that were distinct from one community to the next in Villa Alta and invalidated customs that bound subject communities to cabeceras in Teposcolula.

Finally, and crucially, the case studies featured here in addition to other convenios and compromisos from the archives of Villa Alta and Teposcolula demonstrate that eighteenth-century disputes over commoner labor and servitude produced a contractual understanding of custom upheld by written legal instruments. Claims to antiquity in both cases were vague and rested on shaky ground. What underwrote the validity of the customs in both cases were the contracts that preserved them—their language, genres, provisions and stipulations, and the signatures that attested to the community's consent: what we might call custom's papereality.

In written, contractual form, custom's constructed nature was more readily apparent, as was its relationship to power. Custom as written contract undercut the idea of its timelessness, essentialism, and the notion that its moral authority was rooted in antiquity and long-standing practice. It also framed popular will in a new light. The consent of the community to custom's dictates was not presumed but rather demonstrated by signatures on a page. As the signatories gave way to new generations with new material realities, claims by Native elites to the consent of the community became more tenuous.

Epilogue

MANY YEARS AGO, as a graduate student, I encountered a long and drawn-out legal dispute from eighteenth-century Oaxaca concerning the customary labor that subject communities owed to their parish seat for the celebration of Christian feast days. Competing invocations of custom by the opposing parties caught my attention, especially the ways in which the claimants saddled their versions of custom with distinct temporalities, different interpretations of local history and practice, and contrasting views of social hierarchy and reciprocal obligation. I was fascinated by how custom represented a discursive terrain for the production of local identity and social memory, while serving as a means by which to lay claim to power and resources. How could a concept be so capacious as to hold these many meanings and serve these multiple purposes all at once?

My puzzlement sent me on a journey that resulted in this book. I began with medieval European and Iberian history, where the idea of custom as a legal category was retooled in the service of managing religious difference, centralizing royal power, and systematizing a fragmented world of local laws. From this legal-intellectual foundation, I asked how Spanish theologians, jurists, and administrators harnessed the concept of custom to the purpose of empire, using it as a measure of the civility of America's Indigenous peoples according to European standards and a means by which to incorporate and subordinate Native law within an imperial order. At the same time, I realized that European ideas regarding law, justice, and custom had to be translated into an Indigenous context in order for indirect rule by Mexico's Native elite to function. The missionary enterprise, which was crucial for this process, put priests and Native elites into dialogue regarding the judicial institutions, norms, and moral underpinnings of their respective worlds, resulting in the production of a new vocabulary for negotiating authority and claims to resources. Translation implied alignment of meaning and the production of knowledge. Interpretation of pre-Hispanic law and custom through projects like the Codex Mendoza and the Relaciones geográficas served to sort good from bad customs in the colonial present and define the parameters of Native semisovereignty. The transatlantic concept of the old law as applied to Indigenous polygyny and ritual practice undermined the authority of the hereditary Indigenous nobility while giving meaning to colonial Indian custom, which by the seventeenth century was confined primarily to the realms of landholding, self-governance, and labor. Finally, I examined how through legal disputes in courts of first instance, the norms that regulated these crucial aspects of Native political and economic relations were by the eighteenth century oriented toward economic utility and litigation in pursuit of interests that were purportedly communal. A middling social stratum within Indigenous pueblos composed of principales and, increasingly, of legally literate commoners filled Native offices and guided this process as they administered communal lands, resisted the demands of caciques and cabeceras, and channeled communal resources toward legal disputes. Through litigation, custom became atomized and localized within the realm of single communities, a process that fed into the reconfiguration of the Indigenous world into individual pueblos. In this way, over the course of the colonial period, custom's primary referent changed from the law of the Native nobility and ethnic state to the law of the pueblo, of the community.

By tracing the *longue durée* process of translation, alignment, and moral sorting of Indigenous and Spanish laws and customs and by analyzing how Indigenous litigants used the resulting framework to dispute over land, labor, and political authority, this book shows how global legal orders were localized and then built from the ground up. As I argue throughout, but especially in the first two parts of the book, the Catholic Church's evangelical enterprise played a central part in this story. Missionary priests positioned themselves as the primary interlocutors for Indigenous authorities as they negotiated and adapted to the terms of colonial rule. Through translation and Christian education on the one hand, and violence and extirpation on the other, missionary friars in concert with Native allies laid the foundation for colonial legal consciousness in schools for Native youth, remote Native parishes, and through the repressive arm of the Inquisition. Scholars of colonial Hawai'i and South Africa have centered the Christian mission as a key institution in the production of colonial legal orders.[1] But nowhere was this process as prolonged or intensive as in the case of colonial Mexico.

As much as this book shows how custom gained traction locally, it also demonstrates how local actors participated in and contributed to transatlantic legal history. While Native litigants mobilized the language of custom to haggle over control of Native town councils, the boundaries around common lands, and the labor due to Native and Spanish authorities, they inflected the normative categories of natural law with new meaning resonant with eighteenth-century transformations in legal and political culture in Europe and other parts of the Americas. In doing so, they contributed to debates about the meaning of sovereignty and social contract. At the same time, they participated in the transatlantic processes of property formation, the reconfiguration of the commons, and the long-term transition toward wage labor. Claims to custom sometimes played a conservative role in Native legal disputes, arguing for the perpetuation of older modes of organizing land tenure and labor, as evident in chapter 7. But in other cases, custom could be mobilized to make the case for new forms of collective land tenure, as was seen in the partnership agreements in chapter 5. Custom's malleable relationship to time and its conceptual flexibility provided the legal terrain upon which the variegated local order of colonial Oaxaca could be renegotiated during the late seventeenth and eighteenth centuries and beyond.

Contrary, then, to my initial impressions of custom as local Indigenous practice at odds with Spanish colonial law, my research for this book has taught me that Native custom was an invention of colonial law, produced in spaces of interaction—at times violent and at others collaborative—among diverse historical actors in a broad array of institutional settings. Over time, it became communal patrimony, even property, as claimed by the principales of Tabaá in the dispute over who should build fences to keep livestock out of communal fields. And as time passed, its precise origins, whether Indigenous or Spanish, ancient or recent, became increasingly unimportant in relation to the overwhelming fact of its locality and utility as defined by Native and Spanish authorities and judges.

Custom's slippery origins speak to our current moment in which the question of the historical roots of contemporary injustices—such as dispossession and slavery—has taken center stage in public discourse. The five-hundredth anniversary of the conquest of Tenochtitlan in August 2021 added fuel to these weighty conversations. One response to the contentious question of roots and origins, epitomized by the notion of "decoloniality," has been to mark a historical before and after through the opposition of Western and Indigenous epistemologies and to argue for the recuperation of Indigenous knowledge, communalism, and harmony with nature as the basis for an emancipatory politics and solution to the manifold challenges facing our planet.[2] Decoloniality has been a guiding principle in Indigenous studies and contemporary movements for Indigenous self-determination. In my own work, it has inspired me to read against the grain and deploy Indigenous categories as frameworks for historical analysis. One of the pitfalls, though, of the decolonial vision is that it often rests on a version of Indigeneity disentangled from contact with Europeans, Africans, Asians, and other newcomers to the Americas, thereby casting Indigenous peoples as repositories of a static, insider knowledge rather than as knowledge producers dynamically engaged with history.[3] We should be careful not to draw a false dichotomy between an authentic Indigeneity and a corrupted one or to flatten the categories of "Indigenous" and "Western," when in fact these categories are heterogenous and in deep relationship with one another. Indigenous histories show how, in the face of violence and dispossession, Native people have modified, domesticated, and incorporated foreign knowledge—whether Christianity, law, language, or new forms of agriculture or animal husbandry—into the practice of everyday life. Knowledge production does not respect boundaries or the purported opposition between Indigenous and non-Indigenous; like Indigenous identity itself, it is relational and historically contingent.[4] My hope is that the history of Native custom that I have presented in this book affords some purchase on these conversations about the roots of injustice and the historical complexities and local specificities of Indigeneity in relation to knowledge, power, and colonial culture.

Recent legal reforms in Oaxaca, where Native custom's past and present come together, give concrete form to theoretical debates about decoloniality and Indigeneity. While remaining cognizant of the wide gulf between the present moment and the Spanish colonial period, I am also aware that I formulate my research questions and interpret historical sources in dialogue with the concerns of the present moment. Working in Oaxaca and observing the effects of legal change over the past twenty-five years has nourished this book by providing a broad temporal, cultural, and political framework with which to understand its stakes.

As discussed in the introduction, in 1995 Oaxaca's state legislature recognized *usos y costumbres*, now known as *sistemas normativos indígenas* (Indigenous normative systems), as local law.[5] This move grew out of transformations in Latin America's political economy in earlier decades. During the 1970s, 1980s, and 1990s, neoliberal policies in Latin America and Mexico accelerated changes in rural landholding and undermined the economic solvency of mestizo, African-descent, and Indigenous farmers and laborers. At the same time that the economic situation of the rural and urban working poor became ever more precarious, many Latin American states promulgated multicultural constitutions that recognized the cultural distinctiveness and autonomy of Native peoples and afforded certain kinds of rights based on that recognition, including self-governance and special legal jurisdiction defined by customary law. The confluence of neoliberal reform and official recognition of Native custom was not coincidental. Many critics have argued that far from being progressive, the multicultural constitutions sidestepped growing structural inequality in their nations by replacing the aspirational ideal of political equality under the law—not to mention economic justice—with the legal formalization of cultural difference, which in some ways reproduced the Spanish colonial logic of caste-based jurisdictional separation. Alongside these changes mandated from above, Indigenous social movements like the Ejército Zapatista de Liberación Nacional (EZLN, Zapatista National Liberation Army), based in Chiapas, Mexico, burst onto the scene. Although Indigenous social and political networks had been growing for decades prior, Native leaders and their allies saw an opening in a context in which the idea of Indigenous rights and cultural notions of citizenship were gaining traction on national, regional, and international scales.[6]

Indigenous intellectuals, activists, and nongovernmental organizations (NGOs) declared Latin America's constitutional reforms a victory for Indigenous rights to self-determination and cultural autonomy, arguing that usos y costumbres served as a defensive wall against state and corporate incursions of many kinds. Pointedly, international movements for Indigenous rights cast custom as a bulwark against the "new extractivism" of global corporations that threatens Indigenous-controlled land and natural resources in the Global South.[7] In Oaxaca, Indigenous intellectuals and activists have argued that self-governance according to custom would allow for the manifestation of the principle of *comunalidad*, an Indigenous epistemological concept developed during the 1980s and 1990s by Jaime Martínez Luna and Floriberto Díaz Gómez, Indigenous anthropologists from Oaxaca's Sierra Juárez and Mixe regions. Shared territory, shared governance, shared labor, and shared enjoyment represented the pillars of comunalidad, whose proponents positioned it in opposition to neocolonialism, privatization, and globalized corporate capitalism.[8]

Other local scholars, such as Salvador Aquino Centeno, have nuanced the custom-law and community-state opposition put forward by the proponents of comunalidad, situating Indigenous normative systems as historical and contested and in dynamic interplay with relationships of power within and beyond the community. They point to migration, political change, the expansion of Protestant sects into Indigenous pueblos, community relationships with NGOs, transformations in land use and tenure, and economic relationships at local, national, and global scales as processes in constant interaction and tension with the practice of comunalidad. These processes combined with emergent notions of personhood, gender, and family are necessarily pushing Indigenous communities to reformulate the "harmony ideology" that lies at the foundation of comunalidad and to reconceive of the idea of community more broadly.[9]

In this context, it is not surprising that official recognition of customary law in present-day Oaxaca has produced ambiguous effects. Although it has contributed to greater autonomy and local control in some regions, in other cases it has reinforced and reproduced internal inequalities within Indigenous municipalities, leading to increased electoral violence, the strengthening of the Partido Revolucionario Institucional (PRI, Institutional Revolutionary Party) in electoral politics, and the reinforcement of gender hierarchy.[10] And in some communities in which local leaders built alliances with state representatives and corporations, implementation of usos y costumbres facilitated megaprojects like the giant Eólica del Sur wind farm in the Isthmus of Tehuantepec at the expense of local farmers.[11] These ambiguities complicate arguments about the emancipatory potential of Native custom. None of this is to say that Indigenous customary law is inherently beholden to neoliberalism and the global corporate order or to deny that it is genuinely rooted in local tradition and practice. In fact, many of the institutions that undergird customary law date back centuries to the colonial period when self-governing Indigenous communities aligned local norms with Catholic and Spanish institutions. However, as history has shown and the present moment bears out, custom is not static, nor does it serve all interests in the community equally. Over the *longue durée*, it has represented a strategy for creating, contesting, and rebuilding a normative order in a constantly changing world.

History as a disciplinary practice, then, needs to engage critically with the closely linked ideas of Native custom and Indigeneity. When facing outward, Native custom has been associated with solidarity in the face of state power and violence, while when facing inward, it has reproduced its own forms of inequality and domination. The challenge is how to engage ethically with the entangled histories of colonialism, legal pluralism, and Indigenous identity in the present moment when calls to valorize Indigeneity and decolonize academic practice and law have rightfully disturbed the tranquility of the ivory tower. What an ethnohistory of law can bring to this conversation is a set of questions about how legal institutions and Indigenous legal claims have shaped relationships of power within Indigenous communities over time and how heterogenous Indigenous actors have mobilized law and custom to interface with diverse networks and interest groups beyond the community in pursuit of varied objectives. This is one way in which historians can meet the interpretive demands of their discipline while attending to calls for historical justice.

Notes

Introduction

1. Customary practices of mutual aid and reciprocal labor are glossed as *guelaguetza* in Zapotec.

2. Stephen, *Zapotec Women*, 137–38. For a broader survey of Indigenous customary law in the Tlacolula Valley of Oaxaca during the twentieth century, see Cordero Avendaño de Durand, *Supervivencia de un derecho consuetudinario en el Valle de Tlacolula.*

3. AHJO, VA Civil, Leg. 9, Exp. 15, 1766, Sobre que permanesca el potrero de bestias en Tabaá.

4. Bonfield, "Introduction."

5. Grossi, *El orden jurídico medieval*, 102–3.

6. Miceli, "Derecho consuetudinario y memoria"; Fitzpatrick, *The Mythology of Modern Law*; Fitzpatrick, *Modernism and the Grounds of Law.*

7. Perreau-Saussine and Murphy, "The Character of Customary Law."

8. As early as the 1920s, the anthropologist Bronisław Malinowski mounted this critique. Malinowski, *Crime and Custom in Savage Society.* For foundational work on legal pluralism, see Merry, "Legal Pluralism."

9. Stavenhagen and Iturralde, *Entre la ley y la costumbre.*

10. Burbank, *Russian Peasants Go to Court*; Sommer, *Polyandry and Wife-Selling in Qing Dynasty China.*

11. Grossi, *El orden jurídico medieval*; Howell, *The Marriage Exchange*; Astarita, *Village Justice*; Mauclair, *La justice au village*; Turning, *Municipal Officials*; Hespanha, *Como os jurstias viam o mundo, 1550–1750*; Teuscher, "Document Collections"; A. Wood, *The Memory of the People.*

12. Channock, *Law, Custom and Social Order*; Moore, *Social Facts and Fabrications*; Fitzpatrick, "Custom as Imperialism"; Ibhawoh, *Imperial Justice*; Mamdani, *Citizen and Subject*.

13. Nader, *Harmony Ideology*; Chenaut and Sierra, *Pueblos indígenas ante el derecho*; Sierra and Chenaut, "Los debates recientes y actuales en la antropología jurídica."

14. Motolinía, *Historia de los indios de Nueva España*; Torquemada, *Monarquía indiana*; Zorita, *Relación de los señores de la Nueva España*; Durán, *Historia de las Indias de Nueva España*; Sahagún, *Florentine Codex*.

15. Pomar, "Relación de Texcoco"; Ixtlilxochitl, *Obras históricas de Don Fernando de Alva Ixtlilxochitl*; Schwaller, "The Brothers Fernando de Alva Ixtlilxochitl and Bartolomé de Alva"; Brian, *Alva Ixtlilxochitl's Native Archive*.

16. Betancourt, *Códice Mapa Quinatzin*.

17. Offner, *Law and Politics*; Kellogg, *Law and the Transformation*.

18. Offner, *Law and Politics*, 55–86, 121–282.

19. Offner, *Law and Politics*, 59, 123–24, 147, 250, 285.

20. Lee, *The Allure of Nezahualcoyotl*, 96–127.

21. Kellogg, *Law and the Transformation*, xxvii–xxix; Burkhart, *The Slippery Earth*, 35–38.

22. Menegus Bornemann, *Del señorío indígena*; Sempat Assadourian, *Transiciones hacia el sistema colonial andino*; Sempat Assadourian, "Los señores étnicos"; García Martínez, *Los pueblos de la sierra*; Quezada, *Pueblos y caciques yucatecos*; Mendoza and Augusto, *El cacicazgo muisca*.

23. Seminal studies include Gibson, *The Aztecs under Spanish Rule*; Farriss, *Maya Society under Colonial Rule*.

24. For an overview of the New Philology, see Restall, "A History of the New Philology." The foundational study in the New Philology is Lockhart, *The Nahuas after the Conquest*. For the case of the Maya and the Mixtecs, see Restall, *The Maya World*; Terraciano, *The Mixtecs of Colonial Oaxaca*.

25. Burkhart, *The Slippery Earth*; Townsend, *Annals of Native America*.

26. Puente Luna, "Presentación."

27. Graubart, "Learning from the Qadi"; Graubart, "Competing Spanish and Indigenous Jurisdictions in Early Colonial Lima"; Graubart, "Containing Law within the Walls"; Yannakakis and Schrader-Kniffki, "Between the Old Law and the New"; Premo and Yannakakis, "A Court of Sticks and Branches"; Deardorff, "Republics, Their Customs, and the Law of the King"; Masters, "The Two, the Many, the One, the None."

28. Stern, *Peru's Indian Peoples*; Spalding, *Huarochirí*; Kellogg, *Law and the Transformation*; Yannakakis, *The Art of Being In-Between*; Owensby, *Empire of Law*; Ruiz Medrano and Kellogg, *Negotiation within Domination*; Ruiz Medrano, *Mexico's Indigenous Communities*.

29. Borah, *Justice by Insurance*; Yannakakis, Schrader-Kniffki, and Arrioja Díaz Viruell, *Los indios ante la justicia local*; Traslosheros and de Zaballa Beascoechea, *Los indios ante los foros*; Traslosheros, "El tribunal eclesiástico"; Cutter, *The Protector de Indios*; Cunill, *Los defensores de indios*.

30. Dueñas, *Indians and Mestizos in the "Lettered City"*; O'Toole, *Bound Lives*; Rappaport, *The Disappearing Mestizo*; Echeverri, *Indian and Slave Royalists*; Kellogg, "From Parallel and Equivalent to Separate but Unequal"; Sousa, "Women and Crime"; Premo, "Before the Law"; Premo, "Felipa's Braid"; Uribe-Urán, "Innocent Infants or Abusive Patriarchs"; Pizzigoni, "'Para que le sirva'"; Pizzigoni, "'Como frágil y miserable'"; Masters, "A Thousand Invisible Architects."

31. Serulnikov, *Subverting Colonial Authority*.

32. Puente Luna, *Andean Cosmopolitans*; van Deusen, *Global Indios*.

33. Borah, *Justice by Insurance*. For more recent work on the General Indian Court, see Owensby, *Empire of Law*.

34. Graubart, "Learning from the Qadi"; Graubart, "Competing Spanish and Indigenous Jurisdictions"; Yannakakis and Schrader-Kniffki, "Between the Old Law and the New"; Cunill, "'Nos traen tan avasallados'"; Connell, "'De sangre noble y hábiles costumbres'"; Dueñas, "Cabildos de naturales en el ocaso colonial"; Jones, "Chinamitales"; Puente Luna and Honores, "Guardianes de la real justicia"; Mumford, "Las llamas de Tapacarí"; Premo and Yannakakis, "A Court of Sticks and Branches"; Yannakakis, Schrader-Kniffki, and Arrioja Díaz Viruell, *Los indios ante la justicia local*.

35. Premo and Yannakakis, "A Court of Sticks and Branches"; Belmessous, *Native Claims*. On the centrality of jurisdictional competition to the making of colonial legal orders, see L. Benton, *Law and Colonial Cultures*.

36. On custom in colonial Latin America generally, see Tau Anzoátegui, *El poder de la costumbre*; Traslosheros, "Orden judicial y herencia medieval"; Rosenmüller, *Corruption and Justice in Colonial Mexico*; Rosenmüller, *Corruption in the Iberian Empires*.

37. McKinley, *Fractional Freedoms*; Chira, *Patchwork Freedoms*.

38. Tau Anzoátegui, *El poder de la costumbre*.

39. For an overview, see Herzog, "Immemorial (and Native) Customs."

40. Manzano, "Las leyes y costumbres indígenas."

41. Díaz Rementería, "La costumbre indígena en el Perú hispánico"; Suárez Bilbao, "La costumbre indígena en el derecho indiano"; Ramos Núñez, "Consideración de la costumbre"; Cuena Boy, "La prueba de la costumbre."

42. Menegus Bornemann, "La costumbre indígena en el derecho indiano."

43. Villella, "'For So Long the Memories.'"

44. Cunill and Rovira-Morgado, "Lo que nos dejaron nuestros padres, nuestros abuelos."

45. Ramirez, "Amores Prohibidos."

46. Mumford, "Litigation as Ethnography in Sixteenth-Century Peru."

47. Puente Luna, "That Which Belongs to All."

48. Muñoz Arbeláez, *Costumbres en disputa*.

49. See for example Yannakakis, "Costumbre" for analysis of an eighteenth-century dispute in the district of Villa Alta, Oaxaca in which one side accused the other of inventing new customs in order to overturn old hierarchies, while the other side claimed that their antagonists justified their despotism with claims to ancient

custom. By the time the case concluded, colonial officials were disinclined to respect customary claims and based their decision instead on the presentation of Spanish legal instruments.

50. Puente Luna and Honores, "Guardianes de la real justicia"; Arrioja Díaz Viruell, "Entre costumbres y leyes."

51. Herzog, "Colonial Law and 'Native Customs.'"

52. Premo, "Custom Today"; Premo, *The Enlightenment on Trial*. On centering Spanish America in the history of the Enlightenment, see Cañizares-Esguerra, *How to Write the History of the New World*; and Stolley, *Domesticating Empire*. On centering Indigenous people in eighteenth-century intellectual history, see Díaz, "The Indigenous Archive." For additional work on late eighteenth-century Native custom, see Portillo Valdés, *Fuero indio*.

53. Black, review of *Human Rights and Gender Violence*; Levitt and Merry, "Vernacularization on the Ground"; L. Benton, "Introduction"; L. Benton and Ross, "Empires and Legal Pluralism"; Yannakakis, "Making Law Intelligible"; Yannakakis, "Beyond Jurisdictions"; Duve, "European Legal History"; Duve, "Global Legal History"; Owensby and Ross, *Justice in a New World*; Premo and Yannakakis, "A Court of Sticks and Branches"; Banerjee and Von Lingen, "Law, Empire, and Global Intellectual History."

54. Poole, "Los usos de la costumbre."

55. J. Martínez, *Derechos indígenas en los juzgados*, 58–59; Eisenstadt, "*Usos y costumbres*"; V. García, "Los derechos políticos"; A. Benton, "'Participatory Governance.'"

Chapter One. Custom, Law, and Empire in the Mediterranean-Atlantic World

1. Grossi, *A History of European Law*, 1–38; Hespanha, "The Law in the High and the Late Middle Ages"; Herzog, *A Short History of European Law*; Reynolds, "Medieval Law."

2. Kelley, *The Human Measure*, 109–13.

3. Gilby, *Summa Theologiae*.

4. Gelinas, "Ius and Lex in Thomas Aquinas."

5. Aristotle, *Politics*.

6. Murphy, "Nature, Custom, and Reason."

7. Kelley, *The Human Measure*, 113–21; Brundage, *Medieval Canon Law*.

8. Stein, "Custom in Roman and Medieval Civil Law," 338. Here, Peter Stein cites Cicero's *De inventione*, 2.67.

9. Stein, "The Sources of Law in Cicero," 21–23.

10. Miceli, "Derecho consuetudinario y memoria," 108.

11. Stein, "Custom in Roman and Medieval Civil Law," 339.

12. Freir, *The Codex of Justinian*, Book VIII, Title LII, "What Is an Old Custom" ("Quae sit longa consuetudo"), Bas. 2.1.50–52, Dig. 1.3, 2218–21. See also Fred H. Blume's headnote for "Quae sit longa consuetudo" in his translation of the Justinian

Code online at the University of Wyoming Law Library. Accessed August 15, 2022, http://www.uwyo.edu/lawlib/blume-justinian/_files/docs/Book-8PDF/Book8-52 .pdf.

13. Freir, *The Codex of Justinian*, Book VIII, Title LII, "What Is an Old Custom," Bas. 2.1.50–52, Dig. 1.3, 2218–21.

14. Freir, *The Codex of Justinian*, Book VIII, Title LII, "What Is an Old Custom," Bas. 2.1.50–52, Dig. 1.3, 2218–21.

15. Tomás y Valiente, *Manual de historia del derecho español*, 83–110.

16. Glick, *Islamic and Christian Spain*, 184–219.

17. Glick, *Islamic and Christian Spain*, 184–85, 129.

18. Powers, "Law and Custom in the Maghrib"; Serrano, "Legal Practice in an Andalusī-Maghribī Source."

19. Ibn Harit Al-Jusani, *Historia de los jueces de Córdoba*, cited in Glick, *Islamic and Christian Spain*, 225.

20. Glick, *Islamic and Christian Spain*, 127.

21. Glick, *Islamic and Christian Spain*, 187.

22. Glick, *Islamic and Christian Spain*, 189.

23. Glick, *Islamic and Christian Spain*, 128.

24. Nirenberg, "Muslims in Christian Iberia," 59.

25. Graubart, *Republics of Difference*, 4–7.

26. Glick, *Islamic and Christian Spain*, 188–90.

27. Miceli, "Derecho consuetudinario y memoria," 73–106.

28. Tomás y Valiente, *Manual de historia del derecho español*, 113–54. The redaction of customary law as a means of shoring up local rights and privileges occurred throughout medieval Europe. Ibbetson, "Custom in Medieval Law," 153–55.

29. King Alfonso, *Las Siete Partidas*, 11–23; García-Gallo, "El Libro de las leyes"; Iglesia Ferreiros, "Alfonso X el Sabio y su obra legislative"; Iglesia Ferreiros, "Cuestiones Alfonsinas."

30. Miceli, "Derecho consuetudinario y memoria," 73–106. See in particular her analysis of the fueros of Castile and León.

31. King Alfonso, *Las Siete Partidas*, 1.2.4, p. 11.

32. Miceli, "Derecho consuetudinario y memoria," 204–5.

33. King Alfonso, *Las Siete Partidas*, 1.2.4, p. 11.

34. King Alfonso, ed. *Las Siete Partidas*, 1.2.1, headnote and law p. 10.

35. King Alfonso, *Las Siete Partidas*, 1.2.3, p. 10.

36. King Alfonso, *Las Siete Partidas*, 1.2.3, p. 10.

37. King Alfonso, *Las Siete Partidas*, 1.2.4, p. 11.

38. King Alfonso, *Las Siete Partidas*, 1.2.4, pp. 11–12.

39. King Alfonso, *Las Siete Partidas*, 1.2.7, p. 12.

40. Capdequí, *Manual de historia del derecho español*, 97–99.

41. Lantigua, *Infidels and Empires*, 49.

42. Zavala, *Estudios indianos*, 32–33; Viera y Clavijo, *Noticias de la historia general de las islas*, cited in Borah, *Justice by Insurance*, 17n34.

43. Macías Hernández, "La colonización europea y el derecho de aguas."

44. Gómez, *Compendio de los comentarios extendidos*; Garriga Acosta, "La trama jurídica castellana."

45. Simpson, *The Encomienda of New Spain*.

46. Lantigua, *Infidels and Empires*, 83.

47. Hanke, *The Spanish Struggle*, 23–25; Hussey, "Text of the Laws of Burgos"; Simpson, *The Encomienda of New Spain*, 29–38.

48. Brundage, *Law, Sex, and Christian Society*, 477–79.

49. Duve, "La Escuela de Salamanca."

50. Vitoria expressed these ideas in his lectures "De potestate civile" (ca. 1528), "De potestate ecclesiae prior" (1532), and "De potestate ecclesiastica altera" (1533). English translations are included in Vitoria, *Political Writings*, 1–152; see also Valenzuela-Vermehren, "The Origin and Nature of the State."

51. Vitoria, *Political Writings*, 205–327.

52. Pagden, *The Fall of Natural Man*, 100.

53. Crisp, *Aristotle*, xxiv, xv, 15, 23–24.

54. Murphy, "Habit and Convention at the Foundation of Custom"; Vitoria, *Relectio "De Indis"*; Pagden, *The Fall of Natural Man*, 97–108.

55. Vitoria, *Political Writings*, 293–327; Anghie, *Imperialism, Sovereignty and the Making of International Law*; Grant, "Francisco de Vitoria and Alberico Gentili"; Tierney, "Vitoria and Suarez on *Ius Gentium*."

56. Pagden, *The Fall of Natural Man*, 106–7.

57. Parrish and Weidman, *Las Casas en México*, 9.

58. Las Casas, *Los indios de México*.

59. Adorno, *The Intellectual Life of Bartolomé de las Casas*, 8.

60. Las Casas, *The Devastation of the Indies*.

61. Stevens, *The New Laws of the Indies*; Castro, *Another Face of Empire*.

62. Muro Orejón, *Las Leyes Nuevas de 1542–1543*, fol. 5r (page 12).

63. Puga, *Provisiones, cedulas, instrucciones de Su Magestad*, fols. 53r–56v.

64. Cunill, "El indio miserable."

65. Cunill and Rovira-Morgado, "Lo que nos dejaron nuestros padres, nuestros abuelos," 287.

66. Suárez Bilbao, "La costumbre indígena en el derecho indiano"; Menegus Bornemann, "La costumbre indígena," 156. She cites Hanke, *Los virreyes españoles en América*, 41.

67. Menegus Bornemann, "La costumbre indígena," 157. She cites AGN, "Hospital de Jesús," cuaderno 4, fols. 935–936v, also cited in "La parcela de indios," in Carrasco Pizana, *La sociedad indígena*, 122–23.

68. Villella, "'For So Long the Memories,'" 711.

69. Villella, "'For So Long the Memories,'" 698.

70. Ruiz Medrano, *Reshaping New Spain*.

71. Villella, "'For So Long the Memories.'"

72. Ruiz Medrano and Valle, "Los colores de la justicia."

73. Menegus Bornemann, *Del señorío indígena*; Haskett, *Indigenous Rulers*.

74. Tau Anzoátegui, *El poder de la costumbre*, 71.

75. Kellogg, *Law and the Transformation*.
76. *Recopilación de leyes de los Reynos de las Indias*, 2.1.4, f.126v.
77. Tau Anzoátegui, *El poder de la costumbre*, 71.

Chapter Two. Translating Custom in Castile,
Central Mexico, and Oaxaca

1. In *Africans in Colonial Mexico*, Herman Bennett charts the mutual production of African creole consciousness and legal consciousness.
2. For the case of colonial Mexico, see Burkhart, *The Slippery Earth*; Hanks, *Converting Words*; Christensen, *Nahua and Maya Catholicisms*; Farriss, *Libana*; Farriss, *Tongues of Fire*. For the case of colonial Peru, see Durston, *Pastoral Quechua*; G. Ramos, *Death and Conversion in the Andes*; Salomon and Urioste, *The Huaro-chirí Manuscript*; Estensorro Fuchs, *Del paganismo a la santidad*.
3. Martina Schrader-Kniffki and I are engaged in ongoing collaborative research on this question. Schrader-Kniffki and Yannakakis, "Sins and Crimes."
4. Gonzalbo Aizpuru, *Historia de la educación*, 111–34.
5. Sahagún, *Florentine Codex*.
6. Terraciano, "Introduction."
7. Burkhart, *The Slippery Earth*.
8. Rama, *La ciudad letrada*.
9. Blanch, "Nebrija, primer lingüista moderno"; Sarmiento, "Antonio de Nebrija y la lingüística."
10. Hamann, *The Translations of Nebrija*, 5, 11–13
11. Nebrija, *Vocabulario español-latino*, fol. XXXIv. Compare to Byron Ellsworth Hamann's appendix of changes to subsequent editions: Hamann, *The Translations of Nebrija*, 123–49.
12. Stephens, "The Roman Stoics on Habit," 38.
13. Miceli, "Derecho consuetudinario y memoria," 92–93.
14. Stephens, "The Roman Stoics on Habit," 38.
15. Nebrija, *Vocabulario español-latino*, fol. XXXIv.
16. Covarrubias Orozco, *Tesoro de la lengua castellana o española*, fol. 167v: "El menstruo, en las mugeres, se llama costumbre, por ser ordinario y consueto"; "La costumbre hace ley"; "consuetudo es altera natura"; "No hay más dura ni dificultosa batalla que pelear contra la costumbre"; "A la mala costumbre quebrarle la pierna."
17. Smith-Stark, "Lexicography in New Spain," 29–31; Farriss, *Tongues of Fire*, 204–11.
18. Lockhart, *The Nahuas after the Conquest*, 265; Farriss, *Tongues of Fire*, 217–21.
19. Lockhart, *The Nahuas after the Conquest*, 265–66; Molina, *Vocabulario en lengua castellana y Mexicana* (1571) pt. 1, fol. 73v, pt. 2, fol. 126v.
20. Farriss, *Tongues of Fire*, 213, 220.
21. Farriss, *Tongues of Fire*, 221–22.
22. Molina, *Vocabulario en lengua castellana y Mexicana* (1555), fol. 153v.

23. Molina, *Vocabulario en lengua castellana y mexicana* (1571) pt. 2, *Nahuatl to Spanish*, fol. 4r.

24. Lockhart, *The Nahuas after the Conquest*, 261–84; Hanks, *Converting Words*.

25. Lockhart, *The Nahuas after the Conquest*, 267.

26. Lockhart, *The Nahuas after the Conquest*, 284; Karttunen and Lockhart, *Nahuatl in the Middle Years*, 16–39, 52–91.

27. Molina, *Vocabulario*, pt. 1, fol. 31v, pt. 2, fol. 125v.

28. Sahagún, *Florentine Codex*, 258.

29. Boone, *Stories in Red and Black*.

30. "yn intlamanitiliz catca yn oc yehuantin tlateotocanime / yn tachtoncohcolhuan catca in maca çan tlayohuayan yn oc ce cahuitl ipan onemico." Chimalpahin Cuauhtlehuanitzin, *Codex Chimalpahin*, vol. 2, 118–19, cited in the Nahuatl dictionary at the University or Oregon: https://nahuatl.uoregon.edu/content/tlamanitiliztli.

31. "au inin ca aocmo quinamiqui yn ye uecauh tlamanitiliztli." Reyes García, *Documentos sobre tierras y señorío en Cuauhtinchan*, 198, cited in Cunill and Rovira-Morgado, "Lo que nos dejaron nuestros padres," 292.

32. Mónica Ruiz Bañuls provides a thorough discussion of the debate over the translation of the term *huehuetlatolli* among the major scholars of the form, including Josefina García Quintana, Miguel León-Portilla, and Thelma Sullivan. Ruiz Bañuls, *El huehuetlatolli*, 60–67.

33. Olmos, León-Portilla, and León-Portilla, *Arte de la lengua mexicana*.

34. Ruiz Bañuls, *El huehuetlatolli*, 48–49.

35. Mendieta, *Historia eclesiástica indiana*, Libro II, prólogo, 49.

36. Ruiz Bañuls, *El huehuetlatolli*, 51.

37. Mendieta, *Historia eclesiástica indiana*, Libro II, prólogo, 49; Baudot, "Los franciscanos etnógrafos," 293.

38. Ruiz Bañuls, *El huehuetlatolli*, 50.

39. Farriss, *Libana*.

40. Sahagún, *Florentine Codex*, Books 6 and 9; Sahagún, *Coloquios y doctrina cristiana*.

41. Dehouve, "Un diálogo de sordos."

42. Maffie and Rozo Rondon, "In Huehue Tlamanitiliztli y la Verdad."

43. Segala, *Literatura náhuatl*, 279.

44. Garibay, *Nepantla situados en medio*, 127.

45. Josefina García Quintana, "El huehuetlatolli," 65–66; León-Portilla, *La filosofía náhuatl*; León-Portilla, *"Cuícatl y Tlahtolli*," 94–95; Sullivan, *The Rhetorical Orations*; Sullivan, "Tlatoani and Tlatocayotl," 230.

46. Ruiz Bañuls, *El huehuetlatolli*, 103–234.

47. Calnek, "The Ethnographic Content of the Third Part of the Codex Mendoza."

48. González Obregón, *Proceso inquisitorial*, 52, cited in Lopes Don, "The 1539 Inquisition and Trial," 598.

49. Sepúlveda y Herrera, *Procesos por idolatría al cacique*, 57–68, 89–92.

50. Farriss, *Tongues of Fire*, 145–47.

51. The terms *Zapotec* and *Mixtec* were used by colonial authorities and have been commonly used by modern scholars, state officials, and even by Indigenous peoples to refer to the people and languages associated with these ethnic communities. Tíchzàa and Ñudzahui are the emic categories used by Zapotecs and Mixtecs to refer to themselves and their languages, though they also use the terms *Zapotec* and *Mixtec*. I will use these terms interchangeably throughout the book.

52. López Cruz and Swanton, *Memorias del coloquio Francisco Belmar*.

53. Alvarado, *Vocabulario en lengua misteca*, fol. 136v.

54. Reyes, *Arte en lengua mixteca*, fol. 78.

55. The term *yuhuitayu* is composed of two terms: *yuhui* ("reed mat") and *tayu* ("seat" or "pair," depending on tonal pronunciation). Together, they convey the meaning of the seat of rulership (reed mats symbolized rulership in Ñudzahui pictographic documents; ruling pairs are portrayed seated on reed mats). It was comparable to the Nahua altepetl. Terraciano, *The Mixtecs of Colonial Oaxaca*, 158.

56. Reyes, *Arte en lengua mixteca*, fol. ii.

57. Anders, Jansen, and Pérez Jiménez, *Origen e historia de los reyes mixtecos*.

58. Alvarado, *Vocabulario en lengua misteca*, fol. 56r, col. 1: "costumbre de pueblo"; "costumbre de vida"; "costumbre tener vide abituarse"; "costumbre tener la muger, v. camisa."

59. Alvarado, *Vocabulario en lengua misteca*, fol. 3r, col. 1: "abito costumbre"; fol. 15v, col. 1: "Alçarse la costumbre a la muger"; fol. 55r, col. 2: "Corrupcion de costumbres"; fol. 42v, col. 2: "Camissa por costumbre tener la muger"; fol. 57r, col. 2: "Criarse en buenas costumbres"; fol. 65r, col. 1: "Dañar a otro en las costumbres"; fol. 2v, col. 2: "Abezar poner costumbre. Vide abituarse"; fol. 107r, col. 2: "Estilo o costumbre de la tierra."

60. Alvarado, *Vocabulario en lengua misteca*, fol. 56r.

61. Jansen and Pérez Jiménez, *Voces del Dzaha Dzavui*, 16. Jansen and Pérez Jiménez provide an incredibly useful digitized reverse translation (Ñudzahui-Castellano) of Alvarado's *Vocabulario en lengua misteca*. They modified the entries through standardization of orthography to make the work searchable. I rely on their copious translation work in my analysis.

62. Jansen and Pérez Jiménez, *Voces del Dzaha Dzavui*, 103.

63. Jansen and Pérez Jiménez, *Voces del Dzaha Dzavui*, 14.

64. Smith-Stark, "Juan de Córdova como lexicógrafo," 10. He lists a slightly different figure for entries in Smith-Stark, "Lexicography in New Spain," 25–27 (28,352 entries and 7,780 vocables).

65. Farriss, *Tongues of Fire*, 107.

66. Córdova, *Vocabulario en lengua çapoteca*, fols. 241v–242r.

67. Córdova, *Vocabulario en lengua çapoteca*, fols. 96r–96v.

68. Córdova, *Arte en lengua zapoteca*, fol. 59r.

69. Martina Schrader-Kniffki has written about Zapotec metaphors built around the concept of the soul (*ladzhi*) in late twentieth-century Sierra Norte, Oaxaca. Schrader-Kniffki, "Metáforas de cuerpo del Zapoteco," 34.

70. Farriss, *Tongues of Fire*, 212–15.

71. Córdova, *Vocabulario en lengua çapoteca*, fol. 96r.

72. Córdova, *Arte en lengua zapoteca*, fol. 59v.

73. Córdova, *Vocabulario en lengua çapoteca*, 96r–96v.

74. Córdova, *Vocabulario en lengua çapoteca*, 205r.

75. Córdova, *Vocabulario en lengua çapoteca*, 205r: "Gentil cosa de gentiles ò costumbres de ellos. Xìticha, xichiña, xipèapènipezelào."

76. Lind, *Ancient Zapotec Religion*, 19; Cordova, *Vocabulario en lengua çapoteca*, fol. 141r, col. 1: "Dioses del infierno. Pitào pezèlào."

77. Córdova, *Vocabulario en lengua çapoteca*, fol. 116v.

78. Córdova, *Vocabulario en lengua çapoteca*, fol. 227v.

79. Yannakakis and Schrader-Kniffki, "Between the Old Law and the New."

80. Córdova, *Arte en lengua zapoteca*, fol. 54v.

81. On other notions of time expressed in Zapotec-language calendrical manuals and songs produced during the colonial period, see Oudijk, *La adivinación zapoteca*; Tavárez, *Rethinking Zapotec Time*. On Mesoamerican notions of time more broadly (especially pre-Hispanic), see Jansen and Pérez Jiménez, *Time and the Ancestors*.

82. Alvarado, *Vocabulario en lengua misteca*, 33v, col. 2., 34r, col. 1: "bendecir lo que comían los indios antiguamente"; Jansen and Pérez Jiménez, *La lengua señorial de Ñuu Dzaui*, 236, 334: "ofrecer a Dios; ofrezco a Dios."

83. Gonzalbo Aizpuru, *Historia de la educación*, 103–4.

84. Feria, *Doctrina christiana*, fols. 49r, 112r, cited in Yannakakis and Schrader-Kniffki, "Between the Old Law and the New," 530. On ceremonial style in Feria's *Doctrina christiana*, see Farriss, *Tongues of Fire*, 250–82, and in Zapotec texts more broadly, see Farriss, *Libana*.

85. Silva, *Doctrina cristiana*, 151.

86. Farriss, *Libana*, 145.

87. Feria, *Doctrina christiana*, 22v.

88. Silva, *Doctrina cristiana*, 21, 51–51, 64, 72, 76, 86, 104–6.

89. Córdova, *Vocabulario en lengua çapoteca*, 238v, col. 1: "labor por el trabajo qualqueria. Chína, quelachína, ñaani"; fol. 287v: "oficio pprio del hôbre o servicio. Chijña, quelachijna, xichijñaya."

90. Gonzalbo Arizpuru, *Historia de la educación*, 215–22.

91. Foucault, *History of Sexuality*.

92. Gruzinski, "Confesión, alianza y sexualidad"; Gruzinski, "Individualization and Acculturation"; Harrison, "The Theology of Concupiscence"; Harrison, *Sin and Confession in Colonial Peru*; Sigal, *The Flower and the Scorpion*.

93. Farriss, *Tongues of Fire*, 134–35.

94. Farriss, *Tongues of Fire*, 136.

95. Farriss, *Tongues of Fire*, 136.

96. Harrison, *Sin and Confession in Colonial Peru*.

97. Martínez, *Manual breve*, fol. 2.

98. Martínez, *Manual breve*, fols. 17–21.

99. Martínez, *Manual breve*, fol. 5.

100. Schrader-Kniffki and Yannakakis, "Sins and Crimes."

101. Martínez, *Manual breve*, fols. 22–25.

Chapter Three. Framing Pre-Hispanic Law and Custom

1. Gonzalbo Aizpuru, *El humanismo y la educación en la Nueva España*; Duarte, "The Colegio Imperial"; Mathes, *The America's First Academic Library*; SilverMoon, "The Imperial College of Tlatelolco"; Gonzalbo Aizpuru, *Historia de la educación en la época colonial*.

2. Mundy, *The Mapping of New Spain*.

3. Gómez de Orozco, "Quién fue el autor material," 43–51; Zavala, "Las encomiendas de Nueva España."

4. Gomez Tejada, "Making the Codex Mendoza," 157.

5. Nicholson, "The History of the Codex Mendoza." Jorge Gomez Tejada argues that the translator and author of the Codex Mendoza's Spanish text was in fact Olmos. Gomez Tejada, "Making the Codex Mendoza," 316.

6. Gomez Tejada posits 1547–52 as the period in which the Codex Mendoza was most likely created. Gomez Tejada, "Making the Codex Mendoza," 306–20. Davide Domenici expands the temporal frame further from the 1530s to the 1560s. Domenici, "Nuovi dati per una storia."

7. Gomez Tejada, "Making the Codex Mendoza," 269.

8. Berdan, "The Codex Mendoza," 4–8.

9. Berdan and Anawalt, *The Codex Mendoza*. My analysis in this chapter owes a great debt to this monumental work, especially the descriptive volume.

10. Instituto Nacional de Antropología e Historia, accessed August 8, 2022, https://codicemendoza.inah.gob.mx/inicio.php.

11. Berdan, "The Codex Mendoza," 2.

12. Bleichmar, "Painting the Aztec Past in Early Colonial Mexico," 1368.

13. Bleichmar, "Painting the Aztec Past in Early Colonial Mexico," 1380–84.

14. Berdan and Anawalt, *The Codex Mendoza*, vol. 3.

15. Robertson, *Mexican Manuscript Painting*, 97.

16. Gomez Tejada, "Making the Codex Mendoza," 213, 218.

17. Calnek, "The Ethnographic Content of the Third Part of the Codex Mendoza," 81, 85.

18. Pagden, *The Fall of Natural Man*, 132; Las Casas, *Los indios de México*, 122–94.

19. Gomez Tejada, "Making the Codex Mendoza," 268–99, 311.

20. Boone, *Descendants of Aztec Pictography*, 81.

21. Ferraro, "Childhood in Medieval and Early Modern Times," 68–69.

22. Berdan and Anawalt note a discrepancy in Nahuatl terminology in the glosses for this composition. The school for commoner youths was called the *telpochcalli* (young men's house), dedicated to military training. The cuicacalli was dedicated to the teaching of song, dance, and ritual. She notes that the master of youths ran both the cuicacalli and the telpochcalli, and that children of both gen-

ders and all social ranks attended the first. The curriculum represented on the folios that follow, however, is resonant with the military training of commoner boys at the telpochcalli as attested in other sources like *The Florentine Codex*. Berdan and Anawalt, *The Codex Mendoza*, 2:166–67.

23. McGowan Tress, "Aristotle's Child"; Aristotle, *Nicomachean Ethics*, 1103a lines 23–6.

24. Brundage, *Law, Sex, and Christian Society*, 189.

25. Brundage, *Law, Sex, and Christian Society*, 189.

26. McGowan Tress, "Aristotle's Child"; Kamtekar, "The Relationship between Aristotle's Ethical and Political Discourses."

27. Pearson, "Courage and Temperance," 111.

28. Pearson, "Courage and Temperance," 123–29.

29. Lee Too, "Legal Instructions in Classical Athens," 125.

30. Schroeder, "Aristotle on Law," 20.

31. Kamtekar, "The Relationship between Aristotle's Ethical and Political Discourses," 376.

32. Kamtekar, "The Relationship between Aristotle's Ethical and Political Discourses," 376.

33. Vitoria, *Relectio "De Indis,"* 97, quoted in Pagden, *The Fall of Natural Man*, 80.

34. Pagden, *The Fall of Natural Man*, 104–6.

35. Macuil Martínez, "The *Tlamatque* and Codex Mendoza."

36. Gomez Tejada, "Making the Codex Mendoza," 285–86.

37. Cummins, "From Lies to Truth," 158.

38. Solano, *Cuestionarios para la formación*; Ramos, "La crisis indiana y la Junta Magna de 1568"; Merluzzi, "Religion and State Policies"; Puente, "La política eclesiástica."

39. Acuña, *Relaciones geográficas del siglo XVI*, vol. 2, tomo I, "Prologo," 11–18.

40. Acuña, *Relaciones geográficas del siglo XVI*, vols. 2 and 3, tomos I and II.

41. Ruiz Medrano, *Mexico's Indigenous Communities*, 61–63.

42. Borah, *Justice by Insurance*.

43. Piazza, *La conciencia oscura de los naturales*.

44. Terraciano, "Introduction," 7.

45. Acuña, *Relaciones geográficas del siglo XVI*, vol. 2, tomo I, *Instrucción y memoria*, 19–25.

46. Acuña, *Relaciones geográficas del siglo XVI*, vol.2, tomo I, *Instrucción y memoria*, 22.

47. Pagden, *The Fall of Natural Man*, 13.

48. Pagden, *The Fall of Natural Man*, 18.

49. Fabian, *Time and the Other*.

50. Boesche, "Aristotle's Science of Tyranny," 1–4.

51. *Recopilación de leyes de los Reynos de las Indias*, 6.7.8, fol. 220.

52. Acuña, *Relaciones geográficas del siglo XVI*, vol.2, tomo I, 49, tomo II, 171.

53. Acuña, *Relaciones geográficas del siglo XVI*, vol. 3, tomo II, 151–52.

54. Acuña, *Relaciones geográficas del siglo XVI*, vol.3, tomo II, 555.

55. Acuña, *Relaciones geográficas del siglo XVI*, vol.3, tomo II, 198.

56. Acuña, *Relaciones geográficas del siglo XVI*, vol.2, tomo I, 287.

57. Acuña, *Relaciones geográficas del siglo XVI*, vol.2, tomo I, 51.

58. Acuña, *Relaciones geográficas del siglo XVI*, vol.2, tomo I, 232.

59. Tortorici, *Sins against Nature*; Sigal, *The Flower and the Scorpion*; Chuchiak, "The Sins of the Fathers"; Gauderman, "It Happened on the Way to the Temascal."

60. Acuña, *Relaciones geográficas del siglo XVI*, vol.2, tomo I, 350.

61. Acuña, *Relaciones geográficas del siglo XVI*, vol.2, tomo I, 90.

62. Acuña, *Relaciones geográficas del siglo XVI*, vol.3, tomo II, 233

63. Acuña, *Relaciones geográficas del siglo XVI*, vol.3, tomo II, 185

64. Acuña, *Relaciones geográficas del siglo XVI*, vol.2, tomo I, 215.

65. M. Martínez, "Indigenous Genealogies."

66. Smith, "Why the Second Codex Selden Was Painted." Visual representations of straight-line Indigenous succession also proliferated in colonial-era pictographic images and painting in Central Mexico and Peru. See M. Martínez, "Indigenous Genealogies."

67. Acuña, *Relaciones geográficas del siglo XVI*, tomo II, 134–46.

68. Mundy, *The Mapping of New Spain*, 117.

69. Caso, "El mapa de Teozacoalco"; Mundy, *The Mapping of New Spain*, 114.

70. *Recopilación de leyes de los Reynos de las Indias*, 6.7.3, fol. 219v.

71. Curcio-Nagy, *The Great Festivals of Colonial Mexico City*.

72. Acuña, *Relaciones geográficas del siglo XVI*, vol.2, tomo I, 232.

73. Acuña, *Relaciones geográficas del siglo XVI*, vol.2, tomo I, 233.

74. Kellogg and Restall, *Dead Giveaways*; Christensen and Truitt, *Native Wills from the Colonial Americas*.

75. Acuña, *Relaciones geográficas del siglo XVI*, vol.3, tomo II, 233.

76. Acuña, *Relaciones geográficas del siglo XVI*, vol.3, tomo II, 90.

77. Acuña, *Relaciones geográficas del siglo XVI*, vol.3, tomo I, 48–49.

78. Acuña, *Relaciones geográficas del siglo XVI*, vol.3, tomo I, 102.

79. Berdan and Anawalt, *The Codex Mendoza*, 2:102–5.

80. Acuña, *Relaciones geográficas del siglo XVI*,vol.2, tomo I, 102.

81. Acuña, *Relaciones geográficas del siglo XVI*, vol.3, tomo II, 272.

82. Acuña, *Relaciones geográficas de Michoacán*; Acuña, *Relaciones geográficas de Nueva Galicia*; Muñoz Camargo, *Descripción de la cuidad y provincial de Tlaxcala*.

83. Tavárez, *The Invisible War*, 1–26; Zeitlin, *Cultural Politics in Colonial Tehuantepec*; Piazza, *La conciencia oscura de los naturales*; Hamann, *Bad Christians, New Spains*.

84. Acuña, *Relaciones geográficas del siglo XVI*, vol.3, tomo II, 90.

85. Piazza, *La conciencia oscura de los naturales*; Tavárez, *The Invisible War*.

86. Acuña, *Relaciones geográficas del siglo XVI*, vol.3, tomo II, 143.

87. Acuña, *Relaciones geográficas del siglo XVI*, vol.2, tomo I, 50–51.

88. Hassig, *Polygamy and the Rise and Demise of the Aztec Empire*.

89. Acuña, *Relaciones geográficas del siglo XVI*, vol.2, tomo I, 215.

Chapter Four. The Old Law, Polygyny, and the Customs
of the Ancestors

1. González Obregón, *Proceso inquisitorial*, 41. The original citation for the archival document transcribed by Luis González Obregón is AGN, Siglo XVI, Inquisición, Procesos por proposiciones heréticas, 2. Primera Parte, "Proceso Criminal del Santo Oficio de la Inquisición y del fiscal en su nombre contra Don Carlos, Indio Principal de Tezcuco," Mexico City, 1539.

2. González Obregón, *Proceso inquisitorial*, 52, cited in Lopes Don, "The 1539 Inquisition and Trial," 598. Patricia Lopes Don argues that the language of the testimony suggests that don Carlos's discourse was given in the style of the huehuetlatolli.

3. Lopes Don, *Bonfires of Culture*. For foundational work on the Inquisition in New Spain, see Alberro, *Inquisición y sociedad*; Greenleaf, *The Mexican Inquisition of the Sixteenth Century*.

4. Dahlgren de Jordán, *La mixteca*; Spores, *The Mixtec Kings*; Terraciano, *The Mixtecs*; Sousa, *The Woman Who Turned into a Jaguar*.

5. Schwartz, *All Can Be Saved*, 51–56.

6. M. Martínez, *Genealogical Fictions*, 204.

7. Ruiz Medrano, "Don Carlos de Tezcoco," 171.

8. Greenleaf, *Zumárraga and the Mexican Inquisition*; Alva, "Colonizing Souls"; Arcos, "New Spain's Inquisition for Indians"; Burkhart, *The Slippery Earth*; Cervantes, *The Devil in the New World*; LaFaye, *Quetzalcóatl and Guadalupe*; Gruzinski, *Man-Gods in the Mexican Highlands*; Tavárez, *The Invisible War*.

9. Lopes Don, "The 1539 Inquisition and the Trial"; Lopes Don, *Bonfires of Culture*.

10. Tavárez, *The Invisible War*; B. Benton, *The Lords of Tetzcoco*.

11. Lopes Don, "The 1539 Inquisition and the Trial."

12. González Obregón, *Proceso inquisitorial*, 32–39.

13. González Obregón, *Proceso inquisitorial*, 56; Lopes Don, "The 1539 Inquisition and the Trial," 587.

14. González Obregón, *Proceso inquisitorial*, 38–39.

15. González Obregón, *Proceso inquisitorial*, 33–36.

16. Carrasco, "Royal Marriages in Ancient Mexico."

17. Townsend, "Polygyny and the Divided Altepetl," 93–95.

18. Carrasco, "Royal Marriages in Ancient Mexico," 45–72.

19. Caso, "Land Tenure among the Ancient Mexicans"; Offner, *Law and Politics*, 124–39.

20. Kellogg, *Law and the Transformation*, 93.

21. Burkhart, "Mexica Women on the Home Front."

22. Motolinía, *Memoriales o libro de las cosas de la Nueva España*, 189.

23. Brundage, *Law, Sex, and Christian Society*, 235.

24. Ricard, *The Spiritual Conquest*, 114, 133.

25. Motolinía, *Historia de los indios de Nueva España*, Tratado Segundo, Cap. VII, pp. 124–25.

26. Brian, Benton, and Garcia Loaeza, *The Native Conquistador*.

27. Farriss, *Maya Society under Colonial Rule*; Taylor, *Magistrates of the Sacred*; Ángeles Romero Frizzi, *El sol y la cruz*.

28. *Recopilación de leyes de los Reynos de las Indias*, 6.1.4, fol., 188v.

29. Grijalva, *Cronica de la Orden de N.P.S. Augustin en las provincias de la nueva españa*, Book 1, p. 139–40, cited in Ricard, *The Spiritual Conquest*, 112n16.

30. G. García, *El clero de México*, 37–38.

31. Ricard, *The Spiritual Conquest*, 114nn24–25.

32. Icazbalceta, *Zumárraga*, appendix, 91, cited in Ricard, *The Spiritual Conquest*, 111n6.

33. Granicka, "Marital Practices of the Nahuas."

34. S. Cline, "The Spiritual Conquest Re-examined."

35. Kellogg, *Law and the Transformation*, 52–56.

36. Kellogg, *Law and the Transformation*, 201–4.

37. González Obregón, "Proceso del Santo Oficio contra Tacatetl y Tanixtetl, indios, por idólatras," Mexico City, June 28, 1536, in *Procesos de indios idólatras y hechiceros*, 1–16.

38. González Obregón, "Proceso del Santo Oficio contra Martín Ucelo, indio, por idólatra y hechicero," Temistitán, Mexico, November 21, 1536, in *Procesos de indios idólatras y hechiceros*, 17–51.

39. González Obregón, "Proceso del Santo Oficio contra Mixcoatl y Papalotl, indios, por hechiceros" Mexico City, July 10, 1537, pp. 53–78; "Proceso del Santo Oficio contra Francisco, indio, por casado dos veces, Temixtitán," Mexico City, October 11, 1538, pp. 79–86; "Información contra D. Diego, cacique de Tlapanaloa, por Diversos Delitos," October 19, 1538, pp. 87–98; "Proceso del Santo Oficio Contra los indios Marcos y Francisco," May 30, 1539, pp. 109–14; "Proceso e Información que se Tomo contra Xpobal y su Mujer, por Ocultar idolos y otros Delitos, y contra Martin, Hermano del Primero," August 19, 1539, pp. 141–76; "Denuncia contra Don Juan, cacique de Iguala," July 16, 1540, pp. 201–4; "Proceso Seguido por Fray Andres de Olmos en Contra del Cacique de Matlatlan," 1540, pp. 205–16; "Sumario en Contra de Tomas e Maria, indios, por amancebados," Mexico City, May 16, 1548, pp. 217–20, all in *Procesos de indios idólatras y hechiceros*.

40. Consanguinity: "Proceso del Santo Oficio contra Tacatetl y Tanixtetl"; "Información contra D. Diego, cacique de Tlapanaloa"; "Proceso e Informacion que se Tomo contra Xpobal y su Mujer"; "Denuncia contra Don Juan, cacique de Iguala." Sexual coercion: "Proceso del Santo Oficio contra Tacatetl y Tanixtetl"; "Información contra D. Diego, cacique de Tlapanaloa"; "Denuncia contra Don Juan, cacique de Iguala."

41. B. Benton, *The Lords of Tetzcoco*, 40–42.

42. González Obregón, *Proceso inquisitorial*, 32.

43. B. Benton, "Beyond the Burned Stake."

44. Sepúlveda y Herrera, *Procesos por idolatría al cacique*, 57–68, 89–92.

45. Sepúlveda y Herrera, *Procesos por idolatría al cacique*, 57–68, 89–92.

46. Jiménez Moreno and Mateos Higuera, *Códice de Yanhuitlán*; Dahlgren de

Jordán, *La mixteca*; Spores, *The Mixtec Kings*; Terraciano, *The Mixtecs of Colonial Oaxaca*.

47. Sousa, *The Woman Who Turned into a Jaguar*; Piazza, *La conciencia oscura de los naturales*.

48. Sepúlveda y Herrera, *Procesos por idolatría al cacique*, 119.

49. Sepúlveda y Herrera, *Procesos por idolatría al cacique*, 121.

50. Sepúlveda y Herrera, *Procesos por idolatría al cacique*, 157.

51. Sepúlveda y Herrera, *Procesos por idolatría al cacique*, 162–80.

52. Spores, *The Mixtecs Kings*, 138–39.

53. Spores, *The Mixtecs Kings*, 153.

54. Spores, *The Mixtecs Kings*, 139–54; Terraciano, *The Mixtecs of Colonial Oaxaca*, 172–75.

55. Terraciano, *The Mixtecs of Colonial Oaxaca*, 174.

56. Dahlgren de Jordán, *La mixteca*, 134–35.

57. Sepúlveda y Herrera, *Procesos por idolatría al cacique*, 146–47. Original document: AGN Inquisición, Expediente 7, México-Tenochtitlan, Octubre de 1544, Proceso del fiscal del Santo Oficio contra don Francisco y don Domingo, indios del pueblo de Yanhuitlán, por idólatras, fols. 156r–209v.

58. Spores, *The Mixtec Kings*, 140.

59. Spores, *The Mixtec Kings*, 178–79.

60. *Recopilación de leyes de los Reynos de las Indias*, 6.1.5, fol 188v.

61. Spores, *The Mixtec Kings*, 138–39, 152–53.

62. Zaballa, "Indian Marriage before and after the Council of Trent," 96.

63. Lavrin, "Sexuality in Colonial Mexico," 52; Schwaller, "The Spiritual Conquest of Marriage," 123–30.

64. *Concilio III: Provincial mexicano*, Libro V, Título X, Ley I, "Del concubinato y penas de los concubinarios y alcahuetes," 384.

65. Zaballa, "Promises and Deceits," 62–65. On the persistence of Indigenous marriage customs in colonial Native communities, see Zaballa, "Indian Marriage before and after the Council of Trent"; Dehouve, "El matrimono indio"; Dehouve, "La segunda mujer entre los Nahuas." On historical and contemporary Mesoamerican Indigenous marriage customs, see Robichaux, *El Matrimonio en Mesoamérica*.

66. Menegus Bornemann, *Del señorío indígena*; Quezada, *Pueblos y caciques yucatecos*; Quezada, *Maya Lords and Lordship*; Martínez Baracs, *Un gobierno de indios*; Haskett, *Indigenous Rulers*.

67. Haskett, *Indigenous Rulers*.

68. *Recopilación de leyes de los Reynos de las Indias*, 6.3.16, fol. 200.

69. Yannakakis and Schrader-Kniffki, "Between the Old Law and the New"; Premo and Yannakakis, "A Court of Sticks and Branches."

70. Taylor, *Magistrates of the Sacred*.

71. Chance, *Conquest of the Sierra*, 59.

72. Yannakakis, *The Art of Being In-Between*.

73. Alcina Franch, *Calendario y religión entre los zapotecos*; Yannakakis, *The Art*

of Being In-Between; Piazza, *La conciencia oscura de los naturales*; Tavárez, *The Invisible War*; Oudijk, *La adivinación zapoteca*; Tavárez, *Rethinking Zapotec Time*.

74. Schrader-Kniffki and Yannakakis, "Sins and Crimes"; Schrader-Kniffki and Yannakakis, "Traducción y construcción verbal"; Yannakakis and Schrader-Kniffki, "Between the Old Law and the New"; Yannakakis and Schrader-Kniffki, "Contra Juan Ramos"; AHJO, VA Criminal, leg. 1, exp. 3, 1650–51; leg. 4, exp. 5, 1687; leg. 5, exp. 3, 1695; leg. 5, exp. 4, 1695; leg. 6, exp. 6, 1698; leg. 7, exp. 11, 1703; leg. 7, exp. 6, 1702; leg. 7, exp. 7, 1702; leg. 12, exp. 7, 1727; AHJO, VA Civil, leg. 3, exp. 3, 1690. In some of these files, there are multiple Zapotec-language criminal proceedings. For Zapotec-language records, there are thirty-one letters, reports, petitions, investigations, and testimonies related to crime, which can be found in the previous files and in the following cases as well: AHJO VA Criminal leg. 1, exp. 9, 1659; "Contra Juan Bautista" (uncataloged), 1689; leg. 7, exp. 4, 1704. In addition to the criminal proceedings, this makes a total of forty-eight criminal and crime-related records in Sierra Zapotec languages from 1650 to 1727.

75. Ñudzahui-language criminal proceedings: AHJO, T Criminal, leg. 16, exp. 38, 1669; leg. 20, exp. 9, 1690. The 1690 case includes charges of concubinage against the village constable (alguacil mayor).

76. Terraciano, "Crime and Culture." Ñudzahui-language crime-related records (letters, reports, testimony) can be found in the following files: AHJO, T Criminal, leg. 16, exp. 38, 1669; leg. 18, exp. 3, 1681; leg. 18, exp. 26, 1683; leg. 19, exp. 12, 1686; leg. 19, exp. 16, 1687; leg. 19, exp. 23, 1688; leg. 22, exp. 11, 1701; leg. 26, exp. 26, 1729; leg. 32, exp. 5, 1755.

77. Monzón, *Juicios locales del Michoacán colonial*.

78. AHJO, VA Criminal, leg. 7, exp. 11, 1703, "Causa ynformación de Pascual García," fols. 5–8; AHJO, VA Criminal, leg. 7, exp. 11, 1703, "Causa ynformación de Nicolas Guzmán," fols. 9v–10v; AHJO, VA Criminal, leg. 4, exp. 5, 1687, "Auto de Juan Ramos, 1661," fols. 11–12; AHJO, VA Criminal, leg. 4, exp. 5, 1687, "Auto de Felipe Mendes (1686)," fol. 10.

79. For a fuller analysis of the use of nigolla quie in criminal and notarial records, see Yannakakis and Schrader-Kniffki, "Contra Juan Ramos." The archival records include AHJO, VA Criminal, leg. 4, exp. 5, 1687, "Auto de Juan Ramos, 1661" and "Auto de Felipe Mendes, 1686"; AHJO, VA Criminal, leg. 4, exp. 12, n.d. (the second case in the file), "Baltasar Martín, natural de Juquila contra Juan Francisco, natural de Juquila por muerte de su hija Magdalena"; AHJO, VA Criminal, leg. 7, exp. 4, 1704, "Contra Pascuala Ramos y socios de Yazona por incendarios"; AHJO, VA Criminal, leg. 7, exp. 6, 1702, "Contra Francisco Canseco de Yaee por robo"; AHJO, VA Criminal, leg. 7, exp. 7, 1702, "Francisco de Vargas, principal de San Juan Yaee, contra Nicolás Lorenzo, natural de Tepanzacualco y residente en Yatao, por robo"; AHJO, VA Criminal, leg. 7, exp. 11, 1703, "Contra la república de Taba por varios hechos"; AHJO, VA Criminal, leg. 9, exp. 11, 1708, "Juan Martín, natural de Yagallo contra Gabriel Maldonado, alcalde de Santiago Yagallo."

80. Yannakakis and Schrader-Kniffki, "Between the Old Law and the New"; Yannakakis and Schrader-Kniffki, "Contra Juan Ramos"; "Auto de Juan Ramos,

1661," submitted as evidence in AHJO, VA Criminal, leg. 4, exp. 5, 1687, "Contra don Pablo de Vargas por peculado y robo de la caja común," fols. 11–12.

81. Oudijk, *Historiography of the Bènizàa*.

82. Chance, *Conquest of the Sierra*.

83. See Michel Oudiik's analysis of the Lienzos of Tiltepec and Tabaá in Oudijk, *Historiography of the Bènizàa*.

84. Chance, *Conquest of the Sierra*; Yannakakis, *The Art of Being In-Between*.

85. Don Pablo de Vargas presented evidence of his good Christian conduct and governance as a defense against charges of financial corruption brought against him by fellow villagers. AHJO, VA Criminal, leg. 4, exp. 5, 1687, "Contra don Pablo de Vargas por peculado y robo de la caja común."

86. Dehouve, *Relatos de pecados*, 96.

87. "Auto de Juan Ramos, 1661," fol. 11v: "Rinaao netto Justicia aca naccae christiano ava nezenie santa doctrina cattizo benne golazannaae cattizi leo golaza."

88. "Auto de Juan Ramos, 1661," fol. 12: "Gonna marta de la cruz bixa niha quie goxeno neta iela gotilla acca yoho Dios acca yoho Rey nna yleoo golaza nacca naa racca no gonano golalazi titzanij."

89. Yannakakis and Schrader-Kniffki, "Between the Old Law and the New."

90. Yannakakis and Schrader-Kniffki, "Between the Old Law and the New."

91. For cases from Villa Alta roughly contemporaneous with that of Juan Ramos, see the cases from San Francisco and Santo Domingo Cajonos: AHJO, VA Criminal, leg. 1, exp. 9, 1659, "Contra Jacinto Gabriel por homicidio y adulterio; AHJO, VA Criminal, leg. 1, exp. 6.1, 1667 "Contra Tomás Gonzalo por estar amancebado publicamente con su madrastra." In his study of Native parishes in eighteenth-century Mexico, the historian William Taylor argues that punishment of concubinage and adultery at the hands of Native officials, parish priests, and Spanish magistrates was often harsh. Taylor, *Magistrates of the Sacred*, 348-349.

92. Yannakakis, *The Art of Being In-Between*; Calvo, *Vencer la derrota*.

93. Pedro Carrasco cites ritual purification in rivers as one among several non-Christian ceremonial practices that accompanied investiture of new authorities in the Mixe town of Tamazulapam during the twentieth century: Carrasco, "Ceremonias públicas paganas entre los Mixes de Tamazulapam," 388. For the colonial period, the historian Steve Stern cites other non-Christian customs that accompanied the "entrega de vara" (a customary political ceremony in which the previous year's town authorities pass their staffs of office to the newly elected authorities). In a 1768 case the authorities of the Mixe town of Tepuxtepeque reportedly traveled to a nearby hilltop to sing and conduct animal sacrifices as part of ceremonies of investiture. AEO Obispado, leg.2 exp. 5, 1768, "Ayutla/Tepuxtepec," fols.1v-2 cited in Stern, *Secret History of Gender*, 238.

94. The case against Joseph de Yllescas begins with "A xāna goque alcalde mayor (1683)," AHJO, VA Civil, leg. 3. Exp. 3, 1690, "Las Justicias del pueblo de San Juan Tanetze contra Joseph de Illescas por faltas cometidas a la autoridad," fols. 3–4v.

95. Petition of Pascual García, May 15, 1703, AHJO, VA Criminal, leg. 7, exp. 11, 1703, "Contra la república de Taba por varios hechos," fols. 13–16v.

96. AGI, 882 62-6-28, fols. 254–256v, 296–319. For a transcription of the documentation produced by Bishop Maldonado's investigation, see Oudijk, *La adivinación zapoteca*, vol. 3.

97. AGI, 882 62-6-28, fol. 1171.

98. M. Martínez, *Genealogical Fictions*, 208–11; Tavárez, *The Invisible War*, 179–91.

99. Kellogg, *Law and the Transformation*; Kellogg and Restall, *Dead Giveaways*; Christensen and Truitt, *Native Wills from the Colonial Americas*; Caterina Pizzigoni, *Testaments of Toluca*.

Chapter Five. Custom, Possession, and Jurisdiction
in the Boundary Lands

1. Ruiz Medrano and Valle, "Los colores de la justicia."

2. Kellogg, *Law and the Transformation*, 45–51; Menegus Bornemann, *Del señorío indígena*; Ruiz Medrano, *Mexico's Indigenous Communities*, 31, 38–39; Villella, "'For So Long the Memories.'"

3. Herzog, "Colonial Law and 'Native Customs.'"

4. Borah and Cook, *The Aboriginal Population*; Cook and Borah, *Essays in Population History*; Cline, "Civil Congregations of the Indians in New Spain."

5. García Martínez, *Los pueblos de la sierra*.

6. Solano, *Cedulario de tierras*, 273–74; "Real Cédula (El Pardo, 1 de noviembre de 1591) sobre restitución de las tierras que se poseen sin justos y verdaderos títulos, dirigida a don Luis de Velasco, virrey de la Nueva España," cited in Menegus Bornemann, "Los títulos primordiales de los pueblos de indios."

7. Capdequí, *El régimen de la tierra*; Menegus Bornemann, *Del señorío indígena*.

8. Wood, "The Techialoyan Codices"; Wood, *Transcending Conquest*; Hidalgo, *Trail of Footprints*.

9. Menegus Bornemann, "Los títulos primordiales de los pueblos de indios," 208; Haskett, *Visions of Paradise*; On the primordial titles of Oaxaca, see Oudijk and Ángeles Romero Frizzi, "Los títulos primordiales"; Oudijk, "Espacio y escritura"; Cortés Márquez and Reyes García, "Manuscritos colonials"; Sousa and Terraciano, "The 'Original Conquest' of Oaxaca"; Ángeles Romero Frizzi and Vásquez, "Memoria y escritura"; Ángeles Romero Frizzi and Vásquez, "Un título primordial de San Francisco Yatee, Oaxaca."

10. Megged and Wood, *Mesoamerican Memory*.

11. Rivera Marín de Iturbe, *La propiedad territorial en México*; Florescano, *Estructuras y problemas agrarios*, 44; Torales Pacheco, "A Note on the Composiciones de Tierras"; Goyas Mejía, "Las Composiciones de Tierras de 1643 en la Nueva España"; Borchart de Moreno, "La transferencia de la propiedad agraria indígena"; Glave, "Gestiones transatlánticas."

12. Wood, "The *Fundo Legal*."

13. Carrera Quezada, "Las composiciones de tierras en los pueblos de indios"; Torre Ruiz, "Composiciones de tierras"; Radding, *Wandering Peoples*, 171–207;

Radding, *Landscapes of Power and Identity*, 89–116; López Castillo, *Composiciones de tierras*; López Castillo, *El poblamiento*. For the case of Oaxaca, see Pastor, *Campesinos y reformas*; Menegus Bornemann, "Del usufructo, de la posesión y de la propiedad"; J. E. Mendoza, *Municipios, cofradías y tierras comunales*, 54–59.

14. Owensby, *Empire of Law*, 90–129.

15. Seed, *Ceremonies of Possession*; Greer, *Property and Dispossession*; Saavedra, "The Normativity of Possession."

16. King Alfonso, *Las Siete Partidas*, 3.30.1, 3.30.2, 3.30.3, 3.30.4, pp. 850–51.

17. Herzog, "Immemorial (and Native) Customs in Early Modernity," 24.

18. Saavedra, "The Normativity of Possession," 233.

19. Taylor, *Landlord and Peasant*; Pastor, *Campesinos y reformas*; Chance, *Conquest of the Sierra*; Arrioja Díaz Viruell, *Pueblos de indios*; Menegus Bornemann, *La Mixteca Baja*. In the districts of Teposcolula and Villa Alta, with a few exceptions, Native caciques and communities held their lands throughout the colonial period. In Oaxaca's central valleys, there was a rise of Spanish-owned haciendas and ranches during the late sixteenth and seventeenth centuries, but by the late eighteenth century, Zapotec nobles and communities began to expand back onto the lands.

20. Ángeles Romero Frizzi, *Economía y vida de los españoles*.

21. Dahlgren de Jordán, *La mixteca*; Spores, "Marital Alliance."

22. Spores, *The Mixtec Kings*; Terraciano, *The Mixtecs of Colonial Oaxaca*, 119–20; Martín Gabaldón, "Territorialidad y paisaje."

23. Pastor, *Campesinos y reformas*, 175–78; Terraciano, *The Mixtecs of Colonial Oaxaca*, 124; Martín Gabaldón, "Territorialidad y paisaje."

24. Van Doesburg, "De Linderos y Lugares"; Aguilar Sánchez, "La construcción de espacios sagrados como límites territoriales en los pueblos de la Nueva España"; Aguilar Sánchez, "Ñuu Savi: Pasado, presente y future."

25. Spores, *The Mixtecs in Ancient and Colonial Times*, 210–25.

26. Menegus Bornemann, "Del usufructo, de la posesión y de la propiedad," 184; Menegus Bornemann, *La Mixteca Baja*, 62–72.

27. In my analysis, I use the Ñudzahui-language petition and its Spanish translation transcribed and published in Jansen and Pérez Jiménez, *La lengua señorial*, 338–40. They cite the case as AGN, Tierras 1717, vol. 308, fols. 140–42. The case is also cited as AGN, Tierras, Año 1713–49, vol. 308, exp. 1, fol. 438 "Por los naturales del pueblo de San Juan Sayultepec contra los de San Andrés Sinaxtla sobre propiedad de tierras. Un mapa," in Méndez Martínez and Méndez Torres, *Límites, mapas y títulos* p. 181, item #1015.

28. Zimmerman, *The Law of Obligations*, part IV, ch. 15, Societas, 451, 454–55.

29. Spores, *The Mixtecs in Ancient and Colonial Times*, 98.

30. Jansen and Pérez Jiménez, *La lengua señorial*, 339 for the Mixtec original, and 340 for the Spanish translation.

31. Taylor, "Cacicazgos coloniales en el valle de Oaxaca"; Taylor, *Landlord and Peasant*; Pastor, *Campesinos y reformas*; Terraciano, *The Mixtecs of Colonial Oaxaca*; Menegus Bornemann and Aguirre Salvador, *El cacicazgo en Nueva España y Fili-*

pinas; O'Phelan, *Kurakas sin sucesiones*; Serulnikov, *Subverting Colonial Authority*; Penry, *The People Are King*.

32. Pastor, *Campesinos y reformas*, 166–75.

33. Jansen and Pérez Jiménez, *La lengua señorial*, 339 for the Mixtec original, and 340 for the Spanish translation.

34. Herzog, *Frontiers of Possession*, ch. 3.

35. Blaufarb, "Conflict and Compromise."

36. Carrera Quezada, "Las composiciones de tierras en los pueblos de indios."

37. Torre Ruiz, "Composiciones de tierras en la alcaldía mayor de Sayula," 45–69.

38. AHJO, T Civil, leg. 21, exp. 16.093, 1717, "Petición de licencia, carta de compromiso," fols. 201–10.

39. Spores, *The Mixtecs in Ancient and Colonial Times*, 223 (citing Cook and Borah, *Essays in Population History*, 105).

40. AHJO, T Civil, leg. 21, exp. 16.093, 1717, "Petición de licencia, carta de compromiso," fols. 201–10.

41. Alonso, *La categoría de la obligación "in solidum,"* 51–52.

42. King Alfonso, *Las Siete Partidas*, 5.10.6, 5.10.7, pp. 1086–87.

43. King Philip IV, *Novissima Recopilación de las Leyes del Reino*, Segunda Parte, 5.16.1, fol. 45.

See also the notarial manual Monterroso y Aluarado, Cuesta, and Sarriá, *Pratica civil y criminal y instrucion de escriuanos*, fol. 146, "De la mancomunidad y escussiones, y fuerças dellas."

44. King Alfonso, *Las Siete Partidas*, 5.12.8, p. 1113; Murillo Velarde, *Curso de derecho canónico hispano e indiano*, 3.22, De los Fiadores; Alonso, *La categoría de la obligación "in solidum,"* 59–60.

45. Owensby, *Empire of Law*, 69.

46. The "leyes de duobus reix de vendi" refers to a title of a section in the eighth book of Justinian's Code ("De duobus reis stipulandi et duobus reis promittendi," which in modern editions of the Code corresponds to C. 8.39 or C. 8.40). Authentica "Hoc ita si pactum" is the second provision in this section (C. 8.39/40.2). Authentica "Presente tamen" corresponds to the third provision in this section (C. 8.40/41.3). References to these texts were common in early modern theological and juridical writings about suretyship. Wim Decock, personal communication, November 10, 2018. See also Lessius, *On Sale, Securities, and Insurance*, 140–41. For the incorporation of the Latin into Spanish notarial formulas, see Monterroso y Alvarado, Cuesta, and Sarriá, *Pratica civil y criminal*, 146; Sigüenza and Guasch, *Tratado de clausulas instrumentales*, 51–52. Contracts of mancomunidad were also part of notarial practice in colonial Peru. See Guevara Gil, *Propiedad agraria y derecho colonial*, Cuadro no. 16, "Clausulas Estabilizadas Ubicadas en los Titulos de Propiedad de la Hacienda Santotis," nos. 18 and 19, 302–3. I would like to thank Wim Decock, Otto Danwerth, and Renzo Honores for their generosity in helping me identify the relevant passages in the Justinian Code.

47. Notably, in order to create a multipueblo alliance "de mancomún in solidum" in which all were bound to comply with the entire contract, they needed to re-

nounce the laws of duobus Reis, which were also known as the *laws* of mancomunidad (leyes de mancomunidad) that bound each to comply with a part, or his share.

48. Sigüenza, *Tratado de clausulas instrumentales:* fols. 51v–52, Libro I, Capítulo XVIII, "Sobre la clausula de la mancomunidad, y renunciacion de la Authentica prasente, c. de fide iussoribus, y el Authtentica hoc ita, C. de duobus reis, y renunciacion de la excursion y division."

49. Capdequí, *Manual de historia del derecho español en las indias,* 171–202.

50. These are ubiquitous in the notarial archive of Teposcolula (AHJO, Teposcolula Protocolos).

51. King Alfonso, *Las Siete Partidas,* 7.31, "Concerning Punishments," headnote, 7.31.8, pp. 1463, 1466–67.

52. *El Ordenamiento de Leyes,* Título XVII, Ley Unica, p. 24.

53. Ingold, "Commons and Environmental Regulation in History."

54. Grossi, *El orden jurídico medieval,* 116–18.

55. King Philip IV, *Novissima Recopilación de las Leyes del Reino,* lib. 5, tit. 10.1.7, cited in *Diccionario de Autoridades,* vol. 3 (1732), s.v. "Donación."

56. Zimmerman, *The Laws of Obligation,* 451–54.

57. AHJO, T Civil, leg. 21, exp. 16.099, 1717, "Petición de licencia, carta de compromiso," fols. 215r–217v.

58. Spores, *The Mixtecs in Ancient and Colonial Times,* 220–23.

59. Pastor, *Campesinos y reformas;* Menegus Bornemann, *La Mixteca Baja;* Martín Gabaldón, "New Crops, New Landscapes."

60. Terraciano, *The Mixtecs of Colonial Oaxaca,* 129.

61. AHJO, T Civil, leg. 21, exp. 16.101, 1717, "Petición de licensia, escritura de compromiso," fols. 219v–222r.

62. AHJO, T Civil, leg. 21, exp. 16.108, 1717, "Petición de licensia, escritura de compromiso," fols. 232r–234v.

63. AHJO, T Civil, leg. 21, exp. 16.132, 1718, "Petición de Licensia, escritura de compromiso," fols. 276r–279v. See Mendoza's brief discussion of the composición, effected afterward, and its eventual dissolution years later when the pueblos sought their individual titles. J. E. Mendoza, *Municipios, cofradías y tierras comunales,* 57.

64. Reference to the litigation can be found in AGN, Tierras, vol. 3538, exp. 27, 1791, fol. 2, "Copia del despacho para que el administrador de alcabalas del partido de Tepozcolula conozca acerca de los authos seguidos por los naturales del pueblo de San Mateo Peñasco contra los de San Agustín, por la posesión de tierras," in Méndez Martínez and Méndez Torres, *Límites, mapas y títulos,* p. 160, item #884.

65. AHJO, T Protocolos, leg. 6, exp. 4.17, 1733, "Escritura de convenio 19 de junio de 1733," fols. 25v–30v.

66. AHJO, T Protocolos, leg. 6, exp. 4.17, 1733, "Escritura de convenio 19 de junio de 1733," fols. 25v–30v.

67. Zimmerman, *The Law of Obligations,* 5–6.

68. Berger, *Encyclopedic Dictionary of Roman Law,* vol. 43, pt. 2, p. 603.

69. Zimmerman, *The Law of Obligations,* 5.

70. Menegus Bornemann, "Del usufructo, de la posesión y de la propiedad."

71. Martín Gabaldón, "New Crops, New Landscapes," 44–46; Dahlgren de Jordán, *La mixteca*.

72. Pastor, *Campesinos y reformas*, 181–88; Martin Gabaldón, "New Crops, New Landscapes."

73. Martín Gabaldón, "New Crops, New Landscapes," 63.

74. Martín Gabaldón, "New Crops, New Landscapes," 43, 59.

75. Pastor, *Campesinos y reformas*, 172–73.

76. AHJO, T Protocolos, leg. 4, exp. 2.163, 1714, "Arrendamiento de tierras," fols. 376r–377r; AHJO, T Protocolos, leg. 4, exp. 2.164, 1714, "Arrendamiento de tierras," fols. 378r–379r; AHJO, T Civil, leg. 21, exp. 16.008, 1715, "Arrendamiento de tierras", fols. 27v–30v (a collective agreement in which Chávez rents along with the cabildo of Tlaxiaco); AHJO, T Protocolos, leg. 5, exp. 1.122, 1722, "Arrendamiento de tierras, 30 de octubre de 1722," fols. 241r–243v; AHJO, T Protocolos, leg. 5, exp. 2.43 1723, "Arrendamiento de tierras," fols. 91r–94v; AHJO, T Protocolos, leg. 6, exp. 2.36, 1728, "Arrendamiento de tierras," fols. 63r–65r; AHJO, T Protocolos, leg. 6, exp. 4.04, 1733, "Arrendamiento de tierras," fols. 4r, 7r–10v; AHJO, T Protocolos, leg. 7, exp. 5, 1741, "Escritura de Arrendamiento," fols. 41r–45v; AHJO, T Civil, leg. 30, exp. 29.7, 1742, "Arrendamiento de tierras," fols. 14r–17r; AHJO, T Civil, leg. 30, exp. 29.7, 1742, "Licencia, Arrendamiento de tierras," fols. 14r–17r.

77. AHJO, T Protocolos, leg. 5, exp. 2.43, 1723, "Arrendamiento de tierras," fols. 91r–94v.

78. AHJO, T Protocolos, leg. 7, exp. 5, 1741, "Escritura de Arrendamiento," fols. 41r–45v.

79. AHJO, T Civil, leg. 30, exp. 29.18, 1742, "Contrato de mancomunidad de tierras."

80. AHJO, T Civil, leg. 21, exp. 16.008, 1715 "Arrendamiento de tierras," fols. 27r–30v; AHJO, T Civil, leg. 25, exp 2.15, 1727, "Arrendamiento de tierras," fols. 36v–39v; AHJO, T Protocolos, leg. 6, exp. 4.26, 1734, "Obligación de Pago," fols. 51r–55r; AHJO, T Protocolos, leg. 6, exp. 4.08, 1733, "Arrendamiento de tierras," fols. 12v–17r; AHJO, T Protocolos, leg. 6, exp. 4.09, 1733, "Arrendamiento de tierras," fols. 17r–18v; AHJO, T Protocolos, leg. 6, exp. 4.46, 1734, "Arrendamiento de tierras," fols. 85v–96v.

81. AHJO, T Protocolos, leg. 5, exp. 2.48, 1723, "Poder especial," fols. 104r–106r.

82. AHJO, T Protocolos, leg. 5, exp. 2.89, 1724, "Escritura de convenio y donación," fols. 188r–193v.

83. AHJO, T Protocolos, leg. 5, exp. 2.77, 1724, "Poder especial," fols. 167r–170r.

84. AHJO, T Protocolos, leg. 5, exp. 2.77, 1724, "Poder especial," fols. 167r–170r.

85. AHJO, T Civil, leg. 30, exp. 29.11, 1742, "Escritura de Convenio," fols. 26v–31r.

86. Pérez Castañeda, "Los condueñazgos en México durante el siglo XIX"; Escobar Ohmstede, "Los condueñazgos indígenas en las Huastecas hidalguense y veracruzana"; Ducey, "Liberal Theory and Peasant Practice"; Gutiérrez Rivas, "El proceso agrario en las huastecas hidalguense y veracruzana"; Kourí, *A Pueblo Di-*

vided; Craib, *Cartographic Mexico*; J. E. Mendoza, "De condueñazgo a municipio"; Gutiérrez Rivas, "El condueñazgo de los Moctezuma"; Cruz, "De arrendatarios a condueños"; Neri Guarneros, "Sociedades agrícolas en resistencia"; Fandos, "La formación histórica de condueñazgos."

87. Menegus Bornemann and Cerutti, *La desamortización civil en México y España*; Escobar Ohmstede, "La desamortización de tierras civiles corporativas en México"; Marino, "La desamortización de las tierras de los pueblos"; Escobar Ohmstede, Falcón, and Sánchez Rodríguez, *La desamortización civil desde perspectivas plurales*. For exemplary studies on how Indigenous communities contended with the desamortización civil in Oaxaca, see Sánchez Silva, *La desamortización civil en Oaxaca*; Arrioja Díaz Viruell, *Pueblos de indios y tierras comunales*; J. E. Mendoza, *Municipios, cofradías y tierras comunales*; M. F. Mendoza, *La ley y la costumbre*.

Chapter Six. Custom as Social Contract

1. Haskett, *Indigenous Rulers*, 20–21.

2. Menegus Bornemann, *Del señorío indígena*; García Martínez, *Los pueblos*; García Martínez, "Jurisdicción y propiedad"; Quezada, *Pueblos y caciques yucatecos*; Martínez Baracs, *Un gobierno de indios*. For the case of the Andes, see Sempat Assadourian, *Transiciones hacia el sistema colonial andino*; Sempat Assadourian, "Los señores étnicos."

3. Haskett, *Indigenous Rulers*; Lockhart, *The Nahuas after the Conquest*; Connell, *After Moctezuma*; Terraciano, *The Mixtecs of Colonial Oaxaca*; Restall, *The Maya World*; Ouweneel, "From Tlahtocayotl to Gobernadoryotl."

4. Historian Kevin Terracino surmises that the Codex Sierra (1550–64), a pictographic account book with extensive glosses in Nahuatl from the town of Santa Catalina Texupan in the Mixteca Alta of Oaxaca, was produced with an eye to presenting it to Spanish judges to make legal claims while maintaining legibility for local audiences. Terraciano, *Codex Sierra*, 91.

5. Lockhart, Berdan, and Anderson, *The Tlaxcalan Actas*; Matthew and Oudijk, *Indian Conquistadors*.

6. Lockhart, Berdan, and Anderson, *The Tlaxcalan Actas*, 23–24.

7. Hoekstra, *Two Worlds Merging*, 34–48.

8. On changing and competing referents of time in Indigenous disputes over custom, see Yannakakis, "Costumbre: A Language of Negotiation"; Herzog, "Colonial Law and 'Native Customs'"; Premo, *The Enlightenment on Trial*, 159–90. Tau Anzoátegui highlights Solórzano's conservative attitude toward custom, which he felt should be conserved rather than modified or innovated. Juan de Solórzano Pereira, *Política Indiana* (Madrid: Diego Díaz de la Carrera, 1776 [1647]), cited in Victor Tau Anzoátegui, *El poder de la costumbre*, 183–86.

9. On the concept of utility, see Owensby, "Between Justice and Economics." On how ordinary litigants produced Enlightenment ideas, see Premo, *The Enlightenment on Trial*.

10. Flores-Marcial, "A History of Guelaguetza in Zapotec Communities," 6, 28.

11. Arrioja Díaz Viruell, "Entre costumbres y leyes," 46.

12. On tniño, see Terraciano, *The Mixtecs of Colonial Oaxaca*, 145–50; Sousa, *The Woman Who Turned into a Jaguar*, 177–224. On tniño as communal obligation through service in the cargo system in contemporary Oaxaca, see Monaghan, *The Covenants with Earth and Rain*.

13. Lockhart, *The Nahuas after the Conquest*, 157.

14. See Schwaller, "A Language of Empire."

15. AHJO, VA Penal, leg. 11, exp. 4, 1717, "José Martin y socios de Lachichina acusan a las autoridades de su pueblo de varios hechos."

16. AHJO, VA Civil, leg. 13, exp. 15, 1750, "Queja de los vecinos del pueblo de Lalopa contra sus autoridades quienes les imponen castigos por no asistir a los tequios." For the "custom" of convening ruling councils of notables for tasks of governance, see also AHJO, VA Criminal, leg. 4, exp. 5, 1687, "Contra el cacique Pablo Vargas por peculado, robo de la caja común."

17. Penry, *The People Are King*, 9–15.

18. Gibson, *The Aztecs under Spanish Rule*; Taylor, *Landlord and Peasant in Colonial Oaxaca*; Menegus Bornemann, "El cacicazgo en Nueva España"; Serulnikov, *Subverting Colonial Authority*; Penry, *The People Are King*; Radding, *Wandering Peoples*, 171–207; Radding, *Landscapes of Power and Identity*, 89–116.

19. Tribute and informal payments (nine cases): AHJO, VA Criminal, leg. 1, exp. 7, 1654, "Contra el gobernador de Tonaguia por usurpar un real en cada manta del Real Tributo"; AHJO, T Civil, leg. 13, exp. 13, 1667, "Petición de amparo," fol. 1; AHJO, VA Criminal, leg. 5, exp. 3, 1695, "Contra Don Francisco de Paz, Don Juan de Stgo y Pedro Jiménez Gobernador y alcaldes de Yatzona por derramas económicas, agravios y vejaciones"; AHJO, VA Criminal, leg. 5, exp. 7, 1696, "Contra Miguel Santiago por sedicioso"; AHJO, VA Civil, leg. 5, exp. 7, 1699–1700, "Los Naturales del pueblo de San Francisco Yovego [Bijanos] contra los de San Miguel Tiltepec [Rincón] por tierras"; AHJO, VA Criminal, leg. 11, exp. 4, 1717, "Contra José Martín y José Favian principales de Santa María Lachichina por vejaciones, insulto y abusos de autoridad" (reference to labor for caciques on the part of the commoners); AHJO, VA Civil, leg. 2, exp. 121, 1729, "Protocolo de Instrumentos públicos, Real Provisión sobre el caso de Miguel de Chavez cacique del pueblo de Lachichina contra los oficiales de la República del pueblo de Tiltepec sobre deudos de diverso del arrendamiento de tierras"; AHJO, T Criminal, leg. 42, exp. 4, 1791, "Felipe Bautista contra el alcalde por sedicioso y perjudicia"; AHJO, VA Criminal, leg. 22, exp. 14, 1798, "Abuso de autoridad e injurias, Francisco Macario contra sus justicias por tiranos, San Francisco Cajonos."

20. AHJO, VA Criminal, leg. 5, exp. 3, 1695, "Contra Don Francisco de Paz, Don Juan de Stgo y Pedro Jiménez Gobernador y alcaldes de Yatzona por derramas económicas, agravios y vejaciones" (citation of customary payments of fish and hens to Pedro Boza, the lieutenant of the Spanish magistrate of Villa Alta).

21. Communal labor for public works (ten cases): AHJO, T Criminal, leg. 18, exp. 28, 1683, "Juan Matias de San Andres Xinaxtla contra Diego Gutiérrez (los naturales del pueblo de San Juan cumpliendo con la obligación que deven mandaron hacer un rancho de recibimiento para resevir a vmd como es costumbre)"; AHJO,

VA Civil, leg. 5, exp. 7, 1699–1700, "Los Naturales del pueblo de San Francisco Yovego [Vijanos] contra los de San Miguel Tiltepec [Rincón] por tierras" (reference to cleaning and maintaining road); AHJO, VA Criminal, leg. 11, exp. 4, 1717, "José Martin y socios de Lachichina acusan a las autoridades de su pueblo de varios hechos"; AHJO, T Criminal, leg. 26, exp. 26, 1729, "Contra el Gobernador de San Felipe por abuso de autoridad y azotes"; AHJO, VA Criminal, leg. 14, exp. 9, 1751, "Contra varios individuos de Talea por herir a Marcial Bautista de Analco" (reference to custom of maintaining the hammock bridge); AHJO, VA Civil, leg. 19, exp.14, 1766, "Juan, Nicolas y Antonio Yescas caciques del pueblo de San Juan Yae piden se les exima de trabajos que solo efectuan los macehuales"; AHJO, T Criminal, leg. 42, exp.24, 1795, "Mandamiento de Don Pedro Quevedo exhortando en el al común para que quitase y aboliese las costumbres de nombre mesonero, y los gastos que hazen en sus tequios y comunidades"; AHJO, VA Civil, leg. 32, exp. 11, 1797, "Entre San Juan Yae y Yovego sobre poner la amaca postura del Río Grande que divide sus terrenos"; AHJO, VA Civil, leg. 31, exp. 4.01, 1797, "Petición de comparecencia, San Juan Tabaá contra Yojovi y Solaga sobre construcción de xamaca"; AHJO, VA Civil, leg. 2, exp. 91, 1706, "Gabriel Maldonado y hermanos del pueblo de Yagallo piden se les concedan privilegios de los que gozan los caciques ya que son descendientes de ellos."

22. Public works for divine cult within the community (three cases): AHJO, VA Criminal, leg. 22, exp. 21, 1798, "Narciso de la Cruz y Socios de Lachixila Vijanos acusan a sus justicias de varios hechos"; AHJO, T Criminal, leg. 44, exp. 22, 1799, "Averiguación sobre los golpes y azotes que le dieron a Nicolas y Feliciano López la justicia de San Pedro Quilitongo"; AHJO, VA Civil, leg. 22, exp. 20, 1774, "El escribano de San Juan Yaeé, para dar reglo y convenio sobre sus fiestas."

23. AHJO, VA Civil, leg. 2, exp. 91, 1706, "Gabriel Maldonado y hermanos del pueblo de Yagallo piden se les concedan privilegios de los que gozan los caciques ya que son descendientes de ellos"; AHJO, VA Civil, leg. 19, exp. 14, 1766, "Juan, Nicolas y Antonio Yescas caciques del pueblo de San Juan Yae piden se les exima de trabajos que solo efectuan los macehuales"; AHJO, VA Criminal, leg. 11, exp. 4, 1717, "José Martin y socios de Lachichina acusan a las autoridades de su pueblo de varios hechos"; AHJO, VA Civil, leg. 22, exp. 20, 1774, "El escribano de San Juan Yaeé, para dar reglo y convenio sobre sus fiestas."

24. Cases in which community members denounced their authorities for whipping them for failure to perform tequio during the eighteenth century and into the postindependence era: AHJO, VA Criminal, leg. 8, exp. 13, 1706, "Blas Gómez de Totontepec contra Juan de la Cruz," fol. 11; AHJO, T Criminal, leg. 26, exp. 26, 1729, "Contra el Gobernador de San Felipe por abuso de autoridad y asotes"; AHJO, T Criminal, leg. 43, exp. 15, 1797, "El Gobernador de San Francisco Potlohusta contra las justicias de república por rebelión y azotes, Teposcolula"; AHJO, VA Criminal, leg. 22, exp. 14, 1798, "Abuso de autoridad e injurias, Villa Alta. Francisco Macario contra sus justicias por tiranos, San Francisco Cajonos," fol. 13; AHJO, T Criminal, leg. 43, exp. 40, 1798, "Contra el alcalde Ambrosio de la Cruz por azotes y otro"; AHJO, T Criminal, leg. 44, exp. 22, 1799, "Averiguación sobre los golpes

y azotes que le dieron a Nicolas y Feliciano López la justicia de San Pedro Quili-tongo"; AHJO, VA Criminal, leg. 24, exp. 3, 1805, "Contra el alcalde de Yovego por haber dado de azotes a un individuo, Yovego"; AHJO, VA Criminal, leg. 29, exp. 16, 1828, "Contra el alcalde de Xagalasi por azotes, Xagalasi," fol. 42.

25. AHJO, VA Civil, leg. 5, exp. 7, 1699–1700, "Los Naturales del pueblo de San Francisco Yovego [Vijanos] contra los de San Miguel Tiltepec [Rincón] por tierras"; AHJO, VA Criminal, leg. 14, exp. 9, 1751, "Contra varios individuos de Talea por herir a Marcial Bautista de Analco," fol. 50.

26. Pastor, *Campesinos y reformas*; Yannakakis, *The Art of Being In-Between*, ch. 3; Calvo, *Vencer la derrota*, chs. 2 and 3; Arrioja Díaz Viruell, "Pueblos divididos y no-bles empobrecidos," 203–28.

27. AHJO, T Civil, leg. 13, exp. 26, 1671, "Real Provisión"; AHJO, T Crimi-nal, leg. 19, exp. 19, 1687, "Mandamiento 'para que los naturales de los pueblos de su parte acudiesen a la doctrina y guardasen las costumbres en las avenciones y demas festividades…,'" fol. 1; AHJO, T Protocolos, leg. 3, exp. 8.31, 1707, "Carta de Con-venio 'que los naturales de Yanhuitlán y Chachoapa se han de tratar bien y se han de invitar a sus fiestas titulares y votivas y otras, según su costumbre antigua, acu-diendo a ellas con buena correspondencia como verdaderos amigos'"; AHJO, VA Civil, leg. 3, exp. 101, 1709, "Real Provisión para la celebración de un día de tian-guis en los pueblos de Tanetze y Yaviche"; AHJO, VA Civil, leg. 3, exp. 102, 1709, "Los naturales y común del pueblo de Santiago Lalopa se oponen a ser subordinados del pueblo de San Juan Yaeé"; AHJO, T Protocolos, leg. 4, exp. 2.14, 1714, "Carta de Convenio 'que en las funciones y cosas del culto divino y para el aumento y uti-lidad de su comunidad, han de acudir en cada un año con aquello que lícitamente han tenido de costumbre'"; AHJO, VA Civil, leg. 3, exp. 148, 1735, "Averiguación del porque no asisten a las fiestas de semana santa y otras los naturales de los pueb-los de Yagallo, Lachichina y Yaviche"; AHJO, VA Civil, leg. 4, exp. 188, 1745, "So-bre punto de cabecera"; Rosenbach Museum and Library, New Spain, 462/25, pt. 22, no. 6, 1736–69; Rosenbach Museum and Library, New Spain, 462/25, pt. 21, no. 3, 1744; Rosenbach Museum and Library, New Spain, 462/25, pt. 25, no. 1, 1736–41; Rosenbach Museum and Library, New Spain, 462/25, pt. 21, no. 2, 1735–44; AHJO, VA Civil, leg. 36, exp. 22, 1806, "Entre San Miguel Yotao y San Juan Tanetze por pesos."

28. AHJO, T Criminal, leg. 26, exp. 2, 1721, "Mandamiento"; AHJO, VA Civil, leg. 9, exp. 11, 1731, "Real Provisión"; AHJO, T Civil, leg. 29, exp. 15, 1738, "Bando"; AHJO, VA Criminal, leg. 14, exp. 9, 1751, "Contra varios individuos de Talea por herir a Marcial Bautista de Analco"; AHJO, VA Civil, leg. 27, exp. 21, 1791, "Aran-cel," fol. 27; AHJO, T Criminal, leg. 43, exp. 26, 1799, "Los naturales y república de San Juan Copala contra el gobernador Simon García por arbitrario, despota, y co-brar dos reales por maquila de sembradura."

29. AHJO, T Criminal, leg. 26, exp. 2, 1721, "Mandamiento."

30. AHJO, VA Criminal, leg. 14, exp. 9, 1751, "Contra varios individuos de Talea por herir a Marcial Bautista de Analco." See also accusations against interpreters for charging excessive fees in the following case: Latin American Library, Tulane Uni-

versity, Viceregal and Ecclesiastical Mexican Collection, leg. 8, exp. 28, 1796–1799, Villa Alta, 3 agosto 1796.

31. AHJO, VA Civil, leg. 9, exp. 11, 1731, "Real Provisión."

32. AHJO, T Civil, leg. 29, exp. 15, 1738, "Bando."

33. Tanck de Estrada, *Pueblos de indios y educación*; Arrioja Díaz Viruell, *Pueblos de indios y tierras comunales.*

34. AHJO, VA Civil, leg. 27, exp. 21, 1791, "Arancel."

35. AHJO, VA Civil, leg. 11, exp. 17, 1743, "Visita oficial que hizo el subdelegado Juan Francisco de la Puerta a los pueblos de la jurisdicción de Villa Alta."

36. *Recopilación de leyes de los Reynos de las Indias*, 4.15.1, 4.15.4, fols. 110-110v.

37. AHJO, VA Civil, leg. 10, exp. 10, 1738–1740, "Manuel Gutiérrez del pueblo de Lalopa contra los exalcaldes de Yatzona, Juan Santiago Gómez y socios por deuda de pesos"; AHJO, VA Civil, leg. 11, exp. 13, 1742, "Mandamiento sobre nuevas elecciones de alcaldes en el pueblo de Chuapam" (due to an illegal derrama that they collected to support the parish priest); AHJO, VA Civil, leg. 11, exp. 17, 1743, "Visita oficial que hizo el subdelegado Juan Francisco de la Puerta a los pueblos de la juris. de Villa Alta"; AHJO, VA Criminal, leg. 4, exp. 5, 1687, "Contra el cacique Pablo Vargas por peculado, robo de la caja común"; AHJO, VA Criminal, leg. 5, exp. 3, 1695, "Contra Don Francisco de Paz, Don Juan de Stgo y Pedro Jimenez Gobernador y alcaldes de Yatzona por derramas económicas, agravios y vejaciones"; AHJO, VA Criminal, leg. 11, exp. 4, 1717, "Contra José Martín y José Favian principales de Santa Maria Lachichina por vejaciones, insulto y abusos de autoridad."

38. Personal service (nine cases): AHJO, T Civil, leg. 13, exp. 27, 1671, "Decreto" (states that the parish priest must comply with the obligation to attend to the cabecera without obligating the Natives to construct residences and buildings or other prohibited services); AHJO, VA Civil, leg. 3, exp. 2, 1690, "Real Provisión para que se le presten los servicios necesarios para desempeñar su función al alcalde mayor, Juan Manuel Quiroz"; AHJO, T Civil, leg. 16, exp. 17, 1692, "Mandamientos" (the Natives must comply with the custom to provide for the parish priests of Tlaxiaco); AHJO, VA Criminal, leg. 5, exp. 7, 1696, "Contra Miguel Santiago por sedicioso"; AHJO, T Criminal, leg. 22, exp. 34, 1706, "Contra Juan Mendoza de Topiltepeque por sedicioso" (dispute over whether and what the parish priests should pay for Indigenous labor); AHJO, VA Criminal, leg. 11, exp. 4, 1717, "Contra José Martín y José Favian principales de Santa Maria Lachichina por vejaciones, insulto y abusos de autoridad"; AHJO, T Civil, leg. 36, exp. 19.14, 1765, "Poder especial," fol. 3 (regarding "la costumbre de servicio de los indios" in the sugar-producing estates); AHJO, T Civil, leg. 42, exp. 12, 1776, "Petición" (regarding the custom of personal service for the parish priest); AHJO, T Civil, leg. 45, exp. 28, 1784, "Petición: no sean compelidos los hijos del pueblo a no dar como tenían de costumbre, servicios personales e involuntarios a su gobernador."

39. Zavala, *El servicio personal de los indios en la Nueva España, 1521–1550*, tomo 1, 31.

40. Zavala, *El servicio personal de los indios en la Nueva España, 1700–1821*, tomo 7; Menegus Bornemann, *Los indios en la historia de México*, 41, 43.

41. Customary obligations pertaining to office (twelve cases): AHJO, VA Criminal, leg. 4, exp. 5, 1687, "Contra el cacique Pablo Vargas por peculado, robo de la caja común" (reference to the custom of meeting in the town hall to make decisions pertaining to the governance of the pueblo); AHJO, VA Civil, leg. 3, exp. 3, 1690, "Las Justicias del pueblo de San Juan Tanetze contra Joseph de Illescas por faltas cometidas a la autoridad"; AHJO, VA Criminal, leg. 5, exp. 3, 1695, "Contra Don Francisco de Paz, Don Juan de Stgo y Pedro Jimenez Gobernador y alcaldes de Yatzona por derramas económicas, agravios y vejaciones"; AHJO, VA Criminal, leg. 18, exp. 1, 1765, "Contra Juan Mexia de Santo Domingo Yojovi por lesiones" (a principal from Yoxovi says, "Inmemorial tiempo a esta parte no ha sido costumbre que en nuestro pueblo haya gobernador . . . , pues siempre se ha gobernado como un sujeto de su cabecera . . . por lo que la república se encabeza"); AHJO, T Criminal, leg. 21, exp. 2, 1694, "Contra los autoridades de San Sebastián por malos tratos y perdidos de objetos en perjuicio de Alonso Robles, Teposcolula" (reference to the customs associated with office); AHJO, T Criminal, leg. 43, exp. 10, 1797, "Contra Mariano Guzmán alcalde por haberle faltado a gobernador"; AHJO, T Criminal, leg. 42, exp. 24, 1795, title unknown ("el año de 1794 fingio un mandamiento de Don Pedro Quevedo exhortando en el al común para que quitase y aboliese las costumbres de nombre mesonero, y los gastos que hazen en sus tequios y comunidades . . ."); AHJO, VA Civil, leg. 13, exp. 15, 1750, "Queja de los vecinos del pueblo de Lalopa contra sus autoridades quienes les imponen castigos por no asistir a los tequios"; AHJO, VA Civil, leg. 22, exp. 24, 1774, "Los naturales del barrio de Analco piden se les respeten los privilegios de que gozan de imemorable año"; AHJO, VA Civil, leg. 24, exp. 15, 1778, "Cordillera"; AHJO, VA Civil, leg. 24, 15.02, 1780, "Cordillera,"; AHJO, VA Civil, leg. 24, 15.05, 1782 "Cordillera" (these cordilleras required the Native officials of the region to travel to Villa Alta in order to celebrate Corpus Christi with their "banderas, tambores, clarines, y demás instrumentos músicos y festivos en el modo que ha sido costumbre y puesto el obedicimiento a continuación de este mandamiento"; celebrate the conquest with their regalia and musical instruments [according to custom]; present "una memoria de la milpa del común y las fanegas o cargas que huvieren cosechado de ella"); AHJO, VA Criminal, leg. 15, exp. 10, 1762, "Sobre la libertad que solicitan varios presos de la carcel de Villa Alta" (a case about the requirement that some Native authorities provide a highway patrol to secure the Camino Real through the perilous Monte de Tanga pass between Antequera and the Sierra).

Customary electoral rules and procedures (fourteen cases): AHJO, VA Criminal, leg. 5, exp. 7, 1696, "Contra Miguel Santiago por sedicioso" (reference to custom of local authorities of region's Native towns overseeing the local market); AHJO, VA Civil, leg. 11, exp. 13, 1742, "Mandamiento sobre nuevas elecciones de alcaldes en el pueblo de Chuapam"; AHJO, VA Civil, leg. 22, exp. 17, 1774, "Superior Despacho acerca de elección de fiscales"; AHJO, VA Civil, leg.23 exp.2, 1775, "Los naturales del pueblo de Yaeé anulan las elecciones que se celebraron para elegir a las nuevas autoridades"; AHJO, VA Civil, leg. 24, exp. 15, 15.02, 15.05, 1778, 1780, 1782, "Varias cordilleras sobre elección de justicias y otros asuntos" (reference to custom of closing out the municipal accounts and reference to custom of how and when to conduct elections, as well as who is eligible to be elected); AHJO, T Civil, leg. 36, exp. 41, 1767, "Elecciones"; AHJO, T Criminal, leg. 22, exp. 33.04, 1707, "Elecciones de cantores de capilla"; AHJO, T Penal, leg. 23. exp. 7, 1707, "Petición de elecciones"; AHJO, VA Civil, leg. 20, exp.4, 1768, "Juan, Nicolas y Tomas Hernández del pueblo de Yae piden se les reconosca los privilegios de principales de los cuales siempre han gozado"; AHJO, VA Civil, leg. 18, exp. 15, 1764, "Tomás López Flores y sus hermanos contra la autoridad de San Juan Yae sobre privilegios de nobleza" (dispute over where the caciques and principales enter the cargo system); AHJO, VA Civil, leg. 17, exp. 16, 1760, "Juan López contra la república de Santa María Yavichi" (costumbre as exemption from "oficios bajos" due to principal status); AHJO, VA Civil, leg. 35, exp. 2, 1802, "Nicolás y Salvador Flores contra la república de Santa María Lachichina" (costumbre as everyone doing cargo service from the "más bajo hasta lo más alto"); AHJO, VA Criminal, leg. 22, exp. 16, 1798, "Abuso de autoridad" (the governor and justicias of Camotlan ordered Toribio Pérez y Diego Pérez, indios, principales to be whipped because they did not want their sons to follow the ladder of the cargo system according to custom).

42. AHJO, VA Criminal, leg. 5, exp. 3, 1695, "Contra Don Francisco de Paz, Don Juan de Stgo y Pedro Jimenez Gobernador y alcaldes de Yatzona por derramas económicas, agravios y vejaciones."

43. Bix, *A Dictionary of Legal Theory*, 219.

44. AHJO, T Criminal, leg. 23, exp. 7, 1707, "Petición de elecciones, Sobre elección de gobernadores y república de Teposcolula."

45. Romero Frizzi, *Teposcolula*; Terraciano, *The Mixtecs of Colonial Oaxaca*, 103, 112–13, 118–19, 126, 183, 234, 328, 342.

46. Terraciano, *The Mixtecs of Colonial Oaxaca*, 192–93.

47. AHJO, T Criminal, leg. 23, exp. 7, 1707, "Petición de elecciones, Sobre elección de gobernadores y república de Teposcolula," fol. 8.

48. Terraciano, *The Mixtecs of Colonial Oaxaca*; Lockhart, Berdan, and Anderson, *Tlaxcalan Actas*; Haskett, *Indigenous Rulers*; Ouweneel, *Shadows over Anáhuac*.

49. AHJO, T Criminal, leg. 23, exp. 7, 1707, "Petición de elecciones, Sobre elección de gobernadores y república de Teposcolula," fols. 8–8v.

50. AHJO, T Criminal, leg. 23, exp. 7, 1707, "Petición de elecciones, Sobre elección de gobernadores y república de Teposcolula," fols. 1–2.

51. AHJO, T Criminal, leg. 23, exp. 7, 1707, "Petición de elecciones, Sobre elección de gobernadores y república de Teposcolula," fols. 3–5v.

52. AHJO, T Criminal, leg. 23, exp. 7, 1707, "Petición de elecciones, Sobre elección de gobernadores y república de Teposcolula," fols. 6–7v.

53. Haskett, *Indigenous Rulers*, 33.

54. Miranda, *Las ideas y las instituciones políticas mexicanas*, 122–24.

55. Haskett, *Indigenous Rulers*, 29, 34.

56. AHJO, T Criminal, leg. 23, exp. 7, 1707, "Petición de elecciones, Sobre elección de gobernadores y república de Teposcolula," fols. 9–9v.

57. Owensby, *Empire of Law*, 130–66.

58. AHJO, T Civil, leg. 45, exp. 28, 1784, "Petición, Información del rejidor de San Vicente sobre que su gobernador quiere utilizar en servicio personal a los indios," fol. 1.

59. AHJO, T Civil, leg. 45, exp. 28, 1784, "Petición, Información del rejidor de San Vicente sobre que su gobernador quiere utilizar en servicio personal a los indios," fols. 1v–2.

60. AHJO, T Civil, leg. 45, exp. 28, 1784, "Petición, Información del rejidor de San Vicente sobre que su gobernador quiere utilizar en servicio personal a los indios," fols. 5–6.

61. AHJO, VA Criminal, leg. 22, exp. 21, 1798, "Narciso de la Cruz y socios de Lachixila Vijanos acusan a su justicia de varios hechos," fols. 1–6v.

62. *Diccionario de Autoridades* (1726–39), vol. 2, *1729*, s.v. "corruptela," accessed 8/10/2022 https://apps2.rae.es/DA.html.

63. Owensby, *Empire of Law*, 74; Rosenmüller, *Corruption and Justice in Colonial Mexico*.

64. AHJO, VA Criminal, leg. 22, exp. 21, 1798, "Narciso de la Cruz y socios de Lachixila Vijanos acusan a su justicia de varios hechos," fols. 2–4v.

65. AHJO, VA Criminal, leg. 22, exp. 21, 1798, "Narciso de la Cruz y socios de Lachixila Vijanos acusan a su justicia de varios hechos," fols. 7–9v.

66. AHJO, VA Criminal, leg. 22, exp. 21, 1798, "Narciso de la Cruz y socios de Lachixila Vijanos acusan a su justicia de varios hechos," fols. 10–10v.

Chapter Seven. Prescriptive Custom

1. Reynolds, "Medieval Law," 576.

2. Teuscher, "Document Collections"; Herzog, *A Short History of European Law*, 124–30.

3. Yannakakis, "Costumbre"; Herzog, "Colonial Law and 'Native Customs'"; Premo, "Custom Today"; Muñoz Arbeláez, *Costumbres en disputa*.

4. AHJO, VA Civil, leg. 9, exp. 15, 1766, "Sobre que permanesca el potrero de bestias en Tabaá," fols. 1–1v.

5. Arrioja Díaz Viruell, *Pueblos de indios y tierras comunales*.

6. Dehouve, *Quand les banquiers étaient des saints*; J. E. Mendoza, *Municipios, cofradías y tierras comunales*.

7. Romero Frizzi, "Época colonial (1519–1785)."

8. AHJO, VA Civil, leg. 9, exp. 15, 1766, "Sobre que permanesca el potrero de bestias en Tabaá."

9. AHJO, VA Civil. leg. 9, exp. 15, 1766, "Sobre que permanesca el potrero de bestias en Tabaá," fols. 1–6v.

10. AHJO, VA Civil, leg. 9, exp. 15, 1766, "Sobre que permanesca el potrero de bestias en Tabaá," fols. 3–3v.

11. AHJO, VA Civil, leg. 9, exp. 15, 1766, "Sobre que permanesca el potrero de bestias en Tabaá," fols. 3–3v.

12. AHJO, VA Civil, leg. 9, exp. 15, 1766, "Sobre que permanesca el potrero de bestias en Tabaá," fols. 3–3v.

13. King Alfonso, *Las Siete Partidas*, 5.11.1, p. 1092.

14. King Alfonso, *Las Siete Partidas*, 1.2.5, p. 11.

15. Suárez, *Tractatus de lege et legislatore Deo* in André and Berton, *R. p. Francisci Suarez... Opera omnia*, 7.14.7, p. 190, cited in Tierney, "Vitoria and Suarez on *Ius Gentium*," 118. See also Suárez and Baciero, *Tractatus de legibus ac Deo legislatore* for Latin-Spanish version.

16. Suárez, *Tractatus de lege et legislatore Deo*, 7.3.10, p. 145, cited in Tierney, "Vitoria and Suarez on *Ius Gentium*," 116.

17. Tierney, "Vitoria and Suarez on *Ius Gentium*," 114–19.

18. Dery, "'Papereality' and Learning in Bureaucratic Organizations."

19. Murillo Velarde, *Curso de derecho canónico hispano e indiano*, 1.35, "De los pactos," item 362, p.430: "Los indios, por su miseria y pusilanimidad, gozan del derecho de los menores y de sus privilegios, aunque sean mayores, y, no de otra manera pueden enajenar, no contratar sobre bienes inmuebles y sobre bienes muebles preciosos, mas que con la intervención de la autoridad del juez y con la asistencia de su protector, quien es el mismo fiscal real, u otro especialmente comisionado, sin el cual nada pueden hacer juicio, ni fuera de juicio, ni pueden ser obligados sin él. Y además, pueden, como también los menores, pedir la restitución, si son dañados."

20. Chance, *Conquest of the Sierra*; Baskes, *Indians, Merchants, and Markets*; Hamnett, *Politics and Trade in Southern Mexico*.

21. Autos del pueblo de San Juan Tabaá, 1742–1752, AGN, Tierras 791–92, cited in Carmagnani, *El regreso de los dioses*. See also Baskes, *Indians, Merchants, and Markets*, 24.

22. AHJO, VA Civil, leg. 9, exp. 15, 1766, "Sobre que permanesca el potrero de bestias en Tabaá," fols. 1–6.

23. Grossi, *El orden jurídico medieval*, 117–18.

24. *Diccionario de Autoridades*, vol. 2, *1729*, s.v. "convenio," accessed August 10, 2022, https://apps2.rae.es/DA.html.

25. AHJO, VA Civil, leg. 11, exp. 26.03, 1744, "Carta de Convenio, Santa Catarina Lachatao, San Miguel Amatlán"; AHJO, VA Civil, leg. 19, exp. 13.01, 1766, "Tonaguia and Tepitongo"; AHJO, VA Civil, leg. 30, exp. 14, 1796, "San Juan Yetzecovi, San Juan Tahui." See note 63 in this chapter for nine additional convenios regarding maintenance of the parish priest, church building, and fiesta cycle.

26. AHJO, VA Civil, leg. 9, exp. 15, 1766, "Sobre que permanesca el potrero de bestias en Tabaá," fols. 1–6.

27. *Diccionario de Autoridades*, vol. 2, *1729*, s.v. "compromisso," Accessed August 10, 2022, https://apps2.rae.es/DA.html: "Convención, avenéncia de las partes litigantes, por la qual se da poder y facultad a una o más personas, para que siendo árbitros o arbitradores puedan decidir, resolver o determinar el litígio o controversia sobre que litígan, o quieren litigar. Latín. *Compromissum. Duorum vel plurium con-*

sensus in alicujus peritioris arbitrium. RECOP. lib. 3. tit. 6. l. 9. No reciban él ni sus oficiales compromissos de ningunos pléitos, que ante ellos estuvieren pendientes, ni del que pudieren conocer. BOLAÑ. Comerc. terrest. lib. 2. cap. 14. num. 16. Si en la cáusa del compromisso se huviere de hacer probanza, no la pueden los árbitros ni arbitradores hacer por sí."

28. Chance, *Conquest of the Sierra*, 46–88.

29. AHJO, VA Civil, leg. 9, exp. 15, 1766, "Sobre que permanesca el potrero de bestias en Tabaá," fols. 4–5

30. AHJO, VA Civil, leg. 9, exp. 15, 1766, "Sobre que permanesca el potrero de bestias en Tabaá," fols. 7–7v.

31. AHJO, VA Civil, leg. 9, exp. 15, 1766, "Sobre que permanesca el potrero de bestias en Tabaá," fol. 8.

32. AHJO, VA Civil, leg. 9, exp. 15, 1766, "Sobre que permanesca el potrero de bestias en Tabaá," fols. 8–9.

33. AHJO, VA Civil, leg. 9, exp. 15, 1766, "Sobre que permanesca el potrero de bestias en Tabaá," fols. 10–10v.

34. Chance, *Conquest of the Sierra*; Yannakakis, *The Art of Being In-Between*, ch. 4; Guardino, *The Time of Liberty*, chs. 2 and 3; Premo, *The Enlightenment on Trial*, ch. 5; Arrioja Díaz Viruell, "Pueblos divididos"; Penry, *The People Are King*.

35. AHJO, VA Civil, leg. 9, exp. 15, 1766, "Sobre que permanesca el potrero de bestias en Tabaá," fols. 12–17v.

36. Murillo Velarde, *Curso de derecho canónico hispano e indiano*, 1.35, "De los pactos," item 360, p.428: "es el acuerdo de dos o más en el consentimiento del mismo parecer. Lo que debe darse o hacerse a uno de nosotros, por otro de vosotros."

37. Leonardus Lessius, *De Iustitia et Iure*, lib. 2, acp. 17, dub. 3, num. 18, p. 197, cited in Decock, *Theologians and Contract Law*, 112n410.

38. King Alfonso, *Las Siete Partidas*, 5.6.5, p. 1055.

39. King Alfonso, *Las Siete Partidas*, 5.6.5, p. 1055.

40. Decock, *Theologians and Contract Law*, 107–14.

41. Decock, *Theologians and Contract Law*, 114.

42. Decock, *Theologians and Contract Law*, 199.

43. AHJO, VA Civil, leg. 9, exp. 15, 1766, "Sobre que permanesca el potrero de bestias en Tabaá," fols. 12–17v.

44. AHJO, VA Civil, leg. 9, exp. 15, 1766, "Sobre que permanesca el potrero de bestias en Tabaá," fols. 12–17v.

45. AHJO, VA Civil, leg. 9, exp. 15, 1766, "Sobre que permanesca el potrero de bestias en Tabaá," fols. 12–17v.

46. AHJO, VA Civil, leg. 9, exp. 15, 1766, "Sobre que permanesca el potrero de bestias en Tabaá," fols. 15–15v.

47. Decock, *Theologians and Contract Law*, 44.

48. Decock, *Theologians and Contract Law*, 70–73.

49. AHJO, VA Civil, leg. 9, exp. 15, 1731, "Sobre que permanesca el potrero de bestias en Tabaá," fols. 18–19.

50. AHJO, VA Civil, leg. 9, exp. 15, 1731, "Sobre que permanesca el potrero de bestias en Tabaá," fol. 18v.

51. Kleyn, "The Protection of Quasi-Possession in South African Law," 142–64; Camacho de los Ríos, "Diferencias terminológicas y conceptuales."

52. AHJO, VA Civil, leg. 9, exp. 15, 1766, "Sobre que permanesca el potrero de bestias en Tabaá," fol. 18v.

53. AHJO, VA Civil, leg. 18, exp.15, 1764, "Tomás López Flores y sus hermanos contra la autoridad de San Juan Yae sobre privilegios de nobleza."

54. Teuscher, "Document Collections."

55. AHJO, VA Civil, leg. 9, exp. 15, 1731, "Sobre que permanesca el potrero de bestias en Tabaá," fol. 19.

56. AHJO, VA Civil, leg. 9, exp. 15, 1731, "Sobre que permanesca el potrero de bestias en Tabaá," fol. 20.

57. AHJO, VA Civil, leg. 9, exp. 15, 1731, "Sobre que permanesca el potrero de bestias en Tabaá," fols. 20–21.

58. AHJO, T Civil, leg. 42, exp. 12, 1776, "Petición, Diligencias sobre separación y servicios ymboluntarios."

59. Taylor, *Magistrates of the Sacred*; Terraciano, *The Mixtecs of Colonial Oaxaca*; Farriss, *Tongues of Fire*.

60. Taylor, *Magistrates of the Sacred*, 132–33.

61. Taylor, *Magistrates of the Sacred*, 589n68 (1608, 1609, 1654); Owensby, *Empire of Law*, 131–33 (1609); See p. 208 of *Recopilación Sumaria de los Autos Acordados*: Real Cédula de 15 de Octubre de 1713, CCCLXXXIV. "Que á los Pueblos de Indios se les dé sitio que tenga comodidad de aguas, tierras, montes, salidas, y entradas para que hagan sus labranzas y un exido de una legua donde pasten sus ganados, y que no se les obligue á servicio personal alguno sino por su voluntad, y pagándoles su jornal."

62. Zavala, *El servicio personal de los indios de Nueva España*.

63. AHJO, T Protocolos, leg. 3, exp. 8.31, 1707, "Carta de Convenio, Yanhuitlán y Chachoapa"; AHJO, T Protocolos, leg. 4, exp. 2.14, 1714, "Carta de Convenio"; AHJO, VA Civil, leg. 2, exp. 9.04, 1679, "Convenio, San Juan Lalana, San Juan Teotlacingo"; AHJO, VA Civil, leg. 9, exp. 17, 1731, "Carta de Convenio, Totontepec, Amatepec, Moctún, and Tiltepec"; AHJO, VA Civil, leg. 12, exp. 4, 1745, "Carta de Convenio, Yaeé, Yagallo, Yaviche, Lachichina"; AHJO, VA Civil, leg. 28, exp. 8, 1793, "Juan Pablo, Phelipe Antonio, Ildefonso Josef, Antonio Miguel, Mariano Santiago, Sebastián de la Cruz, Francisco Aparicio y Marcelino Alejandro, naturales del pueblo de Jayacatepec, contra Juan López, alcalde, por haberse comprometido con los del pueblo de Moetún a que los naturales del pueblo de Jayacatepec les ayudarían en la edificación de su iglesia"; AHJO, VA Civil, leg. 28, exp. 12, 1793, "Convenio, San Marcos Moetún and Jayacatepec"; AHJO, VA Civil, leg. 3, exp. 160, 1739, "Compromiso, Protocolos de Instrumentos Públicos, Tanetze, Yae, Lalopa, Talea, Juquila, Yotao, Cacalotepeque, Yaviche, Lachichina, Lahoya, Yatoni"; AHJO, VA Civil, leg. 22, exp. 20, 1774, "Carta de Convenio, San Juan Yaeé" (in this last convenio, the Native authorities and común of Yaeé agreed to the responsibilities

of each social group within their community—caciques, principales, and mace-huales—in the maintenance of the parish priest, church building, and fiesta cycle).

64. Pastor, *Campesinos y reformas*.

65. AHJO, T Civil, leg. 42, exp. 12, 1776, "Petición, Diligencias sobre separación y servicios ymboluntarios," fol. 2.

66. AHJO, T Civil, leg. 42, exp. 12, 1776, "Petición, Diligencias sobre separación y servicios ymboluntarios," fol. 2.

67. S. Cline, *Colonial Culhuacan, 1580–1600*; Terraciano, *The Mixtecs of Colonial Oaxaca*, 194. See Haskett, *Indigenous Rulers*, 98–99, 117, 200, on the catchall role of topiles (*topileque* in Nahuatl) in Indigenous town government in Cuernavaca.

68. Terraciano, *The Mixtecs of Colonial Oaxaca*, 194.

69. Terraciano, *The Mixtecs of Colonial Oaxaca*, 146.

70. AHJO, T Civil, leg. 42, exp. 12, 1776, "Petición, Diligencias sobre separación y servicios ymboluntarios," fol. 2.

71. Terraciano, *The Mixtecs of Colonial Oaxaca*, 191–92.

72. AHJO, T Civil, leg. 42, exp. 12, 1776 "Petición, Diligencias sobre separación y servicios ymboluntarios," fols. 4–4v.

73. AHJO, T Civil, leg. 42, exp. 12, 1776, "Petición, Diligencias sobre separación y servicios ymboluntarios," fols. 4–4v.

74. AHJO, T Civil, leg. 42, exp. 12, 1776, "Petición, Diligencias sobre separación y servicios ymboluntarios," fols. 5–5v.

75. AHJO, T Civil, leg. 42, exp. 12, 1776, "Petición, Diligencias sobre separación y servicios ymboluntarios," fols. 7–8.

76. AHJO, T Civil, leg. 42, exp. 12, 1776, "Petición, Diligencias sobre separación y servicios ymboluntarios," fol. 8.

Epilogue

1. Merry, *Colonizing Hawai'i*; Comaroff and Comaroff, *Of Revelation and Revolution*.

2. Mignolo and Walsh, *On Decoloniality*. For a critique of decoloniality, see Cusicanqui, "Ch'ixinakax utxiwa."

3. van Meijl, "Doing Indigenous Epistemology."

4. Ramos and Yannakakis, *Indigenous Intellectuals*.

5. Cordero Avendaño de Durand, *El derecho consuetudinario indígena en Oaxaca*.

6. Poole, "Los usos de la costumbre"; Johnson, "Indigenizing Self-Determination at the United Nations."

7. Veltmeyer and Petras, *The New Extractivism*.

8. Martínez Luna, "Conocimiento y comunalidad"; Díaz, Robles Hernández, and Cardoso Jiménez, *Escrito*. For a discussion of comunalidad in the context of Oaxaca's legal reform and the movement to bring cell phone service to the Sierra Norte, see J. C. Martínez, *Derechos indígenas en los juzgados*, 58–59; González, *Connected*, 22–23.

9. Aquino Centeno, "Interrogando la costumbre y la legislación indígena." On harmony ideology, see the classic work of legal anthropology: Nader, *Harmony Ideology*.

10. Eisenstadt, "*Usos y costumbres* and Postelectoral Conflicts"; A. Benton, "'Participatory Governance'"; V. García, "Los derechos políticos de las mujeres"; Galar Martínez, "La representación descriptiva y simbólica."

11. Dunlap, "The 'Solution' Is Now the 'Problem.'"

Bibliography

Archives, Libraries, and Collections Cited

Archivo General de la Nación, México (AGN)
Archivo General de las Indias (AGI)
Archivo del Estado de Oaxaca (AEO)
Archivo Histórico Judicial de Oaxaca (AHJO)
      Archivo del Juzgado de Teposcolula (T)
      Archivo del Juzgado de Villa Alta (VA)
Benson Latin American Collection, LLILAS Benson Latin American Studies and
    Collections, the University of Texas at Austin
Latin American Library, Tulane University, Viceregal and Ecclesiastical Mexican
    Collection
Rosenbach Museum and Library, New Spain

Printed or Bound Primary Sources

Note on citation of legal sources: For *Las Siete Partidas*, *Novissima Recopilación
de las leyes del reino*, *Recopilación de leyes de los reinos de las Indias*, I cite in the following order using Arabic numerals: libro (book).título (title).ley (law). For Murillo Velarde, *Curso de derecho canónico hispano e indiano*, I cite libro.título and item
number. For these sources, I also provide the folio or page number for the editions
cited in the bibliography.

Acuña, René, ed. *Relaciones geográficas del siglo XVI: Antequera*. 2 vols. Mexico City:
    UNAM, 1984.
Acuña, René, ed. *Relaciones geográficas de Michoacán*. Mexico City: UNAM, 1987.

Acuña, René, ed. *Relaciones geográficas de Nueva Galicia.* Mexico City: UNAM, 1988.

Al-Jusani, Ibn Harit. *Historia de los jueces de Córdoba.* Edited and translated by Julián Ribera. Madrid: Imprenta Ibérica, 1914.

Alvarado, Francisco de. *Vocabulario en lengua misteca: Hecho por los padres de la orden de predicadores, que residen en ella.* Mexico City: Con licencia, en Casa de Pedro Balli, 1593.

Aristotle. *Nicomachean Ethics.* Cambridge: Cambridge University Press, 2014.

Aristotle. *Politics.* Translated by C. D. C. Reeve. Indianapolis: Hackett, 2017.

Berdan, Frances F., and Patricia R. Anawalt, eds. *The Codex Mendoza.* 4 vols. Berkeley: University of California Press, 1992.

Betancourt, Luz María Mohar. *Códice Mapa Quinatzin: Justicia y derechos humanos en el México antiguo.* Mexico City: CIESAS, 2004.

Chimalpahin Cuauhtlehuanitzin, Domingo Francisco de San Antón Muñón. *Codex Chimalpahin: Society and Politics in Mexico Tenochtitlan, Tlatelolco, Texcoco, Culhuacan, and Other Nahua Altepetl in Central Mexico.* Vol. 2. Translated by Arthur J. O. Anderson and Susan Schroeder. Norman: University of Oklahoma Press, 2016.

Concilio III: Provincial mexicano. Mexico City: Eugenio Maillefert y Compañia, 1859.

Córdova, Juan de. *Arte en lengua zapoteca.* Mexico City: Pedro Balli, 1578.

Córdova, Juan de. *Vocabulario en lengua çapoteca.* Mexico City: Pedro Charte, 1578.

Covarrubias Orozco, Sebastián de. *Tesoro de la lengua castellana o española.* 1611. Reprint, Madrid, 1674. Biblioteca Virtual Miguel Cervantes. http://www.cervantesvirtual.com/obra/tesoro-de-la-lengua-castellana-o-espanola-o.

Durán, Diego. *Historia de las Indias de Nueva España e islas de tierra firme.* Mexico City: Editorial Porrua, 1967.

Feria, Pedro de. *Doctrina christiana en lengua castellana y çapoteca.* Mexico City: En casa de Pedro Ocharte, 1567.

Freir, Bruce W., ed. *The Codex of Justinian: A New Annotated Translation, with Parallel Latin and Greek Text.* Vol. 3. Cambridge: Cambridge University Press, 2016.

García, Genaro. *El clero de México durante la dominación española según el archivo inédito archiepiscopal metropolitano.* Mexico City: Vda. de Ch. Bouret, 1907.

García Icazbalceta, Joaquín. *Don Fray Juan de Zumárraga Primer Obispo y Arzobispo de México.* Mexico City: Andrade y Morales, 1881.

Gilby, Thomas, ed. *Summa Theologiae.* 60 vols. London: Blackfriars, 1964.

Gómez, Antonio. *Compendio de los comentarios extendidos por el maestro Antonio Gómez a las ochentas y tres Leyes de Toro . . . : Lleva tambien cinqüenta y dos advertencias que explican, extienden, alteran ó corrigen las especies á que van llamadas.* D. Joseph Doblado Galiciana: Biblioteca Digital de Galicia, 1785.

González Obregón, Luis, ed. *Proceso inquisitorial del cacique de Tetzcoco.* Mexico City: Eusebio Gómez de la Puente, 1910.

González Obregón, Luis, ed. *Procesos de indios idólatras y hechiceros.* 1912. Fascimile reprint, Mexico City: AGN, 2002.

Grijalva, Juan de. *Cronica de la Orden de N.P.S. Augustin en las provincias de la nueva españa: En quatro edades desde el año de 1533 hasta el de 1592*. 1624. Reprint, Mexico City, 1924–30.

Ixtlilxochitl, Fernando de Alva. *Obras históricas de Don Fernando de Alva Ixtlilxochitl*. Edited by Alfredo Chavero. Mexico City: Editora Nacional, 1965.

Jiménez Moreno, Wigberto, and Salvador Mateos Higuera. *Códice de Yanhuitlán*. Mexico City: INAH, 1994.

King Alfonso X of Castile and Leon. *Las Siete Partidas*. Edited by Robert I. Burns. Translated by Samuel Parsons Scott. Philadelphia: University of Pennsylvania Press, 2001.

King Alfonso XI of Castile. *El Ordenamiento de Leyes que D. Alfonso XI Hizo en las Cortes de Alcalá de Henares en el Año de Mil Trescientos y Cuarenta y Ocho*. Madrid: Libreria de los señores viuda e hijos de D. Antonio Calleja, 1847.

King Philip IV of Spain and Portugal. *Novissima Recopilación de las Leyes del Reino*. Madrid: Diego Díaz de la Carrera, 1626.

Las Casas, Bartolomé de. *The Devastation of the Indies: A Brief Account*. Translated by Herma Briffault. Baltimore: Johns Hopkins University Press, 1992.

Las Casas, Bartolomé de. *Los indios de México y Nueva España: Antología*. Edited by Edmundo O'Gorman and Jorge Alberto Manrique. 7th ed. Mexico City: Editorial Porrua, 1993.

Lessius, Leonardus. *De Iustitia et Iure caeterisque virtutibus cardinalibus*. Lovanii: I. Masii, 1605.

Lessius, Leonardus. *On Sale, Securities, and Insurance*. Translated by Wim Decock and Nicholas de Sutter. Grand Rapids, MI: CLP Academic, 2016.

Martínez, Fray Alonso. *Manual breve y compendioso para enpesar a aprender lengua zapoteca y administrar en caso de necesidad*. 1633. Reprint, Veracruz, Mexico: Veracruz-Llave, 1871.

Mendieta, Gerónimo de. *Historia eclesiástica indiana: Obra escrita a fines del siglo XVI*. Written ca. 1595, first published 1870. Facsimile edition, Mexico City: Porrúa, 1993.

Molina, Alonso de. *Vocabulario en lengua castellana y Mexicana, compuesto por el muy reverendo padre fray Alonso de Molina: Guardian del convento de san Antonio de Tetzcuco de la orden de los frayles Menores*. Mexico City: Juan Pablos, 1555.

Molina, Alonso de. *Vocabulario en lengua castellana y mexicana [en lengua mexicana y castellana], compuesto por el muy Reverendo Padre Fray Alonso de Molina de la orden del bienaventurado nuestro padre san Francisco*. Mexico City: En casa de Antonio de Spinosa, 1571.

Monterroso y Alvarado, Gabriel de, Juan de la Cuesta, and Juan de Sarriá. *Pratica civil y criminal y instrucion de escriuanos: Diuidida en nueue tratados*. Madrid: En casa de Juan de la Cuesta, 1609.

Motolinía, Toribio de Benavente. *Historia de los indios de Nueva España*. Vol. 1 of *Colección de documentos para la historia de México*. Portal de Agustinos no. 3. Mexico City: Libreria de J. M. Andrade, 1858.

Motolinía, Toribio (de Benavente). *Memoriales o libro de las cosas de la Nueva España y los naturales de ella.* Ca. 1541. Reprint, Mexico City: UNAM, 1971.

Muñoz Camargo, Diego. *Descripción de la ciudad y provincia de Tlaxcala.* Edited by René Acuña. San Luis Potosí: El Colegio de San Luis, 2000.

Murillo Velarde, Pedro. *Curso de derecho canónico hispano e indiano.* Zamora: El Colegio de Michoacán, 2006.

Muro Orejón, Antonio, ed. *Las Leyes Nuevas de 1542–1543: Ordenanzas para la gobernación de las Indias y buen tratamiento y conservación de los Indios.* 1543 ("Leyes y ordenanças nuevamente hechas"). Facsimile edition, Seville: Escuela de Estudios Hispano-Americanos, 1961.

Nebrija, Antonio de. *Vocabulario español-latino.* Salamanca, 1495. Biblioteca Virtual Miguel de Cervantes. http://www.cervantesvirtual.com/nd/ark: /59851/bmcvm466.

Olmos, Andrés de, Ascensión H. de León-Portilla, and Miguel León-Portilla. *Arte de la lengua mexicana.* Mexico City: UNAM, 2002.

Pomar, Juan Bautista. "Relación de Tezcoco." In *Varios Relaciones de la Nueva España,* edited by Germán Vázquez and Joaquín García Icazbalceta, 19–99. Madrid: Historia 16, 1991.

Puga, Vasco de. *Provisiones, cédulas, instrucciones de Su Magestad, ordenanças de difuntos y audiencia para la nueva expedición de los negocios y administración de justiçia y governación de esta Nueva España, y para el buen tratamiento y conservación de los yndios desde el año 1525 hasta este presente de 63.* 1563. Reprint, Bloomington: Indiana University Press, 2012.

Recopilación de leyes de los Reynos de las Indias. 1681. Facsimile reprint, Madrid: Ediciones de Cultura Hispánica, 1973.

Recopilación Sumaria de los Autos Acordados de la Real Audiencia de esta nueva españa, que desde el año de 1677 hasta el de 1786 han podido recogerse. México: Don Felipe de Zuñiga y Ontiveros, calle del Espíritu Santo, 1787.

Reyes, Antonio de los. *Arte en lengua mixteca.* Mexico City: En casa de Pedro Balli, 1593.

Sahagún, Bernardino de. *Florentine Codex: General History of the Things of New Spain.* 2nd ed., revised. Translated by Arthur J. Anderson and Charles E. Dibble. Santa Fe, NM and Salt Lake City, Utah: School of American Research and the University of Utah Press, 1981.

Sahagún, Fray Bernardino de. *Coloquios y doctrina cristiana con que los doce frailes de San Francisco enviados por el papa Adriano VI y por el emperador Carlos V, convirtieron a los indios de la Nueva España.* Facsimile edition. Mexico City: UNAM, 1986.

Sepúlveda y Herrera, María Teresa. *Procesos por idolatría al cacique, gobernadores, y sacerdotes de Yanhuitlán, 1544–1546.* Mexico City: INAH, 1999.

Sigüenza, Pedro de. *Tratado de clausulas instrumentales: Vtil y necessario para iueces, abogados, y escrivanos destos Reynos, Procuradores, Partidores, y Confessores, en lo de justicia y derecho.* Madrid: Melchor Sanchez, 1663.

Silva, Francisco Pacheco de. *Doctrina cristiana traducida de la lengua castellana en lengua zapoteca nexitza*. 1687. Reprint, Oaxaca: Juan Mariscal, 1882.

Solórzano Pereira, Juan de. *Politica indiana*. 1647. Reprint, Madrid: Compañía Ibero-Americana de Publicaciones, 1972.

Stevens, Henry. *The New Laws of the Indies for the Good Treatment and Preservation of the Indians*. London: Privately printed at the Chiswick Press, 1893.

Suárez, Francisco. *Tractatus de lege et legislatore Deo*. In *R. p. Francisci Suarez . . . Opera omnia*, 26 vols, edited by M. (Michel) André and Charles Berton. Paris: Vivès, 1856–78.

Suárez, Francisco, and C. Baciero. *Tractatus de legibus ac Deo legislatore*. Madrid: Consejo Superior de Investigaciones Científicas, 2010.

Torquemada, Fray Juan de. *Monarquía indiana*. Mexico City: Editorial Porrúa, 1975.

Vitoria, Francisco de. *Political Writings*. Edited by Anthony Pagden and Jeremy Lawrance. Cambridge: Cambridge University Press, 1991.

Vitoria, Francisco de. *Relectio "De Indis."* Edited by L. Pereña and J. M. Pérez-Prendes. 1539. Reprint, Madrid: Consejo Superior de Investigaciones Científicas, 1967.

Zorita, Alonso de. *Relación de los señores de la Nueva España*. Edited by Germán Vázquez. Madrid: Historia 16, 1992.

Secondary Sources

Adorno, Rolena. *The Intellectual Life of Bartolomé de las Casas*. New Orleans: Graduate School of Tulane University, 1992.

Aguilar Sánchez, Omar. "La construcción de espacios sagrados como límites territoriales en los pueblos de la Nueva España." *Thule* 38/39–40/41 (2015–2016): 689–707.

Aguilar Sánchez. Omar. "Ñuu Savi: Pasado, presente y futuro. Descolonización, continuidad cultural y reapropiación de los códices mixtecos en el Pueblo de la Lluvia." PhD diss. Leiden University, 2020.

Alberro, Solange. *Inquisición y sociedad en México, 1571–1700*. Mexico City: Fondo de Cultura Económica, 2015.

Alcina Franch, José. *Calendario y religión entre los zapotecos*. Mexico City: UNAM, 1993.

Alonso, José Ricardo León. *La categoría de la obligación "in solidum."* Seville: University of Seville, 1978.

Alva, J. Jorge Klor de. "Colonizing Souls: The Failure of the Indian Inquisition and the Rise of Penitential Discipline." In *Cultural Encounters: The Impact of the Inquisition in Spain and the New World*, edited by Mary Elizabeth Perry and Anne J. Cruz, 3–22. Berkeley: University of California Press, 1991.

Anders, Ferdinand, Maarten Jansen, and Gabina Aurora Pérez Jiménez. *Origen e historia de los reyes mixtecos: Libro explicativo del llamado Códice Vindobonen-*

sia: Codex Vindobonensis Mexicanus 1. Graz and Mexico City: Akademische Druck-und Verlagsanstalt and Fondo de Cultura Económica, 1992.

Anghie, Anthony. *Imperialism, Sovereignty and the Making of International Law*. Cambridge: Cambridge University Press, 2007.

Aquino Centeno, Salvador. "Interrogando la costumbre y la legislación indígena: Contribuciones y horizontes de la antropología jurídica en Oaxaca." *Nueva antropología* 26, no. 78 (2013): 87–117.

Arcos, Roberto Moreno de los. "New Spain's Inquisition for Indians from the Sixteenth to the Nineteenth Century." In *Cultural Encounters: The Impact of the Inquisition in Spain and the New World*, edited by Mary Elizabeth Perry and Anne J. Cruz, 23–26. Berkeley: University of California Press, 1991.

Arrioja Díaz Viruell, Luis Alberto. "Entre costumbres y leyes: Las tierras de común repartimiento en una región indígena de México, 1742–1856." *Letras Históricas* 10 (2014): 39–75.

Arrioja Díaz Viruell, Luis Alberto. *Pueblos de indios y tierras comunales: Villa Alta, Oaxaca, 1742–1856*. Zamora: El Colegio de Michoacán, 2011.

Arrioja Díaz Viruell, Luis Alberto. "Pueblos divididos y nobles empobrecidos: Villa Alta (Oaxaca), 1750–1808." In *Los indios ante la justicia local: Intérpretes, oficiales y litigantes en Nueva España y Guatemala (siglos XVI–XVIII)*, edited by Yanna Yannakakis, Martina Schrader-Kniffki, and Luis Alberto Arrioja Díaz Viruell, 203–28. Zamora: El Colegio de Michoacán; Atlanta: Emory University, 2019.

Astarita, Tommaso. *Village Justice: Community, Family, and Popular Culture in Early Modern Italy*. Baltimore: Johns Hopkins University Press, 1999.

Banerjee, Milinda, and Kerstin Von Lingen. "Law, Empire, and Global Intellectual History: An Introduction." *Modern Intellectual History* 17, no. 2 (2020): 467–70.

Baskes, Jeremy. *Indians, Merchants, and Markets: A Reinterpretation of the Repartimiento and Spanish-Indian Economic Relations in Colonial Oaxaca, 1750–1821*. Stanford, CA: Stanford University Press, 2000.

Baudot, Georges. "Los franciscanos etnógrafos." *Estudios de cultura Náhuatl* 27 (1997): 275–307.

Belmessous, Saliha. *Native Claims: Indigenous Law against Empire, 1500–1920*. Oxford: Oxford University Press, 2012.

Bennett, Herman. *Africans in Colonial Mexico: Absolutism, Christianity, and Afro-Creole Consciousness*. Bloomington: Indiana University Press, 2003.

Benton, Allyson Lucinda. "How 'Participatory Governance' Strengthens Authoritarian Regimes: Evidence from Electoral Authoritarian Oaxaca, Mexico." *Journal of Politics in Latin America* 8, no. 2 (2016): 37–70.

Benton, Bradley. "Beyond the Burned Stake: The Rule of Don Antonio Pimentel Tlahuitoltzin in Tetzcoco, 1540–45." In *Texcoco: Prehispanic and Colonial Perspectives*, edited by Jongsoo Lee and Galen Brokaw, 183–200. Boulder: University Press of Colorado, 2014.

Benton, Bradley. *The Lords of Tetzcoco: The Transformation of Indigenous Rule in Postconquest Central Mexico*. Cambridge: Cambridge University Press, 2017.

Benton, Lauren. "Introduction." AHR Forum: "Law and Empire in Global Perspective." *American Historical Review* 117, no. 4 (2012): 1092–100.

Benton, Lauren. *Law and Colonial Cultures: Legal Regimes in World History, 1400–1900*. Cambridge: Cambridge University Press, 2001.

Benton, Lauren, and Richard J. Ross. "Empires and Legal Pluralism: Jurisdiction, Sovereignty, and Political Imagination in the Early Modern World." In *Legal Pluralism and Empires, 1500–1850*, edited by Lauren Benton and Richard J. Ross, 1–17. New York: New York University Press, 2016.

Berdan, Frances F. "The Codex Mendoza: Writing and Re-Writing 'the Last Word.'" In *Mesoamerican Manuscripts: New Scientific Approaches and Interpretations*, edited by Maarten E. R. G. N. Jansen, Virginia M. Lladó-Buisán, and Ludo Snijders, 1–14. Leiden: Brill, 2019.

Berger, Adolf. *Encyclopedic Dictionary of Roman Law*. 1953. Reprint, Philadelphia: American Philosophical Society, 1991.

Bix, Brian. *A Dictionary of Legal Theory*. Oxford: Oxford University Press, 2004.

Black, Mindie Lazarus. Review of *Human Rights and Gender Violence: Translating International Law into Local Justice*, by Sally Engle Merry. *Law and Society Review* 40, no. 4 (2006): 979–81.

Blanch, Juan Manuel Lope. "Nebrija, primer lingüista moderno." In *Memoria del Coloquio La Obra de Antonio de Nebrija y su recepción en la Nueva España, quince estudios nebrisenses (1492–1992)*, edited by Ignacio Guzmán Betancourt and Eréndira Nansen Díaz, 39–46. Mexico City: INAH, 1997.

Blaufarb, Rafe. "Conflict and Compromise: Communauté and Seigneurie in Early Modern Provence." *Journal of Modern History* 82 (September 2010): 519–45.

Bleichmar, Daniela. "Painting the Aztec Past in Early Colonial Mexico: Translation and Knowledge Production in the Codex Mendoza." *Renaissance Quarterly* 72 (Winter 2019): 1362–415.

Boesche, Roger. "Aristotle's Science of Tyranny." *History of Political Thought* 14, no. 1 (Spring 1993): 1–25.

Bonfield, Lloyd. "Introduction: The Dimensions of Customary Law." *Continuity and Change* 10, no. 3 (1995): 331–35.

Boone, Elizabeth Hill. *Descendants of Aztec Pictography: The Cultural Encyclopedias of Sixteenth-Century Mexico*. Austin: University of Texas Press, 2020.

Boone, Elizabeth Hill. *Stories in Red and Black: Pictorial Histories of the Aztecs and Mixtecs*. Austin: University of Texas Press, 2014.

Borah, Woodrow Wilson. *Justice by Insurance: The General Indian Court of Colonial Mexico and the Legal Aides of the Half-Real*. Berkeley: University of California Press, 1983.

Borah, Woodrow, and Sherburne F. Cook. *The Aboriginal Population of Central Mexico on the Eve of the Spanish Conquest.* Berkeley: University of California Press, 1963.

Borchart de Moreno, Christiana. "La transferencia de la propiedad agraria indígena en el corregimiento de Quito hasta finales del siglo XVII." *Cahiers de monde hispanique el luso-brésilien*, no. 34 (1980): 5–19.

Brian, Amber. *Alva Ixtlilxochitl's Native Archive and the Circulation of Knowledge in Colonial Mexico*. Nashville, TN: Vanderbilt University Press, 2016.

Brian, Amber, Bradley Benton, and Pablo Garcia Loaeza, eds. *The Native Conquistador: Alva Ixtlilxochitl's Account of the Conquest of New Spain*. University Park: Pennsylvania State University Press, 2015.

Brundage, James A. *Law, Sex, and Christian Society in Medieval Europe*. Chicago: University of Chicago Press, 1987.

Brundage, James A. *Medieval Canon Law*. New York: Routledge, 2014.

Burbank, Jane. *Russian Peasants Go to Court: Legal Culture in the Countryside, 1905–1917*. Bloomington: Indiana University Press, 2004.

Burkhart, Louise M. "Mexica Women on the Home Front: Housework and Religion in Aztec Mexico." In *Indian Women of Early Mexico*, edited by Susan Schroeder, Stephanie Wood, and Robert Haskett, 45–52. Norman: University of Oklahoma Press, 1997.

Burkhart, Louise M. *The Slippery Earth: Nahua-Christian Moral Dialogue in Sixteenth-Century Mexico*. Tucson: University of Arizona Press, 1989.

Calnek, Edward E. "The Ethnographic Content of the Third Part of the Codex Mendoza." In *The Codex Mendoza*, edited by Frances Berdan and Patricia Rieff Anawalt, 81–91. Berkeley: University of California Press, 1992.

Calvo, Thomas. *Vencer la derrota: Vivir en la sierra zapoteca de México (1674–1707)*. Zamora: Centro de Estudios Mexicanos y Centroamericanos, 2010.

Camacho de los Ríos, Fermín. "Diferencias terminológicas y conceptuales entre Quasi possessio iuris y Quasi possessio rei." *Anales de la Universidad de Alicante: Facultad de Derecho*, no. 7 (1992): 43–60.

Cañizares-Esguerra, Jorge. *How to Write the History of the New World: Histories, Epistemologies, and Identities in the Eighteenth-Century Atlantic World*. Stanford, CA: Stanford University Press, 2001.

Capdequí, José María Ots. *El régimen de la tierra en la América española durante el período colonial*. Ciudad Trujillo: Universidad de Santo Domingo, 1946.

Capdequí, José María Ots. *Manual de historia del derecho español en las indias y del derecho propiamente indiano*. Buenos Aires: Instituto de Historia del Derecho Argentino, 1943.

Carmagnani, Marcello. *El regreso de los dioses: El proceso de reconstitución de la identidad étnica en Oaxaca, siglos XVII y XVIII*. Mexico City: Fondo de Cultura Económica, 1988.

Carrasco, Pedro. "Royal Marriages in Ancient Mexico." In *Explorations in Ethnohistory: Indians of Central Mexico in the Sixteenth Century*, edited by H. R. Harvey and Hanns J. Prem, 41–81. Albuquerque: University of New Mexico Press, 1984.

Carrasco, Pedro. "Ceremonias públicas paganas entre los Mixes de Tamazulapam." In *Fuentes etnológicas para el estudio de los pueblos Ayuuk (Mixes) del estado de*

Oaxaca, edited by Salomón Nahmad Sittón, 387–96. Oaxaca City, Mexico: CIESAS, Oaxaca, 1994.

Carrasco Pizana, Pedro. *La sociedad indígena en el centro y occidente de México*. Zamora: El Colegio de Michoacán, 1986.

Carrera Quezada, Sergio Eduardo. "Las composiciones de tierras en los pueblos de indios en dos jurisdicciones coloniales de la Huasteca, 1692–1720." *Estudios de Historia Novohispana* 52 (2015): 29–50.

Caso, Alfonso. "El mapa de Teozacoalco." *Cuadernos americanos* 47, no. 5 (1949): 145–81.

Caso, Alfonso. "Land Tenure among the Ancient Mexicans." *American Anthropologist* 65 (1963): 863–78.

Castro, Daniel. *Another Face of Empire: Bartolomé de Las Casas, Indigenous Rights, and Ecclesiastical Imperialism*. Durham, NC: Duke University Press, 2007.

Cervantes, Fernando. *The Devil in the New World: The Impact of Diabolism in New Spain*. New Haven, CT: Yale University Press, 1994.

Chance, John K. *Conquest of the Sierra: Spaniards and Indians in Colonial Oaxaca*. Norman: University of Oklahoma Press, 1989.

Channock, Martin. *Law, Custom and Social Order: The Colonial Experience in Malawi and Zambia*. Cambridge: Cambridge University Press, 1985.

Chenaut, Victoria, and María Teresa Sierra, eds. *Pueblos indígenas ante el derecho*. Mexico City: CIESAS, 1995.

Chira, Adriana. *Patchwork Freedoms: Law, Slavery, and Race beyond the Plantation in Cuba*. Cambridge: Cambridge University Press, 2022.

Christensen, Mark Z. *Nahua and Maya Catholicisms: Texts and Religion in Colonial Central Mexico and Yucatan*. Stanford, CA: Stanford University Press, 2013.

Christensen, Mark Z., and Jonathan Truitt. *Native Wills from the Colonial Americas: Dead Giveaways in a New World*. Salt Lake City: University of Utah Press, 2015.

Chuchiak, John F., IV. "The Sins of the Fathers: Franciscan Friars, Parish Priests, and the Sexual Conquest of the Yucatec Maya, 1545–1808." *Ethnohistory* 54, no. 1 (2007): 69–127.

Cline, Howard F. "Civil Congregations of the Indians in New Spain, 1598–1606." *Hispanic American Historical Review* 29, no. 3 (1949): 349–69.

Cline, Sarah. *Colonial Culhuacan, 1580–1600: A Social History of an Aztec Town*. Albuquerque: University of New Mexico Press, 1986.

Cline, Sarah. "The Spiritual Conquest Re-examined: Baptism and Christian Marriage in Early Sixteenth-Century Mexico." In *Families in the Expansion of Europe, 1500–1800*, edited by Maria Beatriz Nizza da Silva, 213–40. Expanding World 29. London: Routledge, 2018.

Comaroff, Jean, and John Comaroff. *Of Revelation and Revolution: Christianity, Colonialism, and Consciousness in South Africa*. Vol. 1. Chicago: University of Chicago Press, 1991.

Connell, William F. *After Moctezuma: Indigenous Politics and Self-Government in Mexico City, 1524–1730*. Norman: University of Oklahoma Press, 2014.

Connell, William F. "'De sangre noble y hábiles costumbres': Etnicidad indígena y gobierno en México Tenochtitlan." *Histórica* 40, no. 2 (2016): 111–33.

Cook, Sherburne Friend, and Woodrow Wilson Borah. *Essays in Population History.* Vol. 1, *Mexico and the Caribbean.* Berkeley: University of California Press, 1971.

Cordero Avendaño de Durand, Carmen. *El derecho consuetudinario indígena en Oaxaca.* Oaxaca, Mexico: Instituto Estatal Electoral de Oaxaca, 2001.

Cordero Avendaño de Durand, Carmen. *Supervivencia de un derecho consuetudinario en el Valle de Tlacolula.* Oaxaca, Mexico: Fondo Nacional para Actividades Sociales, 1982.

Cortés Márquez, Margarita M., and Luis Reyes García. "Manuscritos coloniales de Santa María Tiltepec, Mixe, Oaxaca." *Cuadernos del Sur* 10, no. 20 (2004): 121–36.

Craib, Raymond B. *Cartographic Mexico: A History of State Fixations and Fugitive Landscapes.* Durham, NC: Duke University Press, 2004.

Crisp, Roger, ed. *Aristotle: Nicomachean Ethics.* Cambridge: Cambridge University Press, 2014.

Cruz, Filiberta Gómez. "De arrendatarios a condueños: La lucha indígena contra los Llorente en la Huasteca veracruzana durante el Segundo Imperio." *ULÚA: Revista de Historia, Sociedad y Cultura* 13 (2009): 71–87.

Cuena Boy, Francisco. "La prueba de la costumbre: Del derecho romano al derecho indiano de los indígenas." In *Actas y estudios del XIII Congreso del Instituto Internacional de Historia del Derecho Indiano*, vol. 1, edited by Luis E. González Vales, 119–42. San Juan: Asamblea Legislativa de Puerto Rico, 2001.

Cummins, Thomas B. F. "From Lies to Truth: Colonial Ekphrasis and the Act of Crosscultural Translation." In *Reframing the Renaissance: Visual Culture in Europe and Latin America, 1450–1650*, edited by Claire Farago, 152–74. New Haven, CT: Yale University Press, 1995.

Cunill, Caroline. "El indio miserable: Nacimiento de la teoría legal en la América colonial del siglo XVI." *Cuadernos Intercambio sobre Centroamérica y el Caribe* 8, no. 9 (2011): 229–48.

Cunill, Caroline. *Los defensores de indios de Yucatán y el acceso de los mayas a la justicia colonial, 1540–1600.* Mexico City: UNAM, 2012.

Cunill, Caroline. "'Nos traen tan avasallados hasta quitarnos nuestro señorío': Cabildos mayas, control local y representación legal en el Yucatán del siglo XVI." *Histórica* 40, no. 2 (2016): 49–80.

Cunill, Caroline, and Rossend Rovira-Morgado. "'Lo que nos dejaron nuestros padres, nuestros abuelos': Retórica y praxis procesal alrededor de los usos y costumbres indígenas en la Nueva España temprana." *Revista de Indias* 81, no. 282 (2021): 283–313.

Curcio-Nagy, Linda A. *The Great Festivals of Colonial Mexico City: Performing Power and Identity.* Albuquerque: University of New Mexico Press, 2004.

Cusicanqui, Silvia Rivera. "*Ch'ixinakax utxiwa*: A Reflection on the Practices and Discourses of Decolonization." *South Atlantic Quarterly* 111, no. 1 (2012): 95–109.

Cutter, Charles R. *The Protector de Indios in Colonial New Mexico, 1659–1821*. Albuquerque: University of New Mexico Press in Cooperation with the Historical Society of New Mexico, 1986.

Dahlgren de Jordán, Barbro. *La mixteca, su cultura e historia prehispánica*. Mexico City: Imprenta Universitaria, 1954.

Deardorff, Max. "Republics, Their Customs, and the Law of the King: Convivencia and Self- Determination in the Crown of Castile and Its American Territories, 1400–1700." *Rechtsgeschichte-Legal History* 26 (2018): 162–99.

Decock, Wim. *Theologians and Contract Law: The Moral Transformation of the Ius Commune (ca. 1500–1650)*. Leiden: M. Nijhoff, 2013.

Dehouve, Danièle. *Quand les banquiers étaient des saints: 450 ans de l'histoire économique et sociale d'une province indienne de Mexique*. Paris: Centre National de la Recherche Scientifique, 1991.

Dehouve, Danièle. *Relatos de pecados en la evangelización de los indios de México (siglos XVI–XVIII)*. Mexico City: Centro de estudios mexicanos y centroamericanos, 2013.

Dehouve, Danièle. "Un diálogo de sordos: Los Coloquios de Sahagún." *Estudios de Cultura Náhuatl* 33 (2002): 185–216.

Dehouve, Danièle. "El matrimonio indio frente al matrimonio español (siglo XVI al XVIII)." In *El Matrimonio en Mesoamérica ayer y hoy*, edited by David Robichaux, 75–94. Mexico City: Universidad Iberoamericana, 2003.

Dehouve, Danièle. "La segunda mujer entre los Nahuas." In *El Matrimonio en Mesoamérica ayer y hoy*, edited by David Robichaux, 95–106. Mexico City: Universidad Iberoamericana, 2003.

Dery, David. "'Papereality' and Learning in Bureaucratic Organizations." *Administration and Society* 29, no. 6 (1998): 677–89.

Díaz, Floriberto, Sofía Robles Hernández, and Rafael Cardoso Jiménez. *Escrito: Comunalidad, energía viva del pensamiento mixe*. Mexico City: UNAM, 2007.

Díaz, Mónica. "The Indigenous Archive: Religion and Education in Eighteenth-Century Mexico." *Hispanic Review* 86, no. 2 (Spring 2018): 167–83.

Díaz Rementería, Carlos. "La costumbre indígena en el Perú hispánico." *Anuario de Estudios Americanos* 33 (1976): 189–215.

Domenici, Davide. "Nuovi dati per una storia dei codici messicani della Biblioteca Apostolica Vaticana." *Miscellanea Bibliothecae Apostolicae Vaticanae* 22 (2016): 341–62.

Duarte, Rocío. "The Colegio Imperial de Santa Cruz de Tlatelolco and Its Aftermath: Nahua Intellectuals and the Spiritual Conquest of Mexico." In *A Companion to Latin American Literature and Culture*, edited by Sarah Castro-Klarén, 86–105. Malden, MA: Blackwell, 2008.

Ducey, Michael T. "Liberal Theory and Peasant Practice: Land and Power in Northern Veracruz, Mexico, 1826–1900." In *Liberals, the Church, and Indian Peasants: Corporate Lands and the Challenge of Reform in Nineteenth-Century Spanish America*, edited by Robert H. Jackson, 65–93. Albuquerque: University of New Mexico Press, 1997.

Dueñas, Alcira. "Cabildos de naturales en el ocaso colonial: Jurisdicción, posesión y defensa del espacio étnico." *Histórica* 40, no. 2 (2016): 135–67.

Dueñas, Alcira. *Indians and Mestizos in the "Lettered City": Reshaping Justice, Social Hierarchy, and Political Culture in Colonial Peru*. Boulder: University Press of Colorado, 2010.

Dunlap, Alexander. "The 'Solution' Is Now the 'Problem': Wind Energy, Colonisation and the 'Genocide-Ecocide Nexus' in the Isthmus of Tehuantepec, Oaxaca." *International Journal of Human Rights* 22, no. 4 (2018): 550–73.

Durston, Alan. *Pastoral Quechua: The History of Christian Translation in Colonial Peru, 1550–1654*. Notre Dame, IN: University of Notre Dame Press, 2007.

Duve, Thomas. "European Legal History—Concepts, Methods, Challenges." In *Entanglements in Legal History: Conceptual Approaches*, edited by Thomas Duve, 29–66. Frankfurt: Max Planck Institute for European Legal History, 2014.

Duve, Thomas. "Global Legal History—A Methodological Approach." Max Planck Institute for European Legal History Research Paper Series no. 2016-04. May 20, 2016. https://ssrn.com/abstract=2781104.

Duve, Thomas. "La Escuela de Salamanca: ¿Un caso de producción global de conocimiento? Consideraciones introductorias desde una perspectiva histórico-jurídica y de la historia del conocimiento." *The School of Salamanca: A Digital Collection of Sources and a Dictionary of Its Juridical-Political Language, Working Paper Series*, no. 2 (2018): 2–29.

Echeverri, Marcela. *Indian and Slave Royalists in the Age of Revolution: Reform, Revolution, and Royalism in the Northern Andes, 1780–1825*. Cambridge: Cambridge University Press, 2016.

Eisenstadt, Todd A. "*Usos y costumbres* and Postelectoral Conflicts in Oaxaca, Mexico, 1995–2004: An Empirical and Normative Assessment." *Latin American Research Review* 42, no. 1 (2007): 52–77.

Escobar Ohmstede, Antonio. "La desamortización de tierras civiles corporativas en México: ¿Una ley agraria, fiscal o ambas?" *Mundo Agrario* 13, no. 25 (2012).

Escobar Ohmstede, Antonio. "Los condueñazgos indígenas en las Huastecas hidalguense y veracruzana: ¿Defensa del espacio comunal?" In *Indio, nación y comunidad en el México del siglo XIX*, edited by Antonio Escobar Ohmstede and Patricia Lagos Preisser, 171–88. Mexico City: Centro de Estudios Mexicanos y Centroamericanos, 1993.

Escobar Ohmstede, Antonio, Romana Falcón, and Martín Sánchez Rodríguez. *La desamortización civil desde perspectivas plurales*. Zamora: El Colegio de Michoacán, 2017.

Estenssoro Fuchs, Juan Carlos. *Del paganismo a la santidad: La incorporación de los indios del Perú al catolicismo, 1532–1750*. Translated by Gabriela Ramos. Lima: Instituto Francés de Estudios Andinos, 2003.

Fabian, Johannes. *Time and the Other: How Anthropology Makes Its Object*. New York: Columbia University Press, 2002.

Fandos, Cecilia A. "La formación histórica de condueñazgos y copropiedades en las regiones de las Huastecas (México) y las tierras altas de Jujuy (Argentina)." *Revista de Historia Iberoamericana* 10, no. 2 (2017): 49–79.

Farriss, Nancy. *Libana: El discurso ceremonial mesoamericana y el sermon cristiano.* Mexico City: Artes de México, 2014.

Farriss, Nancy. *Maya Society under Colonial Rule: The Collective Enterprise of Survival.* Princeton, NJ: Princeton University Press, 1984.

Farriss, Nancy. *Tongues of Fire: Language and Evangelization in Colonial Mexico.* Oxford: Oxford University Press, 2018.

Ferraro, Joanne M. "Childhood in Medieval and Early Modern Times." In *The Routledge History of Childhood in the Western World*, edited by Paula S. Fass, 61–77. New York: Routledge, 2013.

Fitzpatrick, Peter. "Custom as Imperialism." In *Law, Society, and National Identity in Africa*, edited by Jamil Abun-Nasr, Ulrich Spellennberg, and UlrikeWanitzek, 15–30. Hamburg: Helmut Buske Verlag, 1999.

Fitzpatrick, Peter. *Modernism and the Grounds of Law.* Cambridge: Cambridge University Press, 2001.

Fitzpatrick, Peter. *The Mythology of Modern Law.* New York: Routledge, 1992.

Flores-Marcial, Xochitl Marina. "A History of Guelaguetza in Zapotec Communities of the Central Valleys of Oaxaca, 16th Century." PhD diss., University of California, Los Angeles, 2015.

Florescano, Enrique. *Estructuras y problemas agrarios de México (1500–1821).* Mexico City: SEP, 1971.

Foucault, Michel. *History of Sexuality.* Vol. 1, *An Introduction.* New York: Vintage Books, 1978.

Galar Martínez, Carina. "La representación descriptiva y simbólica de las mujeres en el proceso de paridad de género en Sistemas Normativos Indígenas de Oaxaca, México." *Revista interdisciplinaria de estudios de género de El Colegio de México* 7 (2021). https://doi.org/10.24201/reg.v7i1.673.

García Quintana, Josefina. "El huehuetlatolli—antigua palabra—como fuente para la historia sociocultural de los nahuas." *Estudios de Cultura Náhuatl* 12 (1976): 61–71.

García-Gallo y de Diego, Alfonso. "El Libro de leyes de Alfonso el Sabio." *Anuario de Historia del Derecho Español*, nos. 21–22 (1951): 345–528.

García Martínez, Bernardo. "Jurisdicción y propiedad: Una distinción fundamental en la historia de los pueblos de indios del México colonial." *Revista Europea de Estudios Latinoamericanos y del Caribe / European Review of Latin American and Caribbean Studies*, no. 53 (December 1992): 47–60.

García Martínez, Bernardo. *Los pueblos de la sierra: El poder y el espacio entre los indios del norte de Puebla hasta 1700.* Mexico City: El Colegio de México, 1987.

Garibay, Javier. *Nepantla situados en medio: Estudio histórico-teológico de la realidad Indiana.* Mexico City: Colegio Máximo de Cristo Rey Centro de Reflexión Teológica, 2000.

Garriga Acosta, Carlos Antonio. "La trama jurídica castellana a comienzos del siglo XVI (Notas y materiales)." In *Las Cortes y las leyes de Toro de 1505*, edited by Benjamín González Alonso, 299–382. Salamanca: Cortes de Castilla and Leon, 2006.

Gauderman, Kimberly. "It Happened on the Way to the Temascal and Other Stories: Desiring the Illicit in Colonial Spanish America." *Ethnohistory* 54, no. 1 (2007): 177–86.

Gelinas, Elmer T. "Ius and Lex in Thomas Aquinas." *American Journal of Jurisprudence* 15 (1970): 154–70.

Gibson, Charles. *The Aztecs under Spanish Rule: A History of the Indians of the Valley of Mexico, 1519–1580*. Stanford, CA: Stanford University Press, 1964.

Glave, Luis Miguel. "Gestiones transatlánticas: Los indios ante la trama del poder virreinal y las composiciones de tierras (1646)." *Revista Complutense de Historia de América* 34 (2008): 85–106.

Glick, Thomas F. *Islamic and Christian Spain in the Early Middle Ages*. Leiden: Brill, 2005.

Gómez de Orozco, Federico. "Quién fue el autor material del Códice Mendocino y quién su intérprete." *Revista Mexicana de Estudios Antropológicos*, no. 5 (1941): 43–51.

Gomez Tejada, Jorge. "Making the Codex Mendoza, Constructing the Codex Mendoza: A Reconsideration of a 16th-Century Mexican Manuscript." PhD diss., Yale University, 2013.

Gonzalbo Aizpuru, Pilar, ed. *El humanismo y la educación en la Nueva España*. Mexico City: Secretaría de Educación Pública, 1985.

Gonzalbo Aizpuru, Pilar. *Historia de la educación en la época colonial: El mundo indígena*. Mexico City: El Colegio de México, 2008.

González, Roberto J. *Connected: How a Mexican Village Built Its Own Cell Phone Network*. Berkeley: University of California Press, 2020.

Goyas Mejía, Ramón. "Las Composiciones de Tierras de 1643 en la Nueva España." *Revista de Historia Iberoamericana* 8, no. 2 (2015): 54–75.

Granicka, Katarzyna. "Marital Practices of the Nahuas and Imposed Sociocultural Change in Sixteenth-Century Mexico." *Ethnohistory* 69, no. 1 (2022): 81–100.

Grant, Daragh. "Francisco de Vitoria and Alberico Gentili on the Juridical Status of Native American Polities." *Renaissance Quarterly* 72 (2019): 910–52.

Graubart, Karen. "Competing Spanish and Indigenous Jurisdictions in Early Colonial Lima." In *Oxford Research Encyclopedia in Latin American and Caribbean History*, edited by Kenneth Mills. Oxford: Oxford University Press, 2016.

Graubart, Karen. "Containing Law within the Walls: The Protection of Customary Law in Santiago del Cercado, Peru." In *Protection and Empire: A Global History*, edited by Lauren Benton, Adam Clulow, and Bain Attwood, 29–46. Cambridge: Cambridge University Press, 2018.

Graubart, Karen. "Learning from the Qadi: The Jurisdiction of Local Rule in the Early Colonial Andes." *Hispanic American Historical Review* 95, no. 2 (2015): 195–228.

Graubart, Karen. *Republics of Difference: Religious and Racial Self-Governance in the Spanish Atlantic World.* New York: Oxford University Press, 2022.

Greenleaf, Richard. *The Mexican Inquisition of the Sixteenth Century.* Albuquerque: University of New Mexico Press, 1969.

Greenleaf, Richard. *Zumárraga and the Mexican Inquisition, 1536–1543.* Washington, DC: Academy of American Franciscan History, 1962.

Greer, Allan. *Property and Dispossession: Natives, Empires and Land in Early Modern North America.* Cambridge: Cambridge University Press, 2018.

Grossi, Paolo. *El orden jurídico medieval.* Madrid: Marcial Pons, 1996.

Grossi, Paolo. *A History of European Law.* Translated by Laurence Hooper. Oxford: Wiley-Blackwell, 2010.

Gruzinski, Serge. "Confesión, alianza y sexualidad entre los indios de Nueva España." In *El lacer de pecar y el afán de normar.* Seminario de Historia de las Mentalidades. Mexico City: Editorial Joaquín Mortiz, 1988.

Gruzinski, Serge. "Individualization and Acculturation: Confession among the Nahuas of Mexico from the Sixteenth to the Eighteenth Century." In *Sexuality and Marriage in Colonial Latin America*, edited by Asunción Lavrin, 96–117. Lincoln: University of Nebraska Press, 1989.

Gruzinski, Serge. *Man-Gods in the Mexican Highlands: Indian Power and Colonial Society, 1520–1800.* Translated by Eileen Corrigan. Stanford, CA: Stanford University Press, 1989.

Guardino, Peter. *Time of Liberty: Popular Political Culture in Oaxaca, 1750–1850.* Durham, NC: Duke University Press, 2005.

Guevara Gil, Jorge Armando. *Propiedad agraria y derecho colonial: Los documentos de la Hacienda Santotis, Cuzco (1543–1822).* Lima: Pontificia Universidad Católica del Perú, Fondo Editorial, 1993.

Gutiérrez Rivas, Ana María. "El condueñazgo de los Moctezuma: Origen y defensa de la tierra, 1880–1929." In *Entretejiendo el mundo rural en el oriente de SLP, siglos XIX y XX*, edited by Antonio Escobar Ohmstede and Ana María Gutiérrez Rivas, 237–62. Mexico City: CIESAS, 2009.

Gutiérrez Rivas, Ana María. "El proceso agrario en las huastecas hidalguense y veracruzana 1825–1874." *Revista Sotavento*, no. 11 (2001–2): 9–38.

Hamann, Byron Ellsworth. *Bad Christians, New Spains: Muslims, Catholics, and Native Americans in a Mediterratlantic World.* New York: Routledge, 2019.

Hamann, Byron Ellsworth. *The Translations of Nebrija: Language, Culture and Circulation in the Early Modern World.* Amherst: University of Massachusetts Press, 2015.

Hamnett, Brian R. *Politics and Trade in Southern Mexico 1750–1821.* Cambridge: Cambridge University Press, 2008.

Hanke, Lewis. *Los virreyes españoles en América durante el gobierno de la Casa de Austria.* Vol. 2, *México.* With Celso Rodriguez. Madrid: Atlas, 1976.

Hanke, Lewis. *The Spanish Struggle for Justice in the Conquest of America.* 1949. Reprint, Philadelphia: University of Pennsylvania Press, 1959.

Hanks, William F. *Converting Words: Maya in the Age of the Cross*. Berkeley: University of California Press, 2010.

Harrison, Regina. *Sin and Confession in Colonial Peru: Spanish-Quechua Penitential Texts, 1560–1650*. Austin: University of Texas Press, 2014.

Harrison, Regina. "The Theology of Concupiscence: Spanish-Quechua Confessional Manuals in the Andes." In *Coded Encounters: Writing, Gender, and Ethnicity in Colonial Latin America*, edited by Francisco Javier Cevallos-Candau, Jeffrey A. Cole, Nina M. Scott, and Nicomedes Suárez-Araúz, 135–150. Amherst: University of Massachusetts Press, 1994.

Haskett, Robert Stephen. *Indigenous Rulers: An Ethnohistory of Town Government in Colonial Cuernavaca*. Albuquerque: University of New Mexico Press, 1991.

Haskett, Robert Stephen. *Visions of Paradise: Primordial Titles and Mesoamerican History in Cuernavaca*. Norman: University of Oklahoma Press, 2005.

Hassig, Ross. *Polygamy and the Rise and Demise of the Aztec Empire*. Albuquerque: University of New Mexico Press, 2016.

Herzog, Tamar. "Colonial Law and 'Native Customs': Indigenous Land Rights in Colonial Spanish America." *The Americas* 69, no. 3 (January 2013): 303–21.

Herzog, Tamar. *Frontiers of Possession: Spain and Portugal in Europe and the Americas*. Cambridge, MA: Harvard University Press, 2015.

Herzog, Tamar. "Immemorial (and Native) Customs in Early Modernity: Europe and the Americas." *Comparative Legal History* 9, no. 1 (2021): 3–55.

Herzog, Tamar. *A Short History of European Law: The Last Two and a Half Millennia*. Cambridge, MA: Harvard University Press, 2018.

Hespanha, António Manuel. *Como os juristas viam o mundo, 1550–1750*. Lisbon: António Manuel Hespanha, 2015.

Hespanha, António Manuel. "The Law in the High and the Late Middle Ages: The Learned Ius Commune and the Vernacular Laws: Southern Europe (Italy, Iberian Peninsula, France)." In *The Oxford Handbook of European Legal History*, edited by Heikki Pihlajamäki, Markus D. Dubber, and Mark Godfrey, 332–57. Oxford: Oxford University Press, 2018.

Hidalgo, Alex. *Trail of Footprints: A History of Indigenous Maps from Viceregal Mexico*. Austin: University of Texas Press, 2019.

Hoekstra, Rik. *Two Worlds Merging: The Transformation of Society in the Valley of Puebla, 1570–1640*. Amsterdam: CEDLA, 1993.

Howell, Martha C. *The Marriage Exchange: Property, Social Place, and Gender in Cities of the Low Countries, 1300–1550*. Chicago: University of Chicago Press, 1998.

Hussey, Ronald D. "Text of the Laws of Burgos (1512–1513) Concerning the Treatment of the Indians." *Hispanic American Historical Review* 12, no. 3 (1932): 301–26.

Ibbetson, David. "Custom in Medieval Law." In *The Nature of Customary Law: Legal, Historical and Philosophical Perspectives*, edited by Amanda Perreau-Saussine and James B. Murphy, 153–75. Cambridge: Cambridge University Press, 2007.

Ibhawoh, Bonny. *Imperial Justice: Africans in Empire's Court.* Oxford: Oxford University Press, 2013.

Iglesia Ferreiros, Aquilino. "Alfonso X el Sabio y su obra legislativa." *Anuario de Historia del Derecho español,* no. 50 (1980): 531–61.

Iglesia Ferreiros, Aquilino. "Cuestiones Alfonsinas." *Anuario de Historia del Derecho español,* no. 55 (1985): 95–150.

Ingold, Alice. "Commons and Environmental Regulation in History: The Water Commons beyond Property and Sovereignty." *Theoretical Inquiries in Law* 19, no. 2 (2018): 425–56.

Jansen, Maarten E. R. G. N., and Gabina Aurora Pérez Jiménez. *La lengua señorial de Ñuu Dzaui: Cultura literaria de los antiguos reinos y transformación colonial.* Oaxaca, Mexico: Colegio Superior para la Educación Integral Intercultural de Oaxaca, 2009.

Jansen, Maarten E. R. G. N., and Gabina Aurora Pérez Jiménez. *Voces del Dzaha Dzavui (Mixteco clásico): Análisis y conversion del Vocabulario de fray Francisco de Alvarado (1593).* Oaxaca, Mexico: Colegio Superior para la Educación Integral Intercultural de Oaxaca, 2009.

Jansen, Maarten and Gabina Aurora Pérez Jiménez. *Time and the Ancestors: Aztec and Mixtec Ritual Art.* Leiden: Brill, 2017.

Johnson, Miranda. "Indigenizing Self-Determination at the United Nations: Reparative Progress in the Declaration on the Rights of Indigenous Peoples." *Journal of the History of International Law* 23, no. 1 (2020): 206–28.

Jones, Owen H. "Chinamitales: Defensores y justicias k'ichee'en las comunidades indígenas del altiplano de Guatemala colonial." *Histórica* 40, no. 2 (2016): 81–109.

Kamtekar, Rachana. "The Relationship between Aristotle's Ethical and Political Discourses." In *Cambridge Companion to Aristotle's Nicomachean Ethics,* edited by Ronald M. Polansky, 370–82. New York: Cambridge University Press, 2014.

Karttunen, Frances, and James Lockhart. *Nahuatl in the Middle Years: Language Contact Phenomena in Texts of the Colonial Period.* Berkeley: University of California Press, 1976.

Kelley, Donald R. *The Human Measure: Social Thought in the Western Legal Tradition.* Cambridge, MA: Harvard University Press, 1990.

Kellogg, Susan. "From Parallel and Equivalent to Separate but Unequal: Tenochca Mexica Women, 1500–1700." In *Indian Women of Early Mexico,* edited by Susan Schroeder, Stephanie Wood, and Robert Haskett, 123–44. Norman: University of Oklahoma Press, 1997.

Kellogg, Susan. *Law and the Transformation of Aztec Society.* Norman: University of Oklahoma Press, 1995.

Kellogg, Susan, and Matthew Restall, eds. *Dead Giveaways: Indigenous Testaments of Colonial Mesoamerica and the Andes.* Salt Lake City: University of Utah Press, 1998.

Kleyn, Duard. "The Protection of Quasi-Possession in South African Law." *Studia Universitatis Babes Bolyai-Iurisprudentia* 58, no. 4 (2013): 142–64.

Kourí, Emilio. *A Pueblo Divided: Business, Property, and Community in Papantla, Mexico*. Stanford, CA: Stanford University Press, 2004.

LaFaye, Jacques. *Quetzalcóatl and Guadalupe: The Formation of National Consciousness, 1531–1813*. Translated by Benjamin Keen. Chicago: University of Chicago Press, 1974.

Lantigua, David M. *Infidels and Empires in a New World Order: Early Modern Spanish Contributions to International Legal Thought*. Cambridge: Cambridge University Press, 2020.

Lavrin, Asunción. "Sexuality in Colonial Mexico." In *Sexuality and Marriage in Colonial Latin America*, edited by Asunción Lavrin, 47–95. Lincoln: University of Nebraska Press, 1992.

Lee, Jongsoo. *The Allure of Nezahualcoyotl: Pre-Hispanic History, Religion, and Nahua Poetics*. Albuquerque: University of New Mexico Press, 2008.

Lee Too, Yun. "Legal Instructions in Classical Athens." In *Education in Greek and Roman Antiquity*, edited by Yun Lee Too, 111–32. Leiden: Brill, 2001.

León-Portilla, Miguel. *"Cuícatl y Tlahtolli": Las formas de expresión en náhuatl*. Mexico City: UNAM, 1983.

León-Portilla, Miguel. *La filosofía náhuatl estudiada en sus fuentes*. Mexico City: UNAM, 1959.

Levitt, Peggy, and Sally Merry. "Vernacularization on the Ground: Local Uses of Global Women's Rights in Peru, China, India and the United States." *Global Networks* 9, no. 4 (2009): 441–61.

Lind, Michael. *Ancient Zapotec Religion: An Ethnohistorical and Archaeological Perspective*. Boulder: University Press of Colorado, 2015.

Lockhart, James. *The Nahuas after the Conquest: A Social and Cultural History of the Indians of Central Mexico, Sixteenth through Eighteenth Centuries*. Stanford, CA: Stanford University Press, 1992.

Lockhart, James, Frances Berdan, and Arthur J. O. Anderson. *The Tlaxcalan Actas: A Compendium of the Records of the Cabildo of Tlaxcala, 1545–1627*. Salt Lake City: University of Utah Press, 1986.

Lopes Don, Patricia. *Bonfires of Culture: Franciscans, Indigenous Leaders, and the Inquisition in Early Mexico, 1524–1540*. Norman: University of Oklahoma Press, 2018.

Lopes Don, Patricia. "The 1539 Inquisition and Trial of Don Carlos of Texcoco in Early Mexico." *Hispanic American Historical Review* 88, no. 4 (2008): 573–606.

López Castillo, Gilberto. *El poblamiento de Tierra de Indios Cahitas*. Mexico City: Siglo XXI and El Colegio de Sinaloa, 2010.

López Castillo, Gilberto. *Composición de tierras y tendencias de poblamiento hispano en la franja costera: Culiacán y Chiametla, siglos XVII y XVIII*. Culiacán, Sinaloa: Centro INAH Sinaloa, 2014.

López Cruz, Ausencia, and Michael Swanton, eds. *Memorias del coloquio Francisco Belmar: Conferencias sobre lenguas Otomangues y Oaxaqueñas*. Vol. 2. Oaxaca, Mexico City: Biblioteca Francisco de Burgoa, UABJO, CSEIIO, Fundación Alfredo Harp Hélu Oaxaca, INALI, 2008.

Macías Hernández, Antonio M. "La colonización europea y el derecho de aguas: Un ejemplo de Canarias, 1480–1525." *Hispania: Revista Española de Historia* 69, no. 233 (2009): 715–38.

Macuil Martínez, Raul. "The *Tlamatque* and Codex Mendoza." In *Mesoamerican Manuscripts: New Scientific Approaches and Interpretations*, edited by Maarten E. R. G. N. Jansen, Virginia M. Lladó-Buisán, and Ludo Snijders, 94–119. Leiden: Brill, 2019.

Maffie, James, and Kevin Daniel Rozo Rondon. "In Huehue Tlamanitiliztli y la Verdad: Las filosofías nahua y europea en Coloquios y doctrina cristiana de Fray Bernardino de Sahagún." *Iberoforum Revista de Ciencias Sociales* 15, no. 30 (2020): 1–40.

Malinowski, Bronisław. *Crime and Custom in Savage Society*. 1926. Reprint, New York: Routledge, 2018.

Mamdani, Mahmood. *Citizen and Subject: Contemporary Africa and the Legacy of Late Colonialism*. Princeton, NJ: Princeton University Press, 2018.

Manzano, Juan Manzano. "Las leyes y costumbres indígenas en el orden de prelación de fuentes del Derecho Indiano." *Revista del Instituto de Historia del Derecho "Ricardo Levene"* 18 (1967): 64–71.

Marino, Daniela. "La desamortización de las tierras de los pueblos (centro de México, siglo XIX): Balance historiográfico y fuentes para su estudio." *América Latina en la Historia Económica* 8, no. 16 (2001): 33–43.

Martínez, Juan Carlos. *Derechos indígenas en los juzgados: Un análisis del campo judicial oaxaqueño en la región mixe*. Mexico City: INAH, 2004.

Martínez, María Elena. *Genealogical Fictions: Limpieza de Sangre, Religion, and Gender in Colonial Mexico*. Stanford, CA: Stanford University Press, 2008.

Martínez, Maria Elena. "Indigenous Genealogies: Lineage, History, and the Colonial Pact in Central Mexico and Perú." In *Indigenous Intellectuals: Knowledge, Power, and Colonial Culture in Mexico and the Andes*, edited by Gabriela Ramos and Yanna Yannakakis, 173–201. Durham, NC: Duke University Press, 2014.

Martínez Baracs, Andrea. *Un gobierno de indios: Tlaxcala, 1519–1750*. Mexico City: Fondo de Cultura Económica, 2008.

Martínez Luna, Jaime. "Conocimiento y comunalidad." *Bajo el Volcán: Revista del Posgrado de Sociología* 15, no. 23 (2016): 99–112.

Martín Gabaldón, Marta. "New Crops, New Landscapes and New Socio-political Relationships in the *cañada* de Yosotiche (Mixteca Region, Oaxaca, Mexico), 16th–18th Centuries." *Historia Agraria* 75 (August 2018): 33–68.

Martín Gabaldón, Marta. "Territorialidad y paisaje a partir de los traslados y congregaciones de pueblos en la Mixteca, siglo XVI y comienzos del siglo XVII: Tlaxiaco y sus sujetos." PhD diss., CIESAS, 2018.

Masters, Adrian. "A Thousand Invisible Architects: Vassals, the Petition and Response System, and the Creation of Spanish Imperial Caste Legislation." *Hispanic American Historical Review* 98, no. 3 (2018): 377–406.

Masters, Adrian. "The Two, the Many, the One, the None: Rethinking the Republics of Spaniards and Indians in the Sixteenth-Century Spanish Indies." *The Americas* 78, no. 1 (January 2021): 3–36.

Mathes, Michael W. *The America's First Academic Library: Santa Cruz de Tlatelolco.* Sacramento: California State Library Foundation, 1985.

Matthew, Laura E., and Michel R. Oudijk, eds. *Indian Conquistadors: Indigenous Allies in the Conquest of Mesoamerica.* Norman: University of Oklahoma Press, 2007.

Mauclair, Fabrice. *La justice au village: Justice seigneuriale et société rurale dans le duché-pairie de La Vallière (1667–1790).* Rennes: Presses Universitaires de Rennes, 2008.

McGowan Tress, Daryl. "Aristotle's Child: Development through Genesis, Oikos, and the Polis." *Ancient Philosophy* 17, no. 1 (1997): 66–80.

McKinley, Michelle A. *Fractional Freedoms: Slavery, Intimacy, and Legal Mobilization in Colonial Lima, 1600–1700.* New York: Cambridge University Press, 2018.

Megged, Amos, and Stephanie Gail Wood. *Mesoamerican Memory: Enduring Systems of Remembrance.* Norman: University of Oklahoma Press, 2012.

Méndez Martínez, Enrique, and Enrique Méndez Torres, eds. *Límites, mapas y títulos primordiales del estado de Oaxaca: Índice del Ramo de Tierras.* Mexico City: Archivo General de la Nación, 1999.

Mendoza, Jesús Edgar. "De condueñazgo a municipio: El caso de Tlacotepec Plumas, Oaxaca, 1863–1911." *Agua y tierra en México, siglos XIX y XX* 1 (2008): 187–208.

Mendoza, Jesús Edgar. *Municipios, cofradías y tierras comunales: Los pueblos chocholtecos de Oaxaca en el siglo XIX.* Oaxaca: Universidad Autónoma Benito Juárez de Oaxaca, 2011.

Mendoza, Jorge Augusto Gamboa, and Jorge Augusto. *El cacicazgo muisca en los años posteriores a la Conquista: Del sihipkua al cacique colonial (1537–1575).* Bogotá: Instituto Colombiano de Antropología e Historia, 2010.

Mendoza, Moisés Franco. *La ley y la costumbre en la Cañada de los Once Pueblos.* Zamora: El Colegio de Michoacán, 1997.

Menegus Bornemann, Margarita. *Del señorío indígena a la república de indios: El caso de Toluca, 1500–1600.* Mexico City: Consejo Nacional para la Cultura y las Artes, 1994.

Menegus Bornemann, Margarita. "Del usufructo, de la posesión y de la propiedad: Las composiciones de tierras en la Mixteca, Oaxaca." *Itinerarios: Revista de estudios lingüísticos, literarios, históricos y antropológicos*, no. 25 (2017): 181–96.

Menegus Bornemann, Margarita. "El cacicazgo en Nueva España." In *El cacicazgo en Nueva España y Filipinas*, edited by Margarita Menegus Bornemann and Rodolfo Aguirre Salvador, 13–69. Mexico City: UNAM, 2005.

Menegus Bornemann, Margarita. "La costumbre indígena en el derecho indiano, 1529–1550." *Anuario Mexicano de Historia del Derecho* 4 (1992): 151–59.

Menegus Bornemann, Margarita. *La Mixteca Baja entre la revolución y la reforma: Cacicazgo, territorialidad y gobierno, siglos XVIII–XIX.* Oaxaca: Universidad Benito Juárez, 2009.

Menegus Bornemann, Margarita. *Los indios en la historia de México: Siglos XVI al XIX: Balance y perspectivas*. Mexico City: Centro de Investigación y Docencia Económica, 2018.

Menegus Bornemann, Margarita. "Los títulos primordiales de los pueblos de indios." *Estudis: Revista de historia moderna*, no. 20 (1994): 207–30. http://hdl.handle.net/10550/34249

Menegus Bornemann, Margarita, and Rodolfo Aguirre Salvador, eds. *El cacicazgo en Nueva España y Filipinas*. Mexico City: UNAM, 2005.

Menegus Bornemann, Margarita, and Mario Cerutti. *La desamortización civil en México y España: 1750–1920*. Mexico City: Senado de la República, LVIII Legislatura, 2001.

Merluzzi, Manfredi. "Religion and State Policies in the Age of Philip II: The 1568 Junta Magna of the Indies and the New Political Guidelines for the Spanish American Colonies." In *Religion and Power in Europe: Conflict and Convergence*, edited by Joaquim Carvalho, 183–201. Pisa: Edizione Plus, Pisa University Press, 2007.

Merry, Sally Engle. *Colonizing Hawai'i: The Cultural Power of Law*. Princeton, NJ: Princeton University Press, 2020.

Merry, Sally Engle. "Legal Pluralism." *Law and Society Review* 22 (1988): 869–96.

Miceli, Paola. *Derecho consuetudinario y memoria: Práctica jurídica y costumbre en Castilla y León (siglos XI–XIV)*. Universidad Carlos III de Madrid, 2012.

Mignolo, Walter, and Catherine E. Walsh. *On Decoloniality: Concepts, Analytics, and Praxis*. Durham, NC: Duke University Press, 2018.

Miranda, José. *Las ideas y las instituciones políticas mexicanas*. Mexico City: UNAM, 1952.

Monaghan, John. *The Covenants with Earth and Rain: Exchange, Sacrifice, and Revelation in Mixtec Sociality*. Norman: University of Oklahoma Press, 1999.

Monzón, Cristina. *Juicios locales del Michoacán colonial en lengua tarasca: Tarecuato 1565 y Uruapan 1602*. Zamora: El Colegio de Michoacán, 2018.

Moore, Sally Falk. *Social Facts and Fabrications: "Customary" Law on Kilimanjaro, 1880-1980*. Cambridge: Cambridge University Press, 1986.

Mumford, Jeremy Ravi. "Las llamas de Tapacarí: Un documento judicial de un alcalde de indios en la Audiencia de Charcas, 1580." *Histórica* 40, no. 2 (2016): 171–85.

Mumford, Jeremy Ravi. "Litigation as Ethnography in Sixteenth-Century Peru: Polo De Ondegardo and the Mitimaes." *Hispanic American Historical Review* 88, no. 1 (2008): 5–40.

Mundy, Barbara E. *The Mapping of New Spain: Indigenous Cartography and the Maps of the Relaciones Geográficas*. Chicago: University of Chicago Press, 1996.

Muñoz Arbeláez, Santiago. *Costumbres en disputa: Los muiscas y el Imperio español en Ubaque, siglo XVI*. Bogotá: Ediciones Uniandes-Universidad de los Andes, 2015.

Murphy, James Bernard. "Habit and Convention at the Foundation of Custom." In

The Nature of Customary Law, edited by Amanda Perreau Saussine and James Bernard Murphy, 53–78. Cambridge: Cambridge University Press, 2007.

Murphy, James Bernard. "Nature, Custom, and Reason as the Explanatory and Practice Principles of Aristotelian Political Science." *Review of Politics* 64, no. 3 (Summer 2002): 469–95.

Nader, Laura. *Harmony Ideology: Justice and Control in a Zapotec Mountain Village.* Stanford, CA: Stanford University Press, 1990.

Neri Guarneros, Porfirio. "Sociedades agrícolas en resistencia: Los pueblos de San Miguel, Santa Cruz y San Pedro, 1878–1883." *Historia Crítica* 51 (2013): 21–44.

Nicholson, Henry B. "The History of the Codex Mendoza." In *The Codex Mendoza*, edited by Frances Berdan and Patricia R. Anawalt, 1–11. 4 vols. Berkeley: University of California Press, 1992.

Nirenberg, David. "Muslims in Christian Iberia, 1000–1526: Varieties of Mudejar Experience." In *The Medieval World*, 2nd ed, edited by Peter Linehan, Janet L. Nelson, and Marios Costambeys, 55–71. New York: Routledge, 2018.

Offner, Jerome A. *Law and Politics in Aztec Texcoco.* Cambridge: Cambridge University Press, 1983.

O'Phelan, Scarlet. *Kurakas sin sucesiones: Del cacique al alcalde de indios (Perú y Bolivia, 1750–1835).* Cuzco: Centro de Estudios Regionales Andinos Bartolomé de Las Casas, 1997.

O'Toole, Rachel Sarah. *Bound Lives: Africans, Indians, and the Making of Race in Colonial Peru.* Pittsburgh: University of Pittsburgh Press, 2012.

Oudijk, Michel R. "Espacio y escritura: El Lienzo de Tabaá I." In *Escritura zapoteca: 2.500 años de historia*, edited by María de los Ángeles Romero Frizzi, 371–76. Mexico City: CIESAS, 2003.

Oudijk, Michel R. *Historiography of the Bènizàa: The Postclassic and Early Colonial Periods (1000–1600 A.D.).* Leiden: University of Leiden, 2000.

Oudijk, Michel R., and María de los Ángeles Romero Frizzi. "Los títulos primordiales: Un género de tradición mesoamericana: Del mundo prehispánico al siglo XXI." *Relaciones* 95, no. 24 (Summer 2003): 19–48.

Oudijk, Michel R. *La adivinación zapoteca* (5 tomos). Mexico City: Universidad Autónoma de México, 2021.

Ouweneel, Arij. "From Tlahtocayotl to Gobernadoryotl: A Critical Examination of Indigenous Rule in 18th-Century Central Mexico." *American Ethnologist* 22, no. 4 (1995): 756–85.

Ouweneel, Arij. *Shadows over Anáhuac: An Ecological Interpretation of Crisis and Development in Central Mexico, 1730–1800.* Albuquerque: University of New Mexico Press, 1996.

Owensby, Brian P. "Between Justice and Economics: 'Indians' and Reformism in Eighteenth-Century Spanish Imperial Thought." In *Legal Pluralism and Empires, 1500–1850*, edited by Lauren Benton and Richard J. Ross, 143–69. New York: New York University Press, 2013.

Owensby, Brian P. *Empire of Law and Indian Justice in Colonial Mexico.* Stanford, CA: Stanford University Press, 2008.

Owensby, Brian P., and Richard J. Ross, eds. *Justice in a New World: Negotiating Legal Intelligibility in British, Iberian, and Indigenous America*. New York: New York University Press, 2018.

Pagden, Anthony. *The Fall of Natural Man: The American Indian and the Origins of Comparative Ethnology*. 1982. Reprint, Cambridge: Cambridge University Press, 1986.

Parrish, Helen Rand, and Harold E. Weidman. *Las Casas en México: Historia y obra desconocidas*. Mexico City: Fondo de Cultural Económica, 1992.

Pastor, Rodolfo. *Campesinos y reformas: La mixteca, 1700–1856*. Mexico City: El Colegio de México, 1987.

Pearson, Giles. "Courage and Temperance." In *Cambridge Companion to Aristotle's Nicomachean Ethics*, edited by Ronald M. Polansky, 110–34. New York: Cambridge University Press, 2014.

Penry, S. Elizabeth. *The People Are King: The Making of an Indigenous Andean Politics*. Oxford: Oxford University Press, 2019.

Pérez Castañeda, Juan Carlos. "Los condueñazgos en México durante el siglo XIX." *Signos Históricos* 20, no. 40 (2018): 178–231.

Pérez Puente, María Leticia. "La política eclesiástica de la junta magna y la creación de los primeros colegios tridentinos en América." In *Poderes y educación superior en el mundo Hispánico: Siglos XV al XX*, edited by Mónica Hidalgo Pego and Rosalina Ríos Zúñiga, 223–41. Mexico City: UNAM, 2016.

Perreau-Saussine, Amanda, and James Bernard Murphy. "The Character of Customary Law: An Introduction." In *The Nature of Customary Law: Legal, Historical and Philosophical Perspectives*, edited by Amanda Perreau-Saussine and James B. Murphy, 1–10. Cambridge: Cambridge University Press, 2007.

Piazza, Rosalba. *La conciencia oscura de los naturales: Procesos de idolatría en la diócesis de Oaxaca (Nueva España), siglos XVI–XVIII*. Mexico City: El Colegio de México, 2016.

Pizzigoni, Caterina. "'Como frágil y miserable': Las mujeres nahuas del valle de Toluca." In *Historia de la vida cotidiana en México el siglo XVIII: Entre tradición y cambio*, edited by Pilar Gonzalbo, 501–30. Mexico City: El Colegio de México, 2005.

Pizzigoni, Caterina. "'Para que le sirva de castigo y al pueblo de ejemplo': El pecado de poligamia y la mujer indígena en el valle del Toluca (siglo XVIII)." In *Las mujeres en la construcción de las sociedades iberoamericanas*, edited by Pilar Gonzalbo Aizpuru and Berta Ares Queija, 193–217. Mexico City: Escuela de Estudios Hispanoamericanos, 2004.

Pizzigoni, Caterina, ed. *Testaments of Toluca*. Stanford, CA: Stanford University Press, 2006.

Poole, Deborah. "Los usos de la costumbre: Hacia una antropología jurídica del Estado neoliberal." *Alteridades* 16, no. 31 (2006): 9–21.

Portillo Valdés, José M. *Fuero indio: Tlaxcala y la identidad territorial entre la monarquía imperial y la república nacional, 1787–1824*. Mexico City: El Colegio de México, 2014.

Powers, David S. "Law and Custom in the Maghrib, 1475–1500: On the Disinheritance of Women." In *Law, Custom, and Statute in the Muslim World: Studies in Honor of Aharon Layish,* edited by Ron Shaham, 17–39. Leiden: Brill, 2007.

Premo, Bianca. "Before the Law: Women's Petitions in the Eighteenth-Century Spanish Empire." *Comparative Studies in Society and History* 53, no. 2 (2011): 261–89.

Premo, Bianca. "Custom Today: Temporality, Customary Law, and Indigenous Enlightenment." *Hispanic American Historical Review* 94, no. 3 (2014): 355–79.

Premo, Bianca. *The Enlightenment on Trial: Ordinary Litigants and Colonialism in the Spanish Empire.* New York: Oxford University Press, 2017.

Premo, Bianca. "Felipa's Braid: Women, Culture, and the Law in Eighteenth-Century Oaxaca." *Ethnohistory* 61, no. 3 (2014): 497–523.

Premo, Bianca, and Yanna Yannakakis. "A Court of Sticks and Branches: Indian Jurisdiction in Colonial Mexico and Beyond." *American Historical Review* 124, no. 1 (2019): 28–55.

Puente Luna, José Carlos de la. *Andean Cosmopolitans: Seeking Justice and Reward at the Spanish Royal Court.* Austin: University of Texas Press, 2018.

Puente Luna, José Carlos de la. "Presentación." *Histórica* 40, no. 2 (2016): 5–8.

Puente Luna, José Carlos de la. "That Which Belongs to All: Khipus, Community, and Indigenous Legal Activism in the Early Colonial Andes." *The Americas* 72, no. 1 (2015): 19–54.

Puente Luna, José Carlos de la, and Renzo Honores. "Guardianes de la real justicia: Alcaldes de indios, costumbre y justicia local en Huarochirí colonial." *Histórica* 40, no. 2 (2016): 11–47.

Quezada, Sergio. *Maya Lords and Lordship: The Formation of Colonial Society in Yucatán, 1350–1600.* Translated by Terry Rugeley. Norman: University of Oklahoma Press, 2014.

Quezada, Sergio. *Pueblos y caciques yucatecos, 1550–1580.* Mexico City: El Colegio de México, 1993.

Radding, Cynthia. *Wandering Peoples: Colonialism, Ethnic Spaces, and Ecological Frontiers in Northwestern Mexico, 1700–1850.* Durham, NC: Duke University Press, 1997.

Radding, Cynthia. *Landscapes of Power and Identity: Comparative Histories in the Sonoran Desert and the Forests of Amazonia from Colony to Republic.* Durham, NC: Duke University Press, 2006.

Rama, Ángel. *La ciudad letrada.* Montevideo: Arca, 1998.

Ramos, Demetrio. "La crisis indiana y la Junta Magna de 1568." *Jahrbuch für Geschichte Lateinamerikas* 23, no. 1 (1986): 1-62.

Ramirez, Susan Elizabeth. "Amores Prohibidos: The Consequences of the Clash of Juridical Norms in Sixteenth Century Peru." *The Americas* 62, no. 1 (2005): 47–63.

Ramos, Gabriela. *Death and Conversion in the Andes: Lima and Cuzco, 1532–1670.* Notre Dame, IN: University of Notre Dame Press, 2010.

Ramos, Gabriela, and Yanna Yannakakis. *Indigenous Intellectuals: Knowledge, Power, and Colonial Culture in Mexico and the Andes*. Durham, NC: Duke University Press, 2014.

Ramos Núñez, Carlos A. "Consideración de la costumbre en la doctrina jurídica virreinal: De la valoración clásica a su impugnación moderna." In *La tradición clásica en el Perú virreinal*, edited by Teodoro Hampe Martíneza, 285–308. Lima: Sociedad Peruana de Estudios Clásicos y Fondo Editorial de la Universidad Nacional Mayor de San Marcos, 1999.

Rappaport, Joanne. *The Disappearing Mestizo: Configuring Difference in the Colonial New Kingdom of Granada*. Durham, NC: Duke University Press, 2014.

Restall, Matthew. "A History of the New Philology and the New Philology in History." *Latin American Research Review* 38, no. 1 (2003): 113–34.

Restall, Matthew. *The Maya World: Yucatec Culture and Society, 1550–1850*. Stanford, CA: Stanford University Press, 1999.

Reyes García, Luis, ed. *Documentos sobre tierras y señorío en Cuauhtinchan*. Mexico City: INAH-CIESAS-Gobierno del Estado de Puebla, 1978.

Reynolds, Susan. "Medieval Law." In *The Medieval World*, 2nd ed., edited by Peter Linehan, Janet L. Nelson, and Marios Costambeys, 568–85. New York: Routledge, 2018.

Ricard, Robert. *The Spiritual Conquest of Mexico: An Essay on the Apostolate and the Evangelizing Methods of the Mendicant Orders in New Spain, 1523–1572*. Berkeley: University of California Press, 1982.

Rivera Marín de Iturbe, Guadalupe. *La propiedad territorial en México, 1301–1810*. Mexico City: Siglo XXI, 1983.

Robertson, Donald. *Mexican Manuscript Painting of the Early Colonial Period: The Metropolitan Schools*. New Haven, CT: Yale University Press, 1959.

Robichaux, David, ed. *El Matrimonio en Mesoamérica ayer y hoy*. Mexico City: Universidad Iberoamericana, 2003.

Romero Frizzi, María de los Ángeles. *Economía y vida de los españoles en la Mixteca Alta, 1519–1720*. Mexico City: INAH, 1990.

Romero Frizzi, María de los Ángeles. *El sol y la cruz: Los pueblos indios de Oaxaca colonial*. Mexico City: INAH, 1996.

Romero Frizzi, María de los Ángeles. "Época colonial (1519–1785)." In *Historia de la cuestion agraria mexicana: Estado de Oaxaca*, edited by Juan Pablos, 107–80. Mexico City: Juan Pablos Editor, 1988.

Romero Frizzi, María de los Ángeles. *Teposcolula: Aquellos días del siglo XVI*. 2008. Reprint, Oaxaca: Secretaría de la Cultura del Estado de Oaxaca y Fundación Alfredo Harp Helú Oaxaca A. C., 2017.

Romero Frizzi, María de los Ángeles, and Juana Vásquez. "Memoria y escritura: La memoria de Juquila." In *Escritura zapoteca: 2.500 años de historia*, edited by María de los Ángeles Romero Frizzi, 393–448. Mexico City: CIESAS, 2003.

Romero Frizzi, María de los Ángeles, and Juana Vásquez. "Un título primordial de San Francisco Yatee, Oaxaca." *Tlalocan* 17 (2011): 85–120.

Rosenmüller, Christoph. *Corruption and Justice in Colonial Mexico, 1650–1755*. Cambridge: Cambridge University Press, 2019.

Rosenmüller, Christoph, ed. *Corruption in the Iberian Empires: Greed, Custom, and Colonial Networks*. Albuquerque: University of New Mexico Press, 2017.

Ruiz Bañuls, Mónica. *El huehuetlatolli: Como discurso sincrético en el proceso evangelizador novohispano del siglo XVI*. Rome: Bulzoni Editore, 2009.

Ruiz Medrano, Ethelia. "Don Carlos de Tezcoco and the Universal Rights of Emperor Carlos V." In *Texcoco: Prehispanic and Colonial Perspectives*, edited by Jongsoo Lee and Galen Brokaw, 165–81. Boulder: University Press of Colorado, 2014.

Ruiz Medrano, Ethelia. *Mexico's Indigenous Communities: Their Lands and Histories, 1500–2010*. Boulder: University Press of Colorado, 2010.

Ruiz Medrano, Ethelia. *Reshaping New Spain: Government and Private Interests in the Colonial Bureaucracy, 1531–1550*. Boulder: University Press of Colorado, 2006.

Ruiz Medrano, Ethelia, and Susan Kellogg. *Negotiation within Domination: New Spain's Indian Pueblos Confront the Spanish State*. Mesoamerican Worlds. Boulder: University Press of Colorado, 2010.

Ruiz Medrano, Ethelia, and Perla Valle. "Los colores de la justicia, códices jurídicos del siglo XVI en la Bibliothèque Nationale de France." *Journal de la Société des Américanistes* 84, no. 2 (1998): 227–41.

Saavedra, Manuel Bastias. "The Normativity of Possession: Rethinking Land Relations in Early-Modern Spanish America, ca. 1500–1800." *Colonial Latin American Review* 29, no. 2 (2020): 223–38.

Salomon, Frank, and George L. Urioste. *The Huarochirí Manuscript: A Testament of Ancient and Colonial Andean Religion*. Austin: University of Texas Press, 1991.

Sánchez Silva, Carlos. *La desamortización civil en Oaxaca*. Oaxaca: Universidad Autónoma "Benito Juárez" de Oaxaca, 2007.

Sarmiento, Ramón. "Antonio de Nebrija y la lingüística en la época del descubrimiento." In *La lingüística española en la época de los descubrimientos: Actas del coloquio en honor del profesor Hans-Josef Niederehe, Treveris, 16 a 17 de junio de 1997*, edited by Beatriz Bagola and Hans-Josef Niederehe, 157–73. Hamburg: Helmut Buske, 2000.

Schrader-Kniffki, Martina. "Metáforas de cuerpo del Zapoteco: Una aproximación etnofilosófica." *THULE: Rivista italiana di studi americanistici*, nos. 14–15 (April–October 2003): 23–49.

Schrader-Kniffki, Martina, and Yanna Yannakakis. "Sins and Crimes: Zapotec-Spanish Translation in Catholic Evangelization and Colonial Law in Oaxaca, New Spain." In *Missionary Linguistics V / Lingüística Misionera V: Translation Theories and Practices*, edited by Otto Zwartjes, Klaus Zimmermann, and Martina Schrader-Kniffki, 161–99. Amsterdam: John Benjamins, 2014.

Schrader-Kniffki, Martina and Yanna Yannakakis. "Traducción y construcción verbal de 'culpa' en textos judiciales del México colonial." In "Legal Language and Legal Translation, Past and Present." Special issue, *Parallèles* 33, no. 1 (2021): 53–70.

Schroeder, Donald N. "Aristotle on Law." *Polis* 4, no 1 (1981): 17–31.

Schwaller, John Frederick. "The Brothers Fernando de Alva Ixtlilxochitl and Bartolomé de Alva: Two 'Native' Intellectuals of Seventeenth-Century Mexico." In *Indigenous Intellectuals: Knowledge, Power, and Colonial Culture in Mexico and the Andes*, edited by Gabriela Ramos and Yanna Yannakakis, 39–59. Durham, NC: Duke University Press, 2014.

Schwaller, Robert C., ed. "A Language of Empire, a Quotidian Tongue: The Uses of Nahuatl in New Spain." Special issue, *Ethnohistory* 59, no. 4 (2012).

Schwaller, Robert C. "The Spiritual Conquest of Marriage: How the Holy Office and Council of Trent Attempted to Reform the Laity of New Spain." *Rechtsgeschichte-Legal History* 27 (2019): 123–30.

Schwartz, Stuart B. *All Can Be Saved: Religious Tolerance and Salvation in the Iberian Atlantic World*. New Haven, CT: Yale University Press, 2014.

Seed, Patricia. *Ceremonies of Possession in Europe's Conquest of the New World, 1492–1640*. Cambridge: Cambridge University Press, 1995.

Segala, Amos. *Literatura náhuatl: Fuentes, identidades, representaciones*. Mexico City: Consejo Nacional para la Cultura y Artes, 1990.

Sempat Assadourian, Carlos. "Los señores étnicos y los corregidores de indios en la conformación del Estado colonial." *Anuario de Estudios Americanos* 44 (1987): 325–426.

Sempat Assadourian, Carlos. *Transiciones hacia el sistema colonial andino*. Lima: Instituto de Estudios Peruanos, 1994.

Serrano, Delfina. "Legal Practice in an Andalusī-Maghribī Source from the Twelfth Century CE: The Madhāhib al-hukkām fī nawāzil all-ahkām." *Islamic Law and Society* 7 (2000): 187–234.

Serulnikov, Sergio. *Subverting Colonial Authority: Challenges to Spanish Rule in Eighteenth-Century Southern Andes*. Durham, NC: Duke University Press, 2003.

Sierra, María Teresa, and Victoria Chenaut. "Los debates recientes y actuales en la antropología jurídica: Las corrientes anglosajonas." In *Antropología jurídica: Perspectivas socioculturales en el estudio del derecho*, 27–59. Mexico City: Universidad Autónoma Metropolitana, 2006.

Sigal, Pete. *The Flower and the Scorpion: Sexuality and Ritual in Early Nahua Culture*. Durham, NC: Duke University Press, 2011.

SilverMoon. "The Imperial College of Tlatelolco and the Emergence of a New Nahua Intellectual Elite in New Spain (1500–1760)." PhD diss., Duke University, 2007.

Simpson, Lesley Byrd. *The Encomienda of New Spain*. Berkeley: University of California Press, 1950.

Smith, Mary Elizabeth. "Why the Second Codex Selden Was Painted." In *Caciques and Their People: A Volume in Honor of Ronald Spores*, edited by Joyce Marcus and Judith Francis Zeitlin, 111–42. Ann Arbor: University of Michigan Press, 1994.

Smith-Stark, Thomas C. "Juan de Córdova como lexicógrafo." *Guchachi' Reza*, no. 58 (May 1998): 2–13.

Smith-Stark, Thomas C. "Lexicography in New Spain (1492–1611)." In *Missionary Linguistics IV / Lingüística misionera*, edited by Otto Zwartjes, Ramón Arzápalo Marín, and T. Cedric Smith-Stark, 3–82. Amsterdam: John Benjamins, 2009.

Solano, Francisco de, ed. *Cedulario de tierras: Compilación de legislación agraria colonial, 1497–1820.* Mexico City: UNAM, 1984.

Solano, Francisco de, ed. *Cuestionarios para la formación de las relaciones geográficas de Indias: Siglos XVI/XIX.* Madrid: Consejo Superior de Investigaciones Científicas, 1988.

Sommer, Matthew H. *Polyandry and Wife-Selling in Qing Dynasty China: Survival Strategies and Judicial Interventions.* Oakland: University of California Press, 2015.

Sousa, Lisa. *The Woman Who Turned into a Jaguar, and Other Narratives of Native Women in Archives of Colonial Mexico.* Stanford, CA: Stanford University Press, 2020.

Sousa, Lisa. "Women and Crime in Colonial Oaxaca: Evidence of Complementary Gender Roles in Mixtec and Zapotec Societies." In *Indian Women of Early Mexico*, edited by Susan Schroeder, Stephanie Wood, and Robert Haskett, 199–214. Norman: University of Oklahoma Press, 1997.

Sousa, Lisa, and Kevin Terraciano. "The 'Original Conquest' of Oaxaca: Late Colonial Nahuatl and Mixtec Accounts of the Spanish Conquest." *Ethnohistory* 50, no. 2 (Spring 2003): 349–400.

Spalding, Karen. *Huarochirí: An Andean Society under Inca and Spanish Rule.* Stanford, CA: Stanford University Press, 1984.

Spores, Ronald. "Marital Alliance in the Political Integration of Mixtec Kingdoms." *American Anthropologist* 76, no. 2 (1974): 297–311.

Spores, Ronald. *The Mixtec Kings and Their People.* Norman: University of Oklahoma Press, 1967.

Spores, Ronald. *The Mixtecs in Ancient and Colonial Times.* Norman: University of Oklahoma Press, 1984.

Stavenhagen, Rodolfo, and Diego A. Iturralde. *Entre la ley y la costumbre: El derecho consuetudinario indígena en América Latina.* Mexico City: Instituto Indigenista Interamericano; San José, Costa Rica: Instituto Interamericano de Derechos Humanos, 1990.

Stein, Peter. "Custom in Roman and Medieval Civil Law." *Continuity and Change* 10, no. 3 (1995): 337–44.

Stein, Peter. "The Sources of Law in Cicero." *Ciceroniana Online* 3 (2015): 19–31.

Stephen, Lynn. *Zapotec Women: Gender, Class, and Ethnicity in Globalized Oaxaca.* 2nd ed. Durham, NC: Duke University Press, 2005.

Stephens, William O. "The Roman Stoics on Habit." In *A History of Habit: From Aristotle to Bourdieu*, edited by Tom Sparrow and Adam Hutchinson, 37–66. New York: Lexington Books, 2013.

Stern, Steve J. *Peru's Indian Peoples and the Challenge of Spanish Conquest: Huamanga to 1640.* 2nd ed. Madison: University of Wisconsin Press, 1993.

Stern, Steve J. *The Secret History of Gender: Women, Men & Power in Late Colonial Mexico*. Chapel Hill: University of North Carolina Press, 1995.

Stolley, Karen. *Domesticating Empire: Enlightenment in Spanish America*. Nashville, TN: Vanderbilt University Press, 2013.

Suárez Bilbao, Fernando. "La costumbre indígena en el derecho indiano." *Anuario de la Facultad de Derecho* 5 (1995): 119–52.

Sullivan, Thelma D. "Nahuatl Proverbs, Conundrums, and Metaphors, Collected by Sahagún." *Estudios de Cultura Náhuatl* 4 (1963): 93–176. https://historicas.unam.mx/publicaciones/revistas/nahuatl/pdf/ecn04/046.pdf.

Sullivan, Thelma D. *The Rhetorical Orations, or Huehuetlatolli, Collected by Sahagún*. Albuquerque: University of New Mexico Press, 1974.

Sullivan, Thelma D. "Tlatoani and Tlatocayotl in the Sahagún Manuscripts." *Estudios de Cultural Náhuatl*, no. 14 (1980): 15–38.

Tanck de Estrada, Dorothy. *Pueblos de indios y educación en el México colonial, 1750–1821*. Mexico City: El Colegio de México, 2010.

Tau Anzoátegui, Víctor. *El poder de la costumbre: Estudios sobre el derecho consuetudinario en América hispana hasta la emancipación*. Buenos Aires: Instituto de Investigaciones de Historia del Derecho, 2001.

Tavárez, David. *The Invisible War: Indigenous Devotions, Discipline, and Dissent in Colonial Mexico*. 2011. Reprint, Stanford, CA: Stanford University Press, 2020.

Tavárez, David. *Rethinking Zapotec Time: Cosmology, Ritual, and Resistance in Colonial Mexico*. Austin: University of Texas Press, 2022.

Taylor, William. "Cacicazgos coloniales en el valle de Oaxaca." *Historia Mexicana* 20, no. 1 (1970): 1–41.

Taylor, William. *Landlord and Peasant in Colonial Oaxaca*. Stanford, CA: Stanford University Press, 1972.

Taylor, William. *Magistrates of the Sacred: Priests and Parishioners in Eighteenth-Century Mexico*. Stanford, CA: Stanford University Press, 1996.

Terraciano, Kevin. "Crime and Culture in Colonial Mexico: The Case of the Mixtec Murder Note." *Ethnohistory* 45, no. 4 (1998): 709–45.

Terraciano, Kevin. "Introduction: An Encyclopedia of Nahua Culture: Context and Content." In *The Florentine Codex: An Encyclopedia of the Nahua World in Sixteenth-Century Mexico*, edited by Jeanette Favrot Peterson and Kevin Terraciano, 1–20. Austin: University of Texas Press, 2019.

Terraciano, Kevin. *The Mixtecs of Colonial Oaxaca: Ñudzahui History, Sixteenth through Eighteenth Centuries*. Stanford, CA: Stanford University Press, 2004.

Terraciano, Kevin. *Codex Sierra: A Nahuatl-Mixtec Book of Accounts from Colonial Mexico*. Norman: University of Oklahoma Press, 2021.

Teuscher, Simon. "Document Collections, Mobilized Regulations, and the Making of Customary Law at the End of the Middle Ages." *Archival Science* 10 (2010): 211–29.

Tierney, Brian. "Vitoria and Suarez on *Ius Gentium*, Natural Law, and Custom." In *The Nature of Customary Law: Legal, Historical and Philosophical Perspec-*

tives, edited by Amanda Perreau Saussine and James Bernard Murphy, 101–24. Cambridge: Cambridge University Press, 2007.

Tomás y Valiente, Francisco. *Manual de historia del derecho español*. 4th ed. Madrid: Editorial Tecnos, 2004.

Torales Pacheco, María Cristina. "A Note on the Composiciones de Tierras in the Jurisdiction of Cholula, Puebla (1591–1757)." In *The Indian Community of Colonial Mexico: Fifteen Essays on Land Tenure, Corporate Organizations, Ideology and Village Politics*, edited by Arij Ouweneel and Simon Miller, 87–102. Amsterdam: Centro de Estudios y Documentación Latinoamericanos, 1990.

Torre Ruiz, Rosa Alicia de la. "Composiciones de tierras en la alcaldía mayor de Sayula, 1692–1754: Un estudio de caso sobre el funcionamiento del Juzgado Privativo de Tierras." *Letras Históricas*, no. 6 (Spring–Summer 2012): 45–69.

Tortorici, Zeb. *Sins against Nature: Sex and Archives in Colonial New Spain*. Durham, NC: Duke University Press, 2018.

Townsend, Camilla. "Polygyny and the Divided Altepetl: The Tetzcocan Key to Pre-conquest Nahua Politics." In *Texcoco: Prehispanic and Colonial Perspectives*, edited by Jongsoo Lee and Galen Brokaw, 93–116. Boulder: University Press of Colorado, 2014.

Townsend, Camilla. *Annals of Native America: How the Nahuas of Colonial Mexico Kept Their History Alive*. Oxford: Oxford University Press, 2016.

Traslosheros, Jorge E. "El tribunal eclesiástico y los Indios en el Arzobispado de México, hasta 1630." *Historia Mexicana* 51, no. 3 (2002): 485–516.

Traslosheros, Jorge E. "Orden judicial y herencia medieval en la Nueva España." *Historia Mexicana* 55, no. 4 (2006): 1105–38.

Traslosheros, Jorge E., and Ana de Zaballa Beascoechea. *Los indios ante los foros de justicia religiosa en la Hispanoamérica virreinal*. Mexico City: UNAM, 2010.

Turning, Patricia. *Municipal Officials, Their Public, and the Negotiation of Justice in Medieval Languedoc*. Leiden: Brill, 2013.

Uribe-Urán, Víctor M. "Innocent Infants or Abusive Patriarchs? Spousal Homicides, the Punishment of Indians and the Law in Colonial Mexico, 1740s–1820s." *Journal of Latin American Studies* 38, no. 4 (2006): 793–828.

Valenzuela-Vermehren, Luis. "The Origin and Nature of the State in Francisco de Vitoria's Moral Philosophy." *Ideas y valores* 62, no. 151 (2013): 81–103.

van Deusen, Nancy E. *Global Indios: The Indigenous Struggle for Justice in Sixteenth-Century Spain*. Durham, NC: Duke University Press, 2015.

Van Doesburg, Sebastián. "De Linderos y Lugares: Territorio y Asentamiento en El Lienzo de Santa María Nativitas." *Relaciones* 86 (2001), 17–83

van Meijl, Toon. "Doing Indigenous Epistemology: Internal Debates about Inside Knowledge in Māori Society." *Current Anthropology* 60, no. 2 (April 2019): 155–73.

Vázquez García, Verónica. "Los derechos políticos de las mujeres en el sistema de usos y costumbres de Oaxaca." *Cuicuilco* 18, no. 50 (2011): 185–206.

Veltmeyer, Henry, and James F. Petras. *The New Extractivism: A Post-neoliberal De-*

velopment Model or Imperialism of the Twenty-First Century? London: Zed Books, 2014.

Viera y Clavijo, José de. *Noticias de la historia general de las islas Canarias*. Edited by Elías Serra Rafols. 3 vols. Santa Cruz de Tenerife: Goya Ediciones, 1950–52.

Villella, Peter B. "'For So Long the Memories of Men Cannot Contradict It': Nahua Patrimonial Restorationism and the Law in Early New Spain." *Ethnohistory* 63, no. 4 (2016): 697–720.

Wood, Andy. *The Memory of the People: Custom and Popular Senses of the Past in Early Modern England*. Cambridge: Cambridge University Press, 2013.

Wood, Stephanie. "The *Fundo Legal* or Lands *Por Razón de Pueblo*: New Evidence from Central New Spain." In *The Indian Community of Colonial Mexico: Fifteen Essays on Land Tenure, Corporate Organizations, Ideology and Village Politics,* edited by Arij Ouweneel and Simon Miller, 117–29. Amsterdam: Centro de Estudios y Documentación Latinoamericanos, 1990.

Wood, Stephanie. "The Techialoyan Codices." In *Sources and Methods for the Study of Postconquest Mesoamerican Ethnohistory*, edited by James Lockhart, Lisa Sousa, and Stephanie Gail Wood, 1–22. https://cpb-us-e1.wpmucdn.com/blogs.uoregon.edu/dist/7/5151/files/2022/01/Wood.pdf.

Wood, Stephanie. *Transcending Conquest: Nahua Views of Spanish Colonial Mexico*. Norman: University of Oklahoma Press, 2012.

Yannakakis, Yanna. *The Art of Being In-Between: Native Intermediaries, Indian Identity, and Local Rule in Colonial Oaxaca*. Durham, NC: Duke University Press, 2008.

Yannakakis, Yanna. "Beyond Jurisdictions: Native Agency in the Making of Colonial Legal Cultures." *Comparative Studies in Society and History* 57, no. 4 (2015): 1070–1082.

Yannakakis, Yanna. "Costumbre: A Language of Negotiation." In *Negotiation within Domination: New Spain's Indian Pueblos Confront the Spanish State*, edited by Ethelia Ruiz Medrano and Susan Kellogg, 137–71. Boulder: University Press of Colorado, 2010.

Yannakakis, Yanna. "Making Law Intelligible: Networks of Translation in Midcolonial Oaxaca." In *Indigenous Intellectuals: Knowledge, Power, and Colonial Culture in Mexico and the Andes*, edited by Gabriela Ramos and Yanna Yannakakis, 79–103. Durham, NC: Duke University Press, 2014.

Yannakakis, Yanna, and Martina Schrader-Kniffki. "Between the Old Law and the New: Christian Translation, Indian Jurisdiction, and Criminal Justice in Colonial Oaxaca." *Hispanic American Historical Review* 96, no. 3 (2016): 517–48.

Yannakakis, Yanna, and Martina Schrader-Kniffki. "Contra Juan Ramos por el delito de concubinato: Traducción cristiana y jurisdicción indígena en Oaxaca, siglo XVII." In *Los indios ante la justicia local: Intérpretes, funcionarios y litigantes en Nueva España y Guatemala (siglos XVI–XVIII)*, edited by Yanna Yannakakis, Martina Schrader-Kniffki, and Luis Alberto Arrioja Díaz Viruell, 131–50. Zamora: El Colegio de Michoacán, 2019.

Yannakakis, Yanna, Martina Schrader-Kniffki, and Luis Alberto Arrioja Díaz Viruell. *Los indios ante la justicia local: Intérpretes, oficiales y litigantes en Nueva España y Guatemala (siglos XVI–XVIII)*. Zamora: El Colegio de Michoacán; Atlanta: Emory University, 2019.

Zaballa Beascoechea, Ana de. "Indian Marriage before and after the Council of Trent: From Pre-Hispanic Marriage to Christian Marriage in New Spain." *Rechtsgeschichte-Legal History* 27 (2019): 90–104.

Zaballa Beascoechea, Ana de. "Promises and Deceits: Marriage among Indians in New Spain in the Seventeenth and Eighteenth Centuries." *The Americas* 73, no. 1 (2016): 59–82.

Zavala, Silvio. *El servicio personal de los indios en la Nueva España*. 7 volumes. Mexico City: El Colegio de México, 1984–1995.

Zavala, Silvio. *Estudios indianos*. 1948. Reprint, Mexico City: Colegio Nacional, 1984.

Zavala, Silvio. "Las encomiendas de Nueva España y el gobierno de Antonio de Mendoza." *Revista Histórica de América*, no. 1 (1938): 59–75.

Zeitlin, Judith Francis. *Cultural Politics in Colonial Tehuantepec: Community and State among the Isthmus Zapotec, 1500–1750*. Stanford, CA: Stanford University Press, 2005.

Zimmermann, Reinhard. *The Law of Obligations: Roman Foundations of the Civilian Tradition*. Oxford: Oxford University Press, 1996.

Index

Page locators in italics indicate figures, maps, and tables.

authorities, Spanish, 4, 6, 37; in cross-cultural networks, 106–7; Native debates with, 73–74, 90, 95; parish priests as, 46–47. *See also* Inquisition

Avila, Alonso de, 115

Aztec Triple Alliance, 5, 84, 102–3, 175

barbarity, concept of, 15, 39, 87, 92–97, 103, 106, 119

Basin of Mexico, 6, 38, 41, 55

Berdan, Frances, 76, 103

Bestia, don Joseph de, 162

Blaufarb, Rafe, 150

Bodleian Library, 75–76

body, 49, 62–63

Borah, Woodrow, 8

Bourbon Reforms, 170, 181–82, 226

Burgos, Laws of, 36–37

cabecera-sujeto model (administrative/parish seat and subjects), 145–46, 159; and election disputes, 190–91; and labor disputes, 180–81, 219–21; municipal office disputes, 184–85; secession cases, 146, 160, 191

cabildos (Native town councils), 7–8, 17, 42, 197; as hybrid institutions, 172; and municipal office holding, 184; as Native tribunal, 128; *propio* (lands used to sustain), 163–64; punishment ordered by, 128–29, 133; staffed by nobility, 128, 171–72; Tlaxcala, 175–76. *See also* authorities, Native

cacicazgos (entailed estates), 42, 139, 145, 148–49, 157; inheritance of, 99, 126; partnership and plural ownership, 163–68; plural, 164–65

caciques (local rulers), 83–84, 94, 103, 139; assimilation to Spanish culture, 173; challenges to, 165–66; declining power of, 148–49; and land tenure, 160; *yya* (lords) as, 145, 187

Cajonos Rebellion (1700), 129–30

calmecac (master of youths), 80, 81, 87

Calnek, Edward, 77–78

calpulli (ward), 114

Canary Islands, 34–35

canon law, Catholic Church, 26, 31; and joint obligation, 155; and polygyny, 36–37, 81, 106, 115

canon law, Islamic, 29

Carlos (Charles) V, 90, 94, 112, 116, 126

caste-based system, 7, 91, 124, 126

Castile, 31–34. *See also* custom, Castilian; law, Castilian

Castilian language, translating custom into, 47–49

catechisms, 53–54, 63–64

Catholic Church: "age of reason" for children, 79–80; canon law, 26, 31, 36–37, 81, 106, 115, 155; confraternities (*cofradías*), 162, 181; Council of Trent, 65, 127, 136; ecclesiastical jurisdiction, 8, 92, 128, 162; fees and labor for divine cults, 178, *179*, 181; fiestas, involuntary labor for, 182, 184, 194–96, 229. *See also* Christianity

Cedulario, 43

Chacón, don Félix (judge), 151, 153, 159, 161

chahui ("good"), 67

Chávez, Miguel, 167

Chávez y Guzmán, don Pedro de (*cacicazgo*), 165–66

chayu (community, variation of "tayu"), 151. See also *yuhuitayu* ("tayu," alliance of two communities)

Chichimecateuctli, don Carlos Ometochtli, 54, 109–13, 117–19, 121, 131–32, 135; denunciation of Christianity, 109–10, 113

china (work, labor, office, obligation), 64, 174–75, 177–78, 203

Chocholtec pueblos, dispute among, 161–62

Christendom, expansion of, 47, 231; custom's role in, 34–43; and *fueros*, 30; Iberian Peninsula, warfare in, 14, 29–31, 34–36, 43, 111; morality of debated, 36–37. *See also* colonialism

Christianity, 14; blessing, concept of, 63; commoner labor for *culto divino*, 178, *179*, 181; divine law, 25, 217; salvation, concern about, 36; syncretic, 45, 65; under Umayyad rule, 29. *See also* Catholic Church; evangelization; missionaries

Christian theologians, 23–25, 37, 43–44, 155

Cicero, 26, 44, 49

civility, Native, 14–15, 45; attributed to Moctezuma, 84; and European standards, 95–97; evaluated by natural law, 74, 78, 87, 89–90, 96, 106–7. *See also* Codex Mendoza; Relaciones geográficas de Antequera; sovereignty, Native

contracts, 13, 17; commercial, 146; custom as, 136, 186; as a form of insurance against expropriation, 156–57; joint liability, 154–56, 163, 168; Ñudzahui, 147–51. *See also* labor agreements, written; land; obligation; partnership contracts; social contract

convenio (written agreement), 210–212, 216, 218, 220–21, 227

co-ownership (*condueñazgo*), 170

Córdova, Juan de, 56, 59–62, 66

Corpus Iuris Civilis. See Justinian Code (*Corpus Iuris Civilis*)

Cortés, Hernán, 38, 115–16, 171, 173

costumbre, juridical concept of, 33–34, 48–49, 57, 60, 203

Council of the Indies, 88, 91

courage, 83, 86

Covarrubias Orozco, Sebastián de, 49, 59

criminal cases, 6, 128–30

Cruz, Ignacio de la (governor of Teposcolula), 192–94

Cruz, Narciso de la (official), 195–96

Cruz, Pascual de la (regidor), 188–89

Cuauhtinchan, altepetl of, 52

cuicacalli (house of song), 80

culturally relative stances, 110, 111–12

custom, 254n93; continuum with law, 9, 34, 85–86; contractual notion of, 136, 186; *costumbre*, juridical concept of, 33–34, 48–49, 57, 60, 203; custom–law opposition, 3–4; flexibility of, 10, 32, 156; and *fueros*, 30; gendered notions of, 49, 57, 61; Iberian aristocracy's use of, 31; *ius consuetudine* (Roman concept), 26–27, 32, 49; as juridical concept, 24; key characteristics in the *Partidas*, 34; as original form of law, 25; and reason, 25, 32–33, 49, 83–88; as "second nature," 44, 49; synthesis of with law, 3–4, 7; territorialization of, 61; translated to normative order, 139; as "unwritten law," 32; usage, 32–33. *See also* antiquity; common good; custom, Native; "good" and "bad" customs; obligation; social contract; timelessness, concept of

custom, Castilian, 14, 23, 47–49

custom, European, in legal revolution of twelfth and thirteenth centuries, 24–27

custom, Native: as binding, 17, 26, 64; as category of European law, 2–3; claims to as

means to contend with change, 5; coexistence of with colonial order, 94; and communal interests, 177; contestation of, 1–2; continuum with law, 9; and expansion of Christendom, 34–43; and gentility, 62, 92–93, 134; at heart of evangelization, 69; hereditary privilege claimed as, 177; as hybrid formulation, 203; Inca, 10–11; inequality reproduced by claims of Native litigants, 3, 12, 163, 233–35; *inter vivos* donations, 158, 168; as invention of, 232; irrationality attributed to, 3; as juridical category, 14; labor obligations justified by, 181, 183, 220; legal battles over meaning of, 17; legal-intellectual history of, 13–14; at local level, 6; Mixtec and Zapotec, translating into, 55–68; Nahuatl, translating into, 50–55; narrowing of ambit of, 5, 15, 43–44, 111; new, establishment of, 33, 197–98, 200–201, 206, 239–40n49; "old" and "new," legal disputes over, 173–74, 176–77; in present-day contexts, 231–35; romanticization of, 3–4, 18, 200; *sistemas normativos indígenas*, 18–19, 232–33; sixteenth and seventeenth century production of, 13; temporal references, shifts in, 11; as tool of European empire, 4; unequal reciprocity grounded in, 17, 172–74, 180, 193–94, 219; *usos y costumbres*, 18, 174, 232–34. *See also* custom; "good" and "bad" customs; labor disputes; written custom

daha (tribute in kind), 224, 225

Danza de la Pluma (reenactment of conquest), 195–96

decoloniality, 232, 235

Delgado, Pedro, 120

derecho indiano school, 9

derrama (supplementary levy), 67, 172–73, *179*, 189

desamortización civil, 170, 260n87

de Soto Guevara, don Alonso (Spanish magistrate), 188, 189

dhimmī status (protected people, People of the Book), 29–30, 35

Díaz Gómez, Floriberto, 233

Diccionario latino-español (Nebrija), 48, 59

dictionaries and grammars: appendices, 60, 61; *Arte de la lengua mexicana* (Olmos),

"good" and "bad" customs, 14, 70, 92–94; "corruption" as "bad" custom, 195; of Nahua society, 38, 40–44, 47, 49, 53; polygyny as "bad" custom, 103–7, 135, 230; sorting of by Castilian writers, 14, 61–64, 67, 73, 92–94. *See also* Codex Mendoza; custom; custom, Native

governors, reelection of, 187–88

Gramática de la lengua castellana (Nebrija), 48–50, 59, 61, 69

Granada, Nasrid Kingdom of, 35, 48

Gratian, 115

Greek traditions, 23, 24, 26, 49, 51

Gualpuyogualcal, Francisco (master of painters), 75

Guanche peoples, 34–35

Guzmán, Gabriel de, 126

Hapsburg Heraldic Shield, *143*

"harmony ideology," 234

heart (*lachi*), 60–61

Herzog, Tamar, 150

Hispania, Roman law applied to, 28

Hispaniola, xii, 35–36, 38

Historia general de las cosas de la Nueva España, 52

huehuetlatolli (high oratory, "archaic word"), 52–54, 59, 77, 87, 250n2; used by don Carlos, 109–10

huey tlatoani (supreme ruler), 54

huidzo sahu (law, "sermon"), 56–57

Iberian Peninsula, 69, 229; *aljama* communities, 30; al-Andalus, 28–30; boundary disputes Andalucía (Spain) and Alentejo (Portugal), 150, 151; Christian expansion in, 14, 29–31, 34–36, 43, 111; ethnic diversity of, 28; Islamic law in, 28–30; Jewish and Muslim converts, 15, 29–30, 44, 111, 134–35; *Leyes de Toro*, 35; *Liber Iudiciorum*, 28, 31; Nasrid Kingdom of Granada, 35, 48; *taifa* principalities, 30; written custom in, 200

"idolatry," 46, 53, 59; as "bad" custom, 103–6; described in Relaciones geográficas, 91–92; extirpation manual, 135; as *quela pezèlào* (the devil's custom), 62; relegated to past, 62–64, 67; in Villa Alta area, 129

imperialism, European, 3

imperial legal orders, Native, 5–6, 8

Indies, laws of, 9

Indigenous people. *See* Native (Indigenous) people

indio ladino, (Hispanized Native), 126

indirect rule, 4, 11, 17, 37, 70, 103, 105, 128, 171, 230. *See also* self-governance, Native

inequality, reproduced by claims of Native litigants, 3, 12, 163, 233–35

inheritance, 13, 17, 97–99, 105–6, 113–17, 124–25; of *cacicazgos*, 99, 126; lateral customs, 97, 115, 117, 124; Spanish customs, 99, 136, 203

Inquisition, 15, 46; cases brought before, 117–18; culturally relative stances in testimony, 110, 111–12; don Carlos Chichimecateuctli, trial of, 54, 109–13, 117–19; and gender relations, 111, 112, 113, 118–19, 121; removal of Native people from jurisdiction of, 111, 127; transatlantic, 111; Yanhuitlan lords, trials of, 104, 120–27, 131, 135. *See also* authorities, Spanish; "old law," discourse of

Instituto Nacional de Antropología e Historia (INAH, Mexico), 76

inter vivos donations, 158

irrationality: attributed to custom, 3

Isabella of Castile, 34, 48

Islamic law, in Iberia, 9–10, 12, 28–30; *dhimmī* status, 29–30, 35

ius commune, 26, 144, 217

ius consuetudine (Roman concept of custom), 26, 27, 32, 49

ius non scriptum (unwritten law), 32

Ixtlilxochitl, Fernando Alva de, 5, 116

Jews, 15, 29–30, 44, 111–12, 134–35

jizya (tax), 29

John the Evangelist, 48

joint jurisdiction, 155, 158, 161, 169–70. *See also* possession, concept of

joint obligation, 154–56, 163, 168

jurados (justices of the peace), 97

juridical codices, 139

jurisdictions: ecclesiastical, 8, 14, 92, 128, 162; Native and Spanish, 7–8; special, for Native litigants, 8. See also *cabildos* (Native town councils)

justice, 6–9, 86; General Indian Court, 8, 91;

Spanish concepts of, 47, 51, 97, 155, 177, 203, 213; *tlamelauacachiualiztli* (Nahuatl term for), 50–51; village, 2, 17, 201

Justinian Code (*Corpus Iuris Civilis*), 23, 25, 31–33, 155, 257n46; Digest, 27, 163; Institutes, 27

Juzgado General de Indios (General Indian Court), 8, 91

Juzgado Privativo de Tierras, 151

Kellogg, Susan, 117

knowledge production, 12, 14–15, 94–95, 232; cross-cultural, 17–18, 230; growing Spanish skepticism of, 200–201; and land title, 140–41; by Native intellectuals, 50, 54–55

labor: custom as justification for involuntary, 94, 179–94, 192, 220–21; *china* (work, office, obligation, duty), 64, 174–75, 177–78, 203; *chinalahui* (work for the community by notables), 176, 185–86; dependent laborers (*terrazgueros*), 164, 165; drafts, 173; *encomienda* system of, 36, 40, 183; fees and head taxes, 178, *179*, 181–83; *guelaguetza* (mutual aid system), 174–75; illegal requisitions of justified by custom, 183, 219; *mayeque*, tribute required from, 90; and public utility, 177–78, 181–82, 184; *repartimiento* (rotational drafts), 90, 209, 220; as social relation, 64; *tequio* (communal labor), 175, 180; *tniño* (work, office, duty, obligation), 175, 177, 224; unequal reciprocity, relations of, 17, 172–74, 180, 193–94, 219. *See also* labor agreements, written; labor disputes; obligation; personal service (*servicio personal*); social contract; tributary relationships

labor agreements, written, 199–201, 226–27; San Juan Tabaá, 1709–1765, 201–19; Yolotepec, Yxcatlan, Tacahua, and Ytnuyucu, 1723–1776, 219–26

labor disputes, 17; civil suits, 202, 209–19, 224–26; fiestas, involuntary labor for, 182, 184, 194–96, 229; intercommunal, 180, 182; labor for community vs. labor for the powerful, 177–84; municipal office holding, 178, 184–86; "old" and "new" customs, litigation over, 173–74, 176–77; opposi-

tion between coercion and free will, 183, 186, 190–91, 196, 221; over personal service, 181, 183–84, 191–94, 197–98, 220–26; San Juan Tabaá, 201–19; selected cases, 178; and self-governance, 184–86; village justice, 2, 17, 201, 203

làchi (heart), 60–61, 66

Lachichina (community), 175

Ladesa, don Juan Antonio de, 166–67

land: *congregación* (*reducción*, forced relocation programs), 140, 145, 164; as nexus for customary claims, 139; plural ownership and *composiciones de tierras*, 151–63; possession, concept of, 141–44, 149–53; pre-Hispanic categories of, 114; primordial titles, 140, 144, 169; *propio* (lands used to sustain *cabildo*), 163–64; special court of land titling, 151; territorialization and reterritorialization, 150; *tierras del común repartimiento*, 164; usufruct rights, 16, 114, 149, 164, 166–69, 203, 218; "voluntary donation" to Crown, 141; *yuhuitayu* ("tayu," alliance of two communities), 57, 59, 124, 145. *See also* communal land; *composiciones de tierras* (royal land titling program); contracts; partnership contracts

land claims, Spanish: royal cédula of 1591, 140; royal cédula of 1687, 146

languages: Castilian, 47–49; Christian-Ñudzahui hybrids, 147; criminal *procesos* in, 130; European, standardization of, 47–48; hybrid constructions, 74, 76, 147, 203; as instrument of empire, 48; Latin, pre-Christian, 48; Otomanguean language family, 56; Spanish-Indigenous grammars and dictionaries, 14, 46, 48; Uto-Aztecan language family, 56. *See also* dictionaries and grammars; Mixtec (Ñudzahui) language; Nahuatl language; translation; Zapotec (Tíchazàa) language

Las Casas, Bartolomé de, 14, 47, 78, 95

Las Casas, Francisco de, 120, 124

last wills and testaments, 99, 136, 158, 203

Latin America: constitutional reforms (1990s), 4, 233; decoloniality, 232, 235; neoliberal policies, 233. *See also* Mexico

Latin America, colonial: custom and law in, 4–13. *See also* Mexico

Latin grammar, 47–49

law: continuum with custom, 9, 34, 85–86; custom as original form of, 25; didactic role of, 85–86; hegemonic function of, 7–8; *ius consuetudinis*, 26–27, 32; language linked with, 5, 60; *lex*, 26, 27, 33; rationality attributed to, 3; synthesis of with custom, 3–4, 7; translations for, 56–57. *See also* law, European; Roman law

law, Castilian, 9; in Americas, 34, 154–57; as first vernacular legal code, 31; *Novissima Recopilación de las Leyes del Reino*, 154, 155, 158; *Ordenamiento de Alcalá*, 34, 156–57. See also *Siete Partidas, Las*

law, European, 13–14, 241n28; custom as category of, 2–3; *ius commune*, 26, 144; and Justinian Code, 25–27, 31; natural law, 17, 23; and Scholasticism, 23–25, 37, 43–44, 155; twelfth-century revolution, 14, 24–27, 31–34

"Law of the Lord," 56–57

legal meaning, production of, 113

legal order, concept of, 13, 51, 112

legal orders, imperial: built from ground up, 18, 230–31; Castilian, 9, 35–36; and expansion of Christendom, 47, 231; interplay of Native and Spanish forms, 8, 74; Native production of, 8; pre-Hispanic custom modified, 119–20. *See also* natural law

legal pluralism, 4, 9, 131; *dhimmī* status, 29–30, 35; in medieval Spain, 28–31

Leo, Emperor, 27

leo golaza (the old law), 132, 134

León, 31

Leyes de Toro, 35

libana (Zapotec ceremonial style), 64

Liber Iudiciorum (Visigothic legal code), 28, 31

lienzos (Indigenous cartographic histories), 146

livestock economy, 1–2, 144, 146, 159, 161–65, 167, 202–19, 231; and cochineal/nopal cactus cultivation, 208–9

local law, 14, 17, 26–28, 30, 201, 207, 229; "custom of the pueblo," 51–52, 57–61, 230; recent changes in Oaxaca, 232–33; and Roman Empire, 26–27. *See also specific locations*

Lopes Don, Patricia, 112, 113

López de Velasco, Juan, 88

Luz y methodo de confesar idolatras, y destierro de idolatrias, debajo del tratado siguiente (Villavicencio), 135

Macuil Martínez, Raul, 87

Maldonado, Francisco (Nahua Christian), 109–10, 111

mancomunidad, laws of, 154–55, 163, 168, 257–58nn46–47

Manual breve y compendioso para enpesar a aprender lengua zapoteca y administrar en caso de necesidad (Martínez), 66–67

Mapa Quinatzin (1546), 5

mapping conventions, Mesoamerican, *98*, 98–99, 140, 146

Maraver, Bachiller Pedro Gómez de (religious official), 121

Marbán, Esteban, 121

marriage, 105–6; consanguineous, 110, 117, 125, 127; couples required to provide labor, 221, 223; "legitimate," 80–81, 106, 115, 125–27; *namiquitiliztli*, 87; Native nobility and Christian ceremonies, 115–16, 121; and natural law, 115; and royal succession, 125. *See also* polygyny

Martínez, Alonso (friar), 66–67

Martínez de Velasco, don Miguel (*cacique*), 176, 185

Martínez Luna, Jaime, 233

Matrícula de Tributos, 77

matrilineal cohorts, 113–14, 124–25

Mendieta, Gerónimo de (friar), 53

Mendoza, Antonio de (viceroy of New Spain), 75, 171

Menegus Bornemann, Margarita, 163–64

menstruation, 49, 62

merit, concepts of, 11

Mesoamerica. *See* pre-Hispanic Mesoamerica

Mesopotamian traditions, 51

Mesquita, Martín de la (religious official), 121

mestizo chroniclers, 5

Mexica society, 74, 75, 78, 114, 175; property, categories of, 114–15; teaching good customs in, 79–83. *See also* Nahua society

Mexico: custom and law in, 4–13; legacy of co-ownership, 170; Native population decline, 90. *See also* Latin America; Latin America, colonial; Oaxaca

Mexico City, 39, 55. *See also* Tenochtitlan

Miceli, Paola, 31–32

Milpa Alta, Oaxaca, 171

miserable, legal category of, 8

missionaries, 5, 44, 230–31; alliances with Native authorities, 116; ambivalence about Native past, 62–63, 68–69, 91; bilingual materials produced by, 14, 46, 48, 50, 63–66; denunciations of abuses, 36, 37; earliest generation of, 62; education of youth by, 45–46, 55–56, 63, 73–74, 247–48n22; humanist philosophy of, 55, 73; Native assistants, 47; Native knowledge valued by, 46; and Native legal culture, 45; polygyny targeted by, 115, 121–27; as translators, 46–55. *See also* Dominican missionaries; evangelization; Franciscan missionaries

Mixteca Alta (Oaxaca), 124–27, 129; cañada de Yosotiche lands, 164–65; livestock economy in, 159; Tlaxiaco district, 164–68

Mixtec (Ñudzahui) language, 245n51; Ñudzahui-language records, 130, 145–47, 154, 175, 187, 221, 224; origin story, 57; translating custom into, 55–68. *See also* Ñudzahui communities

Moctezuma II, 78, 84, 86, 103

modo (mode, style), 60–61

Molina, Alonso de, 50–52, 56–59

Montesinos, Antonio de, 36

Monzón, Cristina, 130

moral dialogue: of labor and servitude, 226–27; Nahua-Christian, 52–55. *See also* Codex Mendoza

morality, of conquest, 6, 36–39

mos maiorum (unwritten norms), 49

Mudejars, 30

Mundy, Barbara, 98

municipal office holding, 178, 183–86

Muñoz Camargo, Diego, 104

Muslims, Iberian Peninsula, 15, 29–30, 44, 111, 134–35; Qur'an, 29; Shari'a (Islamic canon law), 29, 30; Umayyad Caliphate (Córdoba), 28–30

Nahua society: legal culture, 5–6, 12; present-day, 87; *tlacuiloque* (painter-scribes), 5, 15, 52, 73, 75–76, 81, 84, 87, 106, 139. *See also* Codex Mendoza; Mexica society

Nahuatl language: high oratory, 53; *tlamelauacachiualiztli* (justice), 50–51; translating custom into, 50–55

nationalism, 3

Native (Indigenous) people: colonial legal consciousness, development of, 14, 45, 46, 68–69, 106, 226, 230; as heterogeneous, 232; institutions of destroyed by Spanish, 5–6, 52, 55, 104; knowledge of, 11, 46, 50, 57, 89, 140, 200, 232; Laws of Burgos declare freedom of, 36, 37; "natural children" rhetoric, 86–87; population decline, 90, 140, 146, 171; population recovery and growth, 141, 144, 153, 211; as producers of imperial legal orders, 8; and slavery, 9, 36, 38, 40, 220. *See also* authorities, Native; custom, Native; nobility, Native; self-governance, Native; sovereignty, Native

Native tribunals. See *cabildos* (Native town councils)

natural law, 231; in Aristotelian philosophy, 25, 60; and canon law, 115; categories integral to European framework, 17; civility evaluated by, 74, 78, 87, 89–90, 96, 106–7; in Codex Mendoza, 78; custom related to, 32–33; European, 17, 23; and labor disputes, 173; marriage as part of, 115; and sexual crimes, 96; and sovereignty of Native societies, 24, 37; transition to reason from, 25, 26

nature (physis), 25

ndaha ñuu (tributary communities), 187

Nebrija, Antonio de, 48–50, 59, 61, 69

neoliberal policies, 233

New Laws, 40, 88, 183, 220

New Philology, 7

New Spain, viceroyalty of, 10, 15, 88; Audencias of, 41; shifts in administration, 88–90

Nezahualcoyotl (ruler of Tetzcoco), 5–6

Nezahualpilli (lord of Tetzcoco), 118

Nicomachean Ethics (Aristotle), 78, 83, 85

nobility, Native, 5–7; assertions of Native officials against, 13; in *cabildo* posts, 128, 171–72; challenged by commoners, 13, 90; Christian marriage ceremonies, 115–16, 121; compound lordship, 164–65; corporate land rights, 114–15; declining power of, 148–49, 180, 197; demotion of, 133; education of youth by missionaries, 45–46, 110; genealogy, *142*; *huehuetlatolli* and missionaries, 53–54; labor requirements of, 197–98; lesser nobility (*principales*), 97;

Pimentiel, don Hernando, 115
Pius V, 116
Plato, 80
polis, as ideal form of government, 38, 40, 94
political alliances: created by polygyny, 15, 114–15, 124, 135–36; between Spanish and Native authorities, 115–16, 125–28, 135–36. See also *yuhuitayu* ("tayu," alliance of two communities)
political order, Aristotelian, 23, 94
Politics (Aristotle), 78, 85
polygyny: as "bad" custom, 103–7, 135, 230; caste-based, 124, 126; concubinage, 36, 111, 113–19, 126–27, 130–33, 136; continuation of, 116–17, 121–27; criminalization of, 15, 106–7, 113, 126–27; defined as bigamy and concubinage, 111, 119; dismantling of, 13, 15–16, 111; Inquisition's role in dismantling, 111, 121–27; lateral inheritance customs, 97, 115, 117, 124; and Laws of Burgos, 36–37; and matrilineal cohorts, 113–14, 124–25; in the Mixteca, 124–27; "old law," discourse of, 15–16, 110–13, 119–20, 126–27, 132–36, 230; ongoing pronouncements about, 116–17; political alliances created by, 15, 114–15, 124, 135–36; prohibition of in 1530, 116; punishment of, 116, 254n91; women's challenges to, 112, 113, 118–19, 132, 135. *See also* marriage
Portugal, 150, 151
possession, concept of, 141–44, 149–53; joint possession of communal land, 16, 153–60, 163–69, 170
power of attorney, 155–56
pre-Hispanic Mesoamerica: custom and law in, 4–13, 41, 52, 54–55; and imperial legal orders, 119–20; mapping conventions, *98*, 98–99, 140, 146; personal service requirements in, 68, 183; pictographic manuscripts destroyed, 5, 52; religious practices, 54–55, 62–63, 67. *See also* Codex Mendoza; Tenochtitlan
priests, labor for, 219–26
priests, Native, 104–5, 128, 131
primordial titles, 140, 144, 169
principales (village notables), 131, 157; *chinalahui* (work for the community by), 176, 185; commoner competition with, 177; exemptions from labor, 178–79; and labor dis-

putes, 173, 175–79, *179*, 185, 188, 192–93, 201–3, 207–20, 224, 230–31
procesos (criminal proceedings), 130
property, categories of, 114–15
propio (lands used to sustain cabildo), 163–64
prudence (practical wisdom), 86
"pueblo, law of," 51–52, 57–61, 230
punishment, corporal, 180, 185; in Codex Mendoza, 79–80, 81; ordered by cabildos, 128–29, 133; and partnership agreements, 157, 159, 161; in Relaciones geográficas, 95–96

queche (community), 60
quela (essence), 61
quélahualache (essence of the land or country), 61
Quevedo, Pedro de (Spanish magistrate), 191
Quito province (northern Andes), 11

Ramírez de Fuenleal, Sebastián (president of Second Audiencia), 53
Ramos, Juan (*principal*, defendant), 130–33
rationality, 3, 6, 24–25, 43, 49; Codex Mendoza's portrayal of, 78–79
Real Audiencia, 10, 42, 53, 55, 90, 162, 218, 225; cabecera secession cases, 146, 160; and land disputes, 139, 149; polygyny cases, 117
reason (logos), 23, 31–33; transition to from natural law, 25–26
reciprocity, 1–2, 64, 160; changes in over time, 172–77; hierarchical, 183–84; in native languages of Oaxaca, 174–77; and *topil* labor, 191–94, 221; unequal, relations of, 17, 172–74, 180, 193–94, 219. *See also* obligation
"recognition, problem of," 93
Recopilación de leyes de los reynos de las Indias (1680), 43
regidores (aldermen), 187, 193
Relaciones geográficas de Antequera, 15, 74–75, 88–92, 106–7, 230; Christian categories of time in, 93; customs portrayed in negative light, 89–90; maps in, *98*, 98–99; moral classification in, 92–94; sacrifice, idolatry, and polygyny as "bad" customs, 103–6; sartorial distinctions in, 99–102; survey responses and frame of barbarism and civility, 94–103, *98*, *100*, *101*, *102*; translation process, 89

Ten Commandments, 67

Tenochtitlan, *xiv*, 5, 12, 15, 75; artisans, 78, 85; characterized as violent, expansionist, and religious, 6; children's education in, 80; European framing of as republic, 78; five-hundredth anniversary of the conquest of, 239–40; as ideal form of government, 94, 102–3; judicial institutions, 84, 85; Moctezuma's palace complex, 84; Spanish battle for, 115–16; tributary relationships, 77, 102–3. *See also* Codex Mendoza

Teotitlán del Valle (community), 1–2

Teozacoalco, *98*, 98–99, *100*

Teposcolula (administrative center and community), 120, 181, 182, 187–94, 210, 219, 222, 224, 227, *222*; San Vicente, 191–94

Teposcolula-Yanhuitlan (Spanish province), 120, 130, 148, 151

tequigua (courageous warrior), 83

tequitlato (tribute collector), 97

Terraciano, Kevin, 130

Tesoro de la lengua castellana o española (Covarrubias Orozco), 49, 59

testation, 26–27

Tetlahuehuetzquititzin, Pedro, 118

Tetzcoco, *xiv*, 12; Christian marriage ceremonies, 115–16; Christian stance taken by lords of, 119; factional politics, 112, 118–19, 133; pre-Hispanic legal system, 5–6; warfare due to succession claims, 114

Third Mexican Provincial Council, 127, 136

ticha (law), 60, 67

tíchalipéa ("custom," "mode," "style of speech"), 60

tíchapea hualáache (law of the land or country), 61

tierras baldías (*baldíos*), 140, 156, 159, 202

tierras de común repartimiento (communal lands), 202

Tilantongo (*yuhuitayu* and colonial town), 97–99, 148, *100, 102*

timelessness, concept of, 2–3, 4; "denial of coevalness," 93–94; in medieval European custom and law, 26; Mixtec translations for, 59; in Relaciones geográficas, 94–95; "since time immemorial," as stock phrase, 141–44, 157, 164, 179. *See also* antiquity; custom

tlacuiloque (painter-scribes), 5, 15, 52, 139; as

authors, 77–78; and Codex Mendoza, 73, 75–76, 81, 84, 87, 106; "juridical codices" produced by, 139

tlacxitlan (court, "at the feet"), 84

tlamanitiliztli ("custom of the pueblo"), 52, 57–61, 59

tlamatque (sages), 87

tlamelauacachiualiztli (Nahuatl term for justice), 50–51

Tlatelolco, *xiv*, 12

tlatloani (ruler, "speaker"), 5, 112, 114, 118

Tlaxcala (province and city), 173, 175

Tlaxcalan Actas, 173

Tlaxiaco (*yuhuitayu*, colonial administrative district, and town), 164–68, 189

tniño (labor, obligation, duty), 175, 177, 224

tolteca (skilled craftsmen), 78

topil (lower-rank municipal officer), 191–94, 221

Toribio de Benavente (Motolinía), 5, 115, 119

town councils, Native. See *cabildos* (Native town councils)

Tractatus de legibus ac Deo legislatore (*On the Laws and God the Legislator*) (Suárez), 206

transatlantic networks, 14, 111, 135, 151, 158, 230–31

translation, 229–30; "a uso de proceso," 89, 106; and Codex Mendoza, 74, 76–77, 79; and confessional manuals, 64–68; of custom into Mixtec and Zapotec, 55–68; of custom into Nahuatl, 50–55; doublets (pairs of expressions), 51, 61, 203; hybrid works, 74, 76; lack of equivalents, 62; in legal contexts, 76–77; loan words, 51–52, 132, 175, 203; mirroring process, 101–2; missionary context vs. legal context, 76–77; past used to explain Christian message, 62–63; periphrasis, 57–58; of tonal languages, 56. *See also* languages

treasuries, municipal, 181–82, 184

tributary relationships, 77, 94, 102–3, 172; and electoral politics, 188–89; exploited by Native authorities, 178–79; *ndaha ñuu* (tributary communities), 187; and partnership agreements, 147; *tequio* (that which owes tribute), 175, 180; *tequiti* (to perform tribute duty, pay tribute), 175; *tequitl* (tribute, duty), 175. *See also* labor; obligation

Tridentine Council, 127

tyranny, 94, 95, 103, 180
tzahui ("good"), 64, 67

uapaualiztli (education), 87
Ulpiano, Domicio (Roman jurist), 49
United Nations Educational, Scientific and
  Cultural Organization (UNESCO), 74
unwritten norms, 17, 49
usage, 32–33
"use," 59
usos y costumbres, 18, 232–34

Vargas, Pablo de (governor of San Juan
  Yatzona), 131
vecinos (citizen-residents), 178, 187
Velasco, Luis de (the younger), 90–91
Villa Alta, Oaxaca, 16, 56, 239–40n49; Cajonos Rebellion (1700), 129–30; cochineal production, 208–9; extirpation cycle,
  1660s to 1720s, 130; identities of ritual
  specialists exposed, 134; labor disputes in,
  175–76, 178, 181–82; Santa María Asun-
  ción Lachixila Vijanos, 194–96. *See also*
  San Juan Tabaá (community)
Villavicencio, Diego Jaimes Ricardo, 135
virtue, 23, 64, 83–88, 91, 94, 96
Visigothic invasions, 28
Vitoria, Francisco de, 14, 37–40, 86, 112, 242n50
Vocabulario en lengua çapoteca (Córdova),
  56, 59–62
Vocabulario en lengua castellana y mexicana
  (Molina), 50–52, 56–59
Vocabulario en lengua misteca (Alvarado), 56,
  57, 63
Vocabulario español-latino (Nebrija), 48, 50
voluntarism, 186

will (*voluntad*): collective, 26, 189–91, 206;
  free will (*libre voluntad*), 183, 186, 190–91,
  196, 221; of people, 26, 33, 43, 49, 227

women, Native: polygyny, challenges to, 112,
  113, 118–19, 132, 135; property ownership
  by, 114–15, 124
written custom, 4, 31–32, 194, 200–201; *convenios*, 220–21, 227; "papereality" of, 208,
  227; Spanish genres used, 201, 203

xihui ("bad/false"), 67
xitíchaquéche (law; "our community's
  words"), 60

Yanhuitlan (*yuhuitayu*, Mixtec power center),
  55, 104, *122*, 127; Codex of, 223, *223*; lords
  of tried by Inquisition, 104, 120–27, 131,
  135; subject towns of, 160. *See also* Ñudzahui communities
Yllescas, Joseph de (defendant), 134
yoho lahui Audiencia lichi Rey (the
  community and court, house of the
  king), 203
Yolotepec, Yxcatlan, Tacahua, and Ytnuyucu
  litigation, 1723–1776, 219–26
Yosoñama (land area), 166–68
Yrigoyen, Gaspar de (lieutenant), 161
yuhuitayu ("tayu," alliance of two communities): *ñuu* (community) of, 57, 59, 124, 145,
  159, 160; patterns of in later land tenure,
  159, 160; and Spanish partnership concept,
  147; Teposcolula as, 187. See also *cabecera-
  sujeto* model
yya (lords), 145, 164, 187

Zaballa, Ana de, 127
Zahuatlan (community), 155–60
Zapotec (Tíchazàa) language, 51, 245n51,
  246n81; criminal records, 130–34; rec-
  iprocity and communal obligation in,
  174–77; translating custom into, 55–68
Zorita, Alonso de, 5
Zumárraga, Juan de, 52

www.ingramcontent.com/pod-product-compliance
Lightning Source LLC
Chambersburg PA
CBHW071730270326
41928CB00013B/2617